The Alternative Introduction to Biological Anthropology

Second Edition

The Alternative Introduction to Biological Anthropology

SECOND EDITION

JONATHAN MARKS
The University of North Carolina at Charlotte

New York   Oxford
OXFORD UNIVERSITY PRESS

Oxford University Press is a department of the University of Oxford. It furthers the University's objective of excellence in research, scholarship, and education by publishing worldwide. Oxford is a registered trade mark of Oxford University Press in the UK and certain other countries.

Published in the United States of America by Oxford University Press
198 Madison Avenue, New York, NY 10016, United States of America.

For titles covered by Section 112 of the US Higher Education Opportunity Act, please visit www.oup.com/us/he for the latest information about pricing and alternate formats.

Library of Congress Cataloging-in-Publication Data
Names: Marks, Jonathan (Jonathan M.), 1955-
Title: The alternative introduction to biological anthropology / Jonathan
    Marks, The University of North Carolina at Charlotte.
Description: Second edition. | New York : Oxford University Press, 2018. |
    Includes bibliographical references and index.
Identifiers: LCCN 2017007199 | ISBN 9780190490997 (pbk. : alk. paper)
Subjects: LCSH: Physical anthropology.
Classification: LCC GN60 .M32 2018 | DDC 599.9—dc23 LC record available
at https://lccn.loc.gov/2017007199

9 8 7 6 5 4 3 2
Printed by LSC Communications, Inc. Printed in the United States

To my parents, Richard and Renée

CONTENTS

Chapter 5   **Are We Here? If So, Why? (On Issues of Microevolution)   80**

Chapter 6   **Building Better Monkeys, or at Least Different Ones (On Systematics)   101**

Chapter 7   **Is That an Ape in Your Genes, or Are You Just Glad to See Me? (On the Place of Humans in the Natural Order)   121**

Chapter 8   **Apes Run Around Naked, Live in Trees, and Fling Their Poo. Do You? (On the Relevance of Apes to Understanding Humans)   141**

AUTHOR BIOGRAPHY

Jonathan Marks is Professor of Anthropology at the University of North Carolina at Charlotte, where he has taught since the beginning of the present millennium, after brief stretches at Yale and Berkeley. His primary training is in biological anthropology and genetics, but his interests are broad, and he has published widely across the sciences and humanities on the general topics of human origins and human diversity. In 2006 he was elected a Fellow of the American Association for the Advancement of Science. In 2012 he was awarded the First Citizen's Bank Scholar's Medal from UNC Charlotte. In recent years he has been a Visiting Research Fellow at the ESRC Genomics

Photo by Matt Cashore, University of Notre Dame

Forum in Edinburgh, at the Max Planck Institute for the History of Science in Berlin, and a Templeton Fellow at the Institute for Advanced Study at Notre Dame. His work has received the W. W. Howells Book Prize and the General Anthropology Division Prize for Exemplary Cross-Field Scholarship from the American Anthropological Association, and the J. I. Staley Prize from the School for Advanced Research. His most recent books are *Tales of the Ex-Apes: How We Think about Human Evolution* (University of California Press, 2015) and *Is Science Racist?* (Polity Press, 2017).

PREFACE

This book is intended for courses in biological anthropology.

It is hard to write a textbook, and my hat goes off to all those who have successfully published them. But the modern Darwinian market places severe constraints on what textbooks can even attempt, much less accomplish. In the old days a textbook in this field expressed the personality and style of the author. Three classic examples are Earnest Hooton's *Up from the Ape* (1931 and 1946), Ashley Montagu's *Introduction to Physical Anthropology* (1945), and John Buettner-Janusch's *Origins of Man* (1966). (The fact that the author of the last of these died in jail after trying to murder some of his former colleagues, as well as the judge who had convicted him of manufacturing illegal drugs in his laboratory a few years earlier, only adds to the mystique of the olden days.)

Today's textbooks have to strive for market share, which selects to some unfortunate extent for blandness. It also selects for normativity and for the perpetuation of mythologies. By normativity, I mean the tendency not to deviate from a mold, that is to say, from the way things are supposed to be. By mythologies, I mean a set of narratives that explains who we are, where we come from, and where we fit in.

These mythologies include that biological anthropology is unambiguously a science (actually in many universities it is categorized differently, as "just" a social science, and the office next door may house a real-life humanist); that Charles Darwin and Gregor Mendel are its founding founders (actually Thomas Huxley and Aleš Hrdlička had far more to do with it); that we are genetically apes (actually we are genetically humans); and many others.

APPROACH

I wrote this book to present a framework for thinking about biological anthropology as it is, for the most part, *not* presented in contemporary textbooks: principally, as a part of anthropology, and in particular, a part of anthropology that builds a bridge to biology, from which we can see aspects of human biology that may not be visible from too close a vantage point. Like ethnographers, we want to be able to experience human biology as a participant, but also to understand it as an observer. My purpose is to explore, and to some extent to centralize, anthropological issues in the study of our more naturalistic aspects. To that end, I do not feel as though I need to explain things like "mitosis" and "our friend, the femur," which are capably handled in any normative textbook of biological anthropology.

Instead, I focus on more anthropological areas: how we make sense of data about our origins, where our modern ideas come from, our inability to separate natural facts from cultural facts and values as we try to understand ourselves, and the social and political aspects of science as a culturally situated mental activity. This book is structured as a set of pedagogically inflected essays amplifying issues and, hopefully, challenging students to think both critically and anthropologically. The chapters correspond to those in any standard biological anthropology textbook. Each essay draws on and complements—but does not reconstitute, except for the sake of clarity—the data and ideas presented in those standard textbooks.

WHY THIS BOOK?

- It's different, and less straitlaced than other modern presentations. It's mostly just words, but carefully chosen words. In certain places it's even— dare I say it?—funny. It doesn't have color pictures. And that's one reason it's priced lower than other introductory material.
- This book complements traditional textbooks in biological anthropology. I've written this book from a perspective that takes their merits for granted: explanations of basic biological concepts, glossy photos, end-of-chapter questions, and the like. The assets of the present book lie elsewhere, especially in bringing historical and philosophical issues into the picture.
- It gives new slants on familiar ideas. It does not simply mirror what is in the basic textbooks but offers a new spin, fostering critical thinking. Everybody is into critical thinking these days, but it's always about questioning "other" ideas, not the ones in the book. This book tries to explore how to think critically about its own ideas. In anthropology, this is known as "reflexivity."
- To help readers get started, theme statements at the beginning of each chapter introduce the breadth of information covered.
- Further, this book explores connections between biological and general anthropology. For example, the most fundamental intellectual chore is to situate ourselves within a natural order. But there are many ways of ordering nature. We could juxtapose hairy animals (bears and giraffes) against feathered animals (swans and cassowaries). Alternatively, we could juxtapose land-dwellers (lions and snakes) against flying things (bats and mosquitoes). Or striped animals (tigers and bumblebees) against drab animals (llamas and dolphins). Or yummy (duck and lamb) versus yucky (cockroaches and dogs). We will be more interested in the process that yields the first dichotomy, the major adaptations in the history of life. But it's important to recognize

that that is an arbitrary choice, one that interests us scientifically, not aesthetically or gastronomically.

- The discussions offer integration of topics, coherent narratives, and salient examples. The focus here is on the evolution of humans as natural/cultural beings. That involves both examining the primate context of human evolution and the ecological uniqueness of our species. I wrote it from the perspective of someone who has sat on the editorial boards of the *Journal of Human Evolution*, the *Yearbook of Physical Anthropology*, the *International Journal of Primatology*, and the *Journal of the Royal Anthropological Institute*. Like anybody, I have gaps in my knowledge; on the other hand, a lot of people think I know what I'm talking about.

NEW TO THE SECOND EDITION

What's new in this edition? Everything you loved about the first edition is here, plus updated references in every chapter! And new and expanded discussions of the latest issues, such as:

- The Denisovans
- Epigenetics
- *Homo naledi*
- Creationism
- Colonialism
- Race

ACKNOWLEDGMENTS

This book owes debts to many people, through its various incarnations and nicknames, including (but not limited to) *More Biological Anthropology, Biological Anthropology and the Chamber of Secrets*, and *The Un-textbook*.

Thanks first to Jan Beatty, who conceived this project and saw it through its phases of development. Lauren Mine, Sherith Pankratz, Meredith Keffer, and the staff at Oxford University Press were also great to work with.

Special thanks to Karen Strier, Susan McCombie, and my colleagues at UNC-Charlotte, who have charitably allowed me to bounce a wide gamut of ideas off them, and shared theirs with me. For this revised edition, Ella Andrews gave me some very helpful suggestions.

I also thank the following reviewers: Thad Bartlett, University of Texas at San Antonio; Virginia Betz, Phoenix College; Debbie Guatelli-Steinberg, Ohio State University; Amelia Hubbard, Wright State University; Jennifer Mathews, Trinity University; Elizabeth Miller, California State University, Los Angeles; David R. Schwimmer, Columbus State University; Adam Van Arsdale, Wellesley College; and one anonymous reviewer.

And finally, I thank Peta Ann Katz and Abby Marks, who had my last two books dedicated to them and may think this is a demotion, but it isn't.

The Alternative Introduction to Biological Anthropology

What Is Anthropology, What Is Biological Anthropology, and Should I Be Getting Science Credit for This? (On the Philosophy of Science)

THEME

Biological anthropology breaks down the boundaries of traditional academic provinces, being both a scientific and a humanistic endeavor. At some universities, biological anthropology is considered satisfactory fulfillment for a "science" requirement; at others, it is not. Its origin is distinct from that of evolutionary biology because biological anthropology studies the meaning of specifically human differences and origins.

WHAT IS ANTHROPOLOGY?

Anthropology is the scholarly field of inquiry that studies humans as group members. Other fields study humans as individuals (psychology and physiology, for example), but the focus of anthropology is on clusters of people—how they differ in form and behavior from other clusters of people—and how the largest cluster of people, the human species itself, relates to other species.

By "scholarly," I mean that it follows a tradition of rigorous argument, logic, high standards of first-hand evidence, and an understanding and appreciation of the errors earlier generations of students committed in their studies of the subject. It is only by confronting those errors that present generations can come to more comprehensive and accurate understandings of the subject.

In studying humans as group members, anthropology is a field of *mediation*. That is, it takes two entities that look like opposites and finds the areas of connection between them. One obvious area of mediation is "individual" versus "group member." A person is both at the same time. Any person develops from a single egg, containing a genetic program distinct from that of all other people except an identical twin. On the other hand, that person's genetic program is far more similar to that of a chimpanzee than to that of a horse—because they are part of the human species, not a part of the zebra species.

Moreover, that distinct genetic program within the specific human egg will develop into a person in a defined context—a context of biology (such as maternal environment, nutrition, hormones, and drugs), society (the other people already in the world, from the immediate family to one's peer groups), and history (the nonbiological things inherited from ancestors such as money, a home, and a language). Additionally, there exists the suite of experiences lived as an individual, filtered and rendered meaningful through one's own personal history (praise, abuse, attention, abandonment, accidents, relocation).

With so many variables, it is a daunting task to try and explain why any specific person does any specific thing at any specific time. In fact, that is probably a task for astrologers, not scholars.

What we can do, however, is derive some generalizations about the behavior of groups of individuals and contrast them with others.

Such generalizations, of course, must be based on extensive careful observations and analyses of what people in different places at different times actually do—such studies constitute *ethnography*, the firsthand study of a human group in a specific place and situation.

Ethnography is particularly valuable in providing us with the data we need to make reliable statements about the breadth of the human experience. How can we talk sensibly about "what it means to be human," for example, if our only frame of reference is what it means to be human in one particular society, under one particular set of circumstances, at one specific point in time?

Most ethnography, consequently, has involved studying diverse rural, non-Euro-American peoples. Over the course of the last few centuries, these societies have come under the political and economic domination of other, more powerful societies—a set of relationships known as *colonialism*. Thus, while the exotic peoples of Polynesia or Tibet or central Africa have constituted the classical site of ethnography, it has also made anthropology a mediator in the complex relationships between indigenous peoples and colonial powers.

Anthropology assumed this role by demonstrating a mediating role between the *exotic* and the *mundane*. Early twentieth-century anthropologists in the field showed that not only are lives and daily concerns of the people "out there" very much like your own daily life and concerns (resolving disputes among friends, helping friends against enemies, taking care of a family, deriving the means of sustenance, having sex, coping with death, and just getting through the day), but conversely, the concerns and actions that you take for granted in your daily life can seem arbitrary and bizarre when looked at from a distance. Eating three meals a day; blessing someone who has just sneezed; how you dress; reading this English-language page printed in Roman letters rather than in cuneiform, pictograms, or hieroglyphs; adopting a husband's family name; how you spend your day—these are not features of *human* life but specifically of a human life lived here and now, and they might have easily been different. And they could be different.

This mediation—standing between opposites and showing how they are connected—is a fundamental part of anthropology. By looking at the historical origins of particular behaviors and peoples, anthropology mediates the *past* and the *present*. It looks at not only where we have come from but also where other peoples have come from and where we as a species have come from.

In this sense, anthropology also mediates the concept of *human* and *animal*. We are, on the one hand, non-photosynthesizing, multicellular life—animal; and on the other hand, we are a unique form of life that radically transforms its environment and creates its own means by which to survive. We are governed by the needs and instincts of other species—to survive, eat, breathe, and reproduce, among many other things—and yet we are also governed by laws our ancestors made up, which regulate what we can and cannot do as we try to survive and reproduce. We also season our food in locally specific ways that have negligible nutritional value and deliberately inhale substances other than air, such as the burning residue of certain dried leaves, for reasons other than breathing. We are both like other animals and different from other animals.

The classic juxtaposition of animalness and non-animalness, melded into the human and mediated in the study of anthropology, is often represented as a dichotomy of *nature* versus *culture*. "Nature" here would mean the biological core or essence of the human animal; while "culture" would refer to those institutions that are "man-made" or in some sense artificial—not part of our genetic endowment but part of our social endowment. That dichotomy is a classically false one.

Another important site of anthropological mediation is derived from the relations of colonial and indigenous peoples, as mentioned previously. All peoples have knowledge about the world, which serves not only to help them exploit the natural resources available but also to orient them and tell them right from wrong. Science, which emerged in eighteenth-century Europe, is the particular form of knowledge of the world used and valued in modern society. It coexists with other forms of knowledge—such as religion, inspiration, and superstition—but is the knowledge most fundamentally identified with modern society.

And yet, other peoples have knowledge that is useful, effective, and insightful. They know what is dangerous in their own environment; they know how to survive and even thrive where you or I would be virtually helpless. They know the tides, the approaching weather, what to plant and when to plant it; and they also know the spirit world, where they came from, and where they are going after they die.

Here, of course, traditional or folk knowledge may often come into conflict with scientific or technical knowledge. Anthropology also works to mediate these two realms. Often this antagonism is played out as a clash of science versus "belief systems," or in university cultures, as a conflict between science (like physics and geology) and humanities (like literature and history). Sometimes anthropology is part of a middle ground, "social science"—not quite science but not quite arts or humanities either.

In fact, anthropology partakes of both.

THE SUBFIELDS OF ANTHROPOLOGY

Anthropology is an anti-reductive or holistic study of the human species. Its methods range from the scientific to the literary: humans are both physical and mental beings; and so to study their groups rigorously and comprehensively, we are obliged to take an eclectic approach to anthropological data and research. Anthropological research ranges from comparative anatomy and genomics (which shed light on the ways in which human populations differ from one another, how the human species differs from its relatives and ancestors, and how a human cell differs from a gorilla cell) to the analysis of poetry, song, and jokes (which shed light on how groups of people understand themselves in relation to other groups and in varying situations of economic or political inequality).

Biological anthropology represents the most scientific end of the field, devoted to studying the biological history, evolutionary relationships, and adaptive diversity that characterize the human species. The field originally came to be called "physical" anthropology in the nineteenth century, to emphasize the fact that its subject was the physical remains of people—generally their bones and brains—and to contrast with the mental aspects of human life that were becoming the domain of "cultural" anthropologists. In the twentieth century, however, it gradually became clear that there were other things to study that fell within the scope of physical anthropology without being strictly "physical" in the sense that bones are—notably, genes and the behavior of nonhuman primates. Consequently, we commonly refer to the field as "biological anthropology," although the phrase "physical anthropology" remains in use.

Biological anthropology is regarded as one of four intellectual subfields in anthropology. The "four-field" division of anthropology was developed in the United States in the nineteenth century by early anthropologists from the Smithsonian Institution interested in studying Native Americans, who had been finally "pacified" through a combination of genocide and assimilation. No longer a threat to American expansion, they often lived in poor isolated rural communities and yet were directly descended from the original inhabitants of the American continent.

The "four-field" approach began as a system of systematically and comprehensively studying indigenous people. In this case, it involved white scientists going out to study the bodies and bones of Indians, the original occupants of the land; their ancient art and architecture; their customs; and their languages: in other words—physical anthropology, archaeology, cultural anthropology, and linguistics.

In other countries, with different colonial and political histories, anthropology developed differently. In England, archaeology became more closely allied with art history, physical anthropology with human biology, and cultural anthropology with the study of social systems. In France, "anthropology" came to mean physical anthropology, and "sociology" came to mean cultural anthropology.

To the extent that the "four-field" approach is now international, it is derived from the American model. That model, however, arose as a nineteenth-century form of "comprehensive othering"—studying powerless, indigenous people different from yourself. As anthropology has matured beyond that original scope, its approach has matured as well. Anthropology now studies all peoples, not just powerless indigenous ones, and anthropological projects rarely cover more than one subfield; the "four-field approach" is institutionalized but is no longer embodied in the research of any single anthropologist.

THE ANTHROPOLOGY OF SCIENCE

Modern anthropology studies belief systems and practices not only of exotic peoples but also of ourselves. The act of turning the anthropological gaze inward is called *reflexivity*. Classically, it serves to make the acts and thoughts of "modern" people seem exotic—and works like these range from Montesquieu's fictional *Persian Letters* in the eighteenth century (the French as seen through the eyes of a visitor from Persia), through Horace Miner's classic study of the "Nacirema" (spell it backward for the secret message), to modern works such as Rayna Rapp's ethnography of genetic counseling, George Gmelch's ethnography of baseball, and Philippe Bourgois's ethnography of drug dealers.

Science, of course, constitutes a fundamental system of beliefs and practices in modern life and has itself come under the reflexive anthropological gaze. While there is widespread paranoia about "anti-science" attitudes on the part of the public, actually we all make decisions about what bits of science to reject. Some reject evolution, some reject climatology, some reject vaccinations, and some reject scientific racism. Hardly anyone is "anti-science." The anthropology of science is a growing area of study that seeks to stand between science and culture and to analyze science as anthropologists explore other belief systems and the relationship between science itself and the people it affects (society).

Science deals with facts about the world, doesn't it? But where do facts come from? How do ideas become facts? Standard training in science rarely raises such questions. After all, if science is just "reading what's out there in nature," then it can't be wrong, nor have its premises or actions called into question.

And yet science is commonly wrong. Genetics books of the 1940s routinely said that human cells have 48 chromosomes (they only have 46). Scientific books also commonly said that humans diverged from the ape lineage in the early Oligocene (it was in the late Miocene). Indeed in recent years, there have been furious adversarial battles about the scientific evidence for breast implants as a health risk, DNA fingerprinting as a tool for criminal prosecution, and the value and status of stem cells in medical research. If science has the property of being self-correcting—which it does—then it stands to reason that there is something to correct, namely, alternative wrong scientific hypotheses.

It is consequently useful to distinguish among three parts of the scientific subject. *Ontology* is about being—about the state of existence, or of what "really is." But that is not really the domain of science. Science is about *epistemology*—what can be known, and how we can know it.

Consider this question: How many angels are in the room right now?

We'll even simplify it and make it multiple-choice: (a) three or fewer angels; (b) four or more angels; (c) none at all.

Logically, one of those answers must be right. There *is* an answer to the question. But there is no way for science to find it, because angels are not material entities and are not amenable to scientific detection and analysis.

So whatever the answer may be, it cannot be revealed by scientific means. Thus, science is not so much about "reality," or what there "is," as it is about *what we can know*. Science is fundamentally about the kinds of questions one can meaningfully ask, the kinds of data one can collect, and the kinds of answers one can generate. In other words, it is about epistemology.

This distinction between ontology and epistemology—being and knowing—is basic in philosophy but not widely considered in science. Not making the distinction serves to promote the idea that science is simply a continuous revelation of what is true and real, rather than being a series of methods and guidelines, limited by available ideas and technologies.

Not only is there a distinction to be made between what is real and what we can know about it, there is also the fundamental problem of how we communicate it to one another: how we talk, and write, and think about it. We learn that there is a "genetic code"—in other words, that there is something like a language operating in the cell. But this is simply a metaphor devised in 1944 by the biophysicist Erwin Schrödinger; there is no cryptography going on between two communicating, intelligent beings inside the cell. Genetics is *like* a code in some ways—but is not itself a code. This metaphor has been immensely powerful and helpful in conceptualizing the way the cell works, but it is about what the cell is *like*, not what the cell *is*. This is *semiotics,* the domain of meanings, and another fundamental aspect of scientific advance.

We encounter useful metaphors in all parts of science—"black holes" in astrophysics, "bonds" in chemistry, the "adaptive landscape" in biology. It is important, however, to acknowledge that these are aids in conceptualizing and communicating about reality, not descriptions of it. They are no less valuable, but they are units of language and thought, not of external nature.

Ontology, epistemology, and semiotics are all parts of how knowledge is constructed. First, there is some relationship between what is really out there and what science says about it—but that relationship is never obvious or straightforward. Every new discovery, after all, presupposes a prior state of scientific falsehood, which is supplanted by the very discovery. Second, there are ways of discerning aspects of the world, which are bounded by the available instruments and conceptual models. It would be difficult to convince a skeptic about cells without the aid of microscopy, or radioactive decay without calculus. And third, we make sense of the world scientifically through the introduction and use of key metaphors— "genetic code" as noted above, or *"l'homme machine,"* or "natural selection," or even "man the hunter." Each of these helps us to see parts of the world in constructive scientific ways and to frame new questions about how it works.

Finally, there is a process by which ideas become facts. Science is an occupation, and as such, its practitioners face the stresses of life in any other job: promotions, raises, getting the esteem of one's superiors, networking, and protecting one's "turf." Is it any wonder, then, that scientists often promote their own ideas, or those of their friends, or of their professors? As a result, sometimes ideas that are wrong are nevertheless maintained for years after they have been conclusively refuted (for example, that genes are composed of protein rather than of nucleic acid, or that races differ in their innate intellectual capacities); and ideas that are right sometimes have remarkable difficulty getting accepted (for example, Mendel's work on peas; or that *Australopithecus* is a human ancestor).

Just how this occurs is often the subject of careful work by historians. But it does put the lie to the naïve view that science is simply an upward march to truth. It's a march to the truth, but the truth is a negotiation at any point in time between "reality" and "perception," and that march is commonly sideways or backward.

THE NORMATIVE VIEW OF SCIENCE:
SCIENTIFIC METHOD

There is no single method by which science works, to the exclusion of other modes of thought. Nor is science just "glorified common sense," as some have suggested. Rather, science is a set of methods for deriving knowledge about the unknown, beginning with the formulation of an answerable question, and proceeding by paring down the many answers that *might* be true, to the relatively few that *probably are* true. There are many kinds of science, but it is useful to look first at the idealized or normative idea of what science is.

The scientific process begins with the formulation of a problem that needs an answer and can be answered. The choice of a problem to tackle refutes one of the oldest myths about science—that it takes place with a fully open mind, free of preconceptions. Simply choosing a question implies a pre-existing judgment about what is interesting and important, and is thereby worthy of study. A question that is answerable is one for which a class of data can be rigorously collected to settle it. Notice that this criterion excludes studies of the supernatural world, which are not amenable to rigorous data collection.

The articulation of the problem to be studied is known as a *hypothesis:* a statement that may or may not be true, but which can be matched against some information in the real world to help us decide. Hypotheses that do not have this property of *testability*—for which there is nothing you can do to help settle the problem—are metaphysical and outside the domain of scientific investigation. The example we used earlier—How many angels are in the room?—would be such a question, not amenable to scientific analysis. What counts as a scientific question at one time may not count at another—after all, asking about X-rays would have made no sense in the mid-seventeenth century.

The formulation of a testable hypothesis is the creative element in science. Having formulated such a hypothesis, we invoke the empirical part of science—the collection of *data* that bear on the hypothesis. Once again, this is not carried out in an intellectual vacuum: we have made prior judgments about which kinds of information are relevant or not. There is no innocent observation.

In a famous example, Charles Darwin collected birds while in the Galapagos Islands, and upon returning to London, he gave the collection to a distinguished ornithologist named John Gould for study. Gould, interested in the patterns of variation in the beaks and colors of the birds, asked Darwin which island he had collected each specimen from. Darwin, however, did not know for certain. Why? Because for a young biologist educated at Cambridge in the creationist ideas of the 1820s, the assumption was that God had placed creatures in their appropriate settings, and the islands in an archipelago would simply have the same creatures. Darwin had not recorded which island each bird had come from, because he did not think it was important! This would precipitate his interest in *biogeography*— the relationship between life and place—that would ultimately lead to his theory of evolution by natural selection.

The decision about which data to collect or record, then, is crucial to the scientific enterprise. It provides the link to the "real world" that science tries to study. Data can be either in the form of observation (reporting) or experimentation (a controlled activity). In either case, the elimination of extraneous information—control—is crucial to the enterprise, ensuring that the data are in fact relevant to the question at hand. The collection of data cannot be haphazard, but must be done carefully and rigorously.

Thus, for example, there are many old studies that have argued that populations of blacks and whites in America have different average IQs. From this, some investigators have claimed that whites are simply innately smarter than blacks. Others, however, recognizing that whites and blacks in America lead very different lives, insist that you cannot simply compare average IQs of different races, but only average IQs of whites and blacks from the same areas, with similar incomes, and similar family histories. And once you control for these variables, you find that the difference in average IQ disappears—which suggests it was not measuring innate differences in intellectual ability, but differences in the circumstances of growing up black and white in America.

The third part of the normative scientific process is *explanation*—the rational, intellectual enterprise that relates the data collected to the problem formulated. There is never any guarantee that a particular explanation is right, but the most useful scientific explanations have several properties that we can use as guidelines for the formulation of scientific explanations generally.

First, they are concerned with proximate cause, rather than ultimate cause. Proximate cause is mechanism, a "how" question. Ultimate cause is a "why" question, a reason for something. This distinction came to the fore around 1700, when Isaac Newton successfully described gravity in mathematical terms. Prior to that, the fact of apples falling from trees or planets orbiting the sun were disparate phenomena, under the guidance of some heavenly forces that sometimes made apples fall and held planets in check. The Newtonians, however, showed that gravitational attraction was a property of all matter, and that the descent of the apple to the earth was the same as the attraction of the planets to the sun. This did not mean that God didn't exist, or was not responsible for apples and planets, but simply that we now understood *how* the system worked. One could still ask, "What causes gravity?" or "Why does gravity exist?"—and still end up with a Divine answer— but the advance of science has nevertheless displaced the action of God from the immediacies of the physical world and relegated Him to setting up the rules by which the universe works.

In a precisely similar fashion, Darwin formulated an answer to the question "How do different species come to be adapted to their surroundings?"—and his answer was natural selection, the greater proliferation of individuals with certain characteristics. Darwin famously ended his work with this line:

> There is grandeur in this view of life, with its several powers, having been origi- nally breathed into a few forms or into one; and that, whilst this planet has gone cycling on according to the fixed law of gravity, from so simple a beginning end- less forms most beautiful and most wonderful have been, and are being, evolved.

But to the accusation that he was espousing atheism, Darwin added three words to that sentence in the second edition: "having been originally breathed by the Creator into a few forms or into one." His purpose was to try to follow in Newton's footsteps: God may well exist and have a hand in biology, but if so, the mechanism He used to make species differently adapted was an understandable earthly process of natural selection. Darwin was not interested in the origin of life, and his theory was not designed to conflict with the existence of God, but merely to delimit what could be explained by natural, understandable forces. Slightly later, interestingly, he wrote to a friend,

> I have long regretted that I truckled to public opinion, and used the Pentateuchal term of creation, by which I really meant "appeared" by some wholly unknown process. It is mere rubbish, thinking at present of the origin of life; one might as well think of the origin of matter.

Darwin's work was not about the origin of matter or about the origin of life; it was about the origin of *species*, and he didn't care what people thought of the first two, as long as his argument for the third was convincing.

This brings us to a second aspect of scientific explanations, one that has emerged in the century and a half since Darwin struggled with mentioning a "Creator"—namely, that modern science deals exclusively with the natural world, explaining it in terms of itself, without recourse to a supernatural or spiritual world. This is a methodological assumption of science, which strives to under- stand the natural world, assuming that it is knowable; if it is acted upon by occult, capricious forces, then these are by their nature unpredictable and unknowable, and they defeat the purpose of science.

That is not to say they do not exist, for we cannot prove that. They are simply external to modern science. They are also mutually contradictory: if we believe the world was created by a divine being, how can we know which of the many possible divine beings it was?

This assumption of naturalism is useful and has had considerable success in the last few centuries. For example, antibiotics were developed to kill bacteria. The action of antibiotics is predicated on the germ theory of disease, a naturalistic alternative to the "evil spirits" theory of disease. Perhaps antibiotics drive away evil spirits in addition to killing germs—but the value to science has been that they seem to do what they were developed for. There would have been no need to develop antibiotics without the germ theory and no way to explain their curative value either. This obviously makes it likely that a certain class of bacteria, which respond to antibiotics, cause diseases—rather than evil spirits.

Once again this is not to say that evil spirits do not exist, or cause no disease, only that the domain of diseases that can reasonably be ascribed to them is much smaller than it used to be.

A third characteristic of scientific explanations is that they strive to be parsimonious, by which we mean that they try not to be unnecessarily complicated. This principle is commonly known as "Occam's razor"—after a medieval philosopher who believed in trimming away excessive speculations and assumptions. Parsimony, once again, is a useful assumption—given no other information, the simpler explanation is better—but it can easily be itself an oversimplification.

In evolutionary studies, we use Occam's razor in our assumption that major changes (such as bipedalism) generally only occurred once, and that consequently, there is very little parallel evolution—different species evolving into similar forms. We assume, rather, that species who share fundamental traits with each other inherited them from a common ancestor, not independently from diverse ancestors. However, it is also clear that parallel evolution in some traits has indeed happened. For example, a group of primates share a significant feature of the vertebral column, namely, that they lack a tail. We call them "apes," and infer that the loss of a tail was an evolutionary event in a geologically recent ancestor, which they have all inherited. There is also a breed of cats, known as Manx cats, which have lost the tail. Should we infer that Manx cats are apes on this basis? Probably not, because accepting that trait as evidence of intimate ancestry would mean that all the other traits by which a Manx seems to be a cat—retracting claws, carnassial teeth, giving birth to litters, and the like—would have evolved in parallel between cats and "Manx apes." We see the one trait—loss of the tail—as a parallelism, and the cluster of others—the "cat" traits—as more reliable indicators of ancestry. We therefore use the principle of parsimony as a methodological tool to minimize the things that need to be explained away, and we try and invoke evolutionary scenarios that invoke parallel evolution as little as possible.

A fourth characteristic of scientific explanations is that they are probabilistic, not deterministic—that is, they can generally rank outcomes as more-or-less likely given certain boundary conditions, but cannot tell you the future like Nostradamus. This, of course, puts science at a distinct disadvantage to other modes of thought that foretell the future with great clarity, even if not with great accuracy.

It also tends to make scientists poor witnesses in the courtroom, where definitive statements are sought, not qualified statistical outcomes.

However, that is a classic signature of science: uncertainty. Preachers are far more certain than scientists are, which may be why they are often more convincing. But when you are about to have surgery, you may well want an informed assessment of the possible risks and side effects, rather than a glib prediction of the future.

Often a scientific analysis will use statistical tests to see how likely a particular situation is to occur by chance alone. If it is less than 5% likely to be due to chance, we call the situation in question "statistically significant"—and deduce that we are dealing with a nonrandom occurrence, which thus requires an explanation. By that very statistical convention, however, we may be up to 5% likely to be wrong, or likely to be wrong on the average 1 in 20 times.

The last signature of a good scientific explanation is logical rigor. Many nonscientific systems are very logical, but nevertheless wrong—so being logical is no guarantee that you are right. Further, many proper inferences have been drawn from premises that are faulty and thus turn out themselves to be useless. But being logical, and deducing implications rigorously from data and inferences, makes it more likely that you will be right.

THE SOCIAL MATRIX OF SCIENCE

The sociologist Robert Merton devised a famous list of four attributes of science in 1942, which are at best idealizations of the scientific process. The list shows what science should ideally strive for, although it is exceedingly unlikely that it ever has met these standards, and all indications are that it is moving farther away from them. They are known as *CUDOS*.

Science, to Merton, is *communal*—that is, freely shared, in the public record, and available to all. Only a few years later, however, this was undermined by the Manhattan Project, in which the best science suddenly became Top Secret. In more recent times, genetics has become a home for investment capital; and consequently, the scientific research is discussed in far more muted tones, lest a rival company learn too much too soon. A prominent genetics research facility has a sign that says, "Big Blabs Sink Labs."

Merton's second idealized aspect of science is *universalism*—that it should be essentially international and transcend the cultural divisions in society. In practice, though, we commonly find national "schools" in particular sciences—Japanese primatology versus American primatology, for example; or British population genetics versus American population genetics—which makes Merton's idea once again seem oversimplified.

His third aspect is *disinterestedness*—that science should not be for sale to profiteers or ideologues; it should be a fair and open search for truth. But again, we simply do not see that when we look at modern science, for example. Politics looks to science to support its actions, and science is very much for sale in the free market of patenting cell lines and developing new drugs. Indeed, conflicts of interests are now so profound and prolix that many journals and universities are at a loss about how to deal with it.

Merton's fourth aspect is *organized skepticism*—that science relies not on authority, but on doubt, and that the burden of proof falls on the researcher to prove a claim—not on the skeptic to debunk it. In practice, however, we rely greatly on authority, in part because there is simply too much to know and we are obliged to take the word of really smart people; and likewise, much of what we learn about science comes not from scientists themselves, but from journalists. This can have the effect of sidestepping the critical review and organized skepticism of science, so that it is sadly commonplace now for extraordinary claims to enter the popular consciousness—such as the "gay gene" on the X chromosome—and to shift the burden of proof to those who find the claim ludicrous, and force them to waste their time and resources to identify the fatal flaw in the work.

RELATIVIZING SCIENCE

Science is a cultural system in which individuals with common ideas, and their own special language, interact with one another in complex ways. In so doing, they advance themselves, and they advance the cause of science as well. Science has its own reward system, its own standardized set of obligations and expectations, and its own promise of immortality (the citation index, by which a scientist's influence is commonly judged).

Unlike other cultural systems, science appears to advance universally. Our knowledge of the world is indeed continually increasing; more things are being discovered, and virtually nothing is forgotten. This is a rare instance of cultural improvement, which is more commonly a series of trade-offs—for example, an increase in technology with greater fear of the safety hazards associated with that technology, or longer life spans accompanied by greater alienation of the elderly.

But science as a cultural system does advance, and it does so for a simple reason—that is its goal. Science generates origin narratives about the human species, as do all cultural systems; and the principal scientific one is of course the evolution of the human species from the apes of Africa. It is certainly more accurate than any of its alternatives. But does that mean that the alternatives should be suppressed?

The answer is yes, in the context of science classes, and no, in the context of the free market of ideas in the modern world. Some scientists are appalled that so many Americans reject evolution in favor of the diverse strains of Christian creationism. Such an attitude, however, makes science sound as if it were a competing religion, which it should not be.

The difference between the scientific origin myth (evolution) and the Christian one, or any culture's origin myth, is a fundamental one. Science was founded in eighteenth-century European philosophy as a search for a particular kind of truth—truth that can be demonstrated to other people and doesn't require individual revelation or prior commitment to accept. Science has a single goal—to describe and explain the universe most accurately and most fully. Much of scientific method can be thought of simply as ways of attaining that end. And as a result, science indeed provides the most accurate descriptions and explanations of the universe.

The fact that most Americans reject parts of it may not be so much a result of their stupidity but of their possession of different priorities than scientists have. After all, how much does it really matter whether or not you are descended from a late Miocene ape?

Other origin myths have features that science lacks. For example, they bind you to the community. They tell you right from wrong, and give you moral orientation. They tell you that the universe is ultimately just, and benign, and that your life is important. They make you feel good about your place in the spiritual order, and impart meaning to your life and to the events within it.

Science does none of these. It just seeks the most accurate description and explanation of the universe. Because it lacks the other goals that origin myths commonly have, it is hard to say that evolution is "better" than those other myths, if we use *better* in an ordinary and fairly broad sense. Evolution is clearly better, however, if we use the narrow criterion of simply "being the most empirically accurate." But that, of course, is science's own criterion—a highly arbitrary scale of comparison. And it should not be surprising that science fares well by that criterion because that is what scientific methodologies were developed for. It has been said that science is a "self-correcting myth"—that is, a linear narrative continually changing to bring itself into line with reality.

Most science, like most of any industry, consists of boring work—"turning the crank," so to speak. The historian of science Thomas Kuhn called this "normal science." But rarely a revolutionary new idea comes along, one that causes the community, or a large segment of it, to rethink their work and to reinterpret their data. This "paradigm shift" (in Kuhn's phrase) signals a time of great intellectual instability and great creativity, a scientific revolution. Unfortunately, these are only observable in retrospect, and since Kuhn's work appeared in the 1960s, it has become unfortunately too commonplace for scientists to claim to be leading, participating in, or witnessing a paradigm shift in their field.

THE ORIGINS OF ANTHROPOLOGY

Anthropology, however, began with just such a paradigm shift, articulated in 1871 by Edward B. Tylor, a professor at Oxford, in his book *Primitive Culture*. Writing at a time when Darwinism was revolutionizing the biological sciences, Tylor took an interest in the behavioral differences among human groups. The common wisdom of the age was that northern Europe was the most advanced place on earth, both mentally and physically, and its inhabitants had a right—perhaps even a duty—to colonize the rest of the world and to subdue and supplant its indigenous inhabitants. This was justified on the grounds that Europeans were superior beings—morally, mentally, technologically, and physically. And as Darwin had articulated in the subtitle of his most famous book ("The Preservation of Favored Races in the Struggle for Life"), it was the fate of the unfavored races to be eliminated by the favored ones.

Tylor (and his German contemporaries) undermined this argument with a two-part attack that became central to the development of anthropology. The first came to be known as "the psychic unity of mankind"—that people everywhere have pretty much the same intellectual capacities. Geniuses are, by definition, rare; we're not talking about their capacities, just those of the normal folk. Thus, people from Zimbabwe or Tibet or New Zealand can pilot jet planes and splice DNA and write anthropology books, if they are so inclined. There is no good reason to think, when we survey the world's works and the accomplishments of its diverse peoples, that any of them is a substantially superior cluster of organic beings than any other.

The second part of Tylor's attack is one that is so familiar to us now that we hardly can even think it might have been a new idea—namely, that the customs and laws of a people comprise something categorically distinct from their biological natures. He called this "culture"—"that complex whole which includes knowledge, belief, art, law, morals, custom, and any other capabilities and habits acquired by man as a member of society."

The distinction between the learned and the instinctual had been long acknowledged, but Tylor meant something more—specifically, the cumulative social traditions of a group of people, which could even be thought of as having a life of their own.

This new distinction between biology (or nature, or race—all often used synonymously at the time) and "culture" carried a very important political implication. If people's primitive-seeming lifeways did not imply their biological primitiveness or inferiority, then there was no longer a justification in nature for maltreating or exterminating them. And if people everywhere had pretty much the same capabilities for acquiring culture, then the humane and reasonable course of action would be to educate them, not to kill them. Anthropology, wrote Tylor, was "a reformer's science."

In America, the German-born anthropologist Franz Boas gave "culture" its more modern use, as the localized, and generally unconscious, ways that particular groups of people impose meaning on their surroundings, and to some extent construct their world and their lives. "Culture" was to become more than just the social components of "nurture" as opposed to "nature"—it was like the unified spirit of a people, suffusing all aspects of what they did and how they thought about things. It was acquired by growing up with them, and studied by living with them. Most importantly, it was now used as a plural, for each people had their own "culture." And although groups of people differed from one another in their gene pool, in the language they spoke, and in their culture, all three of these features were distinct from one another and could change independently of one another.

THE ORIGINS OF PHYSICAL ANTHROPOLOGY

Physical anthropology, on the other hand, began in no such radical conceptual break. If anything, it began in a far more intellectually primitive climate, one which held that "civilized races" must have better (or at least, bigger) brains than "uncivilized races," and thus began intensively to investigate variation in size and shape of the skull—the bones in which the brain is encased—across the human species.

By the 1840s, early American physical anthropologists were busy studying the skulls of Indians and of other nonwhite peoples in the hopes of finding an organic, "physical" basis for their social and economic inferiority. Some found in this activity a justification for slavery, holding that the heads of Africans were so different from those of Europeans that they must have been the products of separate creations. In France at this time, the first professional society of physical anthropology was founded on such ideas by the great cranial anatomist Paul Broca.

The advent of Darwinism did little to curb such odious science. Where pre-Darwinian students of human form freely associated Africans with apes, as somehow "lower" than Europeans, post-Darwinian racist scholars appropriated their familiar imagery but cloaked the arguments in evolutionary terms. Thus, where previously it might have been maintained that Africans had been created by God as intermediate beings between Europeans and apes, it could now be argued (by first-generation evolutionists such as the German Ernst Haeckel and the English Thomas Huxley) that they had evolved from apes, but just *not as far* as Europeans had.

By the end of the nineteenth century, there was little recognizable as professional physical anthropology. American practitioners had amassed collections of skulls and skeletons from Indian burials; Europeans trained in anatomy were studying the fossils of Neandertals and comparing the bodies of humans and apes. German anthropologists were surveying the human form and measuring the bodies of schoolchildren to assess the "racial" composition of their populations.

One such scholar was Franz Boas, who was trained initially in physics, then in geography, and last in anthropology in Germany. Boas lived among the natives of the Northwest coast of the United States and the neighboring regions in Canada in the 1880s, supporting his studies of their lifeways by selling their goods (and their bones) to museums. Hired in 1897 by Columbia University for his expertise in human body form, he ultimately made his major impact in cultural anthropology and is largely responsible for professionalizing the field of anthropology, with his formalization of the distinctions among race, language, and culture.

The person credited with professionalizing the subfield of *physical* anthropology, however, was a Bohemian-born doctor named Aleš Hrdlička. An avid student of the skeleton and the skull, he studied physical anthropology in France and obtained an appointment at the Smithsonian Institution, building up its collections and becoming the foremost authority on the skeletons of Indians. Hrdlička founded the *American Journal of Physical Anthropology* in 1918 and the American Association of Physical Anthropologists in 1930.

Hrdlička, however, as a museum scientist, did little teaching or training of junior scientists. That part was taken by a classicist from Wisconsin who studied anthropology as a Rhodes Scholar at Oxford and subsequently took a post at Harvard that he held for about 40 years—Earnest Hooton. Hooton trained virtually the entire field of physical anthropologists over those decades and was very much a Harvard celebrity academic.

Much of physical anthropology through World War II consisted in documenting the physical differences among human groups and attempting to classify them on that basis. World War II was a crisis for physical anthropology, however, as its evil German manifestation was both an embarrassment to the field and yet surprisingly difficult to distinguish from its American counterpart. Hooton struggled to differentiate them, largely in vain.

Physical anthropology was essentially rebuilt intellectually in the 1950s by Sherwood Washburn, who had done his doctorate with Hooton in 1940 on the anatomy of monkeys. Washburn slammed the door on the physical anthropology that was centered on measuring people's skulls and relegating them to one group or another—it was static and typological, he argued. It reflected neither modern evolutionary theory nor the reality of human populations. What was needed was a "new" physical anthropology, one focused on the dynamics of evolution and adaptation: one that would be better integrated with modern evolutionary biology. Human evolution, rather than racial classification, would be at the center of the "new" science; and it would be rooted in an understanding of how humans fit into the biology and behavior of the primates. Moreover, the study of presumptively superior or inferior human races would be supplanted by the study of what could be considered a common and primordial heritage in human existence—the biology of human populations, and particularly of hunter-gatherers.

Importantly, Washburn envisioned this as a biological subfield integrated into anthropology. For example, he interpreted the interactions of baboons as socially cohesive forces, as social anthropologists were inclined to do for human societies. Today, a generation later, many of the issues have changed, but Washburn's agenda for biological anthropology has profoundly shaped the field. Most field primatologists work, for example, in concert with local people and government agencies, for primate conservation. Most students of the human form work within the framework of human adaptability studies, documenting the plasticity of the human form under different ecological and economic circumstances. And the study of human evolution is becoming increasingly dominated by a field Washburn nurtured, the study of molecular evolution. Washburn's contemporaries, such as Harvard's William Howells and Oxford's Joseph Weiner, also recognized the need for a "new," reconceptualized physical anthropology. Many practitioners also began to appreciate the non-"physical" nature of many of the subjects it now began to incorporate—such as DNA and primate behavior. "Biological anthropology" began to come into use to encompass the expanding scope of the field.

BIOLOGICAL ANTHROPOLOGY TODAY

At the present time, biological anthropology is a diverse field of study, still centered on the study of the physical aspects of humans as group members. We generally recognize a three-part division in the field: primatology, paleoanthropology, and human variation (or human biology, especially in the United Kingdom).

Each of these areas, however, is highly interdisciplinary, and within each of them, there is considerable variation in the scholarly training and approaches of practitioners. Thus, primatology commonly attracts researchers trained principally in psychology or zoology; paleoanthropology commonly attracts researchers trained in geology or anatomy; and human variation may attract researchers from genetics, forensic sciences, or medicine. On the other hand, it is also quite rare for a university psychology department to house a primatologist, or a geology department to house a paleoanthropologist, or criminal justice department to house a forensic scientist.

Biological anthropology affords a large enough intellectual umbrella for all of these areas of study, for they are all relevant to the field's focus. At the same time, though, this breadth sometimes results in a strong centripetal force—as scholars engaged in biological anthropology research are pulled away from the field's core, anthropology.

Counteracting this is an academic centrifugal force, drawing from contemporary anthropological ideas and themes in our understanding of the field's biological aspects. Many biological anthropologists study the anthropological themes of power, gender, and difference as they are manifested either in the biology of human populations or in our ancestors or primate relatives. Others are involved in analyzing the ways in which modern genetic research is changing our ideas about the body, about who we are, about where we came from, and about who owns body parts. After all, the field took its modern shape with the large-scale collection of Indian bones without much concern for the descendants or even relatives of the people whose bones they were. Federal legislation enacted in 1990, the Native American Graves Protection and Repatriation Act (NAGPRA), makes it clear that the bones have different meanings to different peoples, and the alternatives to the scientific meanings must be acknowledged and respected.

Thus, for example, a biological anthropologist in 1950 could examine a thighbone (femur) and treat it as an object—an "it"—a disembodied piece of dead matter. The old biological anthropologist might well handle it delicately and acknowledge that the femur once was part of a person, but the view of science is that there is a boundary between life and nonlife, and once dead, the femur is an object, not a person.

And yet the boundary between life and nonlife may not be so clear. After all, there is still organic matter—DNA and protein—present in the cells of the bones. And in spite of the reality of the transformation from human to corpse, is the transformation really so profoundly different from other transformations, such as adolescence and old age, that the femur cannot be seen any more as part

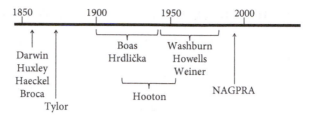

Figure 1.1. Timeline of major works, people, and events discussed in this chapter.

of a person? Could one not make a case that any body part remains a part of that person, even through the transition of death? If your leg remained your leg throughout the profound physical changes associated with birth, childhood, sexual maturity, adulthood, and senescence, why should it cease being your leg just because you have stopped breathing and have begun decomposing?

These are questions confronting modern biological anthropologists, who have to navigate between the sensibilities of peoples and the study of their ancestors' body parts. Similarly, anthropological genetics has had to face such issues in recent years, as its stock-in-trade, the blood of exotic peoples, has come increasingly to be a valuable commodity in pharmaceutical and genomic research. If there are patents to be filed and money to be made, should not the person whose body it came from share in the profit? Alternatively, if the blood belongs only to the researcher after it enters the test tube, why should anyone participate in a genetic study?

These are, of course, issues of property rights and ethics, which have emerged by virtue of new scientific technologies intersecting with economic and political forces. Half a century ago, biological anthropology could shield itself behind a screen of "value-neutral science"—but that privilege no longer exists.

Science is a part of the culture of the modern world and of the global economy. Biological anthropology is consequently bound up in new ideas about science, new ideas about the body, and new ideas about rights. And as such, it is becoming situated once more in an anthropological dialogue, a dialogue of mediation.

REFERENCES AND FURTHER READING

Beckwith, Jonathan R. 2002. *Making Genes, Making Waves: A Social Activist in Science.* Cambridge, MA: Harvard University Press.

Boas, Franz. 1911. *The Mind of Primitive Man.* New York: Macmillan.

Boas, Franz. 1940. *Race, Language and Culture.* New York: Macmillan.

Bourgois, Philippe. 1995. *In Search of Respect: Selling Crack in El Barrio.* New York: Cambridge University Press.

Collins, H. 2014. *Are We All Scientific Experts Now?* Cambridge (UK): Polity Press.

Darnell, Regna. 2001. *Invisible Genealogies: A History of Americanist Anthropology.* Omaha: University of Nebraska Press.

Darwin to J. D. Hooker, March 29, 1863. (http://www.darwinproject.ac.uk/entry-4065)

Fuentes, Agustín. 2010. The new biological anthropology: Bringing Washburn's new physical anthropology into 2010 and beyond—The 2008 AAPA luncheon lecture. *American Journal of Physical Anthropology* 143 (S51):2–12.

Fuller, Steve. 1997. *Science*. Minneapolis: University of Minnesota Press.

Gmelch, George. 2002. Baseball magic. In *Annual Editions, Anthropology 02/03*, ed. E. Angeloni, 171–175. New York: McGraw-Hill/Dushkin.

Goodman, Alan H., and Thomas L. Leatherman, eds. 1998. *Building a New Biocultural Synthesis: Political-Economic Perspectives on Human Biology*. Ann Arbor: University of Michigan Press.

Hooton, E. A. 1946. *Up from the Ape*. New York: Macmillan.

Hrdlička, Aleš. 1914. Physical anthropology in America: An historical sketch. *American Anthropologist* 16:507–554.

Kuhn, T. 1962. *The Structure of Scientific Revolutions*. Chicago: University of Chicago Press.

Kuklick, H., ed. 2008. *A New History of Anthropology*. New York: Blackwell.

Little, M., and K. Kennedy, eds. 2010. *Histories of American Physical Anthropology in the Twentieth Century*. Lanham, MD: Lexington Books.

Marks, J. 2000. Sherwood Washburn, 1911–2000. *Evolutionary Anthropology* 9:225–226.

Marks, J. 2009. *Why I Am Not a Scientist: Anthropology and Modern Knowledge*. Berkeley: University of California Press.

Miner, Horace. 1956. Body ritual among the Nacirema. *American Anthropologist* 54:503–507.

Proctor, Robert. 1991. *Value-Free Science? Purity and Power in Modern Knowledge*. Cambridge, Mass: Harvard University Press.

Rapp, Rayna. 1999. *Testing Women, Testing the Fetus: The Social Impact of Amniocentesis in America*. New York: Routledge.

Spencer, F., ed. 1997. *History of Physical Anthropology: An Encyclopedia*, New York: Garland Press.

Stocking, George W. 1987. *Victorian Anthropology*. New York: Free Press.

Sulloway, Frank J. 1982. Darwin's conversion: The Beagle voyage and its aftermath. *Journal of the History of Biology* 15:325–396.

Tambiah, S. J. 1990. *Magic, Science, Religion, and the Scope of Rationality*. New York: Cambridge University Press.

Tylor, Edward B. 1871. *Primitive Culture: Researches into the Development of Mythology, Philosophy, Religion, Language, Art and Custom*. London: John Murray.

Washburn, S. L. 1951. The new physical anthropology. *Transactions of the New York Academy of Sciences, Series II* 13:298–304.

CHAPTER 2

Where Did Our Scientific Ideas about Ourselves Come From? (On the History of Science)

THEME

Science is a cultural system, but because it has a solitary goal—empirical accuracy—it self-corrects and fares well when compared for its accuracy against other origin myths with additional, conflicting goals. Science is a culturally situated system of knowledge production that emerged in Renaissance Europe. As its rules developed, they were applied to understanding the place of humans in the natural order.

THE BEGINNINGS OF A NEW VIEW OF NATURE

The year 1543 is a good place to start because, far from being an entirely arbitrary year, it is the year that two crucially important works—paradigm-shifting works—were published. Europe was undergoing a rebirth or "renaissance" in art, looking to its classical ancient past for inspiration. The authority of the medieval Catholic Church had been coming under attack since a thirty-four-year-old cleric named Martin Luther had expressed his outrage at its earthly workings in 1517 by posting ninety-five critical theses on the door of his church at Wittenburg. These radical ideas could be disseminated far more rapidly than ever before, since movable type had been in use for several decades, pioneered by a printer named Johannes Gutenberg.

Into this social and political context, an elderly Polish astronomer allowed his radical ideas to be published under his Latinized name Nicolaus Copernicus as he lay dying. Copernicus believed that the existing observational data on the solar system could be explained just as easily by a new approach as it was by the age-old Greek system that held the earth to be constant and motionless and the celestial bodies to revolve around it.

His idea was *heliocentrism,* that the sun—not the earth—is the center of the solar system and that all the planets except the moon revolve around it, rather than around the earth. This idea was radical, although much of his work—*On the Revolutions of the Celestial Spheres*—was not. Copernicus had made no new observations that proved his case (like, for example, Galileo's observation of moons orbiting Jupiter, decades later). Rather, he pleaded his case as a theoretical consistency argument, showing that the available astronomical data could be explained in this new way at least as well as the old way. Like the old view, he believed that heavenly bodies moved in perfect circles (not in odd ellipses, as Kepler would later show) and that they were embedded in perfect solid spheres.

On the other hand, his idea implied that the heavens were considerably larger than they appeared and that the earth was not their center. If true, it implied two things: first, received wisdom might be wrong; and second, since things that do not move are more important than those that do move (you approach the king, not vice-versa) it makes the earth somewhat less important than it formerly was.

The same year, a Flemish physician called Andreas Vesalius published a different kind of work—highly empirical and deliberately provocative—*On the Fabric of the Human Body*. Whereas earlier medical treatises contained highly stylized representations of the human body, Vesalius illustrated his with brilliantly detailed and realistic renderings of the body, musculature, skeleton, and organs. His radicalism was not so much in the implications of a theory but in the methods of acquiring knowledge. How did Vesalius know how to draw the human body? Because he looked inside it, and saw for himself. And his message was, if you look inside the human yourself, this is what you will see. He called for physicians to learn anatomy by dissecting human corpses and seeing it firsthand for themselves.

Also unlike Copernicus, Vesalius boldly demonstrated that the received wisdom from ancient texts was indeed wrong in places. Where the ancient Roman physician Galen had made certain claims about the human body, Vesalius could demonstrate that the claim was based not on the structure of the human body but on that of a pig, or horse, or monkey—because the human body differed from what the ancient text said. *All you had to do was look for yourself.*

THE SCIENTIFIC REVOLUTION

The culmination of the 1543 works of Copernicus and Vesalius was a new approach to the natural world. From Copernicus we learned that new ideas might supersede old ones, and that the human species, and the earth, might not hold such glorified positions in the cosmos. From Vesalius we learned that empiricism was the most direct approach to gaining new knowledge. The empirical approach was the way to gain an accurate description of things; and it might be possible to establish such new knowledge in formalized and generalized ways.

Two such formalizers in the 1600s were the Italian astronomer/physicist Galileo Galilei and the French mathematician/philosopher René Descartes. Among their many contributions, we learned from the former about regularities of motion, and from the latter how to represent geometric shapes as algebraic equations on "Cartesian coordinates." Indeed Descartes formalized the new view of nature as nothing but matter and motion, categorically distinct from mind and spirit. Their contemporary, Francis Bacon, did not write any of Shakespeare's plays (as rumor once had it) but did propagandize extensively for "the new philosophy"—science—which would bring a better life for all, if it were allowed to grow and flourish.

William Harvey was the epitome of the new approach to the human body. He designed and conducted experiments to see whether the heart was really a heater for newly created blood—as ancient wisdom (and contemporary thought) had it, or whether the heart is a pump, with the blood circulating through the body and returning after completing a cycle. Of course, he discovered the latter, setting off a new way of seeing the body—as a machine composed of functioning parts—and a new way of finding about how bodies work: biological experiment.

But the person who came to embody science was Isaac Newton—mathematician, physicist, and mystic. Newton was a very undistinguished school-child until, as legend has it, an apple fell on his head and he got to wondering why things fall. Finding the mathematics of the day inadequate to the task, he invented his own "method of fluxions," which we now know as *calculus*. In his *Principia* (1687), Newton set forth the fundamental laws of motion that are obeyed by all things in the known universe; moreover, he described gravity mathematically, unifying and formalizing the process by which apples fall from trees on earth and planets are kept in motion around the sun in the heavens. The earth and the heavens were not so different after all, if the same mathematical generalizations could be applied to both.

Science after Newton was quite simply different, and he became its epitome—both in good and bad senses. In the bad sense of the modern view of the scientist, Newton was very competitive—he destroyed his perceived enemies and sought full and unshared credit for everything he worked on. Publicly he sounded magnanimous—"If I have seen further, it is because I have stood on the shoulders of giants," he said—but he held strong grudges against other scientists for daring to try and share the intellectual spotlight with him and against the German mathematician Leibniz for inventing calculus independently. He was also an obsessive workaholic with consequent social and mental problems, and a lifelong bachelor with no known romantic interests.

In the good sense of the modern view of the scientist, however, Newton's work defined the domain of science and framed its objectives. In the first place, it was now clear that there was a great deal the Bible had left out: math, the heliocentric solar system, gravity, and motion, just for starters. Clearly there was value in going beyond, or independently of, the Bible in a search for knowledge.

Second, Newton and his followers drew a distinction between proximate cause (processes, mechanisms, and natural laws) and ultimate cause (reasons for things and sources of the laws). While the distinction had been acknowledged since ancient times, the new science brought the distinction to the foreground and made proximate cause the goal of science, demarcating it from theological speculations on ultimate or final causes. The philosophical implications of Newton's unified physics were staggering because they literally redefined the domain of God's work.

If there were great generalizations to be discovered concerning the way in which light, or mass, or gravity worked, then God no longer needed to be invoked in every particular instance of light, or mass, or gravity. Rather, God could be seen as having devised these generalizations at the beginning of time, and then having let the universe run itself. This came to be known as the "mechanical philosophy"— the cosmos as a great machine (an appropriate metaphor for the time, of course), running essentially like a great clock, built by God but no longer requiring His vigorous intervention.

Thus, God came to be seen as the Creator of the laws of matter and motion, which Newton had discovered. If God were a lawmaker, and had endowed humans with the intelligence to study the world, it followed that discovering the laws by which God set the world up was an admirable pursuit. And that became the object of science: to find underlying regularity in nature; specific instances or events were no longer as interesting or important as the underlying law established by God.

Thus, not only was God removed from immediate events, and His domain now restricted, but Nature itself thereby became less mysterious and more fundamentally knowable. It had a divinely established order, set in motion by God. Indeed there was something fundamentally religious about studying Nature, for by coming to study the divine workings as they are manifest in the natural order, you can come to know the mind of God. The power of this view is retained even today. Compare, for example, President Clinton's words when the Human Genome Project announced the human DNA sequence in 1999: "Today we are learning the language in which God created life."

Biology, alas, lagged far behind physics and mathematics when it came to generalizations and laws. There seemed to be little you could learn from studying life that had the spiritual value of studying matter and motion, the fundamental constituents of the universe. Nevertheless, there were some profound changes occurring at this time in certain elements of our understanding of the human condition as well.

THE DECLINE OF DEGENERATION

For well over a thousand years, medieval life had been governed by a view of human existence that was both static and pessimistic. It held that man had sinned in the Garden of Eden (and that it was woman's fault!) and as a result, had "fallen from grace"—so birth was painful, life was tough, and relief could only be expected through death, assuming you were a good Christian. Earth remained in a state of moral decay, reflected in material decay, and would only get better with the return of Christ. Moreover, it was tantamount to sacrilegious to try and improve your lot on earth; God wanted you to focus on the next world, not on this one. This naturally encoded a justification for a stable social hierarchy—and the futility of aspirations to upward mobility that might upset that hierarchy. Life sucked, then you died. (Then, if you were lucky, you went to heaven.)

And yet by the seventeenth and eighteenth centuries, a different and more optimistic view was becoming disseminated. There were lands of great riches, resources, and opportunities, which could provide fortune for an ambitious sailor, merchant, or investor. Science was promoting the value of invention, and the Industrial Revolution was showing how creativity and hard work could change not only *your* life for the better, but *everyone's* life for the better. Maybe things weren't so bad after all!

Consequently, the dour view of degeneration came to be replaced by a more optimistic view of social history as progress. Things could improve on earth, during your lifetime. You could live a better life than your parents had known. Maybe it wasn't life that sucked, but just the feudal political and economic system—and since you could see people becoming freer and wealthier, maybe the purpose of history wasn't to have you look backward with remorse, but to look forward with anticipation.

What the new idea of social progress did was to get people thinking about earthly properties as being important, rather than passively accepting the world as it was passed down to them—and thinking about change as a fundamental part of human history. In other words, a new dynamic social universe was supplanting the old static order of things.

THE ANATOMY OF A "PYGMIE"

Travelogues from ancient times to the eighteenth century had mentioned remote races of people with one eye, or one leg, or no head; those who hissed like snakes, or ate their children, or lived in caves. Sailors had been reporting the existence of bizarre, manlike beasts far away; but then they were known to be great exaggerators, and they also reported mermaids. Ships to the East Indies or Africa occasionally tried to bring an example of these apes home, but the ocean voyage and diet had never permitted it successfully. Finally, in 1698, a young and ailing chimpanzee arrived in England from West Africa.

It died shortly thereafter, but became the subject of one of the most important scientific monographs of the age: Edward Tyson's (1699) *Orang-Outang, sive Homo Sylvestris; or, The Anatomy of a Pygmie, Compared With That of a Monkey, an Ape, and a Man.* Tyson was the leading anatomist in England and provided not only a competent dissection but the first clearly identifiable pictures of an ape (the ape in the title of his work actually refers to short-tailed monkeys, which were well-known).

Tyson made two crucial points in his monograph. The first is that in tabulating the number of observable resemblances between the chimpanzee and a human, versus between the chimpanzee and a monkey, he could identify 48 anatomical resemblances to a human but only 34 to a monkey. But of course it was not human, but an animal that looked more like a human than like anything else. The second crucial point was that its similarity to the human suggested physical continuity between the animals and ourselves. Certainly the resemblances between the human body and those of other animals had long been recognized, but this was something more: a creature more similar to a human than to anything else.

It would no longer be possible to think of humans as distinct from all other forms of life—physically, at least.

The overwhelming structural similarity to the human form directly suggested to Tyson that it had been created to be functionally like a human as well. The bones and muscles of its legs were so similar to those of their human counterparts that Tyson could only imagine that it walked upright, as human do, and that it was made for doing so. And yet he had seen it walking, but it did so on all fours, using the knuckles of its hands. Perhaps, he reasoned, it was only doing that because it was sick. He resolved this paradox by having it drawn neither fully upright nor knuckle-walking, but standing with the aid of a cane. This would encapsulate the symbolic position of the ape—nearly human physically, but not quite—an incomplete person, suggesting a state or a time of subhumanity. Perhaps that is why the cane stuck with pictures of apes for about the next 150 years.

BIBLICAL FALLIBILITY, OR AT LEAST INCOMPLETENESS

Human origins had been rather simple to understand. God created the world in less than a week; and near the end, he created a man ("Adam" is Hebrew for "man") and shortly thereafter took a rib and built a life mate for him ("Eve" or "Chava" is Hebrew for "life"). There was speculation as to whether Adam had a navel or not—if so, then why, for he had no umbilicus; and if not, then he was oddly different from you and me. But by and large, there seemed no compelling reason to question the biblical narrative.

That situation changed in 1492. Clearly there were diverse and unfamiliar people out there, far away. How did they get there? The Bible didn't say. Were they human, with souls and thus requiring salvation? The Bible didn't say. If they were descended from Adam and Eve, how did they come to be as they are? The Bible didn't say. And they must be descended from Adam and Eve, mustn't they?

A papal decree in the early 1500s declared the inhabitants of the New World to be fully human and lost after the Tower of Babel (in which people tried to build a tower to reach heaven, and God responded by destroying the tower and inflicting different languages on the builders, thus confusing them so they could no longer cooperate).

A young, seventeenth-century rabbinical student in Amsterdam named Baruch Spinoza posed a question to the scholars: if Moses wrote the first five books of the Bible, as tradition holds, then how could he possibly have written about his own death and burial in Chapter 34 of Deuteronomy, the fifth book of the Bible? Upon his subsequent excommunication from the Dutch Jewish community, Spinoza adopted the Latin name Benedictus (which, like Baruch, means "blessed") and continued to study philosophy. Spinoza devised a rational philosophical system in which God is seen as the natural order itself, and reason is the key to understanding the process by which that universe brought itself into being. More importantly, however, Spinoza demanded that the Bible be taken as an historical document—not as a document about history but as a document situated within history. His work marks the beginning of the "higher criticism" of the Bible.

It is in this intellectual climate that a French Calvinist scholar and diplomat named Isaac de la Peyrère published a book in 1655 that pales in significance and profundity next to Spinoza, but in fact was read by the young Spinoza and had a considerable impact on the question of interest to us: human origins. La Peyrère's book was called *Pre-Adamites* and raised the possibility that the Bible, being frequently vague, and occasionally self-contradictory, might be compatible with the idea that there were people around before Adam.

In particular, suggested La Peyrère, maybe the Bible is simply describing in Genesis the creation of the ancestors of the Hebrews; and maybe God created the ancestors of other peoples independently and earlier. The importance of La Peyrère's book may lie simply in the fact that it was publicly burned in Paris, and thirty-six refutations of it were published in the next few decades. Clearly it had touched a nerve.

La Peyrère's work has little value for the modern scholar, except as having publicly called into question for the first time the literal truth of the traditional account of the creation of Adam. Oddly, La Peyrère's book would also be invoked as a precursor of a very different, and uglier, idea—that the different races of people were the products of separate creative acts by God, and therefore had no common biological history and should be considered separate species—an idea called *polygenism*.

MONOGENISM

Taking La Peyrère's argument further than he did, one could envision different races being the products of separate creations. If so, then they were different in their very essences and could not be considered members of the same species. This was an interpretation that was greeted with enthusiasm in the American South, prior to the Civil War; after all, if whites and blacks were not really brothers biologically, then slavery might have a scientific argument to justify it. Whites enslaving Africans, in this view, would be different in magnitude, but not in kind, from humans domesticating cattle.

But the term "*species*" was beginning to take on a formal sense by 1700—not two individuals who just looked similar but, rather, who were capable of interbreeding with each other. The implications for understanding the human species were profound. Clearly, humans could interbreed, and were doing so all over the globe; European sailors had demonstrated that beyond reasonable doubt. By that very fact, they must be considered a single species; and if the units of God's creation were species, then all humans must have been the product of a single creative act.

The empirical evidence for monogenism swayed the bulk of the scholarly community, especially in Europe, by the mid-1700s. Polygenism would enjoy a vogue in America just before the Civil War, but except for brief flare-ups at Harvard (in the works of Louis Agassiz in the 1870s and Ruggles Gates in the 1940s), it was effectively dead.

Monogenism, however, carried with it an important implication. Accepting that humans comprised a single species and that the species had its origin in a single creative act, one must still be struck by the physical diversity in the human form over the earth. People looked different from one another; and if Adam and Eve were white (for the sake of argument, the Garden of Eden being in the Near East), then Africans and Asians must have developed their divergent appearances over the course of human history. Therefore, considerable physical change must be possible over the span of biblical time.

The disputation between the monogenists and polygenists is worth considering because the intellectual battle lines were drawn in somewhat different ways than seem familiar to us today. The monogenists held that the human species was a single natural entity, descended from an original single pair of people. They identified that couple as Adam and Eve, taking the Bible as literally true, and used that as an argument for the abolition of slavery. Thus, they were biblical literalists and social liberals.

But they were also obliged, by taking those positions, to accept the mutability of human form and to develop explanations of how biological stocks could change through time. Thus, in addition to being biblical literalists and social liberals, the monogenists were also the first evolutionists: microevolutionists, to be sure—considering changes within species, rather than transpecific change—but the first modern evolutionists nevertheless. The opposition, polygenism, held that different races were the products of separate creations and had always been as they are; thus, they clung to a static creationist view of human origins, invoked it odiously to support the institution of slavery, and rationalized it with a modern, liberal interpretation of the Bible.

CAUSE AND EFFECT

Thinking about the universe as a machine—a powerful metaphor of the age—had another effect: getting philosophers to think more rigorously about why things happen at all. History, for example, could be interpreted as "leading up to" the second coming of Christ. But little of history is thereby explained; if you want to know why the Roman Empire fell, or why the Industrial Revolution occurred, interpreting it in terms of the second coming of Christ will not get you very far. Things happen for reasons in the immediate past, not in the distant future.

What's true for history is also true for physics. A billiard ball moves because of the one that just hit it, not because of the one it's going to hit. This is especially true if we adopt the Newtonian idea that the domain of science is the study of proximate cause. If there is an ultimate cause for the billiard ball moving—for example, the intention of a billiards shooter—that is not the domain of physics and mechanics, but of psychology.

A Scottish philosopher of the eighteenth century named David Hume examined the entire concept of cause and effect in scientific reasoning and concluded that three things were needed to infer that A caused B with any degree of rigor.

The first is some sort of physical contiguity of A and B, such as contact; the second is that A must precede B; and the third is the constant conjunction of the two, by which Hume meant a regular pattern in which A and B occur together. Hume was obviously only interested in cause in the material world—the world of proximate cause and matter and motion. His reasoning had dramatic consequences in biology, however:

- Why did the world come into existence on the first day? So that "man" would have a place to live on the sixth day.
- Why do animals have the features that they do? So that they would be able to survive where they live.
- Why is "man" gifted with the power of reason? So that when a difficulty arises, he can think his way through it.

Each of these questions contains a cause and an effect, but none satisfy Hume's criteria even remotely. Most acutely, they invert the necessary time relations between a cause and an effect: something on day 6 is the cause of something on day 1; human reason is there for its future use. This reasoning is *teleological*— or goal directed. A bullet has a goal in its trajectory—the target at which it was fired; a fertilized egg has a goal—the maturity, reproduction, and senescence of the organism. But does history have a goal? Do things happen today in order to unfold a plan for *tomorrow*? Or do things happen today because of what happened *yesterday*?

Hume would use the idea of causation to attack the popular liberal theology of his age, which saw the hand of the Deity in forming the world and its beings and in giving them goals and purposes for existing. But as Britain's most influential philosopher, he would set in motion the biggest doubts about the quality of these ideas as scientific explanations. Should not explanations about cause and effect in organic beings be framed in tangible, material, natural terms, as the rest of modern thought was clearly heading? And should not biological cause and effect be situated in history, with the past—*not* the future— causing the present?

About this time, too, what had formerly been called "natural philosophy" was coming to be labeled by another, newer term—"*science.*"

THE GREAT CHAIN OF BEING

The structure of the natural world was well understood in medieval times. Just as the social world had a linear hierarchy, with the King at the top and noblemen, knights, and peasants below, so too did the natural world have a linear hierarchy. Humans were obviously the pinnacle of creation, and things that were similar to humans were slightly below them, and so on, stretching down to lizards, fish, and insects. The hand of God gave the species of the world this pattern: species intergraded into one another to form a chain of perfection. It was obvious, it was simple, and it was affirmed by everyday experience.

Except that maybe it was not so obvious. A Swedish botanist-physician named Carl Linnaeus set out to formalize the relations among animals, vegetables, and minerals and published a small pamphlet in 1735 called *The System of Nature*. Linnaeus's "system" involved terse names and descriptions for each form of animal, with an even more obvious, if previously unheralded, structure: different species clustered into groups, and groups of groups clustered as well. Thus, lions and tigers, being similar to one another, could be seen as different species belonging to a common "order" (which he called *Ferae*) whose members had sharp teeth and claws. And this "order" was just one of several that could be clustered into a larger group of hairy, four-footed creatures that nursed their young, which he called a "class"—*Quadrupedia*. And these in turn clustered with birds, amphibians, fish, insects, and worms into the Animal Kingdom.

The new pattern was even more obvious than the Great Chain of Being had been, and caught on nearly overnight in the academic community. God Created, it was said, but Linnaeus Arranged. But these clusterings—which we would now call nested categories of equal rank—had an important consequence in that they obscured the Great Chain of Being. Was there a sense in which falcons were really superior to sharks? Or deer were superior to falcons? Or camels were superior to deer? Or hyenas were superior to camels?

Was every species rankable in terms of their similarity to us? Perhaps Linnaeus could more reasonably aggregate species into restricted groups based on their similarity to *one another*, and then into larger groups of more relaxed similarity.

What Linnaeus was doing here was applying a radical biological relativism to the natural world, tearing down the linear hierarchy of the Great Chain of Being and replacing it with a hierarchy of a very different kind—one wherein all species are equal, and can be more meaningfully arranged in relation to one another than in relation to an imaginary transcendent ideal: presumably, us. The reason we can call it biological relativism is that it parallels ideas that developed in other intellectual fields about the equality of elements in a system for which nonequality had long been taken for granted. In fact, maybe the hereditary aristocratic hierarchies that had existed for centuries weren't so natural after all, and maybe life would be better without them. By the late 1700s, revolutions in America and then in France were promoting the radical relativistic idea that all citizens were equal before the law and perhaps even that everyone was "created equal."

Somewhat later, of course, anthropologists would come to appreciate that like citizens and species, cultures cannot be objectively ranked, except by narrow, arbitrary criteria—a position that they would call "cultural relativism."

And Linnaeus emphasized the point by classifying the human species along with all other animals from the very beginning. By the 1758 edition of *The System of Nature*, humans were a single species (*Homo sapiens*), in contrast to a second species (of Linnaeus's imagination, unfortunately), *Homo troglodytes*; the genus *Homo* was one of four genera in the Order Primates (the others being monkeys, lemurs, and [mistakenly] bats); and the Order Primates was one of several orders within the Class Mammalia.

BUFFON'S OBJECTION TO THE NESTED HIERARCHY

Linnaeus's general view of nature dominated the academic community almost immediately, and the holdouts were few. One such holdout was a respected naturalist outside the university setting, a wealthy independent scholar who took the name of the town he owned, Buffon.

Count de Buffon wrote his own summary of Nature, a work published over several decades in thirty-six volumes, called *Natural History, General and Specific*—one of the most widely read works of the French Enlightenment in the eighteenth century. In it, Buffon describes the different kinds of animals and shows them with elaborate and beautiful woodcuts. His picture of the gibbon, for example, is the first in European literature.

His work was radical in its way. His theory of the earth had it formed by natural means, tens of thousands of years ago—far more than the theology faculty of the University of Paris would permit. They forced him in 1751 to retract some of his more heretical notions about earth history, naturalism, and "truth"—showing how sensitive theologians were already becoming to the difficulties in reconciling nature and scripture.

Unfazed, however, Buffon continued to publish thoughtful musings on natural history with varying degrees of radicalness. He argued explicitly for monogenism, against slavery, and for microevolution—and developed an esoteric theory of the effect of food and the conditions of life on a species' "internal mold" to account for it. For Buffon, the task of the scientist was not just to organize and name things, it was to explain their relationships; and Buffon saw classification as a sterile enterprise if it is unaccompanied by explanation.

He was especially troubled, however, by some of the implications he saw in the Linnaean classification. From comparative anatomy, it was clear that there was a strong correspondence among the bodies of different animals. One could, Buffon noted, convert the skeleton of a horse into that of a human with minimal effort:

> And if it is once admitted that there are families of plants and animals, that the donkey is of the horse family, . . . then one could equally say that man and ape have had a common origin like the horse and donkey. . . .
>
> The naturalists who establish so casually the families of plants and animals do not seem to have grasped sufficiently the full scope of these consequences, which would reduce the immediate products of creation to a number of individuals as small as one might wish. For . . . if it were true that the donkey were but a degenerated horse—then there would be no limits to the power of nature. One would then not be wrong to suppose that she could have drawn with time, all other organized beings from a single being.

Buffon immediately goes on to reject the entire enterprise. In other words, he rejects Linnaean classification because to him it implies macroevolution, which he knows cannot be true. The clustering of cats and dogs and bears into a single group must suggest, to him, the idea of common descent. Paradoxically, Linnaeus himself never drew that conclusion, and both men remained lifelong creationists, nevertheless despising one another.

EXTINCTION

By the end of the 1700s, another set of data was demanding an explanation. The last known dodo, a large flightless bird found only on the island of Mauritius, had been seen in 1684. Had people (in this case, Dutch sailors) driven it to extinction?

If so, this created a theological problem. After all, the hand of God was evident in His works on earth, and one aspect of His bounty was to have populated the world with diverse forms of life that could be arranged into a Great Chain of Being. If almighty God made a chain, how could puny people destroy one of its links? If people could really make species disappear, and undermine God's plan of creation, wrote a prominent naturalist in 1690, that might constitute a "dismemb'ring of the universe"—clearly not something to be considered lightly!

Alas, no more dodos turned up. They did not seem to be hiding anywhere—not on Mauritius, nor in the remotest places people could think of. There were just no more dodos.

Apparently people could indeed make a species go extinct.

This observation settled in about the same time as another one came to light. The Industrial Revolution necessitated the construction of large factories, and building large factories necessitated the excavation of large holes for foundations. And excavating large holes turned up fossils.

Fossils had been known since the Renaissance, and their identity as formerly living things had come gradually to be accepted. Suddenly it became clear that there indeed existed long ago a diverse fauna comprising animals similar to, but distinct from, any living species in the present. Extinction thus became an unavoidable fact of the history of life on earth. But how to make sense of it? What was God's plan for extinction?

Two prominent French biologists tried to explain it in different ways in the early 1800s. The first, Jean-Baptiste de Lamarck, had a surprisingly simple and elegant explanation. Lamarck argued that species have a natural fit to their environments but environments change. When such a change happens, the organism is faced with two options: either die or change itself. He believed that they change according to their needs, and that the physical alterations they effect are stably passed on to their offspring—a theory that came to be known as *the inheritance of acquired characteristics*. Passing on the new body form to the next generation would result in the production of a new species, one slightly improved on its parent, and thus one link higher up on the Great Chain of Being. Thus extinction was something of an illusion: new species succeeded older species, but were actually descended from them.

Lamarck can be credited with producing the first modern theory of macroevolution, the transformation of one species into another, or evolution above the species level.

Georges Cuvier held a different view. He pointed out that the Great Chain of Being was passé, and by implication, any theory that presupposed it could not hold much water. Building on Linnaeus, he argued that there were four kinds of animals, built on entirely different body plans: vertebrates, "Articulata" (including insects), "Radiata" (including animals with radial symmetry), and mollusks (with shells) —and that no amount of argument could permit them to be linearly ranked, for they were so different as to be noncomparable.

Instead, Cuvier looked to the patterns of geological history in which layers of the earth appear to have distinct forms of life within them and appear to have clear boundaries separating them from other ages with other forms of life. This suggested not so much the transformation of species into new species as environments changed, but the wholesale replacement of diverse species alive at one time by a different set of species. Extinction, to Cuvier, was real, and when species died out, in some kind of catastrophe, new species were formed and took their place. Cuvier's theory came to be known as catastrophism, and although he forced the scholarly community to recognize extinction as part of an increasingly complex view of the history of the earth, he nevertheless declined to speculate as to where the new species came from.

But Cuvier was essentially the founder of modern vertebrate paleontology, and after Cuvier, one had to acknowledge that different species came into existence and passed out of existence at different times.

The Napoleonic Wars hindered communication between English and French scientists. In general, the English were more pious than the French and were more preoccupied with trying to reconcile the data of *biology* (Lamarck had coined that term shortly after the turn of the 1800s) with Scripture. The French also tended toward grand theoretical syntheses, while the English were contemptuous of anything that couldn't be directly seen or measured. Consequently, when Cuvier was translated into English, the translator introduced the idea that the most recent catastrophe was described in the Bible as Noah's flood, and this introduction was not noticed for many decades among Cuvier's English readers. Moreover, it left the French with the best understanding of ancient life, but lacking the empirical basis in earth history to make proper sense of it.

The English, for their part, were busy observing, experimenting, and measuring—but lacked a coherent framework or even a philosophical approach for understanding it.

NATURAL THEOLOGY

When Charles Darwin was a student at Cambridge in the 1820s, he was assigned works of natural theology, an English biology movement designed to demonstrate the hand of God in the study of Nature. How did they demonstrate this? By calling attention to the wonders of the natural world and challenging you to imagine how they could have come about in the absence of God.

This God, however, was not the God of the physicists, who set down mathematical laws at the beginning of time and then stepped aside, but rather, a busy craftsman, meticulously molding each species in a demonstration of both His love and bounty, and of His industry. Just as physicists could study the mind of God by inferring regularity in nature, biologists could study it by observing diversity. Imagine finding a watch in the street, went their most famous argument; its intricate complexity tells you that it was made by the hand of a clever craftsman, a watchmaker. Now look at the human eye or an orchid. Doesn't its intricate complexity speak as well of an intelligent designer—a benevolent celestial presence that made it come about?

But a series of devastating arguments were already known, having been formulated first by the skeptical philosopher David Hume. Consider the outline of the shape of your home state. Is it not complex? Aside from Utah, Wyoming, and Colorado, which are simple geometric figures, all the states are so complex that they are hard to draw accurately, and most are consequently instantly recognizable. And yet, they are not the products of a heavenly state maker! They are the products of geological and political forces—complex forces operating over a span of time, but ultimately understandable, unlike miracles.

Thus, the appearance of a complex design doesn't necessarily imply a conscious designer behind it; the forces at work may be blind and undirected, but may be nevertheless comprehensible, and can produce a complex design as well.

A parallel argument was made by an economist named Adam Smith in his book *The Wealth of Nations* (1776). A complex, efficient economy, he argued, develops not through conscious controlled design, but spontaneously by the actions of people pursuing their individual interests. And such a system will tend to run as if guided by an "invisible hand," he wrote. Things apparently could come to exist without top-down creative control. And if economies could seem to exist as if made and regulated by an invisible hand, was it such a stretch to imagine organs and bodies being similar?

And what about the watch lying in the street because it didn't keep good time and was thrown there by a dissatisfied customer? If the existence of a lousy watch implies a lousy watchmaker, doesn't the existence of imperfections—such as degenerative disease, or baldness, or PMS, or birth defects, or acne—imply an incompetent Creator? Yet somehow, natural theologians were not about to criticize the work of God, which shows that they were *assuming* His properties and existence, not *deducing* them.

Thus, neither the observation of order and structure nor the analogy to the attributes of a watch is a valid reason to infer the wisdom or hand of God in operation. God might well exist, but He simply cannot be derived from the properties of living beings on earth. Those features could have arisen by purely natural means—which may be unknown but are ultimately knowable—unlike the actions of God. As the early chemist Robert Boyle argued, in stumping for the New Philosophy—this isn't about what God can do; it's about what Nature can do.

Boyle was, in fact, a very pious Christian, who nevertheless recognized that new knowledge was making it increasingly difficult to take the Bible at face value. And by the time of Paley's *Natural Theology* (1802), an intellectual revolution had already begun in biblical scholarship.

Christians had traditionally imagined Jesus in their own time and place, and relevant to their own lives. But theologians now began to ask what the "historical" Jesus was like. If there was a way to recover the real Jesus from the gospels, it would have to involve engaging with Jewish history, language, and law, which medieval Christian scholars had been reluctant to do. What might the theological implications be, if Jesus turned out to be . . . Jewish? Moreover, what if the Romans really were responsible for his death, and not the Jews, as the gospels strain to suggest?

While Darwinism became a lightning rod for the biblical literalist's reaction against the new trends in science, actually the new biblical criticism was far more threatening to the literalist. By the 1840s, German theologians were grappling with the possibility that the life of Christ, as recorded in the gospels, might not be absolutely accurate. After all, the four canonical gospels are, at very least, frequently contradictory and inconsistent—they give radically different genealogies of Jesus, for a glaring example. Moreover, ancient manuscripts were coming to light, showing that the gospels of Matthew, Mark, Luke, and John were part of a rich tradition of early Christian literature. And by the turn of the twentieth century, the early anthropologist James Frazer could take it as axiomatic that, whatever history lies beneath the gospels, the proper context for understanding them is the myths and legends of the ancient Near East.

UNIFORMITARIAN GEOLOGY

Extrapolating backward from the time of Jesus, pious clerics had attempted to ascertain the time of Creation, given the fact that St. Luke's gospel provides the ancestry of Jesus back to Adam. In 1642, Bishop John Lightfoot calculated that God had been at work at 9 am in 3928 BC creating the universe; and his calculation was revised in 1658 by Bishop James Ussher, who determined that momentous date actually to have been October 23, 4004 BC.

Buffon had speculated in the mid-1700s that the earth was considerably older than the few thousand years the Bible suggests. But English empiricist science would come to make that even more likely, with the maturation of geology in the early nineteenth century. The key figure in that process was Charles Lyell, a Scottish geologist who published a magisterial three-volume summary and synthesis of the field in the 1830s.

Lyell sought to reform geology by giving it a more empirically rigorous basis. We don't see miracles, reasoned Lyell, who was nevertheless a very pious churchman, and therefore we cannot invoke their effects in explaining earth history. As scientists, we can only use the forces we know of, and can study, to explain the geological patterns we encounter.

That raised a serious problem for traditional biblical chronology. After all, the processes we can see and measure, such as erosion, act extremely slowly. Glaciers move, and leave tracks of their movement, but they do so at a glacial pace. The erosion of coastlines by oceans, or riverbeds, can be measured, but this invariably yields results showing very slow movement. Extrapolating backward, one can calculate that the processes that produced the effects we now see must have been going on for a very, very long time, far longer than the 6,000 years allowed by the biblical chronology.

Lyell's approach to geology came to be known as *uniformitarianism,* and subsumed three related ideas: (1) that the only types of process we can use to understand earth history are the ones we see in operation today; (2) that we can only invoke the magnitude of those processes that we see in operation today; and that (3) the earth was consequently very old, so old that it was hard to see when it began, and hard to project when it might end—it just cycled on, with minor perturbations, beyond the human grasp of time. The first idea precluded hypothetical catastrophic events, such as cometary impacts, from playing a major role in the explanation of earth history; the second precluded hypothetical events such as worldwide floods—floods were occasionally severe, but they were local, and not worldwide; and the third was the logical consequence of the first two.

Suddenly the age of the earth was opened up, and geology had some breathing room. Species had time to live, to develop, and to die out; and geological processes had a rock-solid empirical foundation. Lyell's work would have a major impression on the young Charles Darwin, sailing around the world in the *HMS Beagle* as it was being published.

ADAM'S WORLD

This still left one thorny problem for anyone interested in incorporating humans into the history of life on earth. The earth seemed to be old, and displayed a succession of faunas: dinosaurs at one stage and saber-tooth tigers and mammoths at another. Where did humans fit in? There was certainly no evidence to suggest that they lived among the dinosaurs. Humans were clearly geologically very recent, and dinosaurs very ancient.

Natural theologians coyly reconciled earth history and human history by interpreting the formation of the animals by God as recorded in Genesis to be specifically the formation of *modern* animals. What the Bible relates, they reasoned, is the creation of the modern world, prepared by God for Adam and Eve in Eden, loaded up with the animals and plants that we see now. Prior to that was an archaic world, a premodern world, filled with the remote and unfamiliar creatures of paleontology.

This, however, was beginning to have problems as well. All over Europe, ancient remains of extinct mammals were becoming known and were inferred to have been part of the premodern world, before the Garden of Eden. Yet just as ancient geologically as these mammals were chipped rock tools, known as *eoliths,* or "dawn stones." Since humans were the only species known to sharpen the edges of rocks to make cutting tools out of them, it followed that these tools were made by some form of primitive people. Were they "pre-Adamites," or were they modern people in a modern world who existed since the Garden of Eden?

Many scientists favored the latter view, since it removed the teleological reasoning implied by seeing a modern world created as simply the planned precondition for the appearance of humans. One could instead see the history of life intertwining with the history of humans, as ancient life unfolded into modern life, and archaic humans into modern humans. It could be seen as a history, a development, an *evolution*.

Charles Lyell, however, wasn't among those scientists. Although he was the champion of uniformitarianism, and had settled the issue on the age of the earth, he was conservative enough theologically not to be able to imagine tool-making human beings living alongside extinct forms of life. The evidence, he felt, was just insufficient to settle such a crucial issue. In the 1850s, a series of careful archaeological excavations showed incontrovertibly that Lyell's position was no longer tenable. The tools were now being found with the bones of extinct animals, alongside them, scattered among them, and in clear association with them. Some form of human had lived and chipped stone tools on a premodern earth, filled with unfamiliar creatures, long before Adam and Eve and the Garden of Eden on the modern earth.

Lyell himself reluctantly acknowledged it was true.

HUMAN EVOLUTION

The early evolutionary theory of Lamarck was highly speculative and very bold. Lamarck not only applied his theory of acquired characteristics and evolution "up the great chain" to animals but also explicitly recognized that it might apply to humans as well. Clearly, the most similar animals to humans were the apes; could we imagine such a transition from ape to person? Lamarck had written that indeed, we could, in his *Zoological Philosophy* (1809):

> If some race of four-handed animals, especially one of the most perfect of them, were to lose, by force of circumstance or some other cause, the habit of climbing trees and grasping the branches with its feet in order to hold on to them, and if the individuals of this race were forced for a series of generations to use their feet only for walking and to give up using their feet like hands, there is no doubt . . . that these four-handed animals would at length be transformed into two-handed and that the thumbs on their feet would cease to be separated from the other digits.
>
> Furthermore, if they . . . were impelled by the desire to command a large and distant view, and hence tried to stand upright, and continually adopted that habit from generation to generation, there is again no doubt that their feet would gradually acquire a shape suitable for supporting them in an erect posture. Lastly, if these same animals were to give up using their jaws as weapons for biting, tearing or grasping, or as scissors for cutting and feeding on plants, and if they were to use them only for chewing; there is again no doubt that . . . their snout would shorten more and more, and that finally it would be entirely erased so that their incisor teeth became vertical.

Lamarck's ideas never caught on among the scientific establishment in England. But among the literate lay public, there was certainly interest in the problem of the transformation of species.

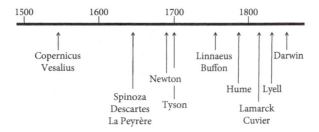

Figure 2.1. Timeline of major scholarly works discussed in this chapter.

One member of the literate lay public was a Scottish publisher named Robert Chambers. He spoke and corresponded with many scientists and read widely; and in 1844 he anonymously published a book, essentially espousing Lamarck's ideas, called *Vestiges of the Natural History of Creation.* Chambers's ideas were crude and far more mystical than academic biologists would tolerate, however. He saw life as a continual progression, and not only imagined humans ascending from apes, but Europeans ascending from nonwhite peoples as well. The work was heretical, racist, and not very well informed biologically.

And yet there was something compelling about the idea of species changing and all life being somehow historically connected. *Vestiges* went through eleven editions and sold 24,000 copies in its first ten years, 1844–1854. (By contrast, *The Origin of Species* would go through six editions and sell only 9,500 copies in its first ten years, 1859–1869.)

Vestiges was scorned widely by scientists throughout its publication history, although it was widely read. Its author was vilified for his ignorance and for his heresy by the experts. If the author's identity had become known, it would have made him a laughingstock and destroyed his career. So if anyone else out there was harboring similar ideas about the transformation of one species into another, or "the development hypothesis" (as it was known), he would do well to keep them to himself.

REFERENCES AND FURTHER READING

Appel, T. 1987. *The Cuvier-Geoffroy Debate: French Biology in the Decades before Darwin.* New York: Oxford University Press.

Buffon, Count de. 1744–1788. *Histoire Naturelle: Générale et Particulière.* http://www .buffon.cnrs.fr/index.php?lang=en#top

Desmond, A., and J. Moore. 2009. *Darwin's Sacred Cause: How a Hatred of Slavery Shaped Darwin's Views on Human Evolution.* New York: Houghton Mifflin Harcourt.

Eddy, J. H., Jr. 1984. Buffon, organic alterations, and man. *Studies in the History of Biology* 7:1–45.

Gillespie, C. C. 1951. *Genesis and Geology: The Impact of Scientific Discoveries upon Religious Beliefs in the Decades before Darwin.* Cambridge, MA: Harvard University Press.

Glass, B., O. Temkin, and W. L. Straus, eds. 1959. *Forerunners of Darwin: 1745–1859*. Baltimore, MD: Johns Hopkins University Press.

Gould, S. J. 1983. Chimp on the chain. *Natural History* 98 (12):18–27.

Gould, S. J. 1984. Adam's navel. *Natural History* 93 (6):6–14.

Gould, S. J. 1990. Darwin and Paley meet the invisible hand. *Natural History* 99 (11):8–16.

Greene, J. C. 1954. Some early speculations on the origin of human races. *American Anthropologist* 56:31–41.

Hall, A. R. 1954. *The Scientific Revolution 1500–1800: The Formation of the Modern Scientific Attitude*. Boston: Beacon Press.

Harris, M. 1968. *The Rise of Anthropological Theory*. New York: Thomas Y. Crowell.

Honigsheim, P. 1942. The philosophical background of European anthropology. *American Anthropologist* 44:376–387.

Koerner, L. 1999. *Linnaeus: Nature and Nation*. Cambridge, MA: Harvard University Press.

Lamarck, J. B. 1809. *Zoological Philosophy*. Chicago: University of Chicago Press, 1984.

Livingstone, D. 2008. *Adam's Ancestors: Race, Religion, and the Politics of Human Origins*. Baltimore, MD: Johns Hopkins University Press.

Lovejoy, A. O. 1936. *The Great Chain of Being*. Cambridge, MA: Harvard University Press.

Lurie, E. 1954. Louis Agassiz and the races of man. *Isis* 45:227–242.

Mayr, E. 1961. Cause and effect in biology. *Science* 134:1501–1506.

Mayr, E. 1982. *The Growth of Biological Thought*. Cambridge, MA: Harvard University Press.

Millhauser, M. 1959. *Just before Darwin: Robert Chambers and Vestiges*. Middletown, CT: Wesleyan University Press.

Montagu, M. F. A. 1943. Edward Tyson, M.D., F.R.S., 1650–1708 and the rise of human and comparative anatomy in England. *Memoirs of the American Philosophical Society* 20.

Radin, P. 1929. History of ethnological theories. *American Anthropologist* 31:9–33.

Rowe, J. H. 1965. The Renaissance foundations of anthropology. *American Anthropologist* 67:1–20.

Rudwick, M. J. S. 1985. *The Meaning of Fossils: Episodes in the History of Palaeontology*. Chicago: University of Chicago Press.

Ruse, M. 1996. *Monad to Man: The Concept of Progress in Evolutionary Biology*. Cambridge, MA: Harvard University Press.

Schiebinger, L. 1993. *Nature's Body*. Boston: Beacon.

Schwartz, J. 1990. Darwin, Wallace, and Huxley, and *Vestiges of the Natural History of Creation*. *Journal of the History of Biology* 23:127–153.

Trautmann, T. R. 1991. The revolution in ethnological time. *Man* 27:379–397.

Turner, J. 2014. *Philology: The Forgotten Origins of the Modern Humanities*. Princeton, NJ: Princeton University Press.

Van Riper, A. B. 1993. *Men among the Mammoths: Victorian Science and the Discovery of Human Prehistory*. Chicago: University of Chicago Press.

Wooton, D. 2015. *The Invention of Science*. New York: Harper.

CHAPTER 3

Can You Tell If You Are a Darwinist?
(On Theories of Evolution)

THEME

Darwinism is a complex set of theories about the productive capability of natural systems. Darwin himself would probably recognize few of the modern invocations of his name, and would likely repudiate some. If Darwinism is used to rationalize oppressive political philosophies, it is bad for science—so it is in our interests to explore and confront the diverse forms that evolutionary theory can take.

Like many students since his time, Darwin was undirected in college, and upon graduation he was not quite sure what he wanted to do, although his father was pushing him toward medicine. He signed up to be ship's naturalist and an educated companion for Captain Robert FitzRoy of the *HMS Beagle*. The *Beagle* set sail for South America on December 27, 1831, and returned to England nearly five years later. Most of that time was spent in or around South America and in the now-famous Galápagos archipelago.

Darwin left England a knowledgeable student of contemporary biology and returned thoroughly confused. Most confusing was the relationship between species and their localities, or biogeography. He had, of course, been educated in pious creationist natural theology at Cambridge, which was already finding difficulty in explaining the distribution of species.

Creationist biogeography was rooted in the biblical story of Noah, who is warned by God of the impending destruction of all life because of the sinful ways of the local people. Noah builds a large ship, after God's specifications, and takes two (Genesis 6) or fourteen (Genesis 7) of every animal, along with his family, to survive the forty days of rain. After the flood waters recede, the ark lands on "the mountains of Ararat," and the world is repopulated by the survivors. The theme of destruction and rebirth of life is common enough in world mythology, and a cognate legend from Babylonia calls the boat builder "Utnapishtim." But it was, by the 1830s, difficult to reconcile with geological data—as all geological formations could not possibly have been laid down in a great worldwide flood a few thousand years ago!

Moreover, there was an unpleasantly unscientific sense to the way in which this theory wrestled with the fit of organisms to their environment. Taking the biblical narrative at face value, one would have to envision penguins and polar bears, adapted to cold weather, alongside camels and scorpions, adapted to hot weather. Assuming for the sake of argument that the ark landed somewhere in west Asia, such as Armenia or Turkey, it was difficult to imagine how those differently adapted kinds of animals could have gotten to where they now live, and are well suited to, without going through a prolonged period of maladaptation in getting there, which they would most certainly not have survived! This was, of course, a classically teleological explanation—the animals were adapted to where they were destined *to end up*, not to where they presumably *were*. And it was seen as highly problematic on that basis.

Darwin was intrigued by the relationships between the extinct fossils he collected in South America and the species he saw there alive—and between the living animals in different South American climates. For example, Darwin knew that horses in the New World had been brought there by the Spanish; but he found evidence that essentially modern horses had been indigenous to the New World and had gone extinct thousands of years ago. "Certainly it is a marvelous event in the history of animals," he later wrote, "that a native kind should have disappeared to be succeeded in after ages by the countless herds introduced by the Spanish colonist!"

Another fact that impressed him was a fossil *glyptodont,* a large extinct animal covered in armor like an armadillo. Glyptodonts were known only from the southern part of the New World. Armadillos were known only from the same regions. Might it be meaningful that two such uniquely similar kinds of mammals would be found together, and nowhere else? And the animals to which they were in turn most similar—sloths and capybaras—were also found in the same area. Was this a miracle, or the signature of an unknown, but interesting, natural process?

Natural theology waved away this issue by saying that God, in His wisdom, created animals to be adapted to their surroundings. One could, of course, thereby predict that South American steppes would have the same kind of animals as West Asian steppes—yet they don't. They seem to have different kinds of animals adapted in different ways to similar environments, likewise with the animals of the South American and Central African rain forests. Further, given that the islands of an archipelago, like the Galapagos, are all environmentally very similar, it is not at all clear, under this theory, why similar animals should differ in form slightly from island to island.

It seemed that geographical proximity and history, not crude environmental similarity, best correlated with the distribution of biological resemblances among fossil and living species. Darwin wrote in his *Journal of Researches,* later known as *The Voyage of the Beagle,* in 1839: "This wonderful relationship in the same continent between the dead and the living will, I do not doubt, hereafter throw more light on the appearance of organic beings on our earth, and their disappearance from it, than any other class of facts."

DARWIN'S ARGUMENT

Darwin returned from his voyage on October 2, 1836, and reestablished contact with the leading biologists of the age, who studied the specimens he had collected. He wrote several books and monographs and developed a reputation as an able and competent biologist himself.

By the mid-1840s, Darwin had satisfied himself that there was a way to explain these biogeographic questions and other diverse issues in biology. The key lay in the writings of a social scientist, Thomas Malthus. In his *Essay on Population* (1798; Darwin read the second edition of 1802), Malthus had observed that people regularly outreproduce their subsistence base. The result was competition, or what Malthus called a "struggle for existence." And if you thought the present was bad, the future would only be worse, given the high reproductive rate of the poor. Malthus called for sexual abstinence (after all, that was where babies came from), and the denial of assistance to the poor (which would only permit them to have more babies, which were, as he saw it, the heart of the problem).

Darwin accepted Malthus's argument of a struggle for existence but wondered why it should only apply to humans. After all, don't mice and dragonflies and sharks multiply faster than their food supply as well, leading to a struggle for existence in them? And at all stages of the life cycle, there are far more cockroaches than can possibly multiply satisfactorily. Only a small proportion of them actually do leave descendants. Perhaps, then, some invisible hand selects those who will leave descendants, out of the many possibilities. And if those "selected" to reproduce preferentially are not perfectly average representatives of their group, the second generation will appear to differ slightly from the first. Thus Darwin transformed Malthus's conservative and static social agenda into a dynamic biological one.

To support his idea, Darwin spoke to real-life selectors, animal breeders. He knew that their predecessors had created diverse breeds of dogs and pigeons in just a few thousand years. Could not the hand of nature mimic the hand of the breeder, although with less intensity and over untold more generations, and thus act as a "natural" selector? It would only require the environment to determine which traits were better and therefore which animals should be favored in the struggle to survive and reproduce. The result would be something like the diversification of the dachshund, Great Dane, terrier, spaniel, bulldog, and Labrador Retriever from one another—only writ large, over the whole history of life. And the fact is, if we didn't know that those domestic stocks were all descended from a common ancestor, we would probably classify them as different species and genera because they are so different from one another!

Darwin named this hypothetical process "natural selection," juxtaposing it against the "artificial selection" of the breeder—although of course the "artificial" selection process was in fact the only one that was known to be real. Further, Darwin didn't postulate the existence of any conscious selective agent for the "natural" selection process—rather, it proceeded *as if* there were an invisible hand guiding it.

The structure of his argument boils down to connecting a simple series of observations and inferences. In the first place, organisms reproduce more than their resources readily permit them to, leading to the "struggle for existence" deduced by Malthus. Since all populations consist of variable members with slightly different features, and those features are often under some hereditary control, it follows that the particular features of those individuals best suited to their conditions of life will predominate in successive generations. The result would thereby be a transformation of the population through time in which specific descendant populations diverged from their ancestors, and from other descendant populations, in ways that fit them to their local environments. Extrapolated over the vastness of geological time, the implication was that all life was genealogically connected, the product of extensive "descent with modification."

Recognizing that his ideas would be controversial, Darwin set about to amass an insurmountable quantity of data in support of his argument, and to convince his friends in the scholarly community. His hand was forced, however, when he received a manuscript from a colleague he had never met, a young naturalist named Alfred Russel Wallace, detailing the same basic ideas as a result of his own reflection on what he had seen of the animals in the Malay archipelago. Darwin consulted with friends, who arranged to present papers jointly by himself and Wallace in 1858 at the Linnaean Society. Then he rushed to get his ideas into print.

The book was published on November 24, 1859, as *On the Origin of Species by Means of Natural Selection, or the Preservation of Favored Races in the Struggle for Life*. The first printing sold out that day. It was, in his own words, "one long argument," making three basic points:

- There exists heritable variation between individuals in any population.
- The nature of the environment causes some individuals to survive and reproduce more successfully than others.
- This changes the composition of the population in later generations, as succeeding generations of the population take on the characteristics of its reproducing members.

WHERE PEOPLE FIT IN

Darwin recognized that the most contentious implication of his theories would be to remove the human species from the direct image of God and situate it zoologically among the primates, where of course Linnaeus had placed it over a century earlier. The difference, however, was that Linnaeus was simply describing a pattern of resemblances, while Darwin was ostensibly talking about historical origins—as indeed Buffon had feared people would.

Darwin, however, sought to defuse that bomb by coyly refusing to deal with humans in the book. The only mention our species gets is in the third-to-last paragraph, when Darwin tells us, "Light will be thrown on the origin of man and his history." In the last edition, Darwin felt secure enough to expand on that thought, and he modified the single mention to, "Much light will be thrown on the origin of man and his history."

Darwin also wrote at a time when the British had outlawed slavery a generation earlier, and the Americans were about to fight a Civil War. The monogenist position (Chapter 2) was the more morally respectable one, for it seemed most compatible with the abolitionist position—we are all one kind, and it is not right to enslave one of your own. It was also the position of biblical literalism, which could trace all people back to Adam and Eve. The polygenist position, however, had something going for it as well. The polygenists held that different races were the products of separate creations, of which the Bible only relates the last one, that of Adam and Eve, presumptive ancestors of the local populations of the Near East. The earlier origins of other races were simply not there in the Scriptures. This implied two other things: that the Bible could not be taken literally at face value and was subject to considerable interpretation, which was attractive to skeptical intellectuals; and that the earth was far older than the Bible seemed to indicate, which was precisely what geology and archaeology were showing. One of Darwin's cultural contributions, then, was to harmonize the morally respectable position, namely, abolition (and his family were indeed ardent abolitionists), with the scientifically respectable position, namely, the antiquity of the earth and the human species. In other words, we all emerge from a common ancestor, but that stock is not from Adam, but from a sort-of chimpanzee.

One member of Darwin's circle was an anatomist who, like Darwin and Wallace, had made a scientific reputation upon returning from a sea voyage: Thomas Huxley. Shortly before its official publication date, Huxley received a copy of *The Origin of Species* from Darwin. Although he had some quibbles with it, he wrote his friend back immediately: "I finished your book yesterday . . . And as to the curs which will bark and yelp—you must recollect that some of your friends at any rate are endowed with an amount of combativeness which (though you have often & justly rebuked it) may stand you in good stead—I am sharpening up my claws and beak in readiness."

Huxley was already involved in a very nasty public dispute with the distinguished anatomist and paleontologist, Richard Owen, over the similarity between the ape's brain and ours. Huxley maintained there was no difference in basic form, just in size; Owen insisted that the human brain had a particular region, the hippocampus minor, that the ape's brain lacked. Darwin's work would mesh nicely with that.

The British Association for the Advancement of Science organized a debate at Oxford University in 1860 so that the followers of Darwin could confront, and be confronted by, their critics. One critic, a friend of Richard Owen, was Samuel Wilberforce, Bishop of Oxford. At the end of his presentation, the story goes, he sarcastically asked Huxley whether he thought he was related to the apes on his grandfather's side or his grandmother's side. Given the choice, replied Huxley, between "a miserable ape for a grandfather" or a clever man who would use his gifts of wisdom and speech in the service of ignorance and prejudice, "I unhesitatingly affirm my preference for the ape."

Huxley himself would write the first book on human evolution in 1863, *Man's Place in Nature*. Our place is, as Linnaeus noted, among the primates, and more specifically among the apes; but now, Huxley argues, we are driven inescapably to recognize that place as being the consequence of an intimate biological history that we share with the apes.

THE SACRIFICE

A new international generation of biologists rallied around Darwinism and expanded on the new biological ideas. Asa Gray in America, Huxley and others in England, and Ernst Haeckel in Germany all wrote extensively in favor of the new biological ideas.

Haeckel in particular developed a single scheme encompassing the biological evolution from amoebas to people, and continuing on to link the transformation of species to the rise of human races and the emergence and domination of modern political states. In other words, he saw the evolution of humans as a rise from the apes, the evolution of Europeans as a rise from the other kinds of people and reaching its zenith with the Germanic nation. There were twelve species of living people, he argued, each a different distance from the apes.

Rudolf Virchow, on the other hand, the most eminent biologist and public intellectual in Germany, thought that evolution did not call for the rise of racist militarist nationalism, and that we are all one species, and consequently took exception to Haeckel's view of evolution. Haeckel's response was telling: he claimed to speak for evolution, and if you didn't buy the whole package, then you were antievolution. Virchow did not buy the whole package, and by the terms of the argument, he became an opponent of evolution. When the fossils of Java Man were discovered in 1891, Virchow would refuse to accept them as human ancestors. Why? Because to admit them as evidence for evolution would have been to accept them as evidence for the political part of Haeckel's evolutionary program, which was far worse.

After Virchow's death, Germans did tend to see evolution just the way Haeckel outlined it. Shortly before the United States entered World War I, the Stanford biologist Vernon Kellogg interviewed educated German officers and found that they invoked Haeckel to rationalize their militarism, much to his dismay. Rudolf Virchow's divorce of biological evolution from social and political forms, however, was picked up by his young German protégé, who would emigrate to the United States in the 1890s, and ultimately be responsible for professionalizing academic anthropology in America—Franz Boas.

But Darwin's first-generation advocates were all faced with a problem when dealing with human evolution—there was virtually no fossil evidence for it. A single skull from Gibraltar that we would now classify as Neandertal, had been found in 1848; and the eponymous skull from the Neander valley in Germany was discovered in 1857. But the Gibraltar skull had not attracted much attention, and it was anyone's guess what the Neander skull was. And yet to link ape and human genealogically, you presumably required something to brandish at the traditional-ists as an intermediate form.

They solved this problem by reviving aspects of an older theory, the Great Chain of Being. Rather than ranking living beings as higher or lower than one another, now it might be "more or less evolved." So where were the missing transitional forms between person and ape? Actually, they're there, said these first-generation Darwinians, most explicitly Ernst Haeckel—the nonwhite peoples of the world grade into the ape on one end and into the European on the other. Even Thomas Huxley, in arguing for the continuity between the ape's brain and the European's brain, would invoke the African's brain as an intermediate form.

The slander was familiar, as Robert Chambers had said as much in 1844's *Vestiges of Creation*; and preevolutionary writers had for decades very casually drawn Africans as "in between" Europeans and apes, so the image itself was a familiar one. But the Darwinians were in a war with an earlier, premodern biological comprehension of the place of humans in the natural order; and so the full humanity of nonwhite peoples would be sacrificed. That would incur a moral debt that biological anthropology will be paying off forever.

IMPLICATIONS FOR PATTERN

The most immediate result of the Darwinian revolution was that it explained the pattern in nature that Linnaeus had discerned over a hundred years earlier. Species clustered together into genera because they shared a recent intimate biological history; genera clustered into families because they shared a more remote common ancestry; and so on.

Where earlier evolutionary theories, such as Lamarck's, had worked within the framework of the Great Chain of Being, there was no way to fit the observed pattern (the nested hierarchy) to the evolutionary process. Suddenly, in Darwin's work, it all became clear—for Darwin's theory incorporated the divergence of species from one another. "I am fully convinced," he wrote, "that species are not immutable; but that those belonging to what are called the same genera are lineal descendants of some other and generally extinct species, in the same manner as the acknowledged varieties of any one species are the descendants of that species."

Darwin here has not only grounded Linnaeus's hierarchy in an underlying evolutionary process but has also linked the production of new breeds or varieties of animals—evolution below the species level, or microevolution—to the production of new species—evolution above the species level, or macroevolution.

IMPLICATIONS FOR SPECIES

Much of modern science is concerned with freeing itself from an ancient philosophical stance known as *essentialism*. This was first formulated by the Greek philosopher Plato in his "Allegory of the Cave" in Book 6 of *The Republic*. Imagine, he suggests, that you are a prisoner chained to a rock in a cave. You cannot see outside, but the fire casts ever-changing shadows on the wall. Since you cannot see outside, you do not know what is causing the shadows, and for all you know, they are all there is. But in fact, says Plato, the shadows are caused by some people or things that are outside of your direct perception—their flickering, dancing, and changing shapes are illusory. They are simply forms caused by real things outside. And your job as a scholar is to see through the apparent variation of the world of forms, to the underlying uniformity in the world of essences—the things of which the shadows are simply pale copies.

His student Aristotle applied this to biology, arguing that the basis of a species lay in just such an essence—a transcendent ideal that existed, perhaps, in the mind of God. All earthly representatives of a species were simply forms, like those shadows on the cave wall. The task of the biologist, then, would be to see beyond the diverse variations that exist in a species and try to imagine what the ideal form, the essence, of that kind of animal would be.

The problem is that this approach subverts the empirical basis of knowledge. It invites you to ignore what you can see, and to imagine what you cannot see—and defines the imaginary part as the true reality. The variations that are part of the world of our experience are here dismissed as mere imperfections, or as degeneracy from the ideal.

Naturalists had, by 1700, begun to reconceptualize species from "animals that look alike and partake of a common essence" to "animals that can reproduce together and share a common history." But these weren't necessarily incompatible; one could still imagine the "idea in the mind of God" on which those real animals that could reproduce together were based. And another important implication of Darwin's work, then, was to stand the old view on its head.

If we accept that a species is really about reproductive compatibility, then the "essence" or "ideal" that they all share is irrelevant. More than that, it is imaginary. The reality lies in the variations themselves, the differences among the animals within a species. These are the qualities that allow an animal to survive and to reproduce in the face of competition from other members of the species. Consequently, the variations should be studied—for they are real and important—and the underlying invariant "essence" is actually neither important, nor even real.

We will encounter essentialism in various guises throughout the study of human diversity, for example, in the study of gender and race (in which you may be defined by a single aspect of your ancestry or makeup, which infuses your entire identity with imaginary properties), and in the Human Genome Project (where the basis of being human would be imagined to reside within a single genetic representative). This of course is a testimony to the power of Plato and Aristotle in shaping European thought. For present purposes, we can just observe that shaking off two millennia of metaphysical speculation about species in favor of an empirical, real-world approach was a major advance in biology: another contribution of Darwin's.

The modern concept of species builds on this distinction. It tells us that a species is not a group, or a set, in which membership is defined by the possession of certain features. Rather, a species is an individual (like an organism or a cell), composed of parts that stand in a specific pattern of relationship to one another. That relationship is participation in a common reproductive community, yielding the ability to share descendants. In the same way that your body is composed of cells, and you don't think of your cells as "members" of your body, but rather as your body's organized subunits, we no longer think of organisms as "members" of a species, but, rather, as "parts" of a species. (However, we do occasionally lapse and articulate it the old way.) This is a genealogical, evolutionary, and hierarchical concept of a species.

IMPLICATIONS FOR BIOLOGICAL HISTORY

Darwinism also explained the cause and effect of adaptation in a way that made sense in the modern scientific sense of the times. Granted that species are adapted to their surroundings, how did that come to be?—especially if they all started out in Noah's ark!

Darwin again reversed the traditional way of thinking about the problem. Rather than thinking of organisms in Noah's ark as built to survive where they will end up—their future circumstances dictating their present structure— Darwinism explained contemporary adaptation in terms of the survival and pro- liferation of ancestors living in the distant past. Thus, it is a theory of biological history, not of biological teleology (in which the end, or *telos*, determines the present state).

This is a far more satisfactory kind of explanation, for philosophical reasons that had been developing for two hundred years, as we have already seen.

This helped establish Darwinism as a more scientific alternative than any of its competing theories. Even the early evolutionary theory of Lamarck, which saw evolution as an "unfolding" in which species responded to ecological pressure by climbing one link up the Great Chain, was still teleological in that the structure of the Great Chain was not of this earth. It was something presumably located in the mind of God. The future state (the next link on the Chain) is what determined the present state, which is not the way things seem to happen.

Darwinism, however, affords a different view. Life is not heading toward the next link, but merely toward survival. Thus, at any time, you are a product of the past, not a slave of the future. You are shaped by what you have inherited from your ancestors, not what you will pass on to your descendants. After all, you definitely had ancestors, but you may not have descendants!

Darwinism was thus a theory in which not only was there a deep history of life, but a deep history of human life as well. There was no knowable future, only a knowable past. It was that past that shaped the way we are today; and it is the way we are today and the conditions we will face that affect what we will become. Thus, it no longer made scientific sense to speak of a "biological destiny" or a "next step" in human evolution.

One still commonly hears this assumption, however—for example, in the question, "What will the person of the future look like?" This question assumes that the future is within us, and only needs to be teased out; and that response to environmental pressures (which we cannot foresee) is irrelevant to answering. We will see later how a modern approach to evolution might frame an answer to that question. For present purposes, we can simply note that Darwinism *historicized* biology and replaced an older teleological explanation for adaptation with a historical one.

IMPLICATIONS FOR RELATING HUMANS
TO OTHER ANIMALS

Humans have always related themselves to the animals. Some of the earliest art, for example, seems to depict half-human, half-animal figures. Mythologies universally give animals human characteristics and teach us how we can become more self-aware when we attend to those traits. In European literature, the master of the genre was Aesop, who wrote in 500 BC about the evil wolf, the honorable mouse, the jealous raven, and the clever monkey, not to mention the wolf in sheep's clothing, the race between the tortoise and the hare, and the goose that laid golden eggs. In modern culture we know, among many others, the smart-aleck bunny ("Bugs"), the irascible duck ("Donald"), and the sly, if unlucky, coyote ("Wile E.").

The idea of blurring the boundary between human and animal is thus an old one. People widely invoke animals to learn about human qualities, or to demonstrate right from wrong, or simply for entertainment. They know that ducks don't really wear four-fingered gloves and the top half of a sailor suit, but there is something self-revelatory about seeing our own characteristics and shortcomings in such a creature.

The human animal, with characteristics of both, is thus a staple of the narrative form. This, of course, is a literary device, a metaphor, telling us that animals are like humans in some interesting and meaningful way. But Darwin showed that there was another way to compare animals and humans that wasn't merely metaphorical, but rather was historical. If humans and apes, for example, shared a recent common ancestry, then their similarities are something of a different order than the similarity of a person to a wise owl or a busy bee. The human–ape similarity is a similarity of biological correspondence due to history. They are similar because not too long ago, geologically speaking, *they were the same thing*.

These relations were later distinguished as *analogy,* a correspondence of fundamentally different structures that are nevertheless superficially similar, such as a mosquito wing and a bat wing, or a centipede leg and a chicken leg, or an octopus arm and a monkey arm; and *homology,* a correspondence of fundamentally similar structures, due to common descent, which may nevertheless be superficially different—such as the paw of a dog and hoof of a horse, or the snout of a pig and the blowhole of a dolphin, or the wishbone of a chicken and the collarbones of a human.

The difference is that the first is still a meaningful symbolic correspondence, but the second is a meaningful biological correspondence. While we can use the same word to denote the "wing" of a mosquito and a bat, that is simply a word game, for the two are fundamentally different structures—developmentally, structurally, and functionally. In both cases, the thing does flap to propel its bearer through the air, but it does so in quite different ways on quite differently built creatures. Conversely, although we may use different words to denote the dog's paw and horse's hoof, they are developmentally, structurally, and functionally very similar. Their relationship of homology isn't a word game, but a reflection of the common biological underpinnings due to common ancestry.

This takes on considerable importance in the post-Darwinian analysis of the evolution of behavior. If a jointed supportive appendage of an ant is not a leg, but a "leg"—that is, an analogy or word game linking two fundamentally different things—then what of slavery in ants? Shouldn't it be "slavery"?

The concept of homology gets another twist when we consider that many organisms are composed of repeated parts, which also develop from a single common ancestral structure. These would include the segments of a centipede, the vertebrae of your backbone, and the relationship between your arm and your leg (a single upper bone, two lower bones, a complex joint, and five radiating digits). This relationship is called *serial homology*. Whereas the serial homology of human bodies is relatively minor, that of the genes is quite extensive, with duplication of genetic structures occurring throughout the chromosomes, whose implications we examine in the next chapter.

PHYLOGENY: THE CORE OF DARWINISM

After recognizing that organisms share a common ancestry to greater or lesser degrees, and that this is why they seem to resemble each other to greater or lesser degrees, the next question is, How do we read the history of life?

To a first approximation, the more similar two species appear, the more closely related they are. This is a simple consequence of the fact that physical differentiation is partly a function of time, and therefore, species that have been separate longer are likely to be more different. To a second approximation, however, rates of evolution are not constant, and therefore, a rapidly changing lineage may leave several slowly changing lineages looking rather similar to one another, while not being very closely related to one another.

Consider, for example, the vervet monkey, spider monkey, and orangutan. While the two monkeys appear to be more generally similar, that is actually a result of the apes having diverged radically from the ancestors of vervet monkeys. In fact, when we zero in on *key* features, we find that the orangutan and vervet monkey match in the details of their teeth, noses, and bony ear chambers more closely than the two monkeys do. The reason that the two monkeys look more similar is because the orangutan has become very different, not because the two monkeys share the most recent common ancestry. Actually, the most recent common ancestry is shared by the vervet monkey and orangutan, which we classify together within the primate infraorder Catarrhini.

This kind of phylogenetic reconstruction is predicated on the fact that above the species level, animal lineages do not grow back together, they only become more separated. Since we define species partly by virtue of their inability to interbreed, it follows that animals belonging to different genera or families cannot interbreed and thereby cannot become more similar to each other that way.

But *below* the species level, however, it can certainly happen. In other words, populations can be similar either because they share recent common ancestry or because they have been in genetic contact. These biological histories are not divergent or dendritic, like classical macroevolutionary tree-like phylogenies, but *reticulate,* like blood vessels, sometimes branching and sometimes reuniting.

There are exceptions to these generalizations, it can be noted—such as the profligacy of plants outside the recognized boundaries of species, or the application of these ideas to viruses and bacteria. Nevertheless, for the organisms of greatest concern to us—large-bodied mammals—the generalizations seem to hold well, at least to a first approximation.

OTHER DARWINISMS

Social Darwinism

As in the days of Haeckel and Virchow at the end of the nineteenth century, we still find that proponents of other theories will claim to speak in Darwin's name and try to legitimate their own ideas by associating them with Darwinian evolution. One such school of thought is called "Social Darwinism," which also had its heyday in the latter part of the nineteenth century. It was more the brainchild of Herbert Spencer, a philosopher-psychologist-sociologist-biologist who developed a theory of the "survival of the fittest"—and then convinced Darwin himself that it was the same as "natural selection."

There were two important differences, however. Spencer's ideas involved seeing "survival of the fittest" as an engine driving species toward increased perfection, rather than just toward greater adaptation. Thus, he saw improvement—not just divergence— as the goal of evolution. Second, he believed a parallel process occurred in society. The fittest thrived, and if you weren't thriving, it was because you just weren't fit.

Combining those ideas, he saw society progressing by virtue of competition, or survival of the fittest. Since it was obvious that wealthy British men were at the top, it followed that they had outcompeted the rest of the world. And since the world was obviously in good shape and getting better all the time, it followed that the social hierarchy that placed colonial powers above other nations, Britain over other colonial powers, and the wealthy above the poor, was a good situation and represented just the playing out of natural processes.

There were two direct social implications. The non-European nations had obviously lost out in the competitive struggle. If they died out, then, it was just the way of the world. So one could easily see in this doctrine a natural justification for colonial oppression, if not outright genocide.

The second implication concerned the relations between social classes in Europe. The poor had obviously lost out in the competitive struggle as well. For whatever reason—bad genes, bad work ethic—they were where they deserved to be. Competition makes the cream rise to the top, said this doctrine. Moreover, any attempt to improve the lot of the poor (much less to stem the greedy practices of the oil, steel, and railroad monopolies) could be seen as tantamount to subverting the laws of nature. Thus, any government regulations to try to improve the lot of the poor, such as child labor laws, or unionization, or even breaking up monopolies, would be bad for both the human species and for the progress of civilization!

By the turn of the twentieth century, it was widely recognized that the social and political ideas piggybacking on Darwinism did not really derive a justification from it. Rather, Social Darwinism seemed just to be a rationalization, by recourse to "the natural way of things," of the vices of the wealthy and powerful—greed, unscrupulousness, and exploitation. However, these ideas do crop up in various forms time and again. In 1994, a best-selling book called *The Bell Curve* argued that (1) IQ is a measure of innate intelligence (false); (2) wealthy people tend to have higher IQs than poor people (true); and, therefore, (3) programs designed to ameliorate educational deficits among the poor should be abolished because they are doomed to failure, as they are thwarted by nature, for people are where they deserve to be (evil). This, clearly, was just a cosmetically altered version of the Social Darwinist ideas in vogue a century earlier.

Neo-Darwinism

Darwin's ideas seemed to run aground on a thorny issue of genetics. Evolution by natural selection began with the *assumption* of a variable population. Darwin didn't know where the variation came from, but for natural selection to act, there must be variation present in the population.

A critic named Fleeming Jenkin, however, pointed out that natural selection would be opposed by the predominant model of heredity at the time, known as *blending inheritance*. Imagine a hypothetical population of yellow creatures and a hypothetical population of blue creatures. They meet and mate. Under blending inheritance, the resulting offspring are all green. The green ones can mate with one another, and their offspring will also be green; or they could mate with some left-over yellows and have chartreuse (greenish-yellow) offspring, or mate with blues, and have teal (greenish-blue) offspring. What Jenkin pointed out, however, was this: variation is being lost every generation. Under blending inheritance, a population moves closer to homogeneity every generation. You can never recover the original blues and yellows!

Losing variation every generation would kill natural selection as an agent of evolutionary change, if natural selection proceeds from the assumption of a variable population. Darwin realized he needed some kind of an engine to crank out more variation as it became blended away and finally sought refuge in Lamarck's theory of the inheritance of acquired characteristics. But the premise of Jenkin's critique was that blending inheritance was the mechanism of heredity, and Gregor Mendel's contribution was to show that was wrong.

By the 1880s, a movement had arisen within biology to jettison Lamarckian inheritance once and for all—even though Mendel's work was not yet known. It might not have been clear where the missing variation might come from, but it wasn't coming from Lamarck; and Darwin was surely right about natural selection, regardless of the theoretical objections from Fleeming Jenkin.

The biological theory that arose shortly before the turn of the twentieth century involved accepting Darwinian natural selection and rejecting Lamarckian inheritance, and came to be known as neo-Darwinism. It has been said that these scientists "out-Darwinned Darwin" in accepting natural selection as the exclusive agent of evolutionary change, and seeing heredity as an unalterable destiny, except through a rare and permanent change called *mutation*. Alternatively (and in the new science of genomics, more realistically), one can envision heredity to be a bit more flexible and responsive. In fact, these were politically inflected viewpoints as well, with aristocrats imagining that heredity is destiny, and the upwardly mobile classes imagining heredity to be more supple, as they reinvented themselves on the way up the social ladder. A great deal of interest is currently directed toward "epigenetics," the study of evolutionary or genetic changes that aren't directly encoded in gene sequences.

The "Synthetic Theory"

In the early 1930s, the field of population genetics was invented in the mathematical work of Ronald Fisher, J. B. S. Haldane, and Sewall Wright. They showed that the study of microevolution could be reduced in principle to a small number of genetic processes, which could be quantitatively analyzed, and which would have predictable effects on natural populations of organisms. Thus was Darwinism "synthesized" with population genetics.

A few years later, a second group of biologists showed that not only was the work of population genetics compatible with what was detectable within real species but also the ideas were compatible as well with something the population geneticists didn't examine—the formation of new species. Led by the Russian-born geneticist Theodosius Dobzhansky, who worked on fruit flies, the ornithologist Ernst Mayr, and George Gaylord Simpson, who worked on fossil mammals, the "Synthetic Theory of Evolution" was in place by midcentury and so-named by the biologist Julian Huxley, the grandson of Thomas.

The Synthetic Theory was Darwinian in two fundamental senses. First, it held that microlevel processes could be extrapolated to explain macrolevel phenomena; thus, the processes by which dog breeds diverged from one another are essentially the same as those by which dogs diverged from cats and bears. And second, it held that species achieve and maintain a fit to their environment through natural selection. However, it went beyond Darwin in integrating advances in cellular and theoretical genetics, and showing that mutation (creating genetic diversity), selection (causing adaptation), genetic drift (causing random change), and gene flow (homogenizing populations) might well be all that one needed to explain the diversity of life.

Evolution at the Molecular Level

Darwin became such a figurehead, much like Newton before him, that he became both myth and symbol. Like Newton, legends developed around him: that the Galápagos finches had convinced him of evolution; that he had accepted Jesus as his personal savior on his deathbed; that he was a rank amateur with no credentials at the time he published *The Origin of Species* (all false). Darwin also became symbolic of the new modern biology, as Newton had been of the new physics: as we have seen, with each generation's pet theorists trying to piggyback on Darwin.

Sometimes a symbol may be so culturally charged that it can be invoked in two seemingly opposite ways. In fact, Darwin became such a powerful symbol that newly emerging schools of biological thought have either aligned themselves *with* him, to exploit his symbolic value as the forward-seeing father of modern biology; or diametrically *against* him, to emphasize Darwin as the originator of the powerful orthodoxy of modern biology.

One such school arose in the study of molecular evolution in the late 1960s, as orthodoxies of all kinds were being attacked, focused on comparing homologous proteins and genes across species. When you compared biomolecules across species, you weren't confronted with evidence of a wise design and precision craftsmanship. Far from it; rather, you were struck by the amount of "slop" in the system.

Diabetics, for example, needed to take injections of insulin. But what they took at the time was pig insulin, which was slightly different in structure from human insulin. And yet it still worked. In other words, you could change the structure and yet not compromise the functional integrity of the hormone. This hardly suggested precise engineering and a perfect fit of the organism to its environment; rather, it suggested the body to be making due with what's there, and the detectable molecular differences between species to be just kind of random, not really critically adaptive.

These two propositions coalesced as the core of a new field of "molecular evolution," which cast itself as "non-Darwinian evolution." If the fundamental changes to DNA, resulting in changes to proteins, were neither harmful nor beneficial to their bearers, but were merely neutral, then they would not (by definition) be affected by natural selection. Rather, they would evolve randomly by a probabilistic process known as genetic drift. Perhaps, then, evolutionary theory had overstated the case for evolution being adaptive; maybe much of it was just random change that at least didn't hurt you, and could allow the body to go on functioning passably. This came to be known as the "neutral theory of molecular evolution," articulated in the 1970s by the Japanese statistical geneticist Motoo Kimura.

While it is now fairly clear that protein structure and function are generally indeed under selective constraints of varying intensities, and thus are indeed often subject to selection, it is also clear that most DNA changes are not even expressed in any form within the cell or the body. Thus, they are indeed neutral, since if they are not expressed as any kind of physical differences, then they cannot have an effect on the survival or reproduction of the organism. Molecular evolution thus constitutes a paradox: the evolution that it studies comprises for the most part neutral, unexpressed, nonadaptive differences between species; but what make evolution interesting are the tangible physical differences that arise between species and affect their form and survival.

Thus the paleontologist George Gaylord Simpson could ridicule non-Darwinian molecular evolution as the study of "the minor features of evolution." He had written a classic book on *The Major Features of Evolution*.

On the other hand, scholars trained in molecular evolution often come to general issues in the field with a healthy skepticism toward the view that organisms are precisely engineered instruments, finely tuned by natural selection. Indeed, in an interesting twist, we find the great French anthropologist Claude Lévi-Strauss explaining the origin of myths in his classic, *The Savage Mind* (1961). Myths, he says, are neither passed on perfectly intact, nor made up from scratch every generation. Rather, they are cobbled together by mythmakers from available motifs and jerry-rigged to be relevant and meaningful to the time and circumstance. Lévi-Strauss called the raw materials *bricolage,* and the mythmaker a *bricoleur,* usually translated as "tinkerer." And when the molecular geneticist François Jacob looked to a metaphor to express his views on molecular evolution, he took inspiration from Lévi-Strauss, declaring that "evolution is like a tinkerer, not like an engineer."

Punctuated Equilibria

Another self-proclaimed anti-Darwinian evolutionary theory arose in the 1980s, with a criticism of Darwin's extrapolation from microevolutionary to macroevolutionary phenomena, spearheaded by the paleontologists Stephen Jay Gould and Niles Eldredge. Rather than a smooth transition from populations through species into genera, perhaps the literal origin of species was accompanied by a break with the direct past, so that different processes may act above the species level than below the species level. We know, for example, that above the species level there is generally no interbreeding, but below the species level there is—perhaps the smooth extrapolation is therefore an oversimplification. Moreover, why should we think that rates of speciation and extinction, which are population-level processes, should be encoded in the DNA of individual organisms? A goal-line defense, after all, cannot be seen in the activity of any specific football lineman, but only in the coordinated activities of all of them.

This was also accompanied by a critique of the engineering implied by seeing natural selection and adaptation as the fundamental processes of evolution. Darwinian theory and its successors generally held species to be continuously adapting to continuously changing environments. This naturally implies that species are in some sense fundamentally unstable, and are always shifting in shape. Instead, however, one could see species as fundamentally stable units (for, say, a few million years) that only changed noticeably at the brief time when they formed (over, say, 50,000 years).

The history of a lineage might then look somewhat different, consisting of long-term stasis or equilibrium, interrupted by short-term change or punctuation.

Its proponents called attention to the fact that even Thomas Huxley, upon reading *The Origin of Species,* privately wrote Darwin to say that he had perhaps relied too heavily on the assumption that *"natura non facit saltum"* (nature does not make a leap). Its detractors derided it as "the theory of evolution by jerks." In fact, much of the theoretical basis for punctuated equilibria could be found in the writings of the synthetic theorists Ernst Mayr (who wrote about rapid speciation accompanied by genetic revolutions) and George Gaylord Simpson (who wrote about variation in evolutionary rates, from very slow [bradytely] to very fast [tachytely]). The argument, however, boiled down to whether species were stable fundamental units through long evolutionary time, or whether they were constantly sensitive to environmental pressures and adapting genetically to each one.

The theory of punctuated equilibria also called attention to other factors shaping the history of life, such as mass extinctions caused by ecological chain reactions (and perhaps triggered by rare astronomical events, such as meteor impacts). Thus it reopened, in a modern way, the issue of catastrophism that had been out of favor since the time of Charles Lyell.

Sociobiology

At just about the same time that the prevalence of adaptation was being called into question both by molecular geneticists and by paleontologists, a "new synthesis" of work in theoretical population genetics and ecology set out to account for the adaptive significance of behavior. While its questions ostensibly were on odd issues—such as why populations regulate their growth and the evolution of particular sterile castes in wasps—its answers cut to the core of Darwinism. Could a behavior evolve for the good of the group?

The answer was straightforward. If it were *for* the benefit of the group and *against* the benefit of the actor, it could not evolve because anything against the actor's interests are selected against, by definition. And if it were for the benefit of the group *and* for the benefit of the actor, then how could you ever say it evolved for the benefit of the group? As a result, a rigorous emphasis was placed on explaining evolutionary phenomena in classically Darwinian terms: the free market struggle of one organism against another in the competition for life and babies. The principal exponent of this school in the 1970s was the entomologist E. O. Wilson.

But there was nevertheless dissent over whether competition occurred the classically Darwinian way, between individuals—or even more basically, between genes. Here, the biologist Richard Dawkins made a case for "the selfish gene"—that is to say, primordial chemicals with no function other than to make copies of themselves. Those that did so remained, and those that didn't ultimately expired without issue. One way that such copying might be aided would be if the gene were capable of producing something to assist it in copying—a protein, perhaps. Once again, those that did so remained, and those that didn't perished—and the result was the development of the cellular apparatus around the genes. Cells thus arose to help the proteins helping the genes make copies of themselves. Later, groups of cells made bodies around themselves, to help them help the proteins helping the genes make copies of themselves. And finally, bodies performed behaviors to help make more bodies, to help make more cells, to help make more proteins help make more genes.

Thus (and the validity of the "thus" is a bit vexing), behaviors exist to help make more copies of genes, and the proper interpretation of a behavior lies in its contribution to the production of genes. William D. Hamilton derived conditions under which a behavior *not* to the benefit of the actor (an "altruistic" behavior) might evolve, if it were directed at *relatives* of the actor. Relatives, of course, have a probability of having inherited the same gene from a common ancestor. Thus, what looks like an altruistic act (against the actor's interests) may actually be in the interests of the actor's genes (and thereby selfish from their perspective). And Robert Trivers derived conditions under which such a superficially altruistic, but genetically selfish, act could evolve, even if directed at nonrelatives.

They pushed strongly to explain all behaviors as adaptations (that is, as something that evolved specifically by natural selection) either from the standpoint of genetic copies or of physical offspring. Coming at a time when the prevalence of adaptation itself was coming into question both in molecular evolution and in macroevolutionary paleontology, it set off an ideological war, being labeled "Darwinian Fundamentalism" in the 1990s by Stephen Jay Gould.

Most controversial, as might be expected, was the perceived need to explain all *human* behavior as ultimately selfish, however altruistic it may seem at face value. Humans, after all, have created social entities that act to coerce people into doing things for the good of the group. Consider the payment of income tax, which began in the United States during World War I. If you give a significant chunk of your earnings away, you must to some extent reduce your probability of survival and reproduction, compared to how much better off you'd be if you had those assets to spend. So why not boycott paying taxes? Because it is against the law, and you may go to jail, which is definitely not in your interests. So the group can compel actors to act against their obvious interests by introducing coercive forces. On the other hand, your taxes do go to paying for civil defense, education, and law enforcement, so there is a sense in which your payment of taxes indeed enhances your own welfare.

Which of those two explanations for why we pay taxes is superior? Is it because we have to or because of the individual benefits it purchases? If both are right, is there a way to tell which is righter? If we take it as an article of faith that everything must be explained as a selfish act, that leaves us with the latter explanation; but why should it be an article of faith? And if humans can and do create cultural institutions that compel individuals to act in the interest of those institutions, does it not seem perverse to deny that people do it?

Universal Darwinism
The attempt to explain all human behavior as selfish, because it must be adaptive and aid in survival and reproduction of self or genetic material for it to be there at all, is undermined by another movement that sprang from sociobiology. Inspired

by the gene-selectionist Richard Dawkins, this movement begins with the proposition that the evolution of human behavior is somewhat different because human institutions *do* perpetuate themselves and *do* compel individuals to act to their benefit. So whether or not angels exist, the *idea* of angels perpetuates itself generation after generation in the minds of people. Dawkins gave the name "memes" to these replicating cultural units. Meme theorists thus explain the behavior of humans in the service of the replication of their own bodies, or their genes in their relatives' bodies, or their memes.

Since this is a metaphorical extension of Darwinism, involving not the competitive survival and proliferation of living organisms, but rather the perseverance of cultural or mental elements, it has been called a theory of "universal Darwinism." Like earlier theories based on the analogy of cultural world to the natural world (such as Social Darwinism), it is not at all clear that this process can be generalized to explain the features of interest in the cultural world sensibly. Is it at all illuminating to say that giving to charity is not "really" a selfless act but rather is a consequence of the spread of the meme for donation (if such a thing even exists)? Darwin wouldn't recognize much of himself in this theory.

But that is precisely the point. Darwinism has come to label many ideas in the course of the last century and a half because it is such as powerful word, calling to mind the modernization of the field of biology and the last great conflict between religious origin narratives and scientific origin narratives.

Atheistic Darwinism

Modern science is predicated on a division between the material world, sensitive to experimental manipulation and the identification of regularity, and the spiritual world, which is impervious to both. This is a very odd view of the universe: To most human beings, the world of spiritual forces interpenetrates the world of mundane existence. Las Vegas, for example, is built on the assumption of such interpenetration (called "luck"). But if we can't rely on our perceptions, or control variables, and if the object of our examination is itself capricious and runs on miracles rather than generalizable laws, then there's very little we can do with it scientifically.

Of course, we could do simulations with random number generators and make statistical predictions about long-term outcomes. But suppose that what looks to us like a random event is really controlled by forces outside our perceptible sphere?

The answer, as the first generation of scientists back in the seventeenth century recognized, is that, whether or not our subject is actually governed only by material forces, science can function under that assumption. Science can't work with the spiritual and the miraculous; but it also can't show their absence. All it can do is proceed as if they are absent and see what comes of it. And of course, what comes of it are antibiotics, vaccinations, and thermonuclear bombs.

That leaves open, however, the question of the spiritual (not to mention the moral) universe. What can we say about it, from the standpoint of science? Quite simply, nothing.

Darwin did not deny miracles. He simply showed that life could multiply in form and adaptation without such interventions. And on the last page of his most famous book, he made it clear that although the origin of life itself might be miraculous, the origin of *species* need not be. He simply cut back on the number of miracles necessary to understand the history and diversity of life—now just "a few . . . or . . . one."

Evangelical atheists quickly adopted Darwin as a figurehead. Swept up in the tide of progress and modernity that overwhelmed late nineteenth-century Europe and America, science has often been invoked as superseding religion—usually in a self-serving fashion that sets the speaker up as a kind of pope.

Concurrently, apologists for science or religion have been known to argue that their domains are entirely separate—despite the obvious and constant introgressions of one on the other. The truth lies somewhere in the middle.

First, human history is not linear and transformative; religion did not supersede magic or superstition, and religion is certainly not being superseded by science. Religion is everywhere flourishing. Second, they do come regularly into contact in the area of origin narratives, at the very least. Science can place constraints on the type of origin narrative, if the only criterion of interest is accuracy. But third, origin narratives are not widely taken as literally as scientists take their own stories, and accuracy may therefore not be the most important criterion for people other than scientists. They might be more interested in whether it instills a feeling of belonging, or of justice—or just whether it rhymes. The heavenly and moral worlds may be just more important to many people than whether they came from monkeys. And indeed, serious modern theologians do engage with the implications of Darwinism for a Christian life.

So, fourth, if science is predicated on a separation of the spiritual from the material realms, then why do scientists conduct periodic forays into areas where they have no expertise or knowledge—like theology (and human history, come to think of it)? Is it possible that with their noteworthy success in developing weapons of mass destruction, scientists have come to feel—dare I say it, arrogantly?—as though they can pronounce authoritatively on subjects outside their domain? Indeed, stimulated by the aggressive atheism espoused by some scientists, like Oxford's Richard Dawkins, an equally embarrassing oppositional genre of scientific pieties has begun to emerge. The Human Genome Project's Francis Collins (now director of the National Institutes of Health) publicly professes his Christian faith, for example, and shows you how he reconciles his faith to his science, as if you should care. Personally, I am as skeptical of geneticists on the subject of theology as I am of theologians on the subject of genetics.

The problem is, with "Darwinism" as a powerful and evocative cultural symbol of modernity and progress, there is rhetorical power in associating it with one's own religious (or irreligious) views. Whether God exists and intervenes actively in the world, or whether He set up laws and then let the world alone to run, or whether He doesn't exist at all—that's simply not the sphere of Darwinism. The responsibility lies with scientists themselves to differentiate answers to questions they do know about from answers to questions they don't know about—but it is rarely in their interests to do so.

REFERENCES AND FURTHER READING

Cartmill, M. 1994. A critique of homology as a morphological concept. *American Journal of Physical Anthropology* 94:115–123.

Claeys, G. 2000. The "survival of the fittest" and the origins of Social Darwinism. *Journal of the History of Ideas* 22:223–240.

Collins, F. 2006. *The Language of God: A Scientist Presents Evidence for Belief.* New York: Free Press.

Cosans, C. 2009. *Owen's Ape and Darwin's Bulldog: Beyond Darwinism and Creationism.* Bloomington: Indiana University Press.

Dawkins, R. 1976. *The Selfish Gene.* New York: Oxford University Press.

Dawkins, R. 1983. Universal Darwinism. In *Evolution from Molecules to Man,* ed. D. Bednall, 403–425. New York: Cambridge University Press.

Dawkins, R. 2006. *The God Delusion.* New York: Bantam.

Dennett, D. C. 1995. *Darwin's Dangerous Idea: Evolution and the Meanings of Life.* New York: Simon and Schuster.

Fuentes, A. 2004. It's not all sex and violence: Integrated anthropology and the role of cooperation and social complexity in human evolution. *American Anthropologist* 106:710–718.

Gould, S. J. 1981. G. G. Simpson, paleontology, and the modern synthesis. In *The Evolutionary Synthesis,* ed. E. Mayr and W. Provine, 153–172. Cambridge, MA: Harvard University Press.

Gould, S. J. 1997. Darwinian fundamentalism. *New York Review of Books,* June 12, 34–37.

Gould, S. J. 2002. *The Structure of Evolutionary Theory.* Cambridge, MA: Harvard University Press.

Graur, D., and W.-H. Li. 2000. *Fundamentals of Molecular Evolution.* 2nd ed. Sunderland, MA: Sinauer.

Hofstadter, R. 1944. *Social Darwinism in American Thought.* Philadelphia: University of Pennsylvania Press.

Jablonka, E., and M. Lamb. 2005. *Evolution in Four Dimensions: Genetic, Epigenetic, Behavioral, and Symbolic Variation in the History of Life.* Cambridge, MA: MIT Press.

Jacob, F. 1977. Evolution and tinkering. *Science* 196:1161–1166.

Kellogg, V. 1917. *Headquarters Nights.* Boston: Atlantic Monthly Press.

Marks, J. 2002. Genes, bodies, and species. In *Physical Anthropology: Original Readings in Method and Practice,* ed. Peter N. Peregrine, C. R. Ember, and M. Ember, 14–28. Englewood Cliffs, NJ: Prentice-Hall.

Massin, B. 1996. From Virchow to Fischer: Physical anthropology and modern race theories in Wilhelmine Germany. In *Volksgeist as Method and Ethic: Essays on Boasian Ethnography and the German Anthropological Tradition,* ed. G. Stocking, 79–154. Madison: University of Wisconsin Press.

Mayr, E. 1982. *The Growth of Biological Thought.* Cambridge, MA: Harvard University Press.

McGrath, A. E. 2013. *Darwinism and the Divine: Evolutionary Thought and Natural Theology.* New York: John Wiley & Sons.

McKinnon, S. 2005. *Neo-Liberal Genetics: The Myths and Moral Tales of Evolutionary Psychology.* Chicago, IL: Prickly Paradigm Press.

Reznick, D. N., and R. E. Ricklefs. 2009. Darwin's bridge between microevolution and macroevolution. *Nature* 457:837–842.

Rose, H., and S. Rose, eds. 2000. *Alas Poor Darwin.* London: Jonathan Cape.

Ruse, M. 1981. *The Darwinian Revolution.* Chicago, IL: University of Chicago Press.

Ruse, M. 1988. *Taking Darwin Seriously.* New York: Basil Blackwell.

Schultz, E. 2009. Resolving the anti-antievolutionism dilemma: A brief for relational evolutionary thinking in anthropology. *American Anthropologist* 111:224–237.

Simpson, G. G. 1949. *The Meaning of Evolution.* New Haven, CT: Yale University Press.

Simpson, G. G. 1953. *The Major Features of Evolution.* New York: Columbia University Press.

Stebbins, G. L., and F. J. Ayala. 1981. Is a new evolutionary synthesis necessary? *Science* 213:967–971.

Tattersall, I. 1999. The abuse of adaptation. *Evolutionary Anthropology* 7:115–116.

Van Huyssteen, J. W. 2009. *Alone in the World? Human Uniqueness in Science and Theology.* Grand Rapids, MI: William B. Eerdmans.

Wilson, E. O. 1975. *Sociobiology: The New Synthesis.* Cambridge, MA: Harvard University Press.

CHAPTER 4

Why Do I Look Like the Cable Guy, Daddy? (On Issues of Human Heredity)

THEME

While Mendel's "laws" are generally presented as the foundation of modern genetics, they are more commonly honored in the breach. Indeed, Mendel's work actually explains remarkably little of modern human genetics. Most significantly, however, cultural meanings and values permeate even the molecular aspects of genetics.

There are four reasons to study genetics in anthropology. The first is to help understand how evolution works. The second is to study how people differ from one another. The third is to understand the relationships of primates through their gene pools. And the fourth is to look at genetics ethnographically, as an example of the way in which scientific knowledge is produced and consumed by modern society.

Although cells had been known since the late 1600s, it wasn't until the middle of the nineteenth century that they were recognized to be the fundamental units of life. The great German pathologist/anthropologist Rudolf Virchow (whom we encountered in the previous chapter for his opposition to the linkage of biological Darwinism to political Darwinism) made a Latin epigram famous: *Omnis cellula e cellula*—all cells come from cells. In other words, life does not get created every generation (this is a denial of the theory of *spontaneous generation*, that living things can continually arise from nonliving matter). Rather, there is a continuity of life; and all living things are literally descended from previously living things. And where that may not be immediately obvious to the eye (as maggots appear to arise on rotting food), it is obvious microscopically.

There were, however, certain attractions of the theory of spontaneous generation. For the materialist, it was a way to argue that there is no basic difference between life and nonlife, for the former can arise from the latter. For the natural theologian, interested in understanding God through nature, spontaneous generation could be seen as a series of miracles, God's creative powers at work in the here and now.

Nevertheless, it is wrong. Obviously life arose from nonlife once—or *at least* once—but all of those semi-living, semi-cells are long gone. Cell division is the way in which living things grow and proliferate today. (Viruses, which parasitize cells, nevertheless cannot reproduce without them.)

A complementary development in the immediately post-Darwinian years was the recognition that there are two kinds of cells, and two kinds of cell division. The body (Greek, *soma*), is composed of "somatic" cells, and grows through a process of cell division called *mitosis*. The cell doubles its parts, then splits in two, and the two daughter cells are genetically identical to each other and to the original cell. This is a *clonal* process of cell proliferation in which the result is an organized mass of genetically identical cells.

The *germ* cells are sequestered in the reproductive organs, and divide in a different way, called *meiosis*, which reduces their genetic constitution by half. Thus, eggs and sperm contain half the amount of genetic material as ordinary cells. This halving is counteracted by the fusion of egg and sperm every generation, the act of fertilization, which restores the proper amount of genetic material to the new zygote, or fertilized egg. The zygote then divides mitotically to develop into the body of the offspring.

In addition to the question of whether life could regularly arise from nonlife, another open question was whether the growth of an embryo involved producing a new functioning body from an undifferentiated mass every generation (epigenesis), or whether instead, a baby was always there in sub-visible form and simply expanded within the maternal womb (preformation). Like all folk theories of heredity, including spontaneous generation, there were social/symbolic/religious implications. After all, knowledge of the world is invariably integrated into knowledge of more important things, like proper behavior and religious duty. Modern science is unique in trying to keep them separate.

If preformationism were true, and embryonic development were simply growth, then men could be seen as contributing substance, and women could be seen as contributing a nurturing environment. This view of human reproduction more or less paralleled traditional European views of domestic life. It also was proved by some of the earliest microscopic studies of sperm, which seemed to show a little fellow, or homunculus, in the sperm head. That little fellow, of course, had to have his offspring preformed in his own tiny germinative organs. Ultimately, then, the entire demographic history of the human species would have been created by God within Adam's genitalia. A different eighteenth-century take focused on Eve's ovaries, and had a mother providing both the form and the nurturing environment for the embryo, while men provided a kind of trigger for its development.

While the nested homunculi would have been infinitesimally small, they would not necessarily have been *impossibly* small. In fact, a belief that Adam and Eve literally embodied the whole human race had the theological attraction of implying that the human species had to end sometime, since Adam and Eve's genitalia were not infinitely large. So there really was an end to history, a "last generation," as the Bible foretold! (And, of course, this might be it!)

But it doesn't happen that way. Fertilization involves an equal contribution of father and mother, with the small exception of the mitochondria, provided by the mother, along with its own DNA. The zygote then divides and develops, and begins to form, as its genetic instructions are implemented, all of the structures and organs it will possess.

This happens every generation. A child is built not from a seed or germ present in the organs of every preceding generation, but from a set of instructions, whose specifics are continually being recombined and reconstituted.

If a child arises from a set of instructions instead of from a seed, the implications are rather different. History is less bounded; the instructions could be there in the indefinite future and the indefinite past. Neither parent necessarily contributes more "substance" to the child; the instructions could (and do) come equally from both.

Another problem that vexed biologists in the late nineteenth century was Lamarck's theory of the inheritance of acquired characteristics. Did organisms absorb the qualities they developed during their lifetimes and pass them on in a stable fashion to their descendants?

The German cell biologist August Weismann showed that they didn't. According to what was already known about cells, they couldn't. After all, the next generation comes from cells of tissues that have already been formed: the testes and the ovaries. There is no way to get information from somatic cells into the next generation; the next generation will be coming from germ cells already set apart early in embryonic life, and only those cells will contribute. Without an efficient mechanism for shunting information from the rest of the body into those particular cells and somehow changing them, there could be no Lamarckian inheritance.

Weismann called this idea "the continuity of the germ-plasm" (Greek *plasma*, meaning tissue). It meant, very simply, that—building on all cells coming from cells—life is a long and unbroken series, when looked at from the standpoint of cells. But there is more to it, for the cells of the body, the somatic cells, constitute a dead end; they will die when the body dies. But there will be another generation of bodies, which will come from germ cells. In other words, it is specifically the unbroken series of germ cells that constitutes the history of life; the somatic cells— the bodies—are mere vessels.

This view is what the English writer Samuel Butler was referring to when he wrote famously in 1877 that "A hen is only an egg's way of making another egg."

Seeing the life processes from the standpoint of cells made Lamarckian inheritance largely meaningless. To drive the point home, a classic experiment is attributed variously to Weismann or to Ivan Pavlov, of salivating dog fame: The experimenter bred mice for fifty generations, and every generation cut the tail off each mouse. Under a regime of Lamarckian inheritance, you would expect the mice's tails to shrivel or dwindle in later generations. Yet the tails of the mice of the fifty-first generation had tails the same length as those of the first generation. No kind of "tail-absence information" was passing from the mouse's body to its gonads; its germ cells, which were unaffected by the surgery every generation, simply transmitted the information on an intact tail each time.

So the development of cell biology in Germany proved to be a valuable addition to the understanding of heredity, and helped to solve some vexing problems, by providing another way to look at them.

THE THEORY OF PARTICULATE INHERITANCE:
MENDEL'S LAWS

The resemblance between family members is acknowledged worldwide and explained in many ways. We are interested in it specifically because the principles of heredity constitute the fundamental backdrop to evolutionary theory when we ask how descendants come to differ from their remote ancestors.

In destroying the basis for the older theories of spontaneous generation and the inheritance of acquired characteristics, the cell theory laid the groundwork for a modern theory of heredity. The third piece of the puzzle was already in place but would go unrecognized until 1900: Mendel's theory of inheritance.

It was certainly appreciated that some traits "run in families"—like diseases, which often show up with equal intensity in all affected family members. Alternatively, some traits "blend away"—for example, the offspring of a dark-skinned person and a light-skinned person would tend to have skin of intermediate shade. In the first case, inheritance would seem to be operating as little particles, transmitted perfectly intact across generations. In the second case, inheritance would seem to be like the mixing of fluids, becoming progressively diluted with each passing generation.

In fact, the latter view, known as "blending inheritance," was a favored theory for inheritance generally. And as we saw in the last chapter, it posed a significant problem for Darwin's theory of natural selection. It was Mendel's contribution to show that heredity is not blending, after all.

Mendel worked with peas, and studied the transmission of seven qualities of pea plants, each inherited in a binary fashion (tall and short; green pods and yellow pods; round and wrinkled; etc.). Mendel's two laws (called "segregation" and "independent assortment") were unknown to him as such and were not even codified until 1916.

Mendelian genetics says that a trait is controlled by a pair of genes, only one of which is passed on to a particular offspring. The fundamental insight here is that nothing happens to the unit of inheritance as it is transmitted across a generation. It is transmitted wholly intact, as a particle, rather than being blended away or diluted, as a fluid. Thus, the critique of natural selection based on blending inheritance is irrelevant because blending inheritance isn't the way things work.

We may observe, however, that some traits, like skin color, do appear to blend. We distinguish here between a blending *pattern* and a blending *process*. The appearance of blending is the result of several different genes entering into different combinations; the *process* is still a particulate one. What is interesting about Mendelian genetics is its generality, for it (somewhat counterintuitively?) applies as well to the inheritance of cystic fibrosis in humans as it does to height in pea plants. Two heterozygous carriers of cystic fibrosis, who do not themselves have the disease, stand a 1 in 4 chance of having a child with the disease by precisely the same logic as Mendel's plants. This shows another important and somewhat counterintuitive consequence of the cell theory. Peas do not eat, breathe, mature, defecate, or speak like humans do. Why on earth should we think that they reproduce like humans do? The answer is that from the standpoint of cells—and *only* from the standpoint of cells—they do indeed seem to reproduce like humans. Those commonalities comprise the most fundamental breakthrough of late nineteenth-century biology: the idea of the "model organism," another species that can be used as a simple surrogate to study what you are really interested in for people.

TEN NON-MENDELIAN LAWS

The Chromosome Theory

Mendel's work was resurrected in 1900, some thirty-five years after it was first published. The reason Mendel's work had been buried was that heredity and development were considered as parts of the same process at the time he wrote. But Mendel worked on transmission without regard for the development of traits. Since he wasn't following the accepted rules of thinking about the subject as they existed in 1865, his work could be readily ignored by the leading scholars. By 1900, however, it had become clear that heredity and development could indeed be seen as distinct processes in different model organisms; the mistake had been in mixing them together (as, for example, Lamarck had). This cast Mendel's work in a new, and better, light. A few years later, they even had a word for this new field: "genetics."

Cell biologists also had begun to realize by the turn of the century that cell division was invariably preceded by the concentration of the diffuse mass of the cell's nucleus into a small number of discrete bodies, which could be stained and seen in the microscope. These *chromosomes* (Greek for "colored bodies") seemed also to be tightly associated with biological inheritance: chromosomal oddities were passed on perfectly intact, and when they were associated with phenotypic features, those were passed on intact, too. But these biologists were working with microscopes, and were differently trained than the plant breeders who were making statistical generalizations about the inheritance of specific features of their organisms. Consequently, the Mendelian theory and chromosome theory had a tense coexistence for several years, as they appeared to be alternatives.

It was the American fruit fly geneticist Thomas Hunt Morgan who put this all together, publishing a series of papers beginning about 1910 that showed that (1) *genes are units of inheritance*, as the followers of Mendel had been arguing; and (2) *each gene occupies a particular place (or locus) on the chromosomes, which are the units that are literally, physically transmitted.*

Human gametes have twenty-three chromosomes. We call this state, having one set of chromosomes, *haploid*. Sperm and eggs, the products of meiosis, are haploid—they have half of the chromosomes that somatic cells have. Human somatic cells, by contrast, are diploid, having two sets of chromosomes, for a total of forty-six.

Another way of thinking about the chromosomes of somatic cells is that they have twenty-three pairs of chromosomes, one of each pair having come from father, and the other from mother. Consequently, the process of meiosis involves sending one representative from each chromosome pair into any particular gamete.

Linkage

Of course there are many genes, and rather few chromosomes. A human sperm or egg, for example, has its 20–25,000 genes distributed over twenty-three chromosomes. A particular chromosome, therefore, may have several thousand genes on it. Genes that are close by, on the same chromosome, will tend to be inherited together because they are parts of a single physical unit, the chromosome.

The transmission of genetic variations together, residing nearby on the same chromosome, is called linkage.

Crossing-Over

Linkage was discovered by Morgan and his students early in the twentieth century, working on fruit flies. Shortly thereafter, they discovered an important addition to the idea of linkage—in essence its opposite, crossing-over.

We now know—thanks to the insightful deduction by Morgan's group—that during the process of meiosis, when gametes are forming, *the homologous chromosomes—that is, chromosome 1 from mother and chromosome 1 from father, and so forth—pair up with one another and actually exchange pieces.* We don't know how they recognize each other in the cell's nucleus, but this pairing and exchange, called *crossing-over* or *recombination*, must happen to every chromosome pair at least once, or else the segregation of chromosomes into haploid germ cells will not be accomplished properly.

Independent assortment describes the fact that any particular one of your gametes will contain a motley combination of chromosomes you inherited from your father and from your mother. Crossing-over ensures that each chromosome itself consists of bits derived from your mother attached to bits derived from your father. This is a system that has evolved to maximize diversity within the limits set by cell division.

Polygenic Inheritance

A fourth non-Mendelian law involves the generalization we can make about phenotypes – or body parts more specifically – in relation to genes. *Everything phenotypically interesting is controlled by more than one gene; the exceptions are trivialities (like ear wax and blood type) and pathologies (like cystic fibrosis).*

Human genetics is complicated by the fact that we are a poor experimental species. We have long generation times, few offspring, and prefer to mate by choice rather than at the request of a geneticist. Consequently, our knowledge of human genetics is considerably more primitive than that of fruit flies or mice. Further, it has tended to be approached through the study of disease.

One of the odd consequences of this is that we know exceedingly little about the genetics of being normal. The genes we have isolated and mapped tend to be biochemicals, such as enzymes, whose general effect on the body is unclear; or major pathologies, such as cystic fibrosis, Tay-Sachs' disease, or Huntington's chorea. Of course, there is no gene whose function is to give you cystic fibrosis. Rather, there is a gene whose function is not well known—in this case, the transport of ions through the cells of the lungs—which, when its effect is compromised, produces cystic fibrosis.

We then employ a shorthand, and call it the cystic fibrosis gene. In this way, we build up a very morbid map of the human genes: arcane biochemicals and diseases. There are some traits in the literature that are believed to be under the control of a single gene, such as earlobe shape, eye color, tongue rolling, and the ability to bend the thumb backward—but these genes haven't been mapped; and in some cases, they are simply untrue. Tongue rolling, for example, was proposed as a single-gene trait by the geneticist Alfred Sturtevant in the 1950s, and retracted shortly thereafter, but it has such utility in genetics classes that it continues to be taught!

And yet, the ability to bend the thumb backward did not allow us to outlast the Neandertals: nor did the shape of our earlobes. We are interested in the traits that make us human—traits like brain size, bipedalism, language, a broad pelvis, long legs, hairlessness, the distribution of sweat glands, and so forth. We don't see genes for these in the human gene map. Why? Because they are all complex features, the products of the interactions of several or many genes.

Although physical features are ultimately caused by genes, and Mendel's laws govern the transmission of genes, Mendel's laws do not directly govern the transmission of physical features. They are the products of many genes interacting together, and consequently, their inheritance is complex.

Environmental Influence on Phenotypes

An important reason to distinguish between genotype and phenotype is that different genotypes may result in the same phenotype, or the same genotype may yield different phenotypes.

We saw earlier that Mendel interpreted "tall plants" versus "short plants" as a consequence of the action of a single gene. Of course, we assume he watered both kinds of plants equally, because if he didn't water the short plants, it's no wonder they turned out that way!

Obviously the height attained by a plant is sensitive to the environmental conditions within which it grows.

Now let's think about people. It has been estimated that the range of normal height is a result of the action of about seven genes. We have not identified them, however. There are also genes known that affect height pathologically. One symptom of Marfan syndrome, for example, is tall stature; and one symptom of achondroplasia is small stature. Both of those genes have been mapped, but they affect the height of relatively few people.

So let us say you are one of the normal people, whose seven major undiscovered genes dispose you to be big. Will you be 5'9", 5'11", or 6'2" tall? That will depend on several factors, from the long-term quality of your diet, to your habits, to your general health, activity level, exposure to sunshine, and possibly many other things, of varying degrees of subtlety. We know, for example, that an average Japanese male of 1995 was nearly 6 inches taller than an average Japanese male of 1955, due presumably to general changes in diet and lifestyle; the Dutch are presently an average of about 8 inches taller than the Dutch people of 150 years ago.

The range of phenotypic variations possible with a single genotype is known as the *norm of reaction*. It is, however, a lot easier to study in model organisms like fruit flies than in humans. As of 2014, genomics had given us over 400 "candidate genes" affecting human height, but together they only accounted for about one-third of the variation in human height.

The point, then, is that a phenotype is the result of a complex mixture of genetics and the conditions of life. Thus, a fifth non-Mendelian law: *Phenotypes are under-determined by genotypes.*

The study of heritable changes that are not encoded in the sequence of DNA bases is known as *epigenetics* (Chapter 6). An environmental stressor (perhaps exercise or famine) induces chemical modifications to the DNA structure, although not to the base sequence itself, which may regulate the expression of the genes. This difference in cell physiology may be passed down across cell and human generations. It seems to afford a way in which the environment can have a direct effect on the phenotype, which can indeed be transmitted to progeny, as the early Lamarckians had imagined.

Unit Characters

A sixth non-Mendelian law involves the relationship between genes and phenotypes. As we saw, Gregor Mendel inferred the binary units of inheritance from the binary traits he examined—tall/short plants, yellow/green seed color, and so forth. The success of his work in simplifying the mechanism of heredity to the transmission of basic informational units was clear after 1900, but it led down a very large blind alley.

They say that when the only tool you have is a hammer, everything tends to look like a nail, and that is a very apt analogy for human genetics in America in the 1910s and 1920s. Human geneticists, led by Charles B. Davenport, began to find binary traits caused by binary genes everywhere. Davenport, for example, held that sailing peoples had a gene for "thalassophilia" (Greek for "love of the sea"). And thus, the next non-Mendelian law: *Although there are units of hereditary information (genes), there are no unit characters of the phenotype that map on to them.*

Consider Davenport's most famous idea, the gene for "feeblemindedness," located in the constitutions of poor people, immigrants, and criminals, and inhibiting them from successful, honest, moral lives. If this sounds ridiculous, consider that the Supreme Court, in the infamous *Buck v. Bell* decision of 1927, upheld the right of the state of Virginia to sterilize a woman against her will, because she, her mother, and her daughter were all judged to be feebleminded. Based on what they believed to be the best scientific, genetic evidence, the Court ruled that "three generations of imbeciles is enough." And genetic testimony about the "feeblemindedness" of Italians and Jews helped pass the immigration restriction act of 1924.

The important point is: Just because you can come up with a name for something, that doesn't mean there's a gene for it. What appear to be nameable entities, whether personality traits or anatomical features, do not correspond to specific genes. Genes build bodies as a system; unit characters don't correspond to units of inheritance. You have elbows and you have a nose, and you have genes, but there is no "elbow" gene, or "nose" gene; much less a "musical talent" gene or "intelligence" gene.

Properties of Heterozygotes

A seventh non-Mendelian law is the recognition that dominance and recessiveness are only two simple relationships to be expressed in the phenotypes of heterozygotes. There are other possibilities, realized in nature, beyond simply one parental phenotype being fully expressed in the heterozygous offspring (dominant) and one parental phenotype being absent in those offspring (recessive).

One can find, for example, instances where the offspring express a phenotype intermediate between the two parents. This would seem to mimic the pattern of blending inheritance, and is known as incomplete, or partial, dominance.

More commonly, *both* parental phenotypes are expressed in the hybrid offspring, a situation known as co-dominance. This is frequently the case for biochemical phenotypes, in which alleles code for two different forms of an enzyme, and a heterozygote expresses them both. In the case of the ABO blood group system, three alleles combine into genotypes six ways. The gene, at the tip of chromosome 9, codes for an enzyme that adds a fifth sugar to a chain of four, attached to a molecule on the surface of a red blood cell. Allele A adds one sugar, allele B adds a different sugar, and allele O adds no sugar at all. Allele O is recessive to A and B (thus genotypes AO and AA yield the same phenotype, and genotypes BB and BO yield the same phenotype), but A and B are co-dominant—hence the AB blood type.

Thus, *the phenotype may not be easily predictable from the combination of alleles present.*

Pleiotropy

While there may be genes that affect those traits in certain predictable ways, there is an important generalization we can make about gene action. Our eighth non-Mendelian law: *Since genes work in nested physiological pathways, they never have just a single effect.* This is called *pleiotropy,* the complex systemic effects of a single gene.

The product of the gene that causes phenylketonuria, or PKU, is involved in metabolizing nutrients; its failure causes a buildup of otherwise transient chemicals called phenylketones. It was recognized in the 1950s that the disease could be treated dietetically; but when left untreated, it becomes a significant genetic cause of intellectual disability. But that's not the only symptom: there are also problems with the skin (eczema), depigmentation, dental anomalies, and personality.

As we will see later, a well-known gene conferring resistance to malaria also causes sickle-cell anemia. And sickle-cell anemia itself has a variety of symptoms, affecting nearly every part of the body. It has also been suggested that a gene conferring resistance to tuberculosis also causes Tay-Sachs disease, more common in eastern European Jews than in other populations.

This throws an important light on popular scenarios of, for example, "intelligence genes." If such genes exist, the question to ask is, What *else* do they do? Make you more likely to develop schizophrenia? Dispose you to heart disease? or alcoholism?

Genes operate within a system, and their effects are trade-offs. You can't change one element without affecting others.

The flip side of pleiotropy (one gene with multiple effects) is *epistasis* (several genes contributing to the same effect) so that one gene may conceal the effect of another gene. In the ABO blood group discussed above, the genetic variation encodes what happens to a fourth sugar at the end of a molecule on the cell surface. But suppose there is no fourth sugar at all because of a mutation in the gene that adds it on (call it the *H* gene, with a recessive allele, *h*). An *hh* individual, with no fourth sugar for the ABO gene's product to work on, would always look like type O antigenically, because although the ABO enzymes may be there waiting to work, they have no substrate on which to work. (This is called the *Bombay phenotype*, after the place it was first discovered.)

Now suppose this person needs a blood transfusion. Matched to type O, suddenly there is blood with cells containing four-sugar chains in the circulatory system. And now the enzymes have something to work on, so they begin converting the type O blood into the recipient's real ABO blood type. But that new blood type is not recognized as "self" by the immune system, because the immune system has never encountered it before, so the body rejects and attacks the new cells.

This is of course life threatening, and is a result of the *h* allele masking the phenotype and genotype of the ABO gene.

Imprinting

Mendel's Laws assume that a gene in a sperm is equivalent to the same (homologous) gene in an egg. Actually, however, patterns of gene expression may differ in the sperm and egg, and some genes require both a male and a female copy of the gene to be present. A small region on the long arm of human chromosome 15 is occasionally deleted, with characteristic pathological results. If the deleted chromosome comes from the father, and the only functional copy is from the mother, the result is Prader-Willi syndrome (characterized by obesity, small hands and feet, and delayed development). If the deleted chromosome is the mother's, and the only functional copy is from father, the result is Angelman syndrome (characterized by seizures, laughing, poor muscle tone, and severe intellectual disability). If the patient has two intact chromosomes 15, but both come from the egg (which rarely happens, a condition known as *maternal uniparental disomy*), Prader-Willi syndrome also results. And if the patient has *paternal* uniparental disomy, the result is again Angelman syndrome.

The explanation seems to be that *the body requires one paternal and one maternal copy of certain genes, and they are different.* Somehow chromosomes are biochemically marked (or imprinted) with their origin as they pass through the genome of a sperm or an egg into the next generation. The imprinting is reversed or reset every generation.

Extra-Nuclear Inheritance

Our last non-Mendelian law involves recognizing that although the nucleus of the cell has the genes sequestered within it, there is still a little bit of genetic information that is inherited along with the cytoplasm of the cell. In particular, the cytoplasm contains organelles called mitochondria whose function is to generate metabolic energy for the cell's function.

Each mitochondrion, however, has its own genes—thirty-seven of them, three orders of magnitude smaller than the number of genes in the nucleus. Several diseases are known to be caused by alterations in these mitochondrial genes.

Mitochondrial genes, being outside the nucleus, are exempted from meiosis and crossing-over. In fact, when sperm and egg unite, the sperm's mitochondria generally do not become incorporated into the new zygote—they come solely from the egg, from mother.

This creates a bizarre situation: although you are genetically equally related to your mother and to your father, that is actually only true for the nuclear genes (which of course constitute the vast majority of what we mean by "genetic.") *Mitochondrially, you are a clone of your mother, and unrelated to your father*—for only the egg contributed your mitochondrial DNA.

Mitochondrial DNA (mtDNA) also changes at a far greater rate than nuclear DNA. Where you are generally about 1%–2% genetically different from a chimpanzee or gorilla, your mtDNA is about 8%–10% different from that of a chimpanzee or gorilla. This also means that there are a few detectable differences from person to person in a segment of mtDNA, where there would be virtually none in a comparable segment of nuclear DNA. Consequently, mtDNA has taken on great significance as a research tool in the study of human genetic history. However, because of its weird manner of transmission, mtDNA challenges our ideas about both genetic ancestry and evolution. Since you are a mitochondrial clone of one of your sixteen great-great-grandparents, and mitochondrially unrelated to the other fifteen, mtDNA does not record ancestry in a familiar sense. Nevertheless, its test results are often sold to consumers as if the ancestry it records were indeed that familiar sense. Further, since only women pass it on, a prolific parent with fifteen children, all boys, is nevertheless mitochondrially extinct. Consequently, the evolution of mtDNA is much more sensitive to random fluctuations in the sex ratios of offspring than to slightly better or worse mutations.

THE MOLECULAR GENOMIC BASIS OF HEREDITY

One of the goals of modern science is reductionism, to explain particular phenomena as just special cases of more general principles. Perhaps the most successful example was Isaac Newton's reduction of diverse examples of gravitational attraction, like apples falling and planets circling, to mathematics. Some biologists believe that since humans are simply a special case of life, all human existence and behavior should only be described by biological laws. This is true only to a limited extent, for although biological laws cover humans, humans also transcend them in certain ways. Those same biologists would be very reluctant to agree that since life is just a special case of chemistry, all things biological should be described and subsumed under chemical laws!

And yet, partly that is what happened during the last half of the twentieth century. The basic principles of heredity were reduced to chemistry, by determining that genes are composed of DNA (deoxyribonucleic acid), and identifying its structure, the famous "double helix." This was accomplished by Watson and Crick in 1953, which ushered in the age of molecular biology, and for which they won the Nobel Prize.

To understand evolution, we need to understand what genes are and how they work, and how they change. The cell's work is carried out by a diverse class of molecules called proteins. Because of their importance, ubiquity, and diversity, it was widely thought into the 1950s that they comprised the genetic instructions themselves. But proteins are the cell's brawn, not the brains. The information is the DNA. The question, then, is, How does the information in the DNA become implemented as protein? Proteins are *polymers*, that is, long chains built up of simple subunits. The subunits are amino acids, of which there are twenty different kinds. Proteins can range in size from a few amino acids to several thousand, and can have any of twenty different options at any position; obviously, then, they can be very diverse.

Molecular genetics makes extensive use of metaphors from language. Physicist Erwin Schrödinger famously suggested in his 1944 book called *What Is Life?* that cellular processes could be understood as a "code," with information in genes communicated to the rest of the cell, regulating its function; the phrase "genetic code" has been with us ever since. And ever since, the dominant metaphors of molecular genetics have been derived from linguistics. Now that we know the genetic "information" is stored in DNA, we talk of it being "transcribed" into messenger RNA (mRNA), "edited" to maturity and functionality, and its "message" "translated" into protein. A gene is an informational segment of DNA, a piece of DNA ultimately responsible for carrying out a biological function. The field of genetics centers on the study of genes.

Thomas Hunt Morgan's research on the relationship between fruit fly genes and chromosomes early in the twentieth century produced an overarching simile to describe that relationship: genes were arrayed on chromosomes *like beads on a string*. That powerful image remained the dominant view until the 1990s and the emergence of a new field, genomics.

The genome is the totality of DNA in a single cell (technically, a haploid cell—a gamete). Genomics, then, is the study of the DNA, not restricted simply to functional entities, or genes. As the genome has been examined, two important observations have overturned the "beads on a string" image. First, the genome has much string and few beads. As we will see shortly, only about 1%–2% of the genome is actually coding sequence. And second, the genes themselves, being stretches of DNA, are simply special cases of the genome. In other words, the beads are themselves made of string.

The Human Genome Project was undertaken in 1989 to generate the entire human DNA sequence, and it accomplished that goal (or nearly so) in 2000. Since about 75% of the human genome consists of intergenic DNA, or the DNA between genes, it is important to understand the other kinds of DNA in the human genome. And of the 25% of the genome that comprises genes, only about 7% of that is coding sequence. For example, the gene called DMD (Duchenne muscular dystrophy) codes for dystrophin, a protein whose failure is the cause of the disease. The gene itself spans 2,400,000 bases—but the functional mRNA is only 14,000 bases. Even within genes, the vast majority of the DNA consists of untranslated regions and introns, which are edited out of the mRNA.

So there is an inefficient use of DNA throughout the genome, with so little DNA—perhaps 2% of the entire genome—actually being translated into protein (and even if we extend the idea of DNA function beyond protein coding, still very little of the DNA actually gets used). Another characteristic of the genome is its pervasive redundancy, which has consequences for the processes of mutation.

There are two broad classes of repetitive DNA: localized and interspersed. About 5% of the human genome consists of regions around the middle of each chromosome, called satellite DNA. It is DNA that has no obvious function in the traditional sense, and can tolerate substantial change with no apparent ill effect. It is generally a simple base sequence, repeated thousands and thousands of times.

Some DNA elements can be removed and reintegrated elsewhere, by a process called *transposition*. These are known as mobile genetic elements, or transposons.

Interspersed repetitive elements are odder still. The best known is a 300-base-pair sequence called *Alu*, of which there are about a million copies, scattered apparently at random throughout the genome, and each one dead, nonfunctional. Alu sequences are still being generated, by a process called *retrotransposition*. Somewhere in the genome, a functional "master Alu" gene is transcribed; its RNA copies are *reverse-transcribed* back into DNA copies, and those are integrated elsewhere in the genome. But the million dead, functionless Alu sequences take up a significantly larger proportion of the genome than DNA coding sequences do!

Even the genes themselves show patterns of redundancy. A gene is generally not found in isolation but rather exists as a part of a gene family, a cluster of functional DNA sequences that tend to make similar products. A fundamental process of change in the genome involves the tandem duplication of a block of DNA, so that two identical genes are now next to one another—in essence, a "rubber stamp" process.

Over many generations, new mutations (changes to the DNA sequence) will spontaneously arise in the duplicated gene. This has three possible consequences. If, for some reason, it is better to have two copies of the gene than just one, then this mutation will be favorable, and the intact duplicated genes will be retained and perpetuated. Alternatively, if it is just as good to have one copy as it is to have two, then mutations might cripple the duplicate gene, with no ill effect to the organism, which still has a functional copy. In this case, we would find a DNA sequence in the genome that looks very much like the gene next to it, but cannot make a functional product; it is called a *pseudogene*. The third option is that mutations to the copied gene might alter the gene product so that it does something slightly different, perhaps in a specialized context. If this is beneficial to the organism, then we would expect to see clusters of similar genes together in the genome.

That ultimately is why we spend some time grappling with molecular genetics. We are interested in evolution, and molecular genetics provides the engine of genetic novelty for evolution. We can see the effects of molecular evolution in the genes for hemoglobin, the best-known genetic system in our species. Hemoglobin consists of an iron-binding porphyrin ring and the protein products of two sets of genes. The beta-globin genes, on chromosome 11, produce half of the hemoglobin protein, the one that is 146 amino acids long. The alpha-globin genes, on chromosome 16, produce the other half, a set of proteins that are each 141 amino acids long.

THE ALPHA-GLOBIN GENE CLUSTER

The alpha (α) globins comprise seven genes, mostly spaced about 4,000 bases (= 4 kilobases, or kb) apart, and scattered among them are over a dozen *Alu* repeats (see Figure 4.1).

The first gene is known as zeta (ζ). Like α, it makes a 141-amino-acid-long hemoglobin component, and three out of every four bases are identical to the α-globin gene. But ζ is only functional early in embryonic life, when the oxygen transport requirements are quite different; α, by contrast, is turned on during the sixth month of fetal life and remains on through adulthood.

Next is a pseudogene of ζ (ψζ1, read as "pseudo-zeta-one"), a very similar copy of it, yet containing a termination codon early in the coding sequence, which prevents it from making a functional globin protein. Then we encounter pseudo-alpha-2 (ψα2), an ancient, beaten-up copy of alpha, whose sequence similarity to alpha was actually discovered by computer analysis. Pseudo-alpha-1 (ψα1), on the other hand, bears a strong similarity to α, although containing numerous features that shut it down. Next come α2 and α1, with identical coding sequences (they differ slightly in noncoding sequence), both making the α-globin component of hemoglobin. And finally, there is theta (θ), a gene about as similar to α as is embryonic ζ, and itself making a protein, but of unknown function.

What we see here are the results of all three consequences of the "rubber-stamp" of tandem duplication at work. The two α genes make the same protein;

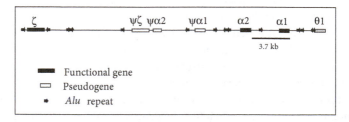

Figure 4.1. The human alpha-globin gene cluster.

ζ and θ make similar, but distinctly different, proteins, and the pseudogenes do nothing. More than that, however, we see how biological novelty is generated genetically: over time, genes can be copied, altered, and put to other uses.

MUTATION

Classical evolutionary theory, as developed in the first half of the twentieth century, begins, as Darwin did, with a genetically variable population. But these variations are the kind that Mendel worked with: changes to the genes. The most basic genetic change is called a point mutation, the substitution of one base for another somewhere in the DNA. Sickle-cell anemia, for example, is caused by a point mutation in the sixth codon of the beta-globin gene on chromosome 11, leading to the substitution of the amino acid valine for glutamic acid in the protein.

Since most DNA is not genic, it follows that most point mutations are not expressed phenotypically. They have no effect, and simply accumulate over time in the species. On the other hand, mutations that occur in genes will tend to affect the functioning of the gene adversely and tend to be weeded out by natural selection. We find, therefore, that when we compare DNA sequences between species, the intergenic DNA is the most divergent, genic noncoding sequences are less different from one another, and coding sequences are the most similar.

Another kind of genetic change involves macroscale breakage and recombination of a chromosome. This is actually visible in the microscope, while point mutations can only be inferred. Thus, a human cell has 23 pairs of chromosomes and a chimpanzee cell has 24 pairs. But humans have a large chromosome (#2) that chimpanzees lack, and chimpanzees have two small chromosomes that humans lack. And when you place the two small chimp chromosomes end to end, you find that they look just like the large human chromosome. Apparently a chromosome fusion has occurred in the human lineage.

This, however, is a marker of the human condition, not a cause of it. It enables you to tell whether the cells you are examining came from a human or a chimpanzee; but it is not the cause of bipedalism, or braininess, or all of the other classic adaptations of the human lineage. It was a random change, with probably no effect at all on the expression of any genes.

Similarly, the gorilla's chromosomes have undergone a translocation in which the chromosomes corresponding to human 5 and 17 have broken and rejoined differently. Thus the gorilla has no chromosome corresponding to human 5 or to human 17; rather, it has one chromosome that is mostly 5 and partly 17, and one that is mostly 17 and partly 5.

In addition to point mutations and chromosome mutations, however, the redundancy of the genome produces another class of mutations: genomic mutations. We have already noted transposition, retrotransposition, and gene duplication. These are three kinds of genomic mutations.

Another kind of genomic mutation is called *strand slippage*. While the precise mechanism is unknown, strand slippage seems to occur in regions where there is already some slight redundancy. It is as if, while the DNA is being copied in preparation for cell division, the cellular machinery "forgets its place" and adds or deletes a few subunits. Thus, a DNA sequence of CTGAAAG might be copied as CTGAAAAAG. This may be at least partly responsible for the genotype of fragile X syndrome, a leading cause of genetic intellectual disability in boys. Here, a bit of the untranslated region of a gene called FMR1 contains a region where CCG is repeated from ten to fifty times in normal people. In some people, however, this is expanded up to two hundred copies, quite possibly by strand slippage. These people are carriers, for they do not manifest the disease. Their children, however, may have 200–500 copies, which impairs translation of the RNA, and causes the syndrome. Other diseases, such as Huntington's chorea and myotonic dystrophy, have similar causes—the expansion or multiplication of a simple repeat in a gene.

Finally, a mode of mutation known as unequal crossing-over may have greater potential for creative effects in the genome. The process of meiosis begins with the intimate pairing of the corresponding maternal and paternal chromosomes, which then cross over and exchange genetic information, thus unlinking allele combinations, as we noted earlier. This exchange is entirely reciprocal—no DNA is gained or lost by either chromosome in the process—and is predicated on the point-by-point genetic correspondence of the appropriate region.

The widespread existence of redundancy, however, especially in gene families, yields a possibility for the pairing mechanism to be briefly "fooled" so that a gene pairs with a similar, but not correct, counterpart. Suppose, during the meiotic processes, the α1 globin gene on the paternal chromosome 16 paired not with the α1 globin gene on maternal chromosome 16, but with α2 just beside it. A crossover would now produce one chromosome with three α-globin genes and one chromosome with just one.

This is precisely how the genotype for α-thalassemia, a blood disease found mostly in East Asia, and (like sickle-cell) conferring resistance to malaria, is generated. It may also be at work in the examples of fragile X, Huntington's chorea, and myotonic dystrophy given previously, complementing the strand slippage.

However, beyond harmful effects, this may also provide a common way to generate more copies of genes that can take on new functions.

The point is that molecular genetics is important as the ultimate source of diversity that drives evolutionary change. Most changes are harmful, but the genetic system is complex, and there are a lot of ways for nature to alter it.

MEANINGS OF THE GENE AND GENETICS

We have been using the word "*gene*" in the sense that it is used in molecular genetics, as a piece of DNA with a recognizable structure and/or function. It is worthwhile to note, however, that other scientists, such as the theoretical biologist Richard Dawkins, use the word *gene* in a very different sense. To Dawkins, a gene is an abstract replicator, something that makes copies of itself to leave in the next generation. While this has spawned a great deal of writing and thought, it is a concept foreign to most geneticists.

There are other, hidden meanings in genes, as well. Genes are often regarded as "uncaused causes"—determinants of appearances and behaviors, as if their expression were invariant, their combinations were unimportant, and the conditions of life did not affect their expression. Perhaps one person has a "gene for violence" or a "gene for shopping." In this sense, genes take on a very pre-Mendelian and pre-scientific meaning, that of an invisible "core" or "essence" that makes you what you are, and that you can neither resist nor transcend. While there is some truth there (such as if you have the alleles for Tay-Sachs disease, you get Tay-Sachs disease), it is very limited.

Most significantly, such a view tends to focus on individual alleles, rather than on genotypes, the diploid pairs that actually exist physically in the cell. The physiological interaction between allele pairs is crucial in determining the phenotype. Often, as in sickle-cell anemia, it is better to be a heterozygote than to be a homozygote of *either* form—which means that neither allele is superior, but their *combinations* are important in determining survival and reproduction.

The older view found its way into the Human Genome Project, which was based on a medical model of the genome in which each gene has a normal allele, and diseases are caused by rare deviant alleles. One could, with this essentialist model in mind, sequence the "normal allele" of each gene and have a map of what a normal human is like—which was precisely what the Human Genome Project proposed to do in the 1980s.

This, however, assumes that diseases are the model for diversity, in which most people share one normal form, and rare deviants have the disease. But there is another model that is probably more realistic. Consider the blood group system, ABO, in which there are three alleles and six genotypes: AA, AO, BB, BO, AB, and OO. None of these alleles is more normal than the others. In what sense, then, would sequencing one of them be meaningful? It would simply (and falsely) suggest that normalcy encompasses a narrow range of DNA sequences, and deviations from that range tend to be pathological, which may be quite the opposite of the truth! Many genetic systems are highly variable, and as we will see in the next chapter, that variation may be good for both the organism and the individual.

More than that, people are diploid, and there appears to be something crucially important about the state of having two sets of genetic information—not one, and not three—whose interactions are not understandable in terms of a single linear DNA sequence. This is known as *dosage*, the body's constraint on having the precise amount of genetic material, deviations from which cannot be easily tolerated. Having a third chromosome of what is normally a pair is generally incompatible with survival, unless it is a very small one, like #21, an extra representative of which leads to Down syndrome. Lacking one chromosome of a pair is even worse.

Thus the combinations into which the genes enter are of vital importance for determining their physiological function and expression. To talk about single alleles as being better or worse than one another, or to talk about a single DNA sequence as being a blueprint for a functioning human cell or body, is to misunderstand and to undervalue critically the real importance of dosage in genetics.

How we talk about genetics is itself important in revealing how we think about it. This is the field of semiotics, or linguistic meanings. Consider the metaphors and analogies we have used in this chapter, which are common in genetic writing and thinking. The cell, whose importance was revealed during the height of the industrial revolution, is like a machine—we talk of the cellular machinery or apparatus. We speak of the genetic "code"—a metaphor so powerful today that we find it hard to talk about genetics any other way. But genetics is not a code, it is *like* a code, in some interesting ways. And we talk about DNA as "information"—a way of thinking that was introduced by mathematicians in the 1950s. These have been immensely helpful as heuristics—devices that help demonstrate the properties of interest. But these are merely linguistic conventions and are not literally true; they will all ultimately reach the limits of their utility and be replaced by new, and more accurate, descriptions and other metaphors.

Finally, there is meaning in genetics that can be seen in an odd question: Is a human egg a body part or a body product?

Approached simply from the standpoint of biology or genetics, the question is meaningless: A human egg is a haploid gamete, a specialized cell.

But in modern society, the question has a great deal of meaning that transcends its genetic meaning. In the United States, you can sell the essentially infinite, replenishable products of your body: notably, blood and sperm. You cannot sell your kidney or your eyeball. (The reason is that it would promote the sale of body parts from poor to rich people, which is now occurring, with often tragic results, in other parts of the world.)

The field of reproductive biology is a booming business, and wealthy infertile couples may be able to spend tens of thousands of dollars for human eggs. Some have advertised $50,000 for eggs from women who meet high standards of intellect, athleticism, and beauty (showing the folk ideas about heredity at work!). However, although eggs are homologous to sperm, they are not as easily accessible. It requires hormone therapy to prime the eggs, and surgery to extract them. So is an egg more like a kidney (in which case you can't be compensated for it), or like sperm (in which case you can)?

The answer, of course, is that an egg is formally recognized as a body product, not a body part. In that sense, however, an egg has become culturally constructed— that is, although it is a natural object, it has assumed meaning not inherent in its biological or genetic properties.

REFERENCES AND FURTHER READING

Barnes, B., and J. Dupré. 2009. *Genomes and What to Make of Them*. Chicago: University of Chicago Press.

Beckwith, J. 1996. The hegemony of the gene: Reductionism in molecular biology. In *The Philosophy and History of Molecular Biology: New Perspectives*, ed. S. Sarkar, 171–183. Dordrecht, The Netherlands: Kluwer.

Beurton, P., R. Falk, and H. Rheinberger, eds. 2000. *The Concept of the Gene in Development and Evolution: Historical and Epistemological Perspectives*. New York: Cambridge University Press.

Collins, F. S., A. Patrinos, E. Jordan, A. Chakravarti, R. Gesteland, and L. Walters. 1998. New goals for the U. S. Human Genome Project: 1998–2003. *Science* 282:682–689.

Condit, C. 1999. *The Meanings of the Gene: Public Debates about Human Heredity*. Madison: University of Wisconsin Press.

Enard, W., and S. Pääbo. 2004. Comparative primate genomics. *Annual Review of Genomics and Human Genetics* 5:351–378.

Falk, R. 1986. What is a gene? *Studies in History and Philosophy of Science* 17:133–173.

Fogle, T. 1987. The phenotypic deception: Influences of classical genetics on genetic paradigms. *Perspectives in Biology and Medicine* 31:65–80.

Gissis, S., and E. Jablonka, eds. 2011. *Transformations of Lamarckism: From Subtle Fluids to Molecular Biology*. Cambridge, MA: MIT Press.

Goodman, A., D. Heath, and M. S. Lindee, eds. 2004. *Genetic Nature/Culture*. Berkeley: University of California Press.

Hubbard, R., and E. Wald. 1993. *Exploding the Gene Myth*. Boston: Beacon.

Lewontin, R. C. 1991. *Biology as Destiny: The Doctrine of DNA*. New York: Harper/Collins.

Marks, J. 1992. Beads and string: The genome in evolutionary theory. In *Molecular Applications in Biological Anthropology*, ed. E. J. Devor, 234–255. New York: Cambridge University Press.

Marks, J. 1995. *Human Biodiversity: Genes, Race, and History*. Piscataway, NJ: Aldine Transaction.

Marks, J. 2009. The construction of Mendel's Laws. *Evolutionary Anthropology* 17:250–253.

Marks, J., J.-P. Shaw, C. Perez-Stable, W.-S. Hu, T. M. Ayres, C. Shen, and C.-K. J. Shen. 1986. The primate alpha-globin gene family: A paradigm of the fluid genome. *Cold Spring Harbor Symposia on Quantitative Biology* 51:499–507.

Miller, W., K. D. Makova, A. Nekrutenko, and R. C. Hardison. 2004. Comparative genomics. *Annual Review of Genomics and Human Genetics* 5:15–56.

Moss, L. 2004. *What Genes Can't Do*. Cambridge, MA: MIT Press.

Müller-Wille, S., and H.-G. Rheinberger, eds. 2007. *Heredity Produced: At the Crossroads of Biology, Politics, and Culture, 1500–1870*. Cambridge, MA: MIT Press.

Müller-Wille, S., and H.-G. Rheinberger. 2012. *A Cultural History of Heredity*. Chicago: University of Chicago Press.

Neel, J. 1994. *Physician to the Gene Pool*. New York: John Wiley.

Pääbo, S. 2003. The mosaic that is our genome. *Nature* 421:409–411.

Pinto-Correia, C. 1997. *The Ovary of Eve: Egg and Sperm and Preformation*. Chicago: University of Chicago Press.

Sarkar, S. 1996. Decoding "coding"—Information and DNA. *BioSystems* 46:857–864.

Scheper-Hughes, N. 2000. The global traffic in organs. *Current Anthropology* 41:191–224.

Spyropoulos, B. 1988. Tay-Sachs carriers and tuberculosis resistance. *Nature* 331:666.

Suarez, E. D. 2007. The rhetoric of informational molecules: Authority and promises in the early study of molecular evolution. *Science in Context* 20:1–29.

Waller, J. 2003. Parents and children: Ideas of heredity in the 19th century. *Endeavour* 27:51–56.

Wood, A. R., Esko, T., Yang, J., Vedantam, S., et al. 2014. Defining the role of common variation in the genomic and biological architecture of adult human height. *Nature Genetics*, 46:1173–1186.

CHAPTER 5

Are We Here? If So, Why?
(On Issues of Microevolution)

THEME

A population is like a superorganism, perpetuating itself across generations and permitting its genetic features to be studied. Genetic theory can explain the existence of specific features that were good and useful (by selection) and of those that were *not* good and useful (by drift). Human genetics is a science with important cultural meanings, however; and investing it with unquestioned authority about kinship and descent—who we are and what we are—can obscure its weaknesses.

DO THINGS EXIST FOR A REASON?

That's not a scientific question, but a philosophical one, and yet one that intrudes to some extent on evolution. Why does this book exist? (1) Without the publisher and printer, it would not exist, but they don't explain the existence of this book in particular; (2) without the author, it would not exist, but all I really did was think it up and type it; (3) without the previous generations of accumulated knowledge of biological anthropology, it would not exist, for I would have had nothing to write about; and (4) if matter and the universe did not exist, neither would this book, although that would be the least of our problems.

Aristotle recognized that all of these are linked into a chain of causality. The production and manufacture of the book and its impression onto wood pulp constitute its efficient and material causes. My writing the book is its formal cause. And whatever compelled me to write it, or at least benignly allowed me to do so, would be its final causes.

Of course, we don't really know if there was a final cause per se, because we don't know whether I wrote the book spontaneously and volitionally, of my own free will, or whether I was compelled to do it by the forces of the universe.

So what this analysis conceals is the complexity of the assumption that there is indeed a reason for everything and that things aren't the way they are for just no reason at all. In other words, is there really a purpose for any specific shit, or does it just "happen"? Much of microevolution is devoted to grappling with that very question.

PRINCIPAL ABSTRACTION: THE GENE POOL

A population can be thought of as a group of organisms that tend to live and breed together. It can be as small as a group of migrants and as large as a species. Microevolution is the study of how such populations perpetuate themselves genetically. As we saw in the last chapter, at a specific genetic site or locus, an organism can be described by a pair of genes, its genotype. By extension, at a specific locus, a population can be described by the proportion of different alleles possessed by its members. Thus, for the ABO blood group locus, a population might have a frequency of 0.65 for the O allele, 0.23 for the A allele, and 0.12 for the B allele.

These numbers describe the genetic composition of the population for that locus, an abstract mathematical summation of all the eggs and sperm, called the *gene pool.* (It is a "pool" in the sense of a betting pool, not in the sense of a swimming pool.) The gene pool is the focus of population genetics, and its dynamics through time constitute the study of microevolution.

The greatest strength of population genetics is also its greatest weakness: it fails to problematize the phenotype. In other words, it takes the phenotype for granted and does not acknowledge that there are questions to be asked about it, like where it comes from—the phenotype here is a non-issue, a non-problem. In focusing on the gene pool, it avoids the entire question of bodies. The gene pool will be tracked through time, and its contents sampled in pairwise combinations representing genotypes, as surrogates for organisms. The simplifying assumption here will be that the phenotype is entirely predictable from the genotype.

The basic principle, from which all other ideas flow in population genetics, was codified in the early 1900s, independently by a British mathematician and a German biologist, Hardy and Weinberg. The Hardy–Weinberg law is an equilibrium law, relating the composition of the gene pool to the organisms (that is, the distribution of genotypes) populating it. It is, in large measure, a simple algebraic extension of Mendel's work.

The Hardy–Weinberg law says, first, *there is a simple relationship between the frequencies of alleles in the gene pool and the frequencies of genotypes in the population*; and second, *this relationship will be perpetuated indefinitely in future generations.* If Mendelian genetics is the only force acting on a gene pool, then it will not change. The allele frequencies and genotype frequencies will be constant and self-perpetuating over the generations, indefinitely—as long as Mendelian genetics is the only factor in operation. In fact, they will remain in the same proportions indefinitely—the Hardy–Weinberg law describes a stable population, a population in equilibrium, unchanging.

Why might the Hardy–Weinberg law *not* be in effect? There were several unarticulated assumptions in the Hardy–Weinberg law that need now to be articulated, so we can look at their effects on the population.

GENE FLOW

One implicit assumption is that the population is genetically isolated from other populations. A wave of immigration might well affect the gene pool and make it different from that of the previous generation's residents. We call this factor *gene flow,* the genetic contact between populations, or interbreeding. The consequence of interbreeding is that different genetic variants may enter the gene pool. Its effect is to make two populations more genetically alike.

In the modern world, of course, gene flow is a major force shaping human populations. It has been estimated that African American populations have (on the average) around 20% of their gene pool descended from Europeans. Similarly, despite having certain distinctions of their own gene pool, everywhere that the gene pool of Jewish populations has been studied, it is more similar to that of neighboring non-Jewish populations than to other Jewish populations. This, of course, suggests long-term genetic contact. Gene flow is consequently also a cohesive force among populations of a single species. For one species to split into two, gene flow will have to be broken.

INBREEDING

Another implicit assumption of Hardy–Weinberg is that all matings are equally likely, a condition called *random mating,* the equal probability of an individual of one genotype mating with any other. In reality, of course, our matings are highly patterned. We tend to mate at higher-than-random frequencies for many features: religion, height, ethnicity, education, and language—to name just a few. This alternative to random mating is known as *positive assortative mating.* Its direct opposite, *negative assortative mating,* or mating at lower-than-random frequencies with people who match us—is hardly known in human populations. Apparently the old saw from physics—that opposites attract—does not apply well to human mating patterns. Mating with relatives would certainly increase the probability of matching for any particular feature—either genetic or not. Mating with relatives is a special and extreme case of assortative mating, and is known as inbreeding.

The result of inbreeding is to drive a population toward homozygosity. This is because homozygotes breed true, but heterozygotes do not. Consequently, if heterozygotes tend to mate with one another, their proportion in the population will actually decrease through time, unlike the proportion of homozygotes.

This does not directly affect the frequencies of alleles in the gene pool, but merely redirects their combinations into genotypes. An inbred population has more homozygotes than would be expected by the Hardy–Weinberg law. The individual product of inbreeding is more likely to be homozygous—having inherited the same allele from a common ancestor on both sides of the family—than a less-inbred individual would be. Consequently, a rare recessive allele is more likely to be expressed in an inbred individual—being homozygous, having inherited the rare allele on both sides from the same ancestor—than in others.

It is important to distinguish inbreeding, a genetic state, from incest, a cultural act. Inbreeding involves reproduction, specifically the progeny of genetic relatives, which is actually a subset of all relatives (who would subsume in-laws and spouses). Incest, on the other hand, is specifically about sexual activity (regardless of whether offspring are produced), and is defined culturally, forbidding relations between in-laws, for example, in spite of not being genetic relatives.

This distinction becomes apparent at the social distance represented by first cousins. Although the progeny of such a union would be inbred, the union itself may or may not be considered incestuous. In Victorian England, it was common for the wealthy classes to marry their first cousins (thus keeping the fortune in the family). As we will see, Charles Darwin married his own first cousin. Indeed, the first cousin is a preferred marriage partner in many of the world's cultures. In some cultures, certain first cousins are preferred partners, and others are considered incestuous matings. Interestingly, a large survey of the progeny of first-cousin marriages failed to detect a significant increase in genetic or general health problems; and a study of Icelanders found that the most prolific couples were about fourth or fifth cousins. The long-term consequence of many generations of cousin marriage, however, may be an increased risk of rare genetic diseases caused by being homozygous.

NATURAL SELECTION

Another Hardy–Weinberg assumption is that the possessors of all genotypes are equally efficient at surviving and reproducing. Perhaps, however, that assumption does not hold. If so, it would represent the genetic equivalent of Darwin's *natural selection:* the differential survival and reproduction of organisms with particular genotypes.

Natural selection, in Darwin's writing, was specifically about phenotypes—features of an organism that give it a greater likelihood of surviving and reproducing. But more importantly, it was about *inherited* phenotypes, those that are passed on over the generations, even though Darwin had no knowledge of modern genetics. In population genetics, we rarely have the ability to link a specific phenotype to its underlying genetic variation. To the extent, however, that there is a relationship between a particular structure or biochemical configuration conferring a benefit, and genetic variation underlying it, the genetic and physical conceptions of natural selection can be considered synonymous.

Although selection is the only mechanism we know of that can produce adaptation in nature, it is remarkably difficult to demonstrate its action rigorously. After all, it operates on slight differences over long periods of time. Consider what we would need to demonstrate it: (1) a consistent bias of survival or reproduction, stretching over several generations; (2) a genetic basis for the feature of interest; (3) a difference between the original and descendant populations; (4) a plausible relationship between the biological feature of interest and the environment, producing the bias; and (5) evidence that the environmental factor related to the biological feature actually did produce the bias.

In practice, it is nearly impossible to demonstrate all of those things together, so we often rely on a combination of observation, experiment, deduction, and partly on arguments of plausibility. Thus, for example, we see in the fossil record that the human brain quadrupled in size over a period of about three million years. We can see this difference between the bipedal *Australopithecus afarensis* and ourselves. We can also be quite confident that this difference is rooted in genetic instructions. We can plausibly relate brain enlargement to intelligence, which could be useful in survival—although the brain enlargement might conceivably have had its advantage in other ways, such as producing language, with its problem-solving capabilities as an added bonus. As for features (1) and (5) above, we just have to take those on faith—and recognize that any explanation other than natural selection for the human brain expansion would have far greater difficulties in being proven.

Even the best-accepted cases of selection in action are less than 100% rigorously proved. One of the chestnuts of biology textbooks is the case of industrial melanism in the peppered moth, *Biston betularia*. Over the course of a century, as soot became deposited on tree trunks in England, the darker form (*carbonaria*) became more prominent because of bird predation on the lighter form (*typica*); as pollution was reduced, the lighter form became more common again, concealed by the lichen (a crusty fungus) on the tree bark. In fact, however, the precise influence of bird predation has never been satisfactorily demonstrated. There is certainly a bias of survival and reproduction, there is certainly a genetic basis to the difference, there is an observable change in the population over time (and in parallel in American moth populations); but it is still unclear exactly what the environmental feature promoting it was. It has something to do with soot and selective predation.

Certainly the selective agency of pesticides is better known in the development of resistant strains of insects. In the European land snail (*Cepaea nemoralis*) the relationship between shell coloration and selection in particular environments by predators is well understood. And a 30-year study of the finch species (*Geospiza fortis* and *Geospiza scandens*) on the Galápagos island of Daphne Major has demonstrated the relationship between environmental changes, food preferences, and size and shape of the beak about as well as anyone could possibly hope.

GENETIC DRIFT

Our last Hardy–Weinberg assumption is that the population size is large enough to avoid random deviations by chance. If you were to flip a coin four times, what would you expect—two heads and two tails, or something other than two heads and two tails? In fact, two heads and two tails is the most likely *single* outcome, but if you sum together all the probabilities of the other alternatives—four heads, three heads and one tail, three tails and one head, and four tails—their combined probability is higher than two heads and two tails. So you are actually more likely to get something *other than* two heads and two tails in four flips than you are to get the two heads and two tails outcome that is your expectation, being the most likely single outcome.

What this means is that perhaps a detectable variation from the Hardy–Weinberg equilibrium is due to a random accident of sampling the gene pool. The smaller the population, the more likely it is to deviate from the mathematical expectations. We call such deviations *genetic drift*. Genetic drift might account for our results simply as sampling error, a run of bad luck, so to speak. It is well known in microevolution in three contexts, all of which are mathematically equivalent: the founder effect, deviations from Mendelian ratios, and the fixation of neutral alleles.

The first case is the founder effect (or Sewall Wright effect, after the American population geneticist who first explored the mathematics of it), and involves the case in which a subpopulation is not a perfect genetic replica of the larger population from which it is derived. This might come about in the context of emigration, or as the aftermath of a population crash.

Imagine a population of 50 people (with 100 total alleles in its gene pool). Two alleles are present: A_1 and A_2. Allele A_1 has a frequency (p) of 0.99, and allele A_2 has a frequency (q) of 0.01. This of course means that the population is composed of 49 A_1A_1 homozygotes and one A_1A_2 heterozygote. We would expect, via the Hardy–Weinberg law, that this population would continue to perpetuate itself indefinitely at the same proportions. But suppose the population crashes—for whatever reason—to 20 people. Now there are 40 total alleles. The question is, did the one heterozygote make it? If so, the A_2 allele is no longer 1 out of 100, but 1 out of 40, so $p = .975$ and $q = .025$. If the heterozygote didn't make it, the allele frequencies have changed to $p = 1$ and $q = 0$. Either way, the gene pool has changed, simply by manipulating the number of individuals.

The magnitude of the change—that is, the extent to which the new, small population deviates from the proportions found in the original population—depends on how small the new population is. If the original population crashes from 50 to 5 people (now with 10 total alleles, rather than 100), then the frequency of A_2 will be either 0 (if the heterozygote did not survive) or .10 (if the heterozygote did survive). And if the frequency of the alleles after the crash is now .90 and .10, that is what the Hardy–Weinberg equilibrium will now tend to preserve.

This random deviation from precisely replicating the original gene pool is identical whether the population crash is due to catastrophe, emigration, or simply subdivision. Many examples of this are known in human populations. For example, porphyria variegata is a genetic disease with a variable range of phenotypic expression, ranging from virtually no symptoms to fits of abdominal pain, dark red urine, and delirium. It is believed to have affected King George III of England and is also found rarely throughout the world. One of the original Dutch settlers of South Africa had the allele, however, and as a result, there is more porphyria among white South Africans of Dutch ancestry (Afrikaners) than in the rest of the world.

Similarly, a mutation in a gene called BRCA1, that predisposes women to breast cancer, is found in people of eastern European (Ashkenazi) Jewish ancestry at approximately twentyfold higher proportions than elsewhere. And although over 300 mutations have been found in this gene worldwide, most Ashkenazi Jews with BRCA1 have either of just two mutations. This strongly suggests a population constriction, which produced a founder effect.

It's the mathematics of genetics. Mendel's ratios are probabilistic: although you can't predict the sex of any specific act of fertilization, you know that about half of all zygotes are XY boys and about half are XX girls, because half of the sperm cells contain an X chromosome and half of the sperm cells contain a Y chromosome. But suppose a couple has just three children? Now they cannot mathematically produce the Mendelian ratios (even if they try!). We all know "Brady Bunch" families in which the three children are all boys or are all girls. As the size of the family increases, the deviations from expected proportions becomes smaller (again, "The Brady Bunch"). Mathematically, this kind of random deviation from expected proportions is equivalent to the founder effect in which the descendant generation is just not a perfectly representative sample of the earlier generation. Here the original population is the very large number of children it is possible to have, and the deviation is represented by the few children actually produced.

Thus, genetic drift can change the gene pool of a population quite significantly. Since it is random, it will make populations different from each other, but it will do so in a non-adaptive way. Its magnitude is inversely proportional to the population size. One of the major consequences of genetic drift is that since it is random, it may govern the spread of a feature that has no net effect (a neutral mutation), or even spread a "bad" feature randomly, which might then be used by the body in a new and different way.

SICKLE CELL

Sickle-cell anemia was described in 1910 by a cardiologist named James B. Herrick, who specifically described red blood cells in his patient that were deformed into the shape of a curved sword, or sickle. It was shown to be transmitted as a single gene in 1941, and shown to be the result of a different structure of the hemoglobin protein in 1948—the first disease reliably assigned to a molecular disturbance. In the mid-1950s, it was shown to be the result specifically of a substitution of the amino acid valine for the amino acid glutamic acid in the sixth position of the 146 amino acids of beta (β) globin, one of the two protein components of hemoglobin.

Homozygotes for the allele express the symptoms of sickle-cell anemia. The change in the amino acid affects the properties of the β-globin molecule so that it does not move freely in the cell, but stacks up. Since a red blood cell, or erythrocyte, is little more than a bag of hemoglobin transporting oxygen inward into the body and other gases outward, the stacked hemoglobin gives the red blood cell different properties. It now assumes a rigid, pointed shape (a "sickle," or perhaps a croissant) instead of the ordinary round, biconcave disc (reminiscent of a bialy, a bread product similar to a bagel).

No longer smooth and rounded, the sickled cells cannot move as smoothly through the capillaries of the circulatory system. They can clog it up, or simply function so poorly that they are removed from the circulatory system through the spleen, whose ordinary function is to recycle red blood cells after their 120-day life span. Of course, that compromises the function of the blood's transportation capabilities. The result is a cascade of variable physical effects: pain and swelling throughout the body, fatigue, jaundice, delayed development, and eye problems are all associated with sickling crises, especially in children. The life expectancy of someone with the disease, without medical interventions discovered only in the last few years, is about 45.

Obviously it is not good to have. So why is 1 in 12 African Americans a carrier of the allele? Why is 1 in 3 people in parts of West Africa likewise a heterozygote? Why hasn't it been eliminated from the gene pool by simple directional selection?

The answer resides in the condition of the heterozygote with respect to a specific environmental agent: malaria. Malaria is caused by a microorganism of the genus *Plasmodium* that spends part of its life cycle in mosquitos and part in human red blood cells. A bite from an infected mosquito leaves traces of the *Plasmodium* parasite, which then enters the liver and then the red blood cells, and proceeds to use them as a temporary home while it reproduces. When the malarial parasites are ready a few days later, the red blood cell bursts and releases thousands more *Plasmodium* cells into the blood stream. The result of this massive attack on the circulatory system is very high fever, chills, sweating, and delirium. After that passes, a few days elapse, and the cycle of symptoms may begin again.

Why are there mosquitos? Because there is standing water in the region.

Why is there standing water in the region? Because of thousands of years of small-scale farming and irrigation. In other words, malaria is an intense threat in many places because of the cultural activity of humans, which ultimately irreversibly transformed their environment.

A heterozygote for sickle-cell anemia has enough circulating normal hemoglobin not to suffer from sickling under ordinary conditions. But under conditions in which the red blood cell is stressed, the sickle hemoglobin it carries will cause the cell to assume the sickled shape, and it will be rapidly eliminated from circulation, via the spleen. It is thought that when a heterozygote is bitten by malaria-carrying mosquito, and the *Plasmodium* parasites enter the red blood cells, they become stressed, and consequently sickled, and are removed from circulation before the malarial parasite has a chance to complete its life cycle.

Thus, in this environment, the health of the sickle-cell homozygote is compromised by the sickle-cell disease, and the health of the "normal" homozygote is compromised by greater susceptibility to malaria. We have just put the word "normal" in quotes because this example leads us to rethink just what "normal" means: possessing two copies of the most common allele is not optimal for survival. What is best is to have one copy of the common allele and one copy of the sickle allele.

We may also observe that neither allele is better than the other, since it is the genotypes that are better or worse for the bearer's survival. And in this case, having both alleles together is optimal for the organism—this is balancing selection, resulting in a *balanced polymorphism* of two common alleles in a population. But since heterozygotes do not breed true, there is a constant replenishment of the suboptimal homozygous genotypes every generation.

Sickle cell is an example of many important concepts: (1) disease as a molecular genetic phenomenon; (2) pleiotropy; (3) balancing selection; (4) genetic adaptation to the environment; (5) adaptation to a problem created or magnified culturally; and (6) how misleading it is to think of alleles as better or worse, when it is really their combinations (genotypes) in particular contexts that are better or worse.

WHY IS THE GENE POOL THE WAY IT IS?

The American geneticist Sewall Wright developed a complex mathematical model for envisioning the synergy between adaptive selection and random genetic drift in evolution. Without the math, it is still a powerful and valuable metaphor: the adaptive landscape.

Let us consider each of the 25,000 or so genes in the genome separately, in a single environmental context. Each one has an optimal set of allele frequencies for that environment. Thus, there is a potential graph one could make, plotting the specific set of possible allele frequencies against the average fitness of the population. The higher the average fitness of the population, the better off it is. If we think of the gene for β-globin, and its allele for sickle-cell anemia, in a malarial context, we can construct a graph of fitness versus allele frequency in which neither allele is superior, but some proportion of both is best for the population. Here, having no sickle-cell alleles is not great but is better than having all sickle-cell alleles; optimally, about 20%–25% sickle cell alleles is best (which is of course what we find in West Africa).

To do this for all the genes in the human genome, and pool the data, would be wonderful, but it would require envisioning a graph in 25,001 dimensions—one for each of the human genes, plotted against average population fitness. That is beyond the capacity of human beings.

So let us simply imagine ourselves high in an airplane, looking down on a mountain range. Points on the ground would be determined by their north-south position, their east-west position, and their up-down position. The north-south dimension and east-west dimensions might stand for the relative allele frequencies for two different genes. Each point on the ground, then, would represent a gene pool, the specific proportions of the alleles at these two loci. The third dimension, altitude, will be a measure of the population's fit to its environment. Peaks represent combinations of allele frequencies with high fitness, and valleys represent combinations of allele frequencies with low fitness or maladaptation. Any point on this geographical grid represents an imaginary population—a specific set of allele frequencies rendered more or less fit by virtue of existing in a particular environmental context. This is what Wright meant by the "adaptive landscape."

The action of natural selection on any population will be to make it better adapted, or to have a higher average fitness. In other words, natural selection will act to "pull" a population up the nearest peak. But that is a small victory for the gene pool. The problem Wright sought to address was: How can a population find a higher peak, a better adapted state, which would require a transient period of maladaptation, as the allele frequencies crossed a valley of poor fitness for several generations?

Of course evolution has no foresight, so there is no way that it can become temporarily less adapted in order to become better adapted later; nor does it have intelligence, so that the population could see the better future for the gene pool if it just became more poorly adapted for the short run. Natural selection is a dumb algorithm.

The answer Wright came up with involved subdividing a population so that each smaller population deviates randomly from the overall allele frequency— what he came to call "genetic drift." Subdivision is the equivalent of splattering paint droplets on the graph around the point of the original parental population. This bit of randomness may be enough to land a small subpopulation at the base of the other, higher, peak, so that natural selection can now pull it up to the top. Thus, the deterministic action of selection and the random action of drift can work together more effectively than either can alone. In Wright's own words,

> Suppose that a person sets out in a dense fog to walk always up the steepest slope in a hilly country. He is almost certain to find himself soon at the top of a rather low knoll with nowhere to go without violating his resolve to go always uphill. If, instead, he had walked wholly at random, he would almost certainly have remained most of the time on somewhat low ground, since the hilltops are relatively few. If, however, he tends in the main to walk uphill but also takes many steps in random directions, he may not reach the actual summit of any hill but will not be brought to a stop on the top of a lower one. Ultimately he will find himself on much higher ground than if rigorously adhering to the steepest slopes.

Wright thus envisions random processes (drift) and deterministic processes (selection) operating synergistically, leading to maximal adaptation. Thus can the two main forces making populations different from one another work together to generate great diversity. But what does this imply about our ability to tell whether any particular feature of the gene pool is there as a result of random historical processes of deterministic biological processes? It certainly complicates the search for a simple historical explanation to explain any particular genetic state.

Indeed, what it seems to imply is that the cases in which it is actually possible to distinguish between those alternatives may be few and far between. The dichotomy itself may be false. And, if we throw in for good measure, the facts that (1) small bands of hunter-gatherers constituted the human species for much of its existence, which would seem to be an ideal situation for genetic drift to run rampant; and (2) in more recent times, technology has increasingly blunted the force of selection; we are left with the recognition that it may be gratuitous to assume that anything we see in humans today actually has an explanation in a supposed beneficial value, as opposed to mere luck.

We know that neutral or unhelpful features can come to prominence in a gene pool, we know what circumstances favor it, and we know that those circumstances have predominated in human prehistory. The assumption that any particular feature of the gene pool, or the body, must be there for a reason (the consistent differential perpetuation of its bearers, or survival of the fittest), as opposed to no reason at all (the vagaries of history, or survival of the lucky), is at best gratuitous.

ADAPTATION OR FOUNDER EFFECT?

Sickle cell is an excellent example of how detailed knowledge of the molecular genetics, physiology, population genetics, and environment can permit us to make a strong inference about adaptive evolution.

Other genetic diseases common in other populations are less well known and thus are harder to identify as adaptations. Of course, they may not be adaptations at all but simply the random result of a founder effect, such as the prevalence of porphyria variegata in South African Afrikaners (see above). Many other such examples are known: an otherwise exceedingly rare genetic disease called Ellis-van Creveld syndrome (characterized by polydactyly or extra fingers, short stature, other skeletal and dental abnormalities, and heart problems), found more commonly in the Pennsylvania Amish (about 13% are carriers) than anywhere else in the world, and traceable to the genes of a single couple who immigrated in 1744.

But the evidence of elevated frequencies of "disease alleles" in diverse populations is usually less clear-cut than the sickle-cell or porphyria cases. How might we tell, for example, whether the elevated frequency of Tay-Sachs disease in Ashkenazi Jews (1 in 26 is a carrier, about ten times the world average, for a degenerative neurological condition that usually kills homozygotes by age three) is a random fluke due to founder effect, or a balanced polymorphism in which heterozygosity confers an advantage against a powerful environmental stressor?

Both options yield predictions. If natural selection is at work, an environmental stressor so powerful it can make a painful ailment like sickle-cell anemia common would probably also elevate the frequencies of other disease alleles that conferred some kind of heterozygous advantage as well. And that is precisely what we find: otherwise rare recessives, such as the Duffy-negative blood group and glucose-6-phosphate dehydrogenase negative (G6PD⁻) alleles, are elevated in malarial areas too. In southeast Asia, where there is malaria, but not sickle cell, a different kind of blood disease called *alpha-thalassemia* attains a high frequency, doing essentially the same thing as sickle cell in heterozygotes. And even the sickle-cell allele itself seems to have arisen and spread at least six separate times, linked to different characteristic DNA variations.

On the other hand, we can predict that a disease allele elevated by chance, and simply inherited from a common ancestral founder, would be almost exactly the same in everyone who has it. Since it is the founder's DNA they all have, it should be virtually identical in all cases.

In the case of Tay-Sachs' disease among Ashkenazi Jews, we find that the gene on chromosome 15 has the same mutation in 79% of the Ashkenazi Jews with the Tay-Sachs allele; and 18% have another mutation. This suggests a more complex scenario with perhaps both founder effect *and* balancing selection working. The fact that there is very little genetic diversity in the mutations causing the disease points to founder effect. The fact that the founder effect would have had to occur at least twice, elevating the separate mutations of the very rare disease to higher frequencies, suggests instead heterozygote advantage. Also suggestive of the latter hypothesis is the fact that Tay-Sachs is just one of a spectrum of diseases of the biochemistry of the nervous system—including Gaucher's, Niemann-Pick's, familial dysautonomia (of whom 99% of the 1 in 30 Ashkenazi carriers have the same allele), and even an adult-onset allele of Tay-Sachs—all elevated in prevalence among Ashkenazi Jews.

It has been suggested that perhaps the Tay-Sachs' allele conferred immunity to tuberculosis on heterozygous carriers, by analogy to sickle-cell anemia. Tuberculosis was a major health problem in crowded urban ghettoes where European Jews were forced to live for hundreds of years. While the hypothesis may be true, the data in support of it are quite spotty—especially since other geneticists argue for a cryptic intellectual advantage, rather than a respiratory one, on the part of its carriers. The point is this: If we cannot really tell that Tay-Sachs is elevated in Ashkenazi Jews because of a deterministic selective bias—fate, as opposed to chance—then it makes no sense to speculate on whether or how the bias accrued to the nervous system rather than to the pulmonary system. If there may be no reason at all for the observation, then spewing out possible reasons is valueless. It's like speculating on the number of angels that can sit on a pinhead, *assuming that there are angels sitting on pinheads.*

Since it is not easy to tell whether drift or selection has been the major force molding the gene pool for a specific locus, it follows that it is hard to say with much security that a specific genetic configuration is an adaptation or not. The elevated frequency of sickle cell in West African and Mediterranean populations is an adaptation; the elevated frequency of porphyria in Afrikaners is not. We have the physiology to support the former story and the historical records to support the latter story. Nevertheless, both groups of people seem to be demographically thriving, in spite of their genetic strengths and weaknesses.

The allele that causes cystic fibrosis (characterized by thick mucus, coughing fits, and respiratory difficulties) is more prevalent in northern Europeans than in other populations—1 in 27 Americans who self-identify as "white" are heterozygotes. Nearly 90% of Danish carriers of cystic fibrosis carry a particular mutation (of the several hundred that have been discovered) known as ΔF508; this figure drops to 75% of Dutch carriers, 70% of French carriers, and 50% of Spanish carriers. It seems to be a combination of both drift (chance) and selection (fitness).

The prevalence of the single ΔF508 allele suggests founder effect, but the genetic heterogeneity otherwise present also suggests an advantage to the heterozygote. Cystic fibrosis affects the cellular transport of chloride ions, as does the bacterial toxin that causes cholera. Perhaps, then, the periodic outbreaks of diarrheal diseases, such as cholera or typhus, throughout urban European history, are the selective agents at work, elevating the frequency of cystic fibrosis in earlier generations; or perhaps not.

ANOTHER POINT ILLUSTRATED BY SICKLE CELL AND PHENYLKETONURIA

In spite of being the first "molecular disease" characterized at the protein level (in the 1950s) and at the DNA level (in the 1980s), sickle-cell anemia remains incurable. When the Human Genome Project—a multibillion-dollar effort to sequence all the DNA in a human cell—was being initially promoted in the 1980s, it was often wrapped in the promise of a cure for genetic diseases. Here the working assumption was that knowing the DNA sequence would allow direct and easy access to the cause, which would in turn suggest a cure.

But the DNA sequence is just a set of instructions for something; the cause of the disease results from knowing what the gene product does and how compromising it leads to the symptoms. And the cure is predicated more technologically on a method of delivery—gene therapy—than on learning the sequence itself.

But there is no gene therapy.

Sickle-cell anemia is well understood both genetically and bio-historically, but remains incurable and nearly untreatable. While it causes considerable pain and can be debilitating at various times, people can live fruitful lives through it: jazz trumpeter Miles Davis lived with sickle cell anemia to age 65.

Thus, knowing the gene sequence does not seem to have been particularly significant in finding a cure. It has recently been found that a drug called hydroxyurea can stimulate the production of fetal hemoglobin, which is ordinarily shut off before birth, but which can provide a useful alternative to sickled adult hemoglobin. Most sickle cell therapy still involves mitigating its symptoms.

On the other hand, phenylketonuria (PKU) is an autosomal recessive allele knocking out the gene for the enzyme phenylalanine hydroxylase, whose DNA sequence was not known until 1986. But it had been treatable since the 1960s, with special diets low in phenylalanine, which cannot be metabolized by people with PKU. Thus, knowing the gene sequence was irrelevant to the treatment of the disease. The DNA sequence is a genotype; the disease is a phenotype; and phenotypes are treatable medically.

Although the course of the ailment is treatable with dietary intervention, homozygous women who had been treated for PKU as children almost invariably give birth to babies with PKU, regardless of the babies' genotype. Apparently the maternal environment plays a major role in the development of the disease.

SICKLE CELL, TAY-SACHS, AND GENETIC SCREENING

In another way, sickle cell also afforded the paradigmatic case of genetics in action, showing the interaction of science and society, as the first mass genetic screening program—and a huge failure.

The story begins with the separate deaths of four black army recruits during basic training at Fort Bliss, Colorado, in 1968–69. A study of their blood at autopsy revealed sickled blood cells (death, or merely removal from living context, is, of course, a stressor on cells, and heterozygotes will commonly be seen to have many sickled cells in the microscope, although not in the bloodstream). Out of the investigation that followed, and an outcry that the funding of research into sickle cell was far lower than that of other (non-black) genetic diseases, President Nixon proposed a war on sickle-cell anemia, initiating a screening program under the National Sickle Cell Anemia Control Act of 1972.

But since the tests of the day just looked for sickled cells, they could not distinguish heterozygous carriers from homozygous anemics—both groups tested positive for sickled cells. Since the goals of the program were not clear, and there were far more heterozygotes than homozygotes, the carriers were the ones targeted, even though they actually didn't express the disease. The great chemist Linus Pauling suggested that they should be branded with forehead tattoos as a public warning of their genetic imperfection.

Small wonder they didn't come in to get screened!

But screening, in many cases, followed them. Many states passed mandatory sickle-cell testing laws just for African Americans (in spite of the fact that many Mediterranean couples are at risk), and many schools and companies instituted mandatory testing as well. And there was no guarantee of confidentiality—other people had access to your test results, sometimes even before you.

As if that were not bad enough, there was little counseling available. People were often not informed about the difference between carriers and homozygotes. Thus, many people who tested positive—since the test didn't make that distinction either—thought they had the disease. Many people came home believing that 10% of their children had sickle-cell disease and would be dead by the age of 20.

Very quickly, insurance rates climbed nearly 25% for anyone who tested positive. African Americans found doors closing to them in the airline industry and the armed forces, who suggested that they would be more prone to sickling crises during high-altitude training, parachuting, and scuba diving. The US Air Force Academy banned all sickle-cell positives from entering flight training, a policy enforced until 1981, when a lawsuit forced them to reverse it.

Since no prenatal diagnosis was yet available, heterozygous couples either had to risk the 1 in 4 chance of having an afflicted child or opt to have no children. Getting screened offered people no benefit and many potential difficulties.

The focus of modern genetic screening is to reduce family tragedy, not to stigmatize large groups of people. Here the purpose of a screening program—helping people—got lost in the combination of inadequate technology, lack of cultural sensitivity, and poor dissemination of adequate information. The accumulation of information outpaced the acquisition of helpful knowledge, and the interests of science superseded the interests of the subjects. The result was widespread harm to people, and little good.

By contrast, the Tay-Sachs screening program, in which heterozygotes have always been detectable and counseling has been available, has reduced the incidence of Tay-Sachs among Jewish couples in America by over 70%.

KINSHIP AS A BIOCULTURAL CONSTRUCTION

Screening programs are targeted for groups at higher risk for certain diseases because of their allele frequencies. This of course capitalizes on people's sense of ethnic identity, that they are more like other people in their group than they are like outsiders. And that is true in many senses: behaviors, attitudes, dress, and speech patterns are all markers of ethnicity. It is important to recall, however, that although sickle-cell anemia is a "black" disease, 11 in 12 African Americans are *not* even carriers of it; 25 of 26 Ashkenazi Jews are *not* carriers of Tay-Sachs. Moreover, there are many non-black cases of sickle-cell anemia and non-Jewish cases of Tay-Sachs, especially among Cajuns and French Canadians. So it can be misleading to associate a disease fully with an ethnic group.

And yet the idea of the genetically unified group is a powerful one. The family is a central unit of social existence everywhere (although many elements of its composition vary). And yet, even where husband and wife are genetically related, they are not part of the same family: Charles Darwin, for example, married his mother's brother's daughter, Emma Wedgwood (of the ceramics family). The most obvious way to reconcile the prohibition on marrying a family member with the desire to marry a relative is to define that relative out of your family. (All humans, after all, are related—the question is where to draw the line!) Consequently, social anthropologists—and many cultures—make a distinction between a *mother's* brother's daughter (like Emma to Charles Darwin), or a cross-cousin; and a *father's* brother's daughter, or parallel cousin, who would in many cases share your last name. In the example shown (Figure 5.1), John Smith has two female cousins. His cousin Jane is the daughter of Dad's brother, Uncle Bob, and shares John's family name. She is a parallel cousin, and a family member. On the other hand, Dad's sister married Polonius Jones, and their daughter Ophelia stands in same genetic relationship to John, but has a different family name.

Kinship is a fundamental aspect of the study of anthropology because it situates a person within the universe of social relations. For most people who have ever lived, it dictates their formal attitudes, obligations, and expectations. The medium of kinship is our orientation into life; it tells us who we are and what we are.

Americans share two common fallacies about kinship: (1) that kinship is a natural property rooted in genetic relationships and (2) that the American means of conceptualizing kinship is based more in genetics than other systems are. But we can see, in the simple example given above, that Uncle Bob and Uncle

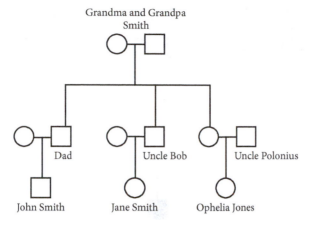

Figure 5.1. To John Smith, Jane and Ophelia are genetically identical, but in many times and places, Jane would be considered an incestuous mating, while Ophelia would be a preferred marriage partner. (This chart uses the stylistic conventions of human genetics, not social anthropology, which are slightly different.)

Polonius are very different relatives, although both are "uncles." And Cousin Jane and Cousin Ophelia are both equally related "by blood" to John Smith, but only Cousin Ophelia might be a suitable partner in many cultures because she is of the Jones, rather than the Smith, lineage. (In American culture, Jane and Ophelia are equally unsuitable, except perhaps on *The Jerry Springer Show.*)

What we see, then, is that kinship is not the same thing as genetic relatedness. It is constructed from two different elements: genetics and law. Every human society is given a set of variables—generation, sex, side of family, and marriage—and weaves a pattern of similarity and difference, which sometimes corresponds to genetics and sometimes does not.

Consider the following business venture to illustrate the complex relationship between cultural ideas about kinship and genetics. For a modest fee, geneticists advertise that they will sample the mitochondrial and Y-chromosome DNA of an African American and tell where in Africa they came from. Those bits of DNA are passed on clonally, for the most part, and thus circumvent the 50/50 chance of being passed on that any ordinary bit of chromosome has. The geneticists say that they will give clients a feeling of connection to Africa. And they well may. But they are not studying ancestry—they are studying a tiny percentage of ancestry. Let us assume for the sake of simplicity that your ancestors were brought to America in 1700, and there are twenty-five years per generation. Then twelve generations have elapsed. You had two ancestors one generation ago (your parents), and four ancestors two generations ago (your grandparents). How many ancestors did you have twelve generations ago? Assuming that you are perfectly outbred, 2^{12} or 4,096. (See Figure 5.2.)

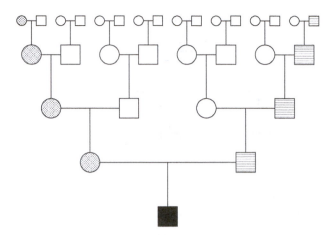

Figure 5.2. Your mtDNA tracks your maternal line; your Y DNA tracks your paternal line; but most of your great-grandparents are entirely invisible to these studies.

And how many of them will be studied? If you have one, your Y chromosome was passed on from father to son; you received yours from your father, who received it from his father, and so forth. It identifies one of your 4,096 ancestors. Likewise, mtDNA, as we noted in the last chapter, is your mother's, and was her mother's, and so on. That identifies a second of the 4,096 ancestors. In Figure 5.2., you can see the relatives identified. Simply among the sixteen great-great-grandparents, you can identify a mitochondrial ancestor, a Y-chromosome ancestor, and fourteen ancestors in that generation who are invisible. Eight generations before that, you would still be able to identify two ancestors, and all the rest would be invisible.

You would not be able to identify the vast majority of biological ancestors in any generation. The two bits of DNA being traced are genetic *markers*, but they are only minimally units of heredity. In other words, this is about kinship—a symbolic linkage to other people—not about the rigorous scientific analysis of your genetic constitution.

And there is an important scientific consequence of this. Suppose you needed to prove your ancestry for some reason. Let us say also that, as a woman, you haven't got a Y chromosome, so you settle for just a mtDNA test. But that test only examines one of your eight great-grandparents. Seven of your eight great-grandparents could be of the "correct" ethnicity, but only a bit of the DNA from your mother's mother's mother is being studied. If it comes out "wrong," you might still have seven-eighths of your ancestry "right" but no way to study it.

For the same reason, it is impossible to establish whether someone is "Native American" or to what tribe they belong on the basis of such data. People are mixed, and labels are not genetically inherited; they are legislated either formally or informally. Who you are and what you are, thus, are only partly facts of nature, established by genetics. The idea that there is a bit of heredity shared by all members of an ethnic group and by nobody else is a relic of essentialist thought. As the Hopi geneticist Frank Dukepoo wrote,

> I call myself a "full-blood" American Indian of Hopi and Laguna heritage. While constructing my own pedigree, I found this is far from the truth: my father (a "Hopi") is a mixture of Hopi, Ute, Paiute, Tewa and Navajo; my mother, on the other hand, (a "Laguna") is a mixture of Laguna, Acoma, Isleta, Zuni and Spanish. Members of other tribes share similar admixture histories as our ancestors raided, traded or kidnapped to ensure survival of their numbers. [I]t is reasonably safe to surmise the same situation for members of other ethnic groups.

GENETIC HISTORY AND THE DIVERSITY PROJECT

Different groups of people may have different allele frequencies for adaptive or nonadaptive reasons. It is reasonable to suppose that a similar constellation of allele frequencies might be an indication of recent common ancestry. And indeed, by the late 1960s, developments in biochemical genetics and statistical analysis dovetailed to the extent that large data sets of allele frequencies could be readily compared and their overall patterns of similarity established.

It could easily be shown that people are genetically similar to those nearby and different from those far away, as is true physically. But much more than that cannot be readily inferred. After all, two populations may be genetically similar because they share recent ancestry or because they have experienced gene flow. These are thus two very different bio-historical explanations for the same genetic pattern.

Further, these differences are subtle to begin with—a few percentage points of one allele or another—and are thus subject to random convergence. And in many cases, where populations have experienced long-term gene flow with several neighboring groups, it makes very little sense to ask which one they are closest to.

And most importantly, human groups come in so many different guises— linguistic (Bantu), national (French), religious (Jewish), racial (white), tribal/ ethnic (Ainu, Apache, Hutu, Roma)—that pooling them into a single study as if they were equivalent categories would be very anthropologically misleading.

In 1991, a group of population geneticists proposed the founding of a Human Genome *Diversity* Project to acquire and study the DNA of diverse populations throughout the world. Why?

1. To find out everyone's evolutionary history. But it was not altogether clear that they could do that, especially given the history of global mixing over the last five centuries. Further, it was not clear that other people were as interested in it as geneticists seemed to be. And moreover, people already had ideas about who they are and where they came from. Why would they wish to help scientists undermine their own ideas?
2. To help cure genetic disease. But genetic information alone—without medical histories to associate with each genotype—won't permit you to

make a diagnosis. And without knowing who had the disease, you can't associate one allele with one state of health and another allele with another state of health. There is, in fact, very little you can do medically with genetic information alone.

3. To preserve the genetic legacy of peoples facing extinction: a noble-sounding goal, but again problematic. After all, if they are really facing extinction, what good does it do them to save their DNA? And what is "extinction" here? Something tragic like genocide, or benign like assimilation? Are the people going extinct, or is their official category going under? If the former, then it sounds awfully cynical to ignore the plight of the people to save their cells; and if the latter, the genes will still be there, but under a different set of ethnic labels.

WHO OWNS THE BODY?

But perhaps the greatest difficulty faced by the Diversity Project came with the emergence of corporate biotechnology at the same time. A man named John Moore was working on the Alaska pipeline when he was diagnosed with a rare form of spleen cancer in 1976. His life was saved by a specialist at UCLA Medical Center, who developed a cell line from the cancer, which he called *Mo-cell*. The cell line turned out to be highly profitable, and the doctor made millions from it—but he didn't tell Moore, nor had Moore even signed a consent form. Moore learned about it in 1984 and sued for a part of the profits derived ultimately from his own body.

In 1990, the California Supreme Court decided the case in a verdict that would establish the domain of corporate biotechnology. John Moore had no claim to the profit from the cell line derived from his spleen. The money had been earned entirely by the person who had invested the labor to make it valuable, the doctor—in spite of the fact that Moore had not even signed a consent form.

Pharmaceutical companies now had the freedom to send doctors out to remote parts of the world in pursuit of the cells of indigenous peoples, and to see if there was anything of value in them—and to owe the natives nothing. It was the opening of a new form of economic exploitation—bio-colonialism.

And just as the Diversity Project was fighting off accusations about its scientific merit and necessity, it became widely known that the National Institutes of Health (NIH) had just filed a claim for a patent on a cell line derived from the blood of a Hagahai man from New Guinea. And there was more in the works—a cell line from a man of the Solomon Islands in Melanesia and from a Guaymí woman from Panama. The Diversity Project had no involvement in this, but it clearly represented a significant economic interest they had not confronted. To many indigenous peoples whom they had hoped to collect blood from, this now sounded like a classic encounter with colonials—they got something valuable and left little or nothing in return. And now American science wanted their very genetic essences.

The Human Genome Diversity Project never got the formal funding it sought, principally because it never acknowledged that the scientific study of human populations is invariably political. This is neither a bad thing, nor a corruption of science, but an intrinsic property of the study of less powerful people, in an economic context of possibly exploitative relations. It requires the conjunction of biology and anthropological knowledge and sensitivities to be accomplished successfully. The patent applications on the cell lines of indigenous peoples were subsequently withdrawn by the NIH; but a successor program, known as the Genographic Project, was launched in 2005 with funding from National Geographic and IBM, and its population geneticists are once again trying to acquire the DNA of indigenous peoples on a large scale. Today ancestry has become a commodity, and recreational genomic ancestry services are its merchants. But as in any marketplace, as the ancient Romans used to say, "*Caveat emptor*" (Let the buyer beware)!

Genomics was transformed as a science as it became absorbed into corporate biotechnology. Henrietta Lacks (Chapter 14) was an African American woman on whose cells many medical advances, reputations, and fortunes have all been made—but whose family never received any acknowledgment, much less a share of the profits. They were abandoned by science, whose goals became simultaneously the advancement of knowledge and the maximization of profit. Today the science of heredity and its cultural meanings and values are so intertwined that we can analyze them as the study of biopolitics; and the nature of moral conduct remains a relevant—but a humanistic, not scientific—question.

REFERENCES AND FURTHER READING

Abu El-Haj, N. 2012. *The Genealogical Science: The Search for Jewish Origins and the Politics of Epistemology*. Chicago: University of Chicago Press.

Annas, G. J. 2006. Anthropology, IRBs, and human rights. *American Ethnologist* 33:541–544.

Barker, J. 2004. The Human Genome Diversity Project: 'Peoples', 'populations' and the cultural politics of identification. *Cultural Studies* 18:571–606.

Bolnick, D. A., D. Fullwiley, T. Duster, et al. 2007. The science and business of genetic ancestry testing. *Science* 318:399–400.

Cain, A. J., and P. M. Sheppard. 1954. Natural selection in *Cepaea*. *Genetics* 39:89–116.

Cavalli-Sforza, L. L., A. C. Wilson, C. R. Cantor, R. M. Cook-Deegan, and M.-C. King. 1991. Call for a worldwide survey of human genetic diversity: A vanishing opportunity for the Human Genome Project. *Genomics* 11:490–491.

Dobzhansky, T. 1971. *Genetics of the Evolutionary Process*. New York: Columbia University Press.

Dukepoo, F. 1998. The trouble with the Human Genome Diversity Project. *Molecular Medicine Today* 4:242–243.

Duster, T. 1990. *Backdoor to Eugenics*. New York: Routledge.

Goldberg, C. 2000. DNA offers link to black history. *New York Times*. August 28.

Grant, P. R., and R. Grant. 2002. Unpredictable evolution in a 30-year study of Darwin's finches. *Science* 296:707–711.

Greene, E., B. E. Lyon, V. R. Muehter, L. Ratcliffe, S. J. Oliver, and P. T. Boag. 2000. Disruptive sexual selection for plumage colouration in a passerine bird. *Nature* 407:1000–1003.

Helgason, A., S. Palsson, and D. Guthbjartsson. 2008. An association between the kinship and fertility of human couples. *Science* 319:813–816.

Karn, M. N., and L. S. Penrose. 1951. Birth weight and gestation time in relation to maternal age, parity, and infant survival. *Annals of Eugenics* 161:147–164.

Kwiatkowski, D. P. 2005. How malaria has affected the human genome and what human genetics can teach us about malaria. *American Journal of Human Genetics* 77:171–192.

Majerus, M. E. N. 1998. *Melanism: Evolution in Action*. New York: Oxford University Press.

Marks, J. 2013. The nature/culture of genetic facts. *Annual Review of Anthropology*, 42:247–267.

Marks, J. 2014. Human Genome Diversity Project. In *Bioethics*, 4th ed, ed. by B. Jennings. Vol. 3, 1578–1583. Farmington Hills, MI: Macmillan Reference.

Murray, R. F. 2001. Social and medical implications of new genetic techniques. In *The Human Genome Project and Minority Communities: Ethical, Social, and Political Dilemmas*, ed. R. A. Zilinskas and P. J. Balint, 67–82. Westport, CT: Praeger.

National Academy of Sciences. 1975. *Genetic screening programs, principles, and research*. Washington DC: NAS Press.

Nelkin, D., and S. Lindee. 1995. *The DNA Mystique: The Gene as a Cultural Icon*. New York: Freeman.

Nelson, A. 2016. *The Social Life of DNA: Race, Reparations, and Reconciliation after the Genome*. Boston, MA: Beacon Press.

Pálsson, G. 2007. *Anthropology and the New Genetics*. New York: Cambridge University Press.

Rutherford, A. 2016. *A Brief History of Everyone Who Ever Lived: The Stories in Our Genes*. Lodon: Weidenfeld and Nicolson.

Sommer, M. 2016. *History Within: The Science, Culture, and Politics of Bones, Organisms, and Molecules*. Chicago: University of Chicago Press.

Tutton, R. 2004. "They want to know where they came from": Population genetics, identity, and family genealogy. *New Genetics and Society* 23:105–120.

TallBear, K. 2013. *Native American DNA: Tribal Belonging and the False Promise of Genetic Science*. St. Paul: University of Minnesota Press.

Wailoo, K., and S. Pemberton. 2006. *The Troubled Dream of Genetic Medicine: Ethnicity and Innovation in Tay-Sachs, Cystic Fibrosis, and Sickle Cell Disease*. Baltimore, MD: Johns Hopkins University Press.

Wailoo, K., A. Nelson, and C. Lee, eds. 2012. *Genetics and the Unsettled Past: The Collision of DNA, Race, and History*. New Brunswick, NJ: Rutgers University Press.

Wald, P. 2006. Blood and stories: How genomics is rewriting race, medicine, and human history. *Patterns of Prejudice* 40:303–331.

Wright, S. 1932. The roles of mutation, inbreeding, cross-breeding, and selection in evolution. *Proceedings of the Sixth International Congress of Genetics* 1:356–366.

Wright, S. 1960. Genetics, ecology and selection. In *The Origin of Life*. Vol. 1 of *Evolution after Darwin*, ed. Sol Tax. Chicago: University of Chicago Press.

CHAPTER 6

Building Better Monkeys, or at Least Different Ones (On Systematics)

THEME

The study of populations below the species level, and the comparisons of species to one another, are epistemologically very different from one another. Nature makes species, but humans organize and arrange them into meaningful groups. The organizing principles of greatest interest to science involve arranging species according to their ancestry.

SPECIATION

The study of the multiplication of lineages and their fates constitutes the domain of macroevolution, in contrast to the study of the transformation of a single biological lineage, or microevolution. Microevolution can often be studied in process, especially in organisms with short generation times. Macroevolution, on the other hand, generally cannot be, and instead our knowledge of it comes from two principal sources: the patterns discernible in the fossil record and the relationships of populations in various stages of diverging from one another.

When we contrast two species, we find that they differ in many ways. They look different, sound different, live in different areas, eat different foods, and have different DNA sequences and different chromosome structures. But how did they come to be that way? At its most basic, the answer is that two separate evolutionary lineages will necessarily adapt to their individual circumstances, as well as diverge randomly from one another, so long as they are not in genetic contact.

What this means is that first and foremost, the gene flow between the two populations must be interrupted. Without genetic contact, the two populations can only become more different from each other; even if they adapt to common environmental problems, they will likely achieve it by different genetic means (as different human populations have responded genetically to malaria, with elevated frequencies of many different blood diseases, of which sickle cell is simply the most famous).

The most obvious way for populations to be removed from genetic contact is geographic separation, or *allopatry*. Once populations are geographically isolated from one another, they cannot interbreed, regardless of whether or not they would like to. Thus, given some time and divergent adapting, if they get back together, they may well discover that they no longer see one another as potential mates.

SPECIFIC MATE RECOGNITION SYSTEMS

We do not understand the basis by which animals recognize some as potential mates and others as not. It is, however, surprisingly difficult actually to mate productively in nature, for many things have to be precisely attuned. First, you have to be able to find a mate, which means you and the mate must occupy the same territory at least part of the time.

Second, you must both be fertile at the same time. In most primates, "fertile" is a near synonym for "interested"—and thus without fertility, there is no sexual engagement.

Third, you must be able to attract the mate with the appropriate signal: this may be achieved through any of the sensory apparatuses. There may be a mating call, or a mating dance, or a stimulus that is olfactory or visual (such as the purple estrus swellings of baboons), or an appropriate behavior, or touch.

Fourth, you must be attractive to the partner. Primates do not mate indiscriminately, and exercise preferences in their choice of mates.

Fifth, you must have the appropriate equipment. Many species of macaques, for example, have oddly shaped penises that are precisely matched to fit oddly shaped vaginas of the same species.

Sixth, you must match the physiology and genetic system of your partner. For example, the alkalinity of the ejaculate must neutralize the acidic conditions of the vagina for the sperm to survive. If sufficient genetically based differences have accumulated, the egg might not be fertilized, or fail to implant, or fail to develop, or fail to gestate, or fail to thrive. And even if the offspring does make it all the way to adulthood, it might end up sterile, like mules (which are only rarely fertile with either horses or donkeys, and never with each other).

Obviously, bearing and raising a sterile offspring represents a lot of wasted effort from the standpoint of evolution, and consequently, selection works to express such incompatibilities at earlier stages. That is, of course, why the situation of sterile mules is so rare in nature, and why most species don't even see each other as potential mates. They have evolved specific mate recognition systems, which permit them to identify their potential partners and to avoid the waste of time and energy in bearing and rearing an offspring that has no hope of perpetuating the lineage.

We know very little of how such recognition systems evolve, but they are likely to involve something like *sexual selection*, a corollary theory proposed by Darwin in 1871. Natural selection was proposed to explain how animal species come to differ from one another. But why might males and females in the same species come to differ from one another? Darwin had, in fact, been thinking about sexual selection when he wrote *The Origin of Species,* but decided to keep that work short (by Victorian standards) and narrowly focused.

The answer Darwin derived was not so much competition for survival and longevity, but competition particularly for mates. In good Victorian fashion, Darwin saw males as nearly universally larger and stronger than females, and imagined that males universally strutted and fought among each other and mated with the waiting female. We now know that scenario to be considerably oversimplified (as well as culturally inflected—reminiscent of Olive Oyl waiting for Popeye and Bluto to slug it out, knowing she'll be satisfied with either one).

Instead, female primates exercise choice, rather than mating indiscriminately with the strongest or fiercest. The choices they make are what drive sexual selection. In some cases, they may mate with the strongest and fiercest, thus presumably perpetuating those traits; or they may mate with the fastest, cleverest, most colorful, or smelliest male. That, in turn, will make males in future generations faster, cleverer, more colorful, or smellier; and they are the traits from which specific mate recognition systems will originate.

Some of our most profound differences from the apes lie specifically in the ways that males of our species differ from females of our species. In chimpanzees and gorillas, for example, the males are essentially just larger, and have larger canine teeth. In humans, however, with male bodies slightly bigger than females (and those differences widely exaggerated culturally), male canine teeth are *not* significantly larger than female canine teeth. Yet men also have beards and body hair; women have little facial and body hair, and those differences are not paralleled in the apes. And women have subcutaneous fat deposits on their hips and under their nipples, and less of their body weight is muscle; neither do ape males and females differ in this way. Since our patterns of sexual dimorphism are so different from those of our primate relatives, it is probably safe to infer that our early ancestors competed for mates in some different manners than apes do today. These ways presumably were cultural, involving locally defined qualities like honor and reputation; but also the development of a peculiar property in a mate that is unknown in other primates: "Someone my parents will like".

GENETIC SYSTEMS PRODUCING INCOMPATIBILITY

Little is known about the genetic production of sterility in primates; however, studies of other species have demonstrated diverse, and fairly simple, mechanisms for doing so.

One well-known example involves bits of DNA called "P elements" in fruit flies. The P element contains a gene that encodes a protein that can be spliced in two ways. Spliced one way, in germ cells, the resulting protein cuts the gene itself out of the DNA ("transposase") so that it can be inserted elsewhere. Spliced another way, the protein inhibits that transposition (repression). A fruit fly with P elements (called a P fly) can mate with others like it. But when it mates with a fruit fly lacking P elements (an M fly), something odd happens. If a female P fly mates with a male M fly, they have normal offspring. If a male P fly mates with a female M fly, however, the offspring have dramatically reduced fertility and extensive mutations (*hybrid dysgenesis*), and offspring of the hybrid have a great deal of chromosome damage and genetic defects.

Why? The P element makes its own repressor proteins, which float around in the cellular cytoplasm. At fertilization, the egg contributes cytoplasm. Thus, a P egg fertilized by an M sperm will have P elements and their repressors; but an M egg fertilized by a P sperm will have no repressors available. In that case, the P elements will make their transposase and "jump" around the genome of the developing fly, causing all genetic hell to break loose.

Is this speciation? No. Both P and M strains are *Drosophila melanogaster*. But P elements have only existed in this species since 1950, apparently introduced from a different species. What this illustrates is the possibility of genomic incompatibilities arising quite suddenly in evolutionary time and promoting the division of gene pools, such that, given sufficient time, speciation might well take place.

Although P-element-mediated hybrid dysgenesis in fruit flies is the best-known example, there are other examples of similar phenomena. And although we don't understand its function, about 5% of the human genome consists of copies of a DNA sequence called L1, which falls within this class of transposable genetic elements.

Somewhat better understood is the way in which large-scale rearrangements of the chromosomes can reduce the fertility of otherwise phenotypically normal people or animals, and thus conceivably produce a genetic barrier between populations. For this we need to recall two aspects of meiosis, the cell division leading to the production of sperm and egg. Meiosis begins with the specific intimate pairing of homologous chromosomes—the two #1 chromosomes pairing with one another, the two #9 chromosomes pairing with one another, and so forth. With a microscope, cytologists can see the twenty-three chromosomal masses thereby formed. At this time, the members of each chromosome pair exchange genetic material—crossing-over. No genetic material is ordinarily gained or lost, since the exchange is simply between different alleles of the "same" chromosomes.

Suppose, however, one of the chromosomes has been structurally rearranged, so that it has the right genes, but in the wrong order. Perhaps the chromosome has broken in two places, and the resulting internal segment has been reinserted upside down. This is known as a chromosomal inversion, and is in fact present in 1 or 2 of every 10,000 human newborns.

A heterozygote for a chromosomal inversion is usually fully healthy in every way but one: they have reduced fertility. Their own meiosis and crossing-over results in gametes with the wrong amount of genetic information—some with too much and some with too little. They themselves have the right genes in the right proportions themselves; but many of their sperm or ova do not.

Another kind of chromosome rearrangement, about 10–15 times more common in humans, involves the breakage of two chromosomes and their reciprocal exchange. This is known as a translocation; in this illustration (see Figure 6.1), involving chromosomes 3 and 9. Once again, since all the genes

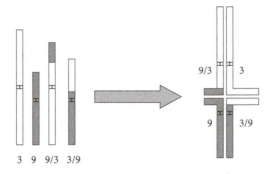

Figure 6.1. A heterozygote for a balanced translocation will undergo meiosis by having its chromosomes pair up in creative ways.

are there and in the right proportions in the heterozygote, the carrier of such a rearrangement is phenotypically normal. But how do the chromosomes undergo meiosis?

They do so by forming a cross-like structure. The problem is that two chromosomes assort into one daughter cell, and two into the other. So which two travel together? *Only if the chromosomes diagonally opposite one another assort together will the gametes have the proper chromosome quantities.* If, on the other hand, the two at the top sort into one daughter cell, and the two at the bottom into the other, then the top gamete will have two copies of most of chromosome 3. With fertilization, the zygote would have three copies of chromosome 3, a situation that is incompatible with life.

Thus, if two populations existed, one with chromosomes 3 and 9 and the other with the translocated chromosomes, they might have long-term difficulties with gene flow since heterozygous hybrids would be reproductively disadvantaged. The chromosome rearrangements might act either to initiate the loss of genetic contact, or to reinforce it, once it has been initiated by other genetic means. Consequently, we find that many primate species differ from their closest relatives by virtue of their chromosome structure.

Humans, gorillas, and chimpanzees differ from one another by perhaps 14 such rearrangements of the chromosomes: a fusion of two chromosomes in the human lineage, a translocation in the gorilla lineage, and about a dozen inversions. Perhaps these served to reinforce the separation of the gene pools in our ancestors 7 million years ago.

The gibbons (family Hylobatidae), on the other hand, have an almost uncountable number of chromosomal rearrangements differentiating the chromosomes of closely related species—very likely, the chromosome rearrangements have been more fundamentally involved in the processes of speciation in gibbons. And in the baboons (family Cercopithecidae), presumably speciation is occurring by other means entirely—well-marked species nevertheless seem to have identical chromosome structures.

SPECIES AS INDIVIDUALS

Classically, as we noted in Chapter 3, a species was considered to be a class or set of creatures that shared one or more key features. Since such an assemblage is timeless and cannot evolve (it can only be redefined), it has very little value today. It is important to note that we can use key features to identify and allocate a specimen to one species or another, but that doesn't help us to understand what a species *is*.

If we see a species, rather, as composed of organisms related to one another through the process of reproduction, or the production of lineage—that is, as potential mates, and as potential common ancestors—then that view of species changes radically. A species is then a unit or an individual (not a class), composed of parts (not members), united by their relationships (not by their attributes). Moreover, this species is capable of evolving, rather than of merely being redefined.

As an individual, a species will easily be seen to possess many familiar properties that it would not have as a class or set. For example, a species will occupy a certain space at a certain time; it will have a beginning, a duration, and an end—analogous to the birth, life span, and death of the individual organism. Here, of course, the beginning is speciation, and the end is extinction. By the same token, a species can split into two—that is, it can reproduce. Moreover, a species interacts with its environment in a specific way—it occupies a *niche* in an ecological system. These properties—interacting with the environment, reproducing, and being bounded in space and time—make a species a thing, a nameable entity, rather than being merely an abstract set defined by the common possession of an essential quality by all its members.

This further places a species at the top of a biological hierarchy of autonomous individuals with the properties we have been discussing: reproduction, spatial and temporal localization, and environmental interaction. This would be a hierarchy of cells, organisms, and species. Each is an organized system composed of the units below it: A species is composed of organisms, and an organism is composed of cells; and yet a species is more than just a collection of bodies, and a body is more than just a flask of cells. The units are organized and related to one another at each level in the hierarchy.

This also permits us to visualize another extension of the Darwinian processes. Classical Darwinian evolution invokes consistent biases in fertility or longevity to explain the diversity of species. Could we not, then, look to the analogies to fertility and longevity in species—namely, rates of speciation and duration of species—to study trends in the history of life?

Indeed we can, and although this kind of work is still young, it addresses questions that seem not be visible otherwise. Why are there so many (over twenty) species of macaques (genus *Macaca*) and so few (only 3–8) of baboons (genus *Papio*, even stretched to include *Theropithecus* and *Mandrillus*), which are closely related to them? Are macaques more prone to form new taxa? Are baboons more prone to go extinct? Why are there 25–30 species of guenons (genus *Cercopithecus*)? Why are there many species of langur monkeys (genus *Presbytis*), but only a handful of the closely related colobus monkeys (*Colobus*)? Why are there many species of gibbons (genus *Hylobates*), but not of orangutans (*Pongo*)?

While these kinds of questions have no ready answers at present, it seems likely that answers will come not from properties of the cells or the bodies of these animals, but rather, from properties of the populations into which they coalesce. This is the same sense in which a birth rate cannot be predicted from aspects of the cells or the bodies (except in a very crude way—a mouse being universally more prolific than a moose, for example), but can only be studied by looking at the population as a "superorganism," and the birth rate as a feature of it.

The idea of the "superorganism" is an old one in biology. It usually arose in discussions of societies, with an ant colony or human culture, for example, being analogized to a single body. With respect to the hierarchical properties of cells, organisms, and species, what gives them special status as individuals is their ability to reproduce or replicate (that is, to make copies or new individuals like themselves, autonomously, given sufficient raw materials) and to interact with the environment (whether that environment is others like them or merely their surroundings). Other things widely identified as units of nature, such as genes, populations, and ecosystems, lack the full extent of these abilities, and thus are not considered individuals. Genes, for example, cannot reproduce without the aid of many external enzymes and cellular features.

LEVELS AND RATES OF EVOLUTION

Although evolution is classically studied with reference to the body, interesting patterns emerge when we compare different biological systems across species. Different species not only have different physical appearances but also have different molecular structures and different chromosomal configurations. This is not unexpected, since the processes of speciation and evolution involve changes in genes, chromosomes, and bodies.

And yet, when we compare genes, chromosomes, and bodies across species, we find that although they all track the same biological histories of the species, they nevertheless have undergone different *kinds* of changes and different *amounts* of changes. Thus, although differences in DNA markers, chromosome structure, and physical form are all in some sense "genetic," we find the first largely nonadaptive and dependent on time; the second involved in speciation; and the third principally in adaptation.

At roughly the same amount of divergence in genetic markers, a macaque and baboon are similar chromosomally, and somewhat different physically; a gibbon and a siamang are also somewhat different physically, but very different chromosomally; and a human and a gorilla are slightly different chromosomally, but quite distinct physically. We might interpret this to mean that each member of the three pairs of species diverged from the other at roughly the same time; the macaque and baboon are similarly adapted, but their speciation did *not* involve chromosome changes; the gibbon and siamang are similarly adapted, and their speciation *did* involve chromosome change; and the human and gorilla are differently adapted, and their speciation is *reinforced* by chromosomal change.

Genetic change is governed principally by the processes of mutation and genetic drift, since most DNA changes are not expressed phenotypically (since most DNA is not genic). Moreover, even within genes, many mutations cause no discernible change to the protein product and thus are "neutral"—or nearly so. By contrast, anatomical variation, which may arise by genetic or physiological means, is not only expressed outwardly (by definition), but also is likely to affect the organism's opportunities to survive and reproduce.

Thus, when comparing their respective subjects in two different species, a geneticist and an anatomist will usually interpret their results quite differently. The anatomist examines the differences between the species and asks what functions are thereby served and what selective pressures may have led to the divergence in form. Change requires an explanation, and stability does not. The anatomist, assuming that if things work then they don't change, does not ask "Why did these creatures remain quadrupedal?" but rather, "Why did this other creature become bipedal?" The answer comes by recourse to directional selection.

The geneticist, on the other hand, assumes mutation is a constant process, and therefore expects two DNA sequences from different species to be different from one another. What requires explanation in the genetic comparison is not the observation of difference between the species, but rather, the observation of similarity. Regions of evolutionary conservation suggest some functional importance, and thus the inability of that particular stretch of DNA to tolerate change like other DNA stretches. The geneticist asks, "Why are these two stretches of DNA more similar than the surrounding sequences?," and answers by recourse to normalizing selection.

DEVELOPMENTAL GENETICS

This, in fact, was the way that the homeobox was discovered, a stretch of about 180 bases of DNA, coding for about 60 amino acids in a protein, which appears virtually intact in species as diverse as fruit flies and people. Since there is little else that appears intact when you compare those species, it stood to reason that these sequences were doing something important. The genes that contained them had bizarre and extraordinary effects when mutated, such as converting a fly's antennas into legs. We now know that the genetic region encodes a protein that binds to DNA, thus switching particular genes "on" and regulating a cascade of physiological events early in the development of the organism. And even though flies and people develop very differently, the genes that control that development have interesting similarities.

The homeobox genes in fruit flies are found in two clusters, known as bithorax and antennapedia, a total of less than ten such genes. In humans, on the other hand, there are four clusters of homeobox genes—on chromosomes 2, 7, 11, and 17—each with about ten such genes, and several more "orphan" homeobox genes scattered throughout the genome, for a total of about fifty. They appear to be intimately involved in establishing the axes of growth and development for the body: front/back (cranial/caudal), top/bottom (ventral/dorsal), and inward/outward (proximal/distal). Each gene in the cluster is turned on in a precise sequence, along these axes—in vertebrates and flies, despite the few resemblances of development between them.

This intersection of molecular genetics, evolution, and developmental biology is known colloquially as "evo-devo," and hopes to resolve the question of how major differences in body form arise. A related field is "epigenetics," which studies not the genes involved in embryonic differentiation, but the developmental origins of phenotypes, which may not involve permanent modifications to DNA, the subjects of "genetics." In a sense, evo-devo does it from the genes up, and epigenetics from the phenotype down.

Central to the study of epigenetics are the concepts of plasticity and canalization, initially formulated by the developmental geneticist C. H. Waddington in the mid-twentieth century. Plasticity is also known as adaptability, the property of the organism to adjust to its particular conditions of life. These adjustments may be short term and reversible, like the adjustment of blood flow to the extremities under temporary conditions of extreme cold; or they may be long term and irreversible, like the adjustment of growth to the conditions of nutrition.

Waddington's insight was to recognize plasticity or adaptability as a genetically controlled system in and of itself, with attendant allelic variation, and therefore subject to selection. In other words, there could be selection for alleles not so much encoding a particular trait, but for facilitating the production of the trait under particular circumstances, thus permitting the organism to react in an adaptive fashion to the shock of the circumstances. For example, when exposed to ether early in development, genetically normal fruit flies frequently die, but sometimes they live and develop a weird pathological condition called "bithorax"—a second thorax behind the first. Since this is stimulated by ether, it is simply an acquired trait. Waddington selected and bred those flies that developed the phenotype readily and began to reduce the dosage of ether needed to induce the trait. Soon he had flies developing the condition under minimal ether stimulation; and in a few generations, he had developed a strain of flies that developed the bithorax phenotype without any ether at all!

Waddington had superficially reproduced the pattern of Lamarck's "inheritance of acquired characteristics"—although within a strictly modern Mendelian framework. He had selected for the genes that control the organism's ability to adapt, or to redirect its development in the face of a particular environmental stimulus. The selection actually consisted of two phases. Initially, the selected flies were the most adaptable, for they had the greatest ability to react—to amend their developmental trajectory—under the altered circumstances (ether), and that feature was selected. The second phase of selection was for the genes that stabilize the production of the new phenotype, so that what was once a weird and rare developmental anomaly became, in this strain of flies, the new "normal" outcome. The genetic system produced the bizarre phenotype under progressively diminishing stimulation.

Waddington called this property "canalization"—a phenotype's genetic buffering, such that it tends to be expressed in spite of the damaging effects of mutation and environment—in other words, the ability of the body to make a "normal" phenotype. In this case, he was able to select for canalization, thus "normalizing" a trait that is ordinarily distinctly abnormal. He invoked the image of a ball rolling along a grooved surface, with each deepening groove symbolizing a developmental trajectory. Early in its course, the ball has a number of options; but the further along it rolls, the deeper its path goes, and the more difficult it is to alter. Plasticity here is the ability to take a different course, early in development; canalization is the property of sticking to that course.

In more tangible terms, one might imagine an ape several million years ago with the ability to walk on all fours, or occasionally upright, as modern apes can. The evolution of bipedalism is consequently genetically problematic, for it is not so much the change from one status (quadrupedalism) to another (bipedalism), but rather a change from facultative bipedalism to obligate bipedalism—an ape that could occasionally walk on two legs eventually evolved into one which can essentially do nothing *but* that. Thus, it seems to involve a choice or decision in an ancient ancestral species that has become ingrained or inscribed into our chromosomes. Genetically, it sounds almost inescapably Lamarckian. But the evolution of bipedalism in human ancestry might not involve changes in a gene "for" an inward pointed knee, a gene "for" an arched foot, a gene "for" an aligned big toe, and for all the other features of human locomotor anatomy—but rather might involve a conceptually simpler system in which genes were selected for their general effects on modeling bones in response to the habit of walking upright (adaptability); and subsequently, other genes were selected for their ability to make this suite of phenotypic features develop regularly and easily (canalization).

ALLOMETRIC GROWTH

Waddington's radical departure here was to recognize the lack of fit between patterns of genetic variation and patterns of phenotypic variation; consequently, his work doesn't try to relate the action of specific genes to specific body parts. Once we acknowledge epigenetics, the systemic genetic control of development, we are in a position to back away from the ordinary modes of thought relating mutant genes to broken bodies, and simply look at bodies in relation to one another.

Physical growth is not simply expansion, like a balloon. Different parts of the body grow at different rates. A young child has a relatively large head; the child's body will grow more over the course of the child's life than its head will. Isometric growth describes an equal rate of growth in different physical structures; allometric growth describes a different rate of growth. Tracking the growth of the body in relation to the head, for example, would be a study of developmental allometry.

Patterns of developmental allometry differ from species to species. The face of a chimpanzee, for example, grows markedly outward over the course of its life.

Thus, a baby chimpanzee, relative to its adult form, has a flat, small face and a large, round skull. And consequently, a baby chimpanzee looks considerably more like a human than an adult chimpanzee does. This has suggested to some researchers that human evolution has involved *neoteny*, the preservation of the infantile form in adults. A classic example of this is the axolotl, a Central American salamander that never actually becomes an adult, but retains its gills and fins into adulthood, and reproduces in what appears to be the larval form of its closest relatives.

And yet, human evolution has followed a quite different trajectory than axolotl evolution. Humans are not ape infants, reproducing without ever entering adulthood; rather, humans grow for a considerably longer period than apes do. Other parts of the body grow quite beyond the ape's growth trajectory; for example, the overall body proportions—which emphasize the trunk in a baby, and the legs in an adult. In fact, the relation of the face to the skull is one of the very few places in the human body where you can actually seem to see neoteny.

Nevertheless, the infant face—with small jaws, small broad nose, big eyes and forehead—seems to resonate with us at a very fundamental level. This is probably why popular images of space aliens so often have these very features.

The most basic kind of allometric growth is functional allometry, the change in form required to preserve equivalent function at a different size. Many physical processes are limited by the relevant geometric area: for example, the respiration of an insect through the exposed surface area of its skin, or the strength of a bone in proportion to its cross-section. And yet, regardless of the biophysical constraints of area (a two-dimensional quantity), animals are three-dimensional beings, with volume and mass.

The problem of functional allometry is simply that as an organism increases in size, a muscle or bone that once functioned efficiently becomes less able to do so. Imagine a creature tripling in every linear measurement: since the strength of a bone is proportional to its cross-sectional area, that bone is now ninefold stronger (the square of the linear measurement). But the work it has to do, to support a mass, has increased 27-fold (the cube of the linear measurement). In order to work as efficiently, the bone must compensate by increasing in width even more than the simple expansion it has already undergone—otherwise, the larger animal will be crushed by its own weight.

This is why if you look at the skeleton of a small mammal and a large mammal reduced to the same size, the bones of the larger animal are still stouter—that is the only way the larger animal can exist in nature. And that is why you cannot have a 50-foot mouse (or a 50-foot person, for that matter), without dramatically changing the design of its body to preserve function at this larger size.

EXTINCTION

The flip side of speciation—the origin of lineages—is extinction, the termination of lineages. We identify two kinds of extinction: background and mass extinction, each with different consequences for the subsequent history of life. Just as speciation (at the species "level") is analogous to birth (at the organismal "level") so, too, is extinction analogous to death.

Background extinction is simply the result of the ordinary course of the struggle for existence. Some fail to survive and die out. Sooner or later, everyone dies, and so do species. In the case of background extinctions, the organismal death rate simply exceeds the birth rate. The reasons for this, of course, may vary from case to case. Here, the extinction of a species has a minimal effect on the ecosystem, since it occurs gradually and has been supplanted by another species filling its ecological niche.

Mass extinction, on the other hand, involves the near-simultaneous termination of many closely and distantly related lineages. This, of course, is superficially similar to what Cuvier had proposed in the early 1800s to be the main engine propelling the history of life on earth. We now realize that while it is a rarity, it is a significant part of evolutionary theory, and it has interesting ecological causes and consequences.

The rarity of mass extinctions is shown by the fact that they occur in intervals on the scale of tens of millions of years. The most famous mass extinction occurred 65 million years ago, eliminating the dinosaurs, as well as many other vertebrates of the air and sea, and diverse kinds of invertebrates as well. However, that mass extinction was small potatoes compared to the one at the end of the Permian era, marking the beginning of the Triassic, about 250 million years ago. That one killed off the trilobites, about 90% of the species living in the seas, and about 70% of land vertebrates, as well as many plant species. Other mass extinctions appear to have occurred at the end of the Ordovician, about 438 million years ago, and at the end of the Triassic, 200 million years ago.

The causes of mass extinctions are still the subject of controversy, but it is widely held that they may be triggered by the impact of an asteroid or meteor with the earth, triggering an ecological catastrophe that only small proportion of species manage to survive. Since the specific nature of the catastrophe is largely unpredictable, the surviving species may be unpredictable as well. Consequently, the role of mass extinctions is far more chaotic than that of background extinctions.

The surviving species that make it through the catastrophe find themselves in an ecological gold rush, with everyone getting rich. With hardly any competition from other species, the surviving species multiply and diversify dramatically to fill the ecological space left vacant. This, of course, is precisely what we see among the mammals, following the extinction of the dinosaurs.

Other mass extinctions have had more mundane causes. The entry of humans into new lands has almost invariably brought with it the elimination of many local species, either hunted out or "squeezed" out by the destruction of their habitats. This was the case in Madagascar about 1,500 years ago, where large mammals and birds disappear from the archaeological record shortly after the arrival of people; and in the New World 12,000 years ago, where many large species of animals disappear shortly after the widespread presence of people.

Since the consequences of a mass extinction are unpredictable, it is a good thing to avoid.

CLASSIFICATION

Perhaps the most basic human thought process is classification, the act of imposing order on a set of data; deciding that *this* is a kind of *that,* and that something new and unfamiliar is actually rather like something already known. Humans do this universally, and anthropologists have long appreciated that understanding how people classify can afford a significant look into how they see the world and react to it.

One important example is how people classify their relatives. There are many ways to do this, involving the intersection of a few key variables: sex, generation, laterality, and marriage. For example, we differentiate between uncle and aunt on the basis of sex, but not between their children, all of whom are "cousins." We give the same term to relatives on mother's side and on father's side (which generally harmonizes with the genetic relationships), but we also give that term to blood relatives (such as our mother's brother) and nonblood relatives (such as the husband of our mother's sister)—which does *not* harmonize with the genetic relationships.

There are, obviously, many ways to juggle these variables to impose some kind of order on social relationships within the family that will be broadly similar to the genetic relationships, but distinct from them. For example, we could decide that all the male children of our paternal grandparents are "father" (as in the system classically called "Hawaiian"); and consequently, all the male children of our "fathers" are "brothers" (even though that would include cousins).

The point here is that no kinship system perfectly reflects natural relationships, and all simply impose order and meaning on the social universe.

Similarly, all human societies classify animals and plants into groups based on their meaningful similarities and differences—which may correspond roughly to their natural properties, but which may be divergent in other ways. Thus, the Bible tells us (in Leviticus 11 and Deuteronomy 14) that the ancient Hebrews classified animals in accordance with two principles: where they lived and how they moved. Their major division was air dwelling, land dwelling, or sea dwelling; and within each category were groups based on the structure of their limbs and how they used them. Within the category of land dwelling, for example, we find those with hooves, those with paws, those that creep or swarm, those that travel on their belly, and those with many feet. Within the category of sea dwelling, they separated those with fins and scales from those without fins and scales; and in the air, they divided those that fly from those that have four feet and swarm, and those with wings and jointed legs that swarm.

The purpose of this classification was to tell people what they could eat. Animals that swarm, with four feet, could not be eaten; while those that swarm, with wings and jointed legs, could be eaten. The latter category includes the grasshopper, locust, and cricket; and some centuries later, we learn that indeed the pious John the Baptist lived in the desert eating locusts (Matthew 3:4).

Of course, this classification produced some results that we would now consider artificial, or even unnatural. For example, the weasel, mouse, gecko, chameleon, lizard, and crocodile are all in a single category, one that subsumes some amphibians, some reptiles, and some mammals. And yet, by the criteria of this classification, the category is an entirely natural one, for it encompasses ground-dwelling animals that swarm or crawl (and forbids their consumption).

SYSTEMATICS AND PHYLOGENY

Science orders species as well, but does so in accordance with different criteria—evolutionary relationships. The general system we use involves the possession of certain key or essential attributes—say, a backbone, or scales, or four limbs—and assigns species to categories based on what they have. This practice goes back at least to Aristotle (ca. 320 BC), and while similar to what the ancient Hebrews were doing, it has a very different purpose—not to tell you what to eat, but to reproduce the general patterns nature has produced and to give us a common vocabulary with which to study and discuss them.

The person who formalized and standardized the scientific classification of animals and plants was an eighteenth-century Swedish botanist and physician, Carl Linnaeus. Linnaeus published under his Latinized name, Carolus Linnaeus; and was ennobled late in life, renamed Carl von Linné. His system involved assigning each species a place within a nested hierarchy, a set of categories beginning with the animal, vegetable, and mineral kingdoms, and becoming increasingly restrictive. At the bottom, the most restrictive category was the species, the smallest category. (See Figure 6.2; in a few very rare cases, including humans, Linnaeus invented subspecies below species, as we see in Chapter 9.)

Modern scientific classification officially dates itself from the tenth edition (1758) of Linnaeus's major work, *The System of Nature*. In it, Linnaeus gave each species a two-part Latin name, a terse description, and a place in the nested natural order. His species *Lemur catta*, for example, was one of three species he recognized within the genus *Lemur*, itself one of the four genera within the order

Animalia					
Mammalia					Other classes
Primates				Other orders	
Lemur		*Homo*		Other genera	
Lemur catta			*Homo sapiens*	Other species	

Figure 6.2. In the Linnaean system, species are assigned a place in relation to one another.

Primates, one of the orders of the class Mammalia, within the kingdom Animalia. (By convention, we give the species and genus names in italics or underlined.) A different species, *Homo sapiens,* was one of two species of *Homo* (Linnaeus named the other *Homo troglodytes,* and mistakenly assigned the more anthropomorphic descriptions of the apes to it), a different genus within the order Primates, class Mammalia, and kingdom Animalia.

It took another century before science was able to explain what that pattern meant. Charles Darwin is the one who accomplished that, being the first to advance the idea that species in the same genus shared a recent common ancestry; those in different genera shared a more remote common ancestry; and those united by falling into even higher taxa shared an even more distant ancestry. This was what Buffon had recognized a century earlier, but rejected (Chapter 2). To a first approximation, then, the Linnaean hierarchy recapitulated evolutionary history. Living species were divergent descendants of now-lost ancestors, which possessed the generalized characteristics of the genus; members of divergent genera were divergent descendants of ancestors that possessed the generalized characteristics of the family (a level that had been introduced between the genus and order by Linnaeus's followers).

The study of the relationships among species is called *systematics*; and obviously "relationships" is a fairly broad term. It might mean that one species is the ancestor of another; or it might mean that they are closely related and look similar; or it might mean that they are closely related but look different because one has diverged radically from the other; or it might mean that whatever similarities they possess are convergences due to adapting to common ecological circumstances. Studying the systematics of the species of interest allows us to understand aspects of their *phylogeny*—the evolutionary history, and the patterns of ancestry and divergence that produced them.

Our goal, of course, is to understand the evolution of the species in question. Understanding their phylogeny is crucial. But two scientific schools of thought exist on how to use that knowledge to organize the species into meaningful categories, as Linnaeus did.

Linnaeus was hampered by the limited knowledge of his day. For example, he believed the bats (*Vespertilio*) were a kind of primate, and placed them in the primate order. To some extent, then, our classification of animals must negotiate a path between the *stability* that permits us to talk about groups without ambiguity and the *flexibility* that allows us to modify our groups as our knowledge of them becomes more clear.

CLASSICAL AND CLADISTIC TAXONOMY

The criteria that people use to construct their classifications—the mental processes behind the act of classifying—constitute *taxonomy*. Obviously different cultural groups have their own taxonomic systems for ordering the species they encounter, and for deciding that "this" is a kind of "that." There are two competing systems of taxonomy in science at present.

The first is known as classical or evolutionary taxonomy, and uses two criteria: descent and divergence. This system attempts to replicate in a classification the phylogenetic relationships among species, yet also acknowledges that there are some times when it may be better *not* to do so. Those times occur when one species evolves very rapidly, and its descendant becomes very different from its closest relatives. In such a case, it may be useful to recognize the divergent group as one category and the ones it left behind as another, even though they may not be each others' closest relatives.

Consider the relationships among living birds, crocodiles, and turtles. We represent those relationships with a basic diagram called a *cladogram* (Figure 6.3), which simply depicts species by their recency of common ancestry. Two species joined by a common node shared a common ancestor not shared by the species outside that node. A cluster of species defined by a node (comprising a "V" in the cladogram) is a clade, and comprises a set of closest relatives.

Detailed studies of the head, pelvis, and genes indicate that crocodiles are more closely related to birds than they are to turtles. The reason birds and crocodiles don't look very similar is that birds diverged radically from their close relatives, and essentially "flew away," leaving a diverse assemblage of scaly, green, crawly creatures behind. Classically, we would place the birds in the class Aves, and the turtle and crocodile in the class Reptilia—nevertheless acknowledging that the organisms constituted by the "reptiles" actually phylogenetically subsume the ones constituted by "birds." In other words, these two groups are not equivalent: birds are a closely related group of species; and reptiles are not, for the birds actually fall within them. Birds here are *monophyletic* (all very closely related), while reptiles are *paraphyletic* (not each others' closest relatives because they are missing some species that diverged from them). Paraphyletic categories are united by sharing ancient, primitive traits or states; one of the most famous paraphyletic categories (no longer widely used) is "invertebrates"—creatures unified by *not* having evolved a backbone, obviously a motley group.

The advantage of this system is that it retains creatures that look rather similar, and are ecologically similar, in the same category. The disadvantage is that it applies criteria inconsistently and creates groups that are not equivalent.

An alternative system of classification is known as *cladistic* classification. Here, a single criterion—proximity of descent—is stringently applied, so that all named

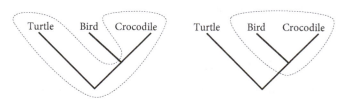

Figure 6.3. Although birds and crocodiles are most closely related, we can associate the turtles and crocodiles as "reptiles" and emphasize the difference of the birds (left) or group the closest relatives together, and incorporate birds into "reptiles" (right).

units (or taxa) comprise a set of closest relatives. Thus, in the example given above, we could not group the turtle and crocodile together, apart from the birds. Rather, we would have to group the birds and crocodiles together, for they are each other's closest relatives here, and separate them from the turtles. A cladistic or phylogenetic classification, then, calls *all three groups* "Reptilia," and places the turtles in one group (Anapsida), and the birds and crocodiles in another (Diapsida).

The advantage of this system is that it applies a single criterion consistently. The disadvantage is that it comes up with weird clusters of animals, who happen to be each other's closest relatives but do not look very much alike—because we are discounting the element of divergence in evolution. Moreover, we create a subtle paradox: Birds are no longer an anatomical contrast to reptiles; birds *are* reptiles.

One is obliged to make a choice, and decide which criteria are more useful, and thus which system to adopt. Here we adopt the position that classical Reptilia (green scaly crawly creatures, or "crocodiles plus turtles minus birds") is a useful group to recognize, even if it is paraphyletic—for the emergence and divergence of birds was a great adaptive step in the history of life. To that extent, emphasizing their adaptive divergence is considered more important than emphasizing the temporal divergence of the turtles. So we opt to use "reptiles" as a paraphyletic, anatomical, and ecological contrast to birds.

By the same token, we classically identify two paraphyletic groups in the primates: the prosimians (which will acknowledge the divergence of the ancestors of monkeys, apes, and humans into a niche of daytime sociality and intelligence); and the great apes (which will acknowledge the divergence of the bipedal ancestors of humans). This is not a quasi-mystical statement, exalting humans apart from other primates, but simply an acknowledgment that, like other great divergences in the history of life, that of humans from the apes constituted a radical and significant evolutionary departure from its close relatives.

PHYLOGENETICS

The most basic question we can ask, as we try to impart some scientific order to the species on earth, is: Of three species, which *two* are most closely related?

One important lesson to be gleaned from the preceding discussion is that overall similarity may not be a good guide to proximity of descent. Two species may be very similar because they are closest relatives, or simply because something else diverged radically from them. Hopefully that was evident in the crocodile-turtle-bird example above.

Now consider a chimpanzee, orangutan, and a human. The chimpanzee and the orangutan have large canine teeth, long arms, long thick body hair, and grasping feet. They are obviously similar kinds of creatures, close relatives. But are they the clos*est* relatives of the three species under consideration?

What we are asking is a very basic question of biological history. Are the features shared by the chimpanzee and orangutan present because they are inheritances from a recent common ancestor that that also shared them, to the exclusion of the human line? Or are they, rather, holdovers from a long period of common ancestry, from which humans have simply diverged?

The difference between these two alternatives can be formalized and generalized. Overall similarity can tell you that species are generally closely related, to a first approximation. But to tell which two species are *most* closely related, overall similarity won't do. A special subset of similarities must be discerned: *derived* similarities, or evolutionary novelties (*synapomorphies*).

Once again, let us look at a single character, canine tooth size. We observe that chimpanzees and orangutans both have large ones, and humans have small ones. Thus, large and small canines constitute two character states. Clearly an evolutionary change has occurred. Either small canines evolved into large canines in the ancestor of chimpanzees and orangutans (which would make large canines a shared derived character), or else they shrank in the ancestor of humans (which would make large canines an ancestral character, retained passively in the other two lineages). We need to establish the polarity of the evolutionary event: Was it a change from small to large canines, or from large to small canines?

The basic test is an *outgroup comparison*. Its logic goes like this. We know (because we find two character states) that an evolutionary event occurred within the group constituted by chimpanzees, orangutans, and humans—whose precise relationships we are trying to work out. The character state that came first, the ancestral state, should be preserved in species that diverged before the group under consideration, and which is consequently now somewhat more distantly related to them. If we examine such a species—say, a baboon—we will see that it has large canines. Thus, large canines represent the ancestral state for the group we are interested in—chimpanzees, orangutans, and humans. That, in turn, means that the evolutionary event in question was a reduction in canine size in humans; and thus, the possession of large canines in chimpanzees and orangutans is merely an ancestral retention, and thereby not a reliable indicator that they are closest relatives.

This logic can be applied to any kind of comparative data. For example, if we examine the fine structure of the enzyme carbonic anhydrase I, we find that the 38th amino acid in the human form of the enzyme is threonine. It is also threonine in the chimpanzee. But in the orangutan's form of that enzyme, the 38th amino acid is alanine. Here we see again two character states, but the shared state is between human and chimpanzee. Is this a shared evolutionary novelty (synapomorphy), or an ancestral retention?

Once again, we look to the baboon for guidance, in the expectation that it will retain the ancestral state, since it presumably diverged from these three before the evolutionary event that occurred among them took place. The corresponding amino acid in the baboon's form of the protein is alanine. (See Table 6.1.)

Thus, the character state shared by human and chimpanzee (threonine) is the derived one, which in turn implies that the evolutionary event was a change from alanine to threonine in a recent common ancestor of human and chimpanzee. Thus, humans and chimpanzees are probably closest relatives, by this bit of data.

Table 6.1. The distribution of two characters in three taxa and an outgroup (baboons).

	CANINE SIZE	CARBONIC ANHYDRASE I AMINO ACID #38
Human	Small	Threonine
Chimpanzee	Large	Threonine
Orangutan	Large	Alanine
Baboon	Large	Alanine

LIMITATIONS OF THE PHYLOGENETIC METHOD

Like all manners of producing knowledge, the outgroup method of establishing the polarity of an evolutionary event—to determine whether the features shared by species are derived or ancestral, and thus reliable determinants of a recent common ancestry—works well to a first approximation. It does, however, make some crucial assumptions that must always be considered.

For example, we are assuming that evolution is parsimonious, or sparing, in its activity. In other words, we assume that evolutionary events are fairly infrequent and, consequently, that specific similarities are more likely to be the result of a single evolutionary event in a common ancestor than of two different evolutionary events occurring in parallel in separate lineages. The evolution of a similarity in different lineages independently is called *homoplasy.*

Suppose we use "moustaches" as a character, and examine humans, baboons, and moustache tamarins. The two animals that share this trait are humans and moustache tamarins, even though virtually everything else shows that humans and baboons are each other's closest relatives. We don't find any other primates with this character, either, so it doesn't seem to be an ancestral retention (that is, a result of the loss of moustaches in early baboons, leaving the humans and moustache tamarins). Rather, it seems to be something that was independently acquired in *both* the human and in the moustache tamarin lineages.

The choice of the outgroup may not be simple, and must be made carefully. Ideally, the outgroup should be the "next-closest" relative to the species under consideration. In the human-chimpanzee-orangutan example, the gorilla would be a very bad choice of outgroup, for it would in fact be an ingroup, that is, falling among the species under consideration. There would thus be no reason to think that the gorilla's character state is likely to be the ancestral one (although in the case of the canine teeth, it is). In a similar fashion, if the chosen outgroup falls too far outside the species being considered, the outgroup is likelier to have been subject to parallel evolution of the trait in question. A mouse, for example, is in a different taxonomic order (Rodentia), and has lost its canine teeth entirely; it is thus valueless in the example of canine size in the apes.

Additionally, not all characters are equally useful in such a study. Ideally you need a character that exists in two states among the three species being considered;

but you don't want it to be too variable in other species. The more the trait varies among species generally, the less likely is the chosen outgroup to be retaining its conservative, ancestral state. Thus, a trait like "hair coloration" is rather too diverse to be of value in a cladistic study, without many other assumptions about its evolution: it varies from dark to pale in humans, is dark in chimpanzees and gorillas, red in orangutans, and is quite variable in gibbons.

REFERENCES AND FURTHER READING

Carroll, S. B. 2005. *Endless Forms Most Beautiful*. New York: W. W. Norton.

Dupré, J. 1995. *The Disorder of Things: Metaphysical Foundations of the Disunity of Science*. Cambridge, MA: Harvard University Press.

Eldredge, N., and J. Cracraft. 1984. *Phylogenetic Patterns and the Evolutionary Process: Method and Theory in Comparative Biology*. New York: Columbia University Press.

Flatt, T. 2005. The evolutionary genetics of canalization. *Quarterly Review of Biology* 80:287–316.

Godfrey, L. R., and J. Marks. 1991. The nature and origins of primate species. *Yearbook of Physical Anthropology* 34:39–68.

Gould S. J. 2002. *The Structure of Evolutionary Theory*. Cambridge, MA: Harvard University Press.

Graur, D., and Li Wen-Hsiung. 2000. *Fundamentals of Molecular Evolution*. 2nd ed. Sunderland, MA: Sinauer Associates.

Groves, C. 2004. The why, what, and how of primate taxonomy. *International Journal of Primatology* 25:1105–1126.

Hull, D. L. 1970. Contemporary systematic philosophies. *Annual Review of Ecology and Systematics* 1:19–54.

Marks, J. 2007. Anthropological taxonomy as both subject and object: The consequences of descent from Darwin and Durkheim. *Anthropology Today* 23:7–12.

Martin, R. 1990. *Primate Origins and Evolution: A Phylogenetic Reconstruction*. London: Chapman and Hall.

Mayr, E. 1963. *Animal Species and Evolution*. Cambridge, MA: Harvard University Press.

Peterson, E. L. 2016. *The Life Organic: The Theoretical Biology Club and the Roots of Epigenetics*. Pittsburgh, PA: University of Pittsburgh Press.

Schwartz, J. H. 2005. *The Red Ape*. New York: Basic Books.

Serrelli, E., and N. Gontier, eds. 2015. *Macroevolution: Explanation, Interpretation and Evidence*. New York: Springer.

Shubin, N., C. Tabin, and S. Carroll. 2009. Deep homology and the origins of evolutionary novelty. *Nature* 457:818–823.

Simpson, G. G. 1961. *Principles of Animal Taxonomy*. New York: Columbia University Press.

Tattersall, I., and N. Eldredge. 1977. Fact, theory, and fantasy in human paleontology. *American Scientist* 65:204–211.

Waddington, C. 1942. Canalization of development and the inheritance of acquired characters. *Nature* 150:563–565.

Waddington, C. H. 1957. *The Strategy of the Genes*. London: Allen and Unwin.

CHAPTER 7

Is That an Ape in Your Genes, or Are You Just Glad to See Me? (On the Place of Humans in the Natural Order)

THEME

The study of primate diversity and origins is the beginning of our scientific narrative of who we are and where we came from. As such, it is a narrative of kinship, the culturally specific knowledge that orients people in their universe, and is often contested. A scientific narrative of kinship carries cultural authority, and consequently must be invoked very judiciously.

Our primate origins are not very surprising. Our resemblances to the primates are recorded in many native terms for the primates who live around them: "man of the woods," "ghosts of the forest," and the like. Cicero records that around 200 BC, Quintus Ennius commented on "how similar we are to monkeys, the most horrid of creatures." Nearly two millennia later, Linnaeus quoted that line in *The System of Nature*.

The issue, it seems, is not so much our similarity to the primates but what that similarity means. To Linnaeus's generation, in the mid-eighteenth century, it meant that our corporeal or bestial side connected us to the animals, while our rational or spiritual side connected us to God. But a hundred years later, to the generation after Darwin, both our brains and our bodies would have to connect us to the animals, and we would have to see ourselves as connected to them historically and genetically.

There is still wiggle room, however. Since Darwinism is about descent and divergence, not just descent, we can see our relation to the apes as one that incorporates extensive divergence. The human, after all, is the one walking and talking, at the very least.

On the other hand, what would it mean if we could train an ape nearly to walk, or nearly to talk? Might it mean that, no matter how different we think we are, we are never beyond the control of our "inner ape"? Or that we are governed more than we realize by "nature"? And that even our historical injustices and modern inequalities are "just" irremediable expressions of a subcutaneous simian—one that we may not like, but that we are stuck with?

Indeed, it might mean all that, and more. Decades of scientific best sellers, from *African Genesis* (1961) through *The Naked Ape* (1967), *The Third Chimpanzee* (1992), and *Demonic Males* (1996), have overemphasized the similarities between human and ape, to construct an apparently scientific argument for the "naturalness" of things like aggression, social hierarchies, gender roles, and even war. Even admitting a broad swath of naïveté, it is hard to believe that the authors are entirely innocent of the political implications of their writings. Using "nature" as a bludgeon against the poorest and weakest elements of society, after all, was the core of the "social Darwinist" agenda even before World War I.

And thus we find the apes as pawns in a larger philosophical contest over human nature—is injustice really unjust, or is it just life? In other words, should we bother working to improve society, or just leave it alone, warts and all? Of course, you can probably guess how the warts themselves would vote—to leave it alone. And if they could recruit the primates to support them, they might make a persuasive case for a conservative social agenda.

Consequently, our place among the primates is invariably highly contested biocultural terrain. Not just scientifically and religiously, but politically and socially as well. We assign to primatology the job of patrolling the boundary of what it means to be human—certainly an important symbolic marker—and consequently, we invest a lot of cultural power in it. As a result, it is hard even to imagine a "value-neutral" primatology; virtually any pronouncement that comes out of the field has meaning that directly bears on where we came from and, by implication, who and what we are.

PRIMATE CLASSIFICATION

Ultimately, classification is a cultural act. We make judgment calls about the criteria to apply (do we use phylogeny exclusively, or phylogeny and divergence, or something else?), about the rank at which to acknowledge those criteria (is a clade of three related animals a single genus with three species, or a single family with three genera?), and even about the number of groups to be recognized. For example, the same assemblage of animals might be grouped into four small clusters (say, four genera with one species apiece) or into two large clusters (say, two genera with two species apiece).

Even the natural units themselves, the species, which are rather less arbitrarily defined, are still subject to expansion and contraction. This is especially true in the study of paleoanthropology, where the data on which to base systematic judgments is restricted to incomplete skeletal material. We call systematic decisions to keep the number of taxa small "lumping" (for here we are lumping diverse and possibly different creatures into the same few categories), and we call decisions to construct many taxa to accommodate a group of organisms "splitting" (for here we are splitting similar and possibly conspecific creatures into separate categories).

Primate taxonomy is particularly sensitive to cultural influences. Not only is the reward system in paleoanthropology structured toward splitting (Chapter 8), but even the taxonomy of living primates is culturally inflected as well. Consider this: Primatology textbooks published in the mid-1980s tabulated about 170 living species of primates. Two decades later, there were about twice that; and now there are well over 400 living primate species formally recognized.

What is the cause of this explosive increase in the number of primate species? Are new species being discovered? Are primates undergoing extensive speciation?

Actually, the number of new species discovered is quite small, and the amount of time under consideration (about 30 years) is hardly sufficient for speciation. What is at play in this multiplication of species is very important, but only minimally biological.

Most primates live in arboreal environments, that is, in trees. Many of them live in countries in which the human societies are economically developing, and part of that development involves building farms, factories, and houses—often at the expense of forests. Much of the model here is based on the history of the United States, where the conservation movement arose at the end of the nineteenth century, after the indigenous peoples had been "pacified," the bison had been all but exterminated, native forests had been destroyed, and Niagara Falls was an industrialized eyesore.

Now, however, we recognize the importance of conservation—not just for such mundane things as acid rain, or the ozone layer of the atmosphere, which filters out harmful ultraviolet rays, but also for the balance that ecosystems maintain, with each species filling its own role, and for the irrecoverable loss incurred by extinction, and especially for an understanding of primate diversity and adaptation.

Given the interest in conservation both nationally and internationally, it should not be surprising that primates are often the centers of attention. The mountain gorillas studied by Dian Fossey in Rwanda have come to be known all over the world; and the woolly spider monkeys (or muriquis) studied by Karen Strier in Brazil have shown that they can rebound from extensive habitat disturbance—although still highly endangered. That shows the immediacy of conservation issues: there is a window of opportunity to save endangered primates, but it is closing.

Conservation is the key to understanding why there are so many species of primates. Since much of conservation legislation is written at the species level, it is strongly in the conservationists' interest (and the primates' interest) to be splitters, and to regard local populations as distinct species. In that way, particular populations of endangered species have their own chance at survival, and bureaucrats (acting on behalf of industrial patrons) can't protect just one population of a species and feel as though the entire species itself is protected satisfactorily. With so much at risk, the number of species has grown extensively.

Thus, the number of natural evolutionary units of primates (which we defined as species in Chapter 6) is certainly overestimated by the number of formally designated, named units of primates. The abstract species we discussed in Chapter 6 were units of ecological genetics, bounded by their gene pools; the living species of primates in this chapter are units of conservation, bounded by a compromise between gene pools and politics. That isn't necessarily bad, but is simply an ac-knowledgment that the material needs of the primates are more urgent than the abstract interests of scientists—and that the apparent facts of nature are facts of culture as well.

PROBLEMS OF UNIFORMITARIANISM

We take as a general guide to research in the historical sciences that the present is the key to the past. This guideline was established by Charles Lyell in the nine-teenth century, and named "uniformitarianism" in a review of his book, *Principles of Geology*. Like all guidelines, however, it isn't always right, and sometimes can be positively misleading. Three cautionary examples may be useful.

In the 1960s, a prominent paleontologist sought to make sense of the Miocene (23.5–5.3 million years ago) fossil record of apes. Starting with the recognition that there are three forms of African "apes" alive today—humans, chimpanzees, and gorillas—he grouped the Miocene fossils into three categories as well, which he thought represented the ancestors of the three living groups. In this case, however, the diversity of apes alive today was not a reliable guide to the diversity of Miocene apes. The ape species that survive today are a sad and pathetic relic of a once-broad and diverse radiation of such creatures. We now recognize about thirty genera of Miocene apes.

A second example is the lemurs of Madagascar, which are all fairly small crea-tures today, ranging in size from the tiny mouse lemur, up to the size of a small dog, about 25 lbs. And yet it would be misleading to think of lemurs only as small crea-tures. When humans first arrived on the island of Madagascar about 1,500 years ago—in historical times!—there were actually lemurs weighing 150 lbs. Shortly after the arrival of humans, the largest Madagascan birds and mammals died out. Thus, the lemurs alive today are a skewed sample of the physical diversity of this group, skewed probably by human agency, driving them to extinction in recent times.

As a final example, we note that modern higher primates of the Old World are grouped into three categories—quadrupedal monkeys, brachiating apes, and walking humans. Each of these categories represents a broad and successful radia-tion of species, and has several other anatomical and behavioral correlates. The monkeys, for example, tend to have crests connecting the cusps on their molar teeth, the better to shear their plant food with; apes tend to have long arms; and humans to walk erect. Since these are the "packages" that our modern primates fall into, it is only natural, when we encounter a fossil primate, to seek to assign it to one of those three categories. Yet extinct primates are not necessarily constrained by the same pigeonholes into which we can sort their surviving cousins. In *Oreo-pithecus,* an 8-million-year-old primate from Italy, we find teeth similar to those of living monkeys, long arms similar to those of living apes, and adaptations of the feet similar to living people. Which of these features is the "real" one, which allows us to find the proper pigeonhole for *Oreopithecus*? Current opinion sees

Oreopithecus as an odd member of the adaptive radiation of apes, converging dietarily and dentally with monkeys, and converging as well on the upright posture of humans—but as ample testimony to the confusion incurred by trying to assign extinct primates to the established categories of living primates.

Thus, while the present may be the best and most reliable guide we have for understanding the past, the past must also be understood on its own terms.

GENETIC AND ANATOMICAL DATA

Classically, the relationships among groups of animals were, and are, established by a detailed comparison of their bodies, especially their musculoskeletal systems (as that is the only system accessible in the case of extinct species). Using the phylogenetic method discussed in Chapter 6, and formalized explicitly in the 1970s, we have been able to ascertain the relationships of the major groups of primates with a considerable degree of resolution. In some cases, however, anatomical data may be ambiguous. Since the 1960s, however, these data have been increasingly augmented with molecular genetic data, principally protein and DNA structure, which provide an independent suite of traits to analyze phylogenetically. The advantages of using molecular data to analyze phylogenetic relationships are that they are not as sensitive to adaptive convergence (superficial resemblance due to common circumstances) as anatomical characters are; they can be readily treated quantitatively; and they provide many characters for analysis. The principal disadvantages are that there are few character states (you can only be A, T, C, or G in DNA, for example), which leads to a great deal of random parallel mutation; there may be multiple mutations at the same site, so that one observable nucleotide difference between two species may be the result of more than one evolutionary change, which cannot be seen; and except for fortuitous preservation of recent materials, the fossil record is not amenable to genetic study—and yet it constitutes the totality of our knowledge of the history of life.

Usually the relationships of living creatures as deduced from anatomical studies match very well with the relationships as deduced from biomolecular studies. When they don't, however, each set of data has to be carefully re-examined to see what assumptions may be incorrect and what methods are more reliable in the particular case. Closely related groups may often yield ambiguous phylogenetic results from whatever data are being analyzed, which is an indication that perhaps the model we are imposing on the evolutionary history of the species is a bit too simple. Thus, the relationships among the woolly monkey (*Lagothrix*), the spider monkey (*Ateles*), and the woolly spider monkey (*Brachyteles*) do not seem to be readily resolvable into two closest relatives and an outgroup. Perhaps, then, it was the result of a three-way split, the nearly simultaneous divergence of three gene pools from one another—the kind of situation that may not represent the simplest case, but is not terribly improbable, either.

Since we focus on derived features to establish patterns of descent, we sometimes end up focusing on things that may seem minuscule or arcane. Here we need to remember that for our purposes, these derived features are simply mark-ers of relationship; only in some cases do they reflect fundamental adaptive changes.

THE MAMMALS

The world of 100,000,000 years ago was quite a bit different. As you emerged from your time machine to examine the wildlife, you might notice the complete lack of familiar-looking trees (angiosperms), but forests composed of other kinds of plants—ferns and palms. You might find the air a bit invigorating, as the oxygen content of the atmosphere would be perhaps 40% higher than what you evolved to expect. The large land animals could be broadly divided into two classes—those that ate plants and those that ate the animals eating plants—rather like the wilde-beest and zebras of the African plains on the one hand, and the lions and hyenas tracking them on the other.

But of course, the two classes of animals you'd be seeing would be dinosaurs.

Scurrying underfoot, however, would be a strange group of different kinds of creatures, covered neither with scales, nor with feathers, but with hair. If you found a nest of them, you would see that their young were born live, and suckled from glands on their mother's abdomen, rather than being hatched from eggs. You might also notice aspects of their teeth and bones; but altogether, they would not seem like a particularly impressive group of animals, compared with the diverse and large dinosaurs atop the proverbial food chain.

About 65 million years ago, perhaps stimulated by a meteor impact, an ecological catastrophe dramatically altered the shape of life on earth. The large-bodied dinosaurs died out, along with many other groups of plants and animals. Some mammals managed to survive, however, and found a world liberated of the great reptilian competitors and predators. Within about 10 million years, they had expanded and diversified into most of the general kinds of mammals we are fa-miliar with today, one of which is our group, the Order Primates. However, this diversification was so explosive that tracing back the relationships of particular mammalian orders is very difficult; it is consequently often called a "star phylog-eny," with many different modern lineages developing at roughly the same time.

Although we tend to focus on lactation as "the" key mammalian trait, in fact, the mammals share several interesting features of the skeletal and reproductive system. Perhaps the most significant of these is our skin, which has hair and sweat glands. Another is the differentiation of our teeth into groups with diverse func-tions: incisors for biting, canines for slashing, premolars for chewing, and molars (with more than one root) for grinding. Yet another is the development of the embryo inside its mother, rather than in an egg, encased by a shell. To a paleontolo-gist, however, the most significant mammalian feature is the construction of our jawbone, which is made up of several elements in other vertebrates, but of only a single element in mammals. The other bones have become the hammer, anvil, and stirrup of our middle ear—and the reduction and migration of these bones can be tracked in the skulls of the "mammal-like reptiles," whose skeletons link us to the other vertebrates of the Jurassic era.

This might raise a question about our official designation as "mammals." Given that the term denotes a natural group distinguished on the basis of several key adaptive features, why do we privilege the breast, something functional in only half of the species, and rarely even in them? Why would *National Geographic* feature a mother–infant dyad on the cover of a special issue on the mammals in April 2003 rather than their hair, or skin, or teeth, or ears? Is there some reason why we should consider ourselves fundamentally specialized breast-feeders, as opposed to fundamentally specialized chewers, or hearers, or sweaters?

There is a reason, and it helps us to see the interaction of scientific facts and social history. We "became" mammals in the canonical tenth edition of Linnaeus's *System of Nature* (1758); prior to that time, he had called the group "Quadrupedia" and noted that it was characterized by a "hairy body, four limbs, and females give birth to live young and lactate." For example, in his 1746 description of the animals of Sweden, Linnaeus grouped them into Quadrupedia (mammals), Aves (birds), Amphibia (including reptiles), Pisces (fish), Insecta, and Vermes (worms). In the 1750s, however, Linnaeus became involved in a social controversy: women in urban Europe were increasingly sending their newborns to the country to be wet-nursed. This permitted the new mothers greater freedom to work in an industrializing society, although it exposed the baby to higher health risks. Linnaeus was among those who did not like this change in maternal behavior; and in fact, he wrote a pamphlet condemning the practice. The tenth edition of *Systema Naturae*, with its change from "Quadrupedia" to "Mammalia," was the very next thing he wrote.

Linnaeus was encoding a social message in his biological classification. He was saying, "It is the natural role of woman to nourish her child." By emphasizing disproportionately the basic role of the "mammal" as maternal caretaker, he simultaneously discredited wet-nursing as unnatural and led many generations of biology students to accept lactation as the key feature of the group at the expense of all the other adaptive features the group possesses.

Once again, apparently natural facts are also cultural facts.

OUR PLACE IN PRIMATE SYSTEMATICS

Among the mammals, primates are known principally for two suites of features—their hands and their eyes. Those adaptations appear to be related to arboreal life, to catching insects, and to eating fruit in the branches of flowering trees. While we rarely eat insects or climb trees to eat fruit, we can nevertheless identify these adaptations in the human body.

Dividing the living primates into two groups is problematic because of the ambiguous position of the tarsier—sharing primitive traits with the lemurs and lorises (such as grooming claws on the toe), derived traits with anthropoids (such as a whiskerless dry nose, single upper lip, uterine structure, enclosed eye socket, and the inability to synthesize vitamin C), and possessing their own unique traits (such as elongated ankle bones and very large eyes). A traditional classification sorts the tarsier along with the lemurs, lorises, and galagos (Prosimii), as opposed to monkeys and apes (Anthropoidea). This has the advantage of acknowledging the adaptive success of a diurnal, social arboreal quadruped—the earliest monkeys. (See Figure 7.1.)

An alternative, cladistic classification takes the phylogenetic position of the tarsier as the basis of reclassifying the primates by removing the tarsiers from the prosimians and clustering them instead with the anthropoids. The resultant groups would be Strepsirrhini (lemurs, lorises, and galagos) and Haplorhini (tarsiers, monkeys, apes, and people).

This is not widely adopted for much the same reason that biologists have not enthusiastically tossed out "Reptilia." The adaptive divergence of the contrasting group—in this case Anthropoidea; in that case, Aves—is considered more important than phylogenetic consistency. In other words, phylogeny is good, but obsessing about it is probably unhealthy.

The Eocene (ca. 45 MYA, or million years ago) is the epoch in which the first familiar-looking primates evolved—with the suite of classic specializations found in living primates. Two well-known families, the Adapidae and Omomyidae, nevertheless also have uncertain relationships to modern primate families—showing nicely the lack of fit between "finding many fossils" and "understanding where they go," as well as the prominence of "transitional forms"—for what is a transitional form, if not an animal that is unclassifiable for its mixture of features? A fossil nicknamed "Ida" enjoyed some recent transient fame as an anthropoid ancestor, but other features appear instead to link it to the lemurs and lorises.

We group the anthropoids into two infraorders: Platyrrhini of Central and South America, and Catarrhini of Europe, Asia, and Africa. An important taxonomic consequence of this separation between platyrrhines and catarrhines is that the category "monkey" is paraphyletic, for it unites distantly related creatures—"monkeys" of the New World, and "monkeys" of the Old World. Actually the monkeys of the Old World are more closely related to apes and humans (by virtue of having the key catarrhine features) than they are to the monkeys of the New

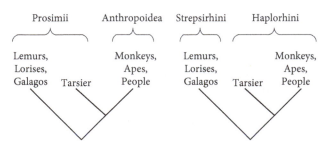

Figure 7.1. A traditional classification recognizes the paraphyletic prosimians; a cladistic classification would define them out of existence.

World. The reason the two groups of "monkeys" resemble one another is that these primates share basic skeletal adaptations for arboreal quadrupedalism: walking and running on, clinging to, and leaping from, branches in trees.

THE LIVING APES

The natural history of apes has proven a fertile ground for mythologizing. In inventing the genre of the crime story in 1841, Edgar Allan Poe had an orangutan commit "The Murders in the Rue Morgue." Franz Kafka used the ape-transformed-into-human as a metaphor for the assimilated Jew in early twentieth-century Europe. The modern humorist James Gorman ironically likens the personalities of Jane Goodall's Gombe chimpanzees to those of particular televangelists.

The scientific presentation of the apes was satirized as early as 1931 by the *New Yorker* writer Will Cuppy. Of our best-known nonhuman primate, Cuppy wrote,

> The Baboon is entirely uncalled for. Some people like baboons but something is wrong with such people. Baboons lose their tempers. There are more baboons than you might think. The baboon is not an Anthropoid Ape. He has a tail, though not a good one, and so he is a Lower Ape. In fact he is more of a Monkey. The Arabian Baboon as the name implies is found in Abyssinia. Baboons have highly colored ischial callosities. Scientists tell us that all animals who sit down a great deal have ischial callosities. That is a lie. The Mandrill is the worst especially when going South. Baboons bark. It seems as though there would be no female Baboons but there are. The family life of the Baboon is known as hell on earth. . . . Never call anyone a baboon unless you are sure of your facts. Baboons have flat feet.

After reading such inspired nonsense, it is hard to take any pedagogical discussion of the primates seriously. Nevertheless, to a great extent, our place in nature is predicated on how we understand our place in the hominoid radiation of the Miocene. We begin with the gibbons, of whom Cuppy wrote, "Those thin long-waisted types with no head to speak of are generally Gibbons. . . . The Hoolock of Upper Assam cannot swim. Gibbons are noted for the number and variety of things they cannot do. It is believed that the Gibbon could be taught to swat flies. . . . Gibbon authorities do not know whether the Gibbon is interested in sex. But you know and I know."

Living only in Southeast Asia and some of the neighboring islands, the gibbons are known colloquially as "lesser apes" for their small body size, weighing generally less than 20 lbs. Although the most distantly related members of the Hominoidea to us, they are also curious among the Catarrhini generally for their monogamous, nuclear-family-oriented social structure. They are also very speciose as apes go, with at least nine species generally recognized, differing principally in size, coloration, and quite strikingly in chromosome structure. Classically, we group them all into a single genus, *Hylobates,* of which the siamang (*H. syndactylus*) is the largest, with the most distinctive anatomical features, and yet can still hybridize with other gibbon species (although the hybrids are probably sterile, like mules). Newer classifications may split the gibbons into as many as four genera.

A gibbon was first described scientifically in 1766 by the French naturalist Buffon, who was impressed by its enormously long arms, which appear to able to touch the ground even when the animal stands upright. When on the ground, it assumes a bipedal stance, balancing with arms stretched out to the side, much like a trapeze artist.

Because gibbons live high in the treetops, they have not been as extensively studied as the more terrestrial great apes. However, they are noteworthy for their lack of sexual dimorphism, both in body size and canine teeth. This is presumably a result of reduced competition for mates brought on by the monogamous social structure; catarrhine species in which males and females are not pair bonded, but mate more promiscuously, tend to have greater amounts of sexual dimorphism as a result of males having to compete for reproductive access to females.

And yet those monogamous gibbons are known to cheat on their partners, as recent DNA studies have shown.

Like many arboreal primates, the gibbons are highly territorial and signal their spatial positions in relation to one another with a series of loud calls. In fact, the different species rarely overlap in geographic distribution. They are unique, however, in the way they move through the trees, swinging acrobatically with their long, strong arms, and hook-like hands. It is unclear whether they are the most basic brachiators (from which the larger apes diverged), or the most highly derived and specialized brachiators, but one thing is certain—they do it very well.

Classically, there is but a single species of orangutans, divided into two subspecies: *Pongo pygmaeus pygmaeus* on Borneo and *Pongo pygmaeus abelii* on Sumatra (although again, newer classifications may elevate them to species). They got there during times of lowered sea levels, and the remains of orangutans are known on the Asian mainland as well as on other islands. Orangutans are, curiously, among the least social of primates, generally traveling alone and entering into few obvious long-term social relationships. Their bodies are covered with long reddish hair, and their close-set eyes give them an appearance more human-like than the other apes, which is why the local people called them "people of the woods"—the loose translation of "orangutan." Although they do come down to the ground sometimes, most of their lives are spent in the trees, where they move slowly and deliberately, a locomotion known as "clambering." On the ground, their clambering movements translate into a slow four-limbed gait in which they bear their weight partially on their clenched fists.

Orangutans are very highly sexually dimorphic, with males developing large pads on the sides of their face, in addition to the common catarrhine patterns of body size and canine size dimorphism. Since we tend to find high levels of sexual dimorphism in more terrestrial species, and in more highly social species, the orangutan remains a bit of an enigma.

Since their discovery in the mid-nineteenth century, the gorillas have been perhaps the most highly mythologized living creatures. Confined now to small patches of forest in central and western Africa, they are allotted to one (*Gorilla gorilla*) or two (*Gorilla beringei*) species. The different gorillas are ecologically differentiated into eastern lowland, western lowland, and mountain. Paradoxically, the mountain gorilla is the rarest, but the most familiar, because of the pioneering researches of Dian Fossey at the site of Karisoke in Rwanda, the subject of the popular movie *Gorillas in the Mist*.

The charismatic paleontologist Louis Leakey sponsored the initial researches of Dian Fossey on mountain gorillas, as well as Jane Goodall on chimpanzees and Biruté Galdikas on orangutans. Those three women came to be known as the "trimates"—each doing field research on one of the three genera of the great apes. Fossey, however, had a temperament less well disposed to the economic, social, and political rigors of her fieldwork. Living among desperately poor people, she seemed to sympathize more with the plight of the gorillas, which were all too commonly the victims of poaching, a tragic part of the local economy. Fossey embraced the rumor that she was a witch, in order to protect the gorillas from poaching, but witchcraft is taken very seriously in much of Africa; and she met a gruesome end one night in her camp at Karisoke. The simplistic moral of the movie *Gorillas in the Mist*—along the lines of "people bad, gorilla good"—ignores the network of political and economic forces that placed the gorillas in such jeopardy at the hands of the local people. This was certainly reinforced by the civil war in Rwanda in the 1990s, which left hundreds of thousands of people dead, and some mountain gorillas as well.

Of the great apes, the gorilla is the only one known to be very strictly vegetarian in the wild. Living in small groups with a single adult male, several adult females, and subadults, gorillas are the largest living primates, and also highly sexually dimorphic, with males weighing up to 600 pounds. Younger peripheral males will occasionally try to take a female away from an adult "silverback" male, resulting in most of the violence that is recorded in gorilla interactions.

When they descend to the ground, gorillas (and chimpanzees) move about in an odd way. The long arms and strong flexor muscles of the fingers that serve brachiators so well in the trees are employed as the ape bears its weight on the knuckles of its hands. This "knuckle-walking" is a very unique way of getting around, and it is not known whether it represents a derived trait shared by the African apes, an independent acquisition in the taxa that do it, or a primitive ancestral condition of human bipedalism.

Gorillas are also not widely known to use tools or to have local behavioral traditions, as chimpanzees and orangutans appear to. This does not mean they all behave the same way, of course—lowland gorillas, for example, are now known to spend far more time in the trees than mountain gorillas.

More is known about chimpanzees (*Pan troglodytes*) than about the other living apes, principally because they are more common and have been the subject of a well-known continuous study, now spanning over five decades, by Jane Goodall and her colleagues, at the site of Gombe in Tanzania.

Jane Goodall's first book, *In the Shadow of Man* (1971), was based on a decade of fieldwork and gave an idyllic view of the Gombe chimpanzees. Each had a name and a personality. Despite the occasional jockeying for dominance, they lived generally peaceful lives, and mostly spent their time sitting around and eating. Goodall also observed them to select a twig, strip the leaves off it, wet it, poke it into a termite hole, and retrieve and eat the termites that clung to the twig. This was celebrated as the first discovery of tool manufacture and use in another primate species (although other clever species had long been known to modify elements of their environment to assist them in obtaining food).

But darker times lay ahead for the Gombe chimpanzees. Two females, Passion and Pom, went on a brief, violent infanticidal spree. Later, the community fissioned, and over the course of a few years, the males of the Kasakela group opportunistically killed the males of the Kahama group, one by one, as any of them ventured too close to Kasakela turf. Such nastiness lies at the core of the "Demonic Males" theory, based on the study of the Gombe chimpanzees. Whether this representation of chimpanzees is more accurate, or more real, than the earlier one is currently unknown.

One thing is clear: it is certainly a mistake to essentialize chimpanzee behavior, and to imagine that there is a single narrow "natural" chimpanzee way of living, which is independent of the history, social milieu, and environment of any specific population of chimpanzees. We now know, for example, from long-term studies at other sites, that chimpanzees greet one another differently, have different food preferences, hunt differently, and use different kinds of tools at different sites. By implication, the same is probably true of the other, more poorly known, ape species.

Perhaps the most interesting feature of chimpanzees is their hunting. Although primarily vegetarian, chimpanzees will opportunistically eat small vertebrates, and one of their favorites is the red colobus monkey. The degree of coordination in the chase is unclear, and may vary between different sites, but several individuals, mostly males, will wait for a young monkey to stray far enough away from an adult and then chase it through the trees with the ruthless pursuit of an intelligent predator. If a monkey is caught, it is dashed against a tree branch or lethally bitten, and its carcass is begged for and divided among the members of the hunting party, and the meat is apparently savored by all participants.

Chimpanzees are also unique among the apes for their prominent displays of female fertility, marked by the visually striking pink swelling of the genitalia. This is also known among some cercopithecine monkeys, such as baboons. Other apes have more subtle behavioral and olfactory changes during the period of female fertility, which leads her to solicit and accept sexual overtures—a period known as estrus.

Bonobos are generally placed in their own species, *Pan paniscus,* and are clearly very similar to chimpanzees and differ from them in subtle physical ways, for example, bonobos having long black hair on their head, parted in the center; and their vocalizations are like squeaks. Behaviorally, however, the two species of *Pan* are different in fascinating manners. Unlike common chimpanzees, the bonobos form female coalitions, which prevent individual females from the physical intimidation that larger male chimpanzees often inflict on smaller female chimpanzees.

These female bonobo coalitions are reinforced by non-reproductive sexual activity between females. They also appear to have more human-like limb proportions, which gives them better balance when they assume a bipedal posture—although like chimps and gorillas, their gait on the ground is usually knuckle-walking.

These apparent similarities to humans, however, are balanced by dissimilarities: bonobos use tools far less than common chimpanzees, nor do they hunt much. Phylogenetically, bonobos and chimpanzees are each other's closest relatives, so the lesson here is fundamentally about the great breadth of behavior observable in the genus *Pan*.

THE AFRICAN APE CLADE

In the 1960s, the first applications of molecular genetic techniques to the relations of the Hominoidea showed that humans fell in with a cluster of the African ape genera, leaving the orangutan as a more distant relative. Indeed, among humans, chimpanzees, and gorillas, the genetic relations are so close that they appear to be nearly indistinguishable (for example, the hemoglobins of human and chimpanzee are identical), and the phylogeny intractable—they appeared to have split three ways simultaneously 4–8 million years ago, an "unresolvable trichotomy."

In the 1980s, these results were augmented by the application of other genetic data, especially the actual DNA sequences themselves. Some, such as mitochondrial DNA sequences, suggested that humans and chimpanzees shared an especially intimate chunk of biological history—they might actually be each other's sole closest relatives. This would leave out the gorilla, which nevertheless seems to have much in common with chimpanzees, such as knuckle-walking and aspects of chromosome structure—which would now be difficult to interpret. Thus, far from clarifying the picture, the new data suggest, rather, that our strictly bifurcating models may be too simple to represent the actual bio-history of the hominoids. (See Figure 7.2.)

While it is clear that the plurality of genetic data support the association of chimpanzee and human over any of the other pairwise schemes, it is also clear that *any* strict pairwise scheme does not flow from the data particularly well. Nearly

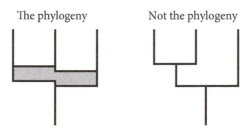

The phylogeny   Not the phylogeny

Figure 7.2. The split of human, chimp, and gorilla in the late Miocene was more interesting and complicated than two successive bifurcations.

every genetic study that shows the chimpanzee to be "closer" to the human than to the gorilla also shows the statistical error bar to be broader than the little bit of biological ancestry ostensibly separating the gorilla; or infers substantial introgression from the gorilla lineage subsequent to its speciation.

What seems to have happened about 6–7 million years ago is something both micro- and macroevolutionary, leaving a trail of complexly linked populations. In this way, the discordant genetic and anatomical data might not be wrong, but merely evidence of somewhat more complex ecological events than just successive simple divergences of the gorilla, then the chimpanzee, from the human lineage.

Consider an ancient species of ape, widely distributed across equatorial Africa about 7 million years ago, and physically similar to chimpanzees. In a small part of its central-western range, a founding population begins to evolve into gorillas. Roughly simultaneously, on the eastern part of its range, a larger founding population begins to evolve into humans. The broad middle evolves into chimpanzees. (See Figure 7.3.)

What patterns would we expect to see when we compared them millions of years later? Probably most data would fail to detect two closest relatives (for there aren't two closest relatives); but some data would link chimpanzee and gorilla (for these shared a unique biological history geographically removed from human ancestors). More data would link chimpanzee and human (for these shared a unique biological history geographically removed from gorillas, and over a broader area), and rather limited data would link humans and gorillas (for these share no biological history with each other distinct from chimpanzees).

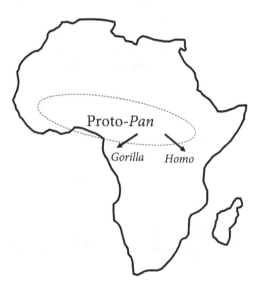

Figure 7.3. The nearly contemporaneous separation of gorilla and human ancestors from a founding population of chimp ancestors would account well for the biological patterns we find.

This model fits the general pattern of data more closely than the simply bifurcating model, and is a variant of the "East Side Story" scenario proposed by the French paleontologist Yves Coppens.

There are attractions of the specific human-chimpanzee model, however. For example, it might considerably simplify the interpretation of many traits in which chimpanzees and gorillas differ, permitting us to regard the chimpanzee as in effect a living human ancestor—our sole closest relative. In this way, their multimale social group and frontier male violence might be specific antecedents of human behavior. Considering chimpanzees and gorillas to be equally closely related to us would suggest instead that neither of these forms can be reliably inferred as ancestral to us.

Another crucial feature affected by the phylogenetic interpretation is the evolution of human bipedalism. If it really were a complex three-way split, then knuckle-walking might be a part of the brief local history shared by chimpanzees and gorillas. Human bipedalism, then, would not have evolved from knuckle-walking, but from a more general form of locomotion, from which *both* knuckle-walking and bipedalism are separately derived. If it really were resolved as chimp-human, on the other hand, then knuckle-walking must either be an independent acquisition in the chimpanzee and gorilla, or a primitive character of the human-chimp-gorilla clade. The latter interpretation would make it likely that bipedalism evolved *from* knuckle-walking.

Since the interpretation of the direct antecedent state of human bipedalism is contingent on the phylogeny, and the phylogeny is contested, it is difficult to say much with confidence about the specific origins of human bipedalism.

CLADISM, REDUCTIONISM, AND THE RISE OF THE HOMININS

In 1962, struck by the genetic similarity of humans and African apes, the biochemist Morris Goodman began to suggest reforming the classification of the apes. His first argument was that the genetic similarity demanded that humans not be separated from apes at a taxonomic level as high as the Family, but at a lower one. His second argument was that since chimps and gorillas are more closely related to humans than to orangutans, we should not classify chimps, gorillas, and orangutans together (as great apes, or Family Pongidae), but rather, we should classify chimps, gorillas, and humans together—to reflect the phylogenetic relationships. Goodman was an early advocate of a cladistic classification.

Neither suggestion was accepted well by the leading biologists of the age. The great mammalogist George Gaylord Simpson flatly rejected Goodman's suggestion on the grounds that "*Homo* is both anatomically and adaptively the most distinctive of all hominoids" and "[c]lassification cannot be based on recency of common ancestry *alone*." Indeed, the biologist Julian Huxley suggested around the same time that humans be separated from other multicellular life at the subkingdom level, as Psychozoa—mental life.

The issue was how the complex information about evolutionary history is to be employed. Anatomically, mentally, and ecologically, humans are quite different from apes. There is, obviously, a lot of apeness recoverable in the human body and behavior, but certainly even the most incompetent observer could hardly miss the fact that in a group of apes in their representative habitats, our species is the only one walking, talking, sweating, shaving, weeping, cooking, praying, building, marrying, bartering, bathing, covering themselves, reading, driving, seasoning their food, drinking things other than water and inhaling things other than air, using material culture (stripped twigs notwithstanding), and inheriting.

The question is, Why should a scientific classification choose to ignore that? What is more scientific about privileging the temporal divergence of the orangutan over the anatomical, ecological, and behavioral divergence of the human? I like orangutans as much as the next fellow, but their separation from humans, chimps, and gorillas is simply not as biologically significant as the separation of humans, whose unique behavior and ecology has driven the other hominoids to the brink of extinction!

What is left unarticulated in all this is the assumption that somehow genetically determined relationships are the "realest" and that the "best" representations of reality should reflect those relationships. But sez who? The geneticists? Why should genetics be the primary criterion for a scientific classification? After all, if you can't tell a human from a chimp by looking at their genes, all you really have to do is just look at something else!

It is one thing to acknowledge the genetic similarity and phylogenetic proximity of humans, chimps, and gorillas to one another. But it is another thing entirely to say that that information is more important to express in a classification than the divergence of humans.

Divergence, after all, is what Darwin wrote *The Origin of Species* about. Evolution is the production of difference. To deny the significance of the differences evolution has produced is, well, weird.

Unfortunately, however, the cladistic classification—prioritizing phylogeny over divergence—has also become widely adopted in recent years. That is why textbooks now say "hominins," while professors say "hominids" to refer to the same group of species.

The traditional classification, using the paraphyletic family Pongidae, separates living humans (and their close extinct relatives) as the family Hominidae, or colloquially as "hominids." The cladistic/genetic classification, which adopts Morris Goodman's suggestion, sinks the family Pongidae, and instead puts all the extant large-bodied apes in the family Hominidae, and separates the orangutan from human-chimp-gorilla at the subfamily level. The separation of humans and their fossil relatives from the chimps and gorillas is now reduced to an even lower level, the Tribe Hominini, or colloquially as "hominins." (See Table 7.1.)

Using the "hominin" system presumably means that you agree with its principles: that a scientific classification should be constructed on descent alone, and not at all on divergence; and that the cryptic genetic similarity is more important

Table 7.1. Alternative classifications.

The traditional classification

Superfamily Hominoidea
      Family Hylobatidae
            Genus *Hylobates*
      Family Pongidae
            Genus *Pongo*
            Genus *Gorilla*
            Genus *Pan*
      Family Hominidae ("hominids")
            Genus *Homo*

The cladistic/genetic classification

Superfamily Hominoidea
      Family Hylobatidae
            Genus *Hylobates*
      Family Hominidae
          Subfamily Ponginae
                  Genus *Pongo*
          Subfamily Homininae
             Tribe Gorillini
                  Genus *Gorilla*
             Tribe Panini
                  Genus *Pan*
             Tribe Hominini ("hominins")
                  Genus *Homo*

---

to encode than the striking physical, behavioral, and ecological differences. That seems antithetical to both Darwinian evolution (which is fundamentally about adaptive divergence) and to anthropology itself (which is predicated on the special interest accorded to humans in the panoply of nature). As we will see in Chapter 10, the newer classification also has an adverse effect on the handling of our extinct relatives. That is why I don't use it.

WHAT DOES IT MEAN TO BE 98% GENETICALLY CHIMPANZEE?

It is now widely known that when we compare the DNA bases of a chimpanzee to those of a human, over 98% of them will match. Given this genetic correspondence, it is easy to slip into the conclusion that we are "nothing but" slightly made-over chimpanzees. It is important, therefore, to look carefully at the true meaning of the 98% genetic similarity. There are three points that may not be immediately obvious but are crucial for the proper interpretation of the 98% genetic similarity to chimpanzees.

First, there is still much room for tremendous difference to have arisen between the two species. Remember that the size of a mutation does not predict the size of its effect—the smallest change in a piece of DNA can result in either no problem, or a life-threatening disease, or anything in between. And since the genome is composed of 3,200,000,000 nucleotides, a 1% difference would mean 32,000,000 different nucleotides. There is certainly no problem in generating the biological changes responsible for the differences between a chimpanzee and a human.

Second, it should not be that surprising to learn that we are 98% genetically identical to chimpanzees. After all, life on earth comes in amazingly diverse forms. Simply among the primates, we have noted features like the rotating shoulder and absence of a tail that show how similar physically we are to chimpanzees. But if we broaden our scope and compare humans and chimpanzees to starfish, we will find that bone for bone, nerve for nerve, muscle for muscle, organ for organ, the human and the chimpanzee match—and the starfish (an echinoderm) does not. In the great scope of life on earth, humans are certainly at least 98% physically similar to chimpanzees—so the 98% genetic similarity seems hardly out of place.

And finally, our ideas of similarity and difference are culturally loaded. We think of a scale of similarity ranging from 0% (completely different) to 100% (completely the same), with 98% being close to the same. Yet DNA doesn't work that way. Recall that DNA is a polymer, a long string of simple subunits, and that there are only four subunits—A, G, C, and T. What this means is that any nucleotide has a one in four chance of matching any other nucleotide *purely at random*. Put another way, two randomly generated DNA sequences are statistically constrained to match 25% of the time. If we look at two strings of 60 nucleotides, we randomly expect them to match in 15 places.

While you could generate two DNA sequences that would match nowhere, that would not be a random comparison—and a random comparison is our baseline. Given that randomness generates a 25% DNA match, it follows that human DNA and DNA-based life anywhere else in the universe, with no genealogical connection to us, would be constrained to match 25% of the time. Or, more earthbound, our DNA must match any other DNA from any species on this planet over 25% of the time, since all life on earth is ultimately linked by common ancestry, which generates more similarity than pure randomness.

In other words, while our DNA matches that of a chimpanzee at over the 98% level, it matches the DNA of the banana the chimpanzee is eating at over the 25% level. Yet there is hardly any way we can imagine ourselves to be over one-quarter banana—except in our DNA.

All of which is not to deny the 98% genetic identity of human and chimpanzee, but to show that it contains a lot of cultural information as well, and has no stand-alone self-evident biological meaning. The seeming paradox—that humans and chimps are so different physically, yet so similar genetically—is a consequence of two factors: our familiarity with chimp bodies, and our unfamiliarity with genomes. DNA similarity is simply one way of comparing things, no more meaningful or meaningless than other ways of comparing. The relationships of species may simply not be reducible to relationships of their DNA.

REFERENCES AND FURTHER READING

Arnold, M. 2008. *Reticulate Evolution and Humans: Origins and Ecology.* New York: Oxford University Press.

Campbell, C. J., A. Fuentes, K. C. MacKinnon, M. Panger, and S. K. Bearder. 2011. *Primates in Perspective.* 2nd ed. New York: Oxford University Press.

Chaline, J., B. Dutrillaux, J. Couturier, A. Durand, and D. Marchand. 1991. Un modèle chromosomique et paléogeographique d'évolution des primates supérieurs. *Geobios* 24:105–110.

Cuppy, W. 1931. *How to Tell Your Friends from the Apes.* New York: Horace Liveright.

Dupré, J. 2003. *Darwin's Legacy: What Evolution Means Today.* New York: Oxford University Press.

Fleagle, J. 2013. *Primate Adaptation and Evolution.* 3rd ed. San Diego: Academic Press.

Fossey, D. 1983. *Gorillas in the Mist.* New York: Houghton Mifflin.

Goodall, J. 1971. *In the Shadow of Man.* New York: Houghton Mifflin.

Gorman, J. 1989. *The Man with No Endorphins: And Other Reflections on Science.* New York: Penguin.

Groves, C. P. 2014. Primate taxonomy: Inflation or real? *Annual Review of Anthropology,* 43:27–36.

Hagen, J. B. 2009. Descended from Darwin? George Gaylord Simpson, Morris Goodman, and primate systematics. In *Descended from Darwin: Insights into the History of Evolutionary Studies, 1900–1970,* ed. J. Cain and M. Ruse, 93–109. Philadelphia, PA: American Philosophical Society.

Harris, E. E. 2015. *Ancestors in Our Genome: The New Science of Human Evolution.* New York: Oxford University Press.

Henke, W., and I. Tattersall, eds. 2015. *Handbook of Paleoanthropology* (online). doi: 10.1007/978-3-642-27800-6. Berlin: Springer.

Holliday, T. 2003. Species concepts, reticulation, and human evolution. *Current Anthropology* 44:653–673.

Hrdy, S. B. 1999. *Mother Nature.* New York: Pantheon.

Kafka, F. 1917. *Ein Bericht für eine Akademie* [Report to an Academy]. http://records.viu.ca/~johnstoi/kafka/reportforacademy.htm

Marks, J. 2005. Phylogenetic trees and evolutionary forests. *Evolutionary Anthropology* 14:49–53.

Marks, J. 2009. What is the viewpoint of hemoglobin, and does it matter? *History and Philosophy of the Life Sciences* 31:239–260.

Rosenberger, A. L. 2012. New World Monkey nightmares: Science, art, use, and abuse (?) in platyrrhine taxonomic nomenclature. *American Journal of Primatology,* 74:692–695.

Sayers, K., and C. O. Lovejoy. 2008. The chimpanzee has no clothes. *Current Anthropology* 49:87–114.

Scally, A., J. Y. Dutheil, L. W. Hillier, et al. 2012. Insights into hominid evolution from the gorilla genome sequence. *Nature,* 483:169–175.

Schiebinger, L. 1993. *Nature's Body*. Boston, MA: Beacon.

Sommer, M. 2008. History in the gene: Negotiations between molecular and organismal anthropology. *Journal of the History of Biology* 41:473–528.

Strier, K. B. 2017. *Primate Behavioral Ecology*. 5th ed. Upper Saddle River, NJ: Pearson.

Strum, S. C., and L. M. Fedigan. 2000. *Primate Encounters: Models of Science, Gender, and Society*. Chicago, IL: University of Chicago Press.

Thorpe, S., R. Holder, and R. Crompton. 2007. Origin of human bipedalism as an adaptation for locomotion on flexible branches. *Science* 316:1328–1331.

Wrangham, R., and D. Peterson. 1995. *Demonic Males*. New York: Houghton Mifflin.

Yoon, C. K. 2009. *Naming Nature: The Clash between Instinct and Science*. New York: W. W. Norton.

CHAPTER 8

Apes Run Around Naked, Live in Trees, and Fling Their Poo. Do You? (On the Relevance of Apes to Understanding Humans)

THEME

Human nature has a dual character, being both derived from primate biology and yet also divergent from it. There are very few things we can learn about humans from studying apes that we can't learn better by studying humans, for the importance of the apes for evolutionary studies lies in their contrast with the human condition. The major issues in primatology today focus on conserving primates in the wild, and ensuring that they are treated humanely and sensitively in captivity.

WHAT PRIMATES CAN AND CAN'T TELL US

Primates, and especially apes, hold a special symbolic place in the natural world, being the creatures that most obviously connect us to the rest of the animal kingdom. As a result of that symbolic significance, primates are also vested with political relevance that other animals lack. For example, the supposed resemblance of black people to apes was emphasized in the nineteenth century by defenders of slavery, as a way of dehumanizing the slaves. That historical use of the apes to satirically dehumanize people is still a sensitive issue. Consequently, in the twenty-first century, political opponents of President George W. Bush routinely caricatured him as looking like a simian; but political opponents of President Barack Obama had to find other outlets for their satirical urges.

The political and symbolic power that apes hold makes it particularly difficult to establish what they "really" are like, for it means that any attempt to understand them must inevitably be refracted through cultural lenses. The best-known primates in the world, the chimpanzees of Gombe, Tanzania, studied by Jane Goodall and her colleagues, show this very strikingly. Goodall's famous 1971 book, *In the Shadow of Man*, was a chronicle of her first decade there. She gave each chimpanzee a name and identity and showed chimp life to be largely carefree—concerned with life, food, social interactions, attachment to one another, and of wild sexual abandon at the appropriate times. It resonated as a happy hippie commune. In the next decade, pathologies began to appear—episodes of infanticide, cannibalism, and even the elimination of the members of one community by their neighbors. This all sounded rather like the Ewings of *Dallas* or the Carringtons of *Dynasty*—the two most popular prime-time soap operas of the era. By the 1990s, what had formerly been pathological was now considered strategic; and the differences in behavior of different groups of chimpanzees mirrored the multiculturalism of American society. And finally, in the twenty-first century, as polls show about half of adult Americans don't accept evolution, the Gombe chimpanzees now show just how much "like us" they really are.

Granted that chimpanzees are doing the things as the primatologists report—groups of males going on patrol to defend a turf, like a primitive version of *West Side Story,* but without the score, dialogue, or choreography—the question is, how do we know what that behavior means? It is hard enough to figure out what is going on in the head of someone of a different sex, much less someone of a different culture, and very much less someone of a different species. But that is the question at the heart of contemporary studies of "wild" chimpanzees.

The situation is not much different for the study of captive chimpanzees, either. Chimpanzees in zoos and those reared in a human home have been valuable sources of information about the cognitive abilities of apes. But the cost is that the information has been very hard for humans to understand because raising a chimpanzee in a human environment is essentially very intensive training. And if you train a chimpanzee to act human, does it not stand to reason that the chimpanzee will show you some amazing similarities? Circus trainers for generations have shown us that chimps can ride tricycles and sip tea and smoke cigarettes—but they didn't purport to tell us that they had shown anything scientific at all about its mental or behavioral relation to humans.

So what are we to make of the stories of apes raised in human environments, under constant human stimulation, which end up acting in recognizably human fashions? Do they tell us anything about ourselves? Do they tell us anything about themselves? Or do they simply show that development and maturation is a biosocial activity, and after rearing the apes in an aberrantly human context, you will readily be able to see human qualities in them?

Intertwined in all of this is the fact that the apes are all endangered species, threatened by the encroachment of human societies, ranging from deforestation to consuming primates as food, or "bushmeat." On the one hand, we would be very loath to see any human being starve to death for the sake of an ape; but on the other hand, it would be nice to be able to offer an inducement to anyone willing to forgo that baby gorilla sandwich for a tray of Big Macs. Moreover, their genetic similarity to people makes the apes especially prone to come down with infectious diseases from humans, which is another reason why their numbers are precipitously declining.

Ironically, one of the few human diseases that chimpanzees do not readily get is AIDS. While it might conceivably be useful to discover just what chimpanzees have, which prevents the HIV virus from destroying their immune systems, there is currently no AIDS research on chimpanzees going on in the United States or Europe. Heightened sensitivity to the conditions of chimpanzees in captivity and to their lives as experimental subjects has simply wiped this research program off the scientific map. This raises the issue of the moral economy of apes in research: How can we balance the welfare of apes against the welfare of humans? Ape lives have already saved human lives: for example, a mysterious disease known in Papua New Guinea as kuru was the focus of the (ultimately Nobel Prize–winning) work of D. Carleton Gajdusek. At the outset of the research, the incidence of kuru had shown some consistency with both a genetic pattern and a contagious pattern. It was very specifically the ability to induce the symptoms in a chimpanzee which led to the recognition that it was infectious (and indeed, the first example of a prion disease, in the same category as Mad Cow) and was being spread by funerary practices.

Can we find a way to use chimpanzees humanely in research to help develop treatments for a disease that does not manifest itself in them clinically, but may manifest itself in millions of people? Right now we are not even trying. Even worse, infectious diseases like Ebola are still decimating ape populations in the wild, and without biomedical research, their prospects are grim.

PRIMATE FIELDWORK

The most fundamental difference among studies of the nonhuman primates is the conditions under which they are studied. Captive studies are those in which primates are studied under conditions that are highly constructed: notably, zoos and laboratories. Wild studies are those in which primates are studied under conditions of minimal disturbance—as they are "naturally." Of course, most primate habitats are disturbed to some extent; and the ubiquitous presence of humans, sometimes provisioning the animals, sometimes hunting the animals, means that a state of complete "naturalness" is an illusion.

The advantages of wild studies are obvious—you get a glimpse of what the behavior of the primates is like under the most normal conditions of their existence. But there are disadvantages as well. Primates at their "wildest" are not too fond of being observed by large bipedal creatures with binoculars, and must be habituated to accept a human presence. In the most extreme cases, this may take several frustrating months. Note the paradox: to study primates *au naturel*, you must transform them fundamentally by making them tolerate your presence.

The difficulties of wild studies are also worth considering. First, there is the general rigor of fieldwork, living far from the comfort of home, with a minimum of conveniences. Second, there is the fact that most fieldwork must be conducted in poor countries, in rural areas, with little governmental presence or protection—so not only is it inconvenient, it is often dangerous. Third, the animals are often hard to locate—even habituated ones. Fourth, setting up experiments, even if feasible, defeats the purpose of studying them "in their native habitat"—so you can really only watch and record what they do, and not really know what they would do under slightly different circumstances. Fifth, to obtain enough data for statistical treatments, you generally have to be in the field for several years. And sixth, it's frightfully expensive.

A captive study also has advantages and disadvantages. The major advantages are that it is cheap and convenient (as long as you don't figure in the costs and travails of establishing and maintaining the captive population yourself!). The animals are always there, and consequently you don't have to spend time looking for them. Moreover, they can't flee very far from you. Because they are there, you can also study them much more extensively and under more controlled conditions. You can see them enough times to do statistical studies, and can give them psychological tests. On the other hand, captive primates may be different from their wild conspecifics. Because they are provisioned, they exercise less and eat more, and thus are commonly bigger and fatter than wild primates. Their social group size may be a simple consequence of the number of animals the zoo was able to procure, which may affect their behavior.

In general, we have to acknowledge that wild studies tell us what primates do; captive studies tell us what they are capable of.

Another important distinction is between short-term and long-term studies. The advantage of long-term studies lies in the scope of data: rainy season versus dry season, annual fluctuations, life cycles, demographics. The disadvantages lie in the logistics—generating enough funding over a long enough period of time, usually under unstable political conditions, as well as the sometimes scattershot quality of the data. A well-focused, short-term study has value in yielding a sharply focused answer to a narrow, specific question—more "bang for the buck." But the long-term data contain the keys to the primates' survival in the face of ecological and demographic disruptions.

In some ways, primate fieldwork may seem superficially like ethnography—you visit a group in a remote place and record what they do. So what if the group is monkeys, not people?

Actually, however, the differences between primatology and ethnography are more striking than the similarities. After all, ethnographers get most of their data from talking to the people they work with. For not only is an ethnographer interested in recording what people do, but also in what they *think* they're doing, what they think they *ought* to do, and what they *wish* they could do but can't. Further, the ethnographer learns about other people in the group—which is why it has been remarked that ethnographers trade in gossip, and why they get drawn into the social politics of their subjects. The ethnographer usually lives with the people studied, actively participates in their daily lives, and requires their explicit permission to work there. This is all obviously quite different from the work that primatologists do.

PRIMATES IN GROUPS

Primates navigate a sea of costs and benefits in group life: groups repel predators but also attract them; groups can find food sources more easily but must share them; groups permit mates to be readily available but may create a need to compete for access to them.

How do primates know where they belong in their groups? In fact, the group behavior of primates consists of highly variable ranges of affiliative and antagonistic interactions, with some primates hardly interacting with one another beyond their basic minimal interests to stick together. In the more social species, a primate learns a dominance hierarchy, which primatologists infer by studying the interactions between pairs of individuals, and evaluating them across the social group. These interactions may range from actual fights to the subtle ability of one individual to displace another (to compel that individual to get up and walk away)—or simply the sangfroid to ignore a threat directed one's way.

The dominance hierarchy has often been regarded as a result of males striving to reproduce most efficiently, by competing for the best opportunities to fertilize the best females. But evidence relating position in a dominance hierarchy to reproductive success has not been easy to come by. The "pecking order" among male primates is often sufficiently ephemeral as to render very temporary any preferential access to mates; and the extent to which rank affects a female's ability to survive and reproduce is also unclear. Primates commonly form "coalitions" to demote an animal with a high rank, thus shifting the relationships throughout the hierarchy. Furthermore, the relationships within the hierarchy are commonly not linear—so that one monkey may dominate a second, and the second may dominate a third, but the third may dominate the first.

Thus, dominance is regarded by primatologists as a state, rather than as a trait. It changes through time, and a primate's social skills and temperament may have a greater effect upon it than crude size and strength. Consequently, although some scientists believe that there is an intimate relationship between dominance and reproductive success in human ancestry, it has proven difficult to demonstrate a consistent effect of the one upon the other in primate societies. Other factors, from mate choice to strategic coalitions, act to level the reproductive playing field.

Another way in which dominance relationships are expressed is in threat displays. The extent to which these are effective at getting another primate to back down or go away is another marker of the primate's position in the dominance hierarchy. Different primate species accomplish this in different ways—a ring-tailed lemur waves its conspicuous tail, a squirrel monkey brandishes his penis, a baboon yawns to show its formidable canine teeth, and a gorilla thumps its chest. Other displays may accompany the stereotyped behavior—shaking branches, jumping, piloerecting (having the hair bristle), and vocalizing. It could be argued that the analog of this behavior in modern society is threatening to call your lawyer.

SOCIAL BEHAVIOR AND ECOLOGY

Primates live longer than most other mammals, particularly when species of the same body weight are being compared. As a result, primates spend more time acquainting themselves with the physical and social universe, learning how to manipulate it, and one another, to achieve their ends.

Living primates span a considerable range in body size, from the mouse lemur to the gorilla, and many particulars of primate life history are related to body size. Most primates give birth to one offspring at a time, the exceptions being principally galagos and callitrichids, who tend to have twins. A primate infant thus does not have to compete for attention against littermates, as many mammalian infants must. Further, in comparison to other mammalian infants, a primate is very altricial—poorly developed and unable to function well on its own and thus needing more attention and assistance for a longer period of time than other young mammals. This long period of relatively slow development compels a primate to be a good learner—not only in relation to its environment, where it will have to learn what to eat and where to find it, but also in relation to other members of its group, who may be new immigrants or aggressive competitors, or the stable residents of a new community with whom it must coexist.

Being born is the first thing any primate does, and usually it is not too difficult. Most other primates do not seem to have so difficult a time as humans do, because their heads are smaller and consequently pass through the mother's birth canal more easily. A primate mother generally gives birth to her infant alone, without assistance, and eats the placenta shortly thereafter. Like many mammals, a primate mother sensitizes her newborn to her smell and her presence by licking it clean. The baby can cling to its mother's fur and suckle from her nipple, and she will shield it from other members of the group, however curious they may be, for at least a few days. Gradually the infant will be exposed to its mother's relatives; it will not know its biological father, but will after a while be exposed to the resident males, any of whom might well be its father. In general, the amount of male care a baby receives is roughly proportional to the likelihood that the particular male is the child's father: strongly pair-bonded primate species tend to have much care given by the male, while more promiscuous primate species have little.

Very young primates are almost wholly dependent on their mothers for their survival—but survival is more than just nutrition: it is comfort as well. The psychologist Harry Harlow studied young rhesus monkeys in the 1950s to test whether they identified as "mother" simply whatever they derived nutrition from (such as a wire doll with a bottle) or whether they went for something soft and warm. Soft and warm won, hands down.

In many species, the newborn has a distinctive appearance, such as a different color coat pattern, that allows it to be seen and identified readily. They tend to lose this characteristic coloration around the time that they distinguish strangers from more familiar kin or friends. If something happens to the mother after weaning, it is not uncommon for a maternal relative to take care of the infant, a behavior called "alloparenting." As an infant (with a mother) matures, alloparenting becomes common in many primate species, and other adults in the group may "babysit"—although this is quite variable from species to species.

However, without a mother, a primate infant is at great risk. Certainly the most famous "mama's boy" in the primate literature is a Gombe chimpanzee named Flint, whose mother Flo was quite old when he was born and was unable to wean him successfully. Flo had another baby, but could not coerce 5-year-old Flint away from her nipple. When the baby died, Flint remained at his mother's side. When Flint was 8 years old, Flo died—and to the extent that we can infer grief from chimpanzee behavior, he grieved over her corpse. And Flint himself died just a few weeks later of symptoms that looked, for all intents and purposes, like depression.

In general, the birth of a new infant is a signal for the older infant to become more independent—socialize more with age-mates and other group members, and to be weaned from the mother's supply of milk. This marks the transition from an infant to a juvenile. Juvenile primates begin to develop sex-specific roles, with males generally involved in more mock-aggressive play and females involved in more mock-maternal play. Some juvenile play also involves sexual activity, although neither sex is mature or fertile yet. A primate that nears sexual maturity, and is nearly fully grown, is called a subadult. In many species, this is a time of considerable tension, as the subadult male baboon begins to rise in the dominance hierarchy, while at the same time is becoming marginalized from his troop. Male baboons transfer into new troops when they reach adulthood; in chimpanzees, it is the females who transfer. Transfer out of the natal group may occur shortly before or after sexual maturity. Obviously, the social consequences and experiences of the primate who transfers into a new group will be different from those of a primate who remains in the same social group for its whole life.

In general, primates interact preferentially and most agreeably with those with whom they are most intimately familiar. This interaction can subsume simple toleration, through mutual grooming, to the sharing of food. In practice, this preference is extended principally to those group members who are most closely related to its mother—her own siblings and their offspring—the ones the mother has known and trusted enough to allow near her infant as it grows.

The size and composition of the group depends upon several factors. One is genetics: some species naturally associate in very small groups (such as marmosets) or considerably larger groups (such as chimpanzees). Some naturally form monogamous pair-bonds (like gibbons), and others form groups with one adult male and several adult females, anthropomorphically sometimes called harems (like hamadryas baboons). In some primates, like chimpanzees and spider monkeys, groups periodically divide or coalesce, a social arrangement called "fission/fusion." Other factors that influence group size are food preference (species that eat diverse diets, or preferentially eat things that are abundant, such as leaves, tend to associate in larger groups than primates that eat, for example, insects—which are too hard to catch, and too small to nourish a lot of primates at the same time), habitat (a continuous habitat, such as the ground, makes it easier to sustain a larger population than a discontinuous or patchy forest does), the kinds of predators in the area (five male baboons may induce a leopard to back off, whereas one male baboon might not be able to), and activity patterns (diurnal primates, active in the daylight, tend to live in larger groups than nocturnal primates—presumably living in large groups would defeat the evolutionary advantage of being nocturnal, that is, being less detectable to predators). With so many factors at work, it is difficult to predict the group size of any particular primate species at any particular time accurately, without actually observing them. Moreover, we have very little information on the range of variation exhibited in behaviors of different populations of the same species.

Groups of primates organize themselves socially in surprisingly diverse ways, analogous to the various forms of social organization anthropologists study among different human societies. There are two crucial differences, however. First, basic aspects of the social organization of a primate species appear to a considerable extent to be "hardwired" or determined instinctively. In a famous disaster, scientists at the London Zoological Gardens in 1927 put 30 female hamadryas baboons into what had previously been an all-male group, in a circumscribed area—not realizing that male hamadryas baboons physically coerce females into harems by nature. Within a month, half of the females were dead, literally torn to pieces by competing males simultaneously trying to establish harems. Humans, of course, can adopt different forms of social organization readily, and have indeed done so over the millennia and across the continents, and consequently cannot be labeled as having any particular kind of natural social form.

The second crucial difference is the human difference of creating social bonds from the fabricated world of laws, which are comparable in power to the bonds that emerge from nature. Thus, the roles of "husband," "genitor," "provider," "protector," "head of household," "children's disciplinarian," and "mother's sexual partner" may not refer to the same person at any given time. Likewise, a "mate" and a "spouse" are not equivalent—the latter is a legal status, the former a sociobiological role. And of course, the status of "in-laws" has no parallel in nonhuman primates.

Bearing those differences in mind, however, we can see social forms in the nonhuman primates that are quite easy to identify with. Among the smallest primates of the New World, we find commonly that an adult female will have two or three regular mates. This seems to be related to the difficulty that small primates have in giving birth (with the offspring being relatively large compared to the mother) and the callitrichid habit of having twins. Being bonded to multiple males seems to be their way of ensuring that the babies are adequately provisioned and carried safely—an interpretation that is supported by the fact that even older siblings help out with the infants.

The range of social behaviors in primates is staggering. On one end are generally unsocial primates, such as the orangutan, potto, and some lemurs. On the other end lies primate species in which several males ordinarily consort with several adult females—a multimale group—found in rhesus monkeys, savanna baboons, and chimpanzees, as well as in muriqui monkeys of Brazil and the lemur-like sifaka of Madagascar. In between lie monogamous primates, or a social unit including only one adult male and one adult female, characteristic of the gibbons as well as some callitrichids and prosimians; species of callitrichids in which several males attend to a single female; and species that ordinarily have one adult male with several females and offspring. Even here, however, new DNA technologies are showing high rates of "cuckoldry" or "cheating"—the resident adult male may not be the sire of all the offspring.

Since macaques, baboons, and chimpanzees are the best-studied primate species, there has been a tendency to overemphasize their social systems at the expense of the diversity of social forms found in other primates, and indeed even in other primates that associate in multimale groups. The primatologist Karen Strier calls this disproportionate focus on the macaque, baboon, and chimpanzee society "the myth of the typical primate"—the idea that they represent the essence of primate social organization, rather than representing simply how intensively these few species have been studied.

FOOD

Primates derive their sustenance from their surroundings, like all species. And like all species, they need principally proteins for cell growth and carbohydrates for energy. How they get these, however, turns out to vary quite extensively.

Few primates rely exclusively on one or a few foods but rather eat eclectically what is readily available. Most primate species have decided preferences in foods, but they are adaptable enough that some monkeys are now exploiting the resources offered by human farms or by human garbage as a primary food source. This sometimes has the troublesome side effect of having local people regard them as pests.

Species with highly specialized diets often have adaptations that facilitate the processing or digestion of their food. Thus folivorous (leaf-eating) langur monkeys have a biochemical convergence in the structure of the enzyme lysozyme (which breaks down the cell walls of plants) that gives their enzyme some of the properties of the cow's version of the enzyme. They also have symbiotic bacteria in their stomachs to help detoxify their food. Gorillas, also folivorous, have extended passageways for their food, to maximize their ability to extract its nutrients. Some primates have adapted behaviorally to specialized diets by eating clay or charcoal, which detoxifies some of the vegetable matter they also consume. Certainly the most extraordinary of these specializations is that of the golden bamboo lemur, who somehow manages to live on a diet that contains more cyanide than any other species could tolerate!

In general, insectivory is an augmentation to a large-bodied primate's diet—as insects are small, hard to catch, and hard to digest. The primates that have a major component of their diet consisting of insects tend to be small bodied. On the other hand, insectivory has a hallowed place in primatology, as it was in getting termites to eat that a chimpanzee named David Graybeard was seen by Jane Goodall to take a twig, trim it, moisten it, and use it to probe inside the mound—a chimp making and using a tool in the wild.

Folivory (eating leaves) can provide the bulk of protein in a primate's diet, but only if the primate can digest the leaves efficiently. As noted above, mountain gorillas and some colobines eat principally leaves. Gramnivory (eating seeds) is also a difficult way for a primate to subsist, as seeds are hard, small, and tough to digest. It is likely that our extinct relatives, the robust australopithecines, had a lot of seeds in their diet, as their molar teeth were large and thickly enameled and their chewing muscles very strong. No living primate subsists principally on such foods, but some—notably, baboons—do supplement their diets with seeds. Gumnivory (eating sap and gum) is another way to augment the diet, as these are foods rich in carbohydrates, and readily available, if you have the means to get it. This would require the ability to gouge or gnaw, or to scrape the bark of a tree, as some prosimians and callitrichids do. Eating things that grow underground, like roots and tubers, is a way that some primates (like baboons) supplement their diets with a potentially rich source of carbohydrates. However, being underground, they are not very easy to locate, and pigs are far better at it than primates. It is also hard for a primate to dig them up—and some anthropologists have advanced the idea that human ancestors successfully exploited this resource with their earliest tools.

Frugivory (eating fruit) is the most generalized theme of the primate diet, providing even the familiar stereotype of the chimpanzee with a banana. Most primates have some part of their diet consisting of fruit. Fruits are very nutritious; however, they have the disadvantage of being distributed in a very patchy and unpredictable manner. Indeed, some anthropologists argue that exploiting such a resource successfully is what precipitated the development of the long period of learning that characterizes the primate life cycle.

Finally, carnivory (meat eating) is a small component of the primate diet generally, but it is of interest to us because our species eats more meat than other primates do. Meat has the advantage of being very nutritious and coming in large packages—and the disadvantages of running away when you try and get it, or even fighting back. Meat is consequently a high-risk and high-reward food. It was once thought that a taste for meat was unique to our species, but it is now clear that many other primate species—for example, baboons—will eat some meat, and will even occasionally hunt and kill something to eat it.

Much attention has been focused on hunting behavior in the chimpanzees, as this was once thought to separate human behavior from that of other primates. We now know, however, that (alone among the apes) chimpanzees enjoy meat in their diet, and will even seek it out. It is not a major part of their diet, but a regular one, and one that involves some behaviors that seem familiar and bizarre.

The favored prey of a chimpanzee is the red colobus monkey (although they have been observed to kill and eat over 30 other different mammalian species), and at some sites, chimpanzees seem to derive the taste for flesh primarily during the dry months of summer. The chimps begin by working themselves up into an apparent frenzy, with very characteristic movements and vocalization, then they take off after the group of monkeys they want. The hunting party consists mostly of males, who seem to have different strategies of attack in different sites. At Taï, a forest site in the Ivory Coast, the chimpanzees work in a coordinated fashion, some driving the prey, some circling the prey, some chasing, and some blocking their avenues of escape. At Gombe in Tanzania, on the other hand, the chimpanzees work together but in a seemingly less coordinated fashion—they all seem to be doing the same things, which still allows them to nab and devour a monkey.

Tool use, which characterizes human hunting, doesn't come into play commonly among the chimpanzees. They go after prey, grab it, and tear it to bits. And unlike the way they eat vegetable foods, the carcass of the monkey is divided up among the hunting party. The chimpanzees make very special begging gestures and sounds, and the killer of the monkey distributes bits and pieces. And the chimps served first tend to be the closest friends, relatives, and allies of the successful hunter. Some chimpanzees have been observed to "spear" bushbabies, by essentially treating them as if they were large termites.

Chimpanzee meat consumption also extends to eating dead infants of their own species. The extent and meaning of primate infanticide is still a hotly contested topic in anthropology (see below), but when it occurs in chimpanzees, it appears to be uniquely accompanied by the consumption of the dead infant. Oddly, chimpanzees never eat dead adult chimpanzees.

Beyond the gruesome fascination with chimp hunting, carnivory, and cannibalism, however, perhaps the most interesting aspect of primate diets presently is the apparent ability of some primates to medicate themselves. Several primate species have now been observed to walk long distances to eat a plant they don't ordinarily ingest, walking by perfectly edible things to get to it, and appear not to be enjoying it as they eat it. Then chemical studies are used to show that these plants have some medicinal properties, and medical studies show that some ailment (such as intestinal parasites) that the animals previously had is now abated. Obviously we cannot read their minds, but certainly a good circumstantial case can be made for zoopharmacognosy—the knowledge possessed by another species about the beneficial effects of certain things in their environment.

SEXUAL ACTIVITY AND PARENTHOOD

The most important social knowledge that a primate has is the reproductive status of the group's females. The vast majority of sexual activity in primates occurs at the time of female fertility, which is generally the only time that females are interested in sex; in many species, the males are not sexually interested at other times either; and in some, the male's testes are resorbed into his body when the females are infertile. The cues for female receptivity are commonly behavioral and olfactory, and sometimes spectacularly visual.

In fertile female chimpanzees and baboons, for example, the skin around the genitalia, or perineum, expands greatly and turns bright pink—a "sexual swelling." At this time, she will generally solicit and receive a great deal of sexual attention from the resident adult males. Often the female will copulate with many males, but research in recent years has shown that the females do not mate haphazardly. Some go off and mate with a single "friend" or "consort"; some go off and mate furtively with males from other groups; and many do express preferences about whom they mate with within the group—a good protector, a food sharer, or simply the most dominant males at the time.

In many primate groups, the general levels of tension and aggression rise with the onset of signals of female fertility. Copulation is usually brief, less than half a minute, with little tactile exploration. (Spider monkeys have been known to copulate for up to twenty minutes, but that is quite rare among the primates.) In some primates with multimale, multifemale social systems, the male ejaculate can coagulate and form a "sperm plug," keeping the sperm of other males out. This of course, puts a premium on mating with a female early during her estrus period; alternatively, some male primates reach in and remove a sperm plug before copulating.

In theory, this may be an expression of "sperm competition." Where several males copulate with a single fertile female, a male with a higher sperm count might have a reproductive advantage over the others. If there is genetic variation for it, then selection could act on the population to raise the sperm counts of the males, since the ones with higher sperm counts would be disproportionately fathering the children. The coagulation of seminal fluid might just be another way of beating out the other fellow's sperm.

And indeed, we do find that chimpanzees have testes considerably larger than those of humans or gorillas, just as this scenario would predict. On the other hand, chimpanzees also have very big ears, and we don't have a good selective explanation for that. Big ears are considered just "one of those things"—and a good reminder that it is often easy to come up with a plausible story for the origin of a particular trait, but hard to tell whether the story is really true. Nor do the chimpanzees seem to be one of the primate species that actually have sperm plugs.

MODELS FOR HUMAN EVOLUTION

The nature of being human has a dual character, being both derived from primate biology and yet also divergent from it. While studying primate behavior has traditionally held out the hope of illuminating some aspects of human behavior, it has become less clear just what it does show or can show about human behavior. However, even in the most pessimistic view, studying primate behavior is certainly valuable for demonstrating the breadth of variation possible in a flexible, intelligent, and adaptable group of animals, like humans. Obviously the "big question" for primate behavior—and of course, for its inclusion in anthropology curricula— is, What do we learn about humans from the primates?

The answer is not as readily apparent as might immediately be suggested. With grasping hands, large brains, and long lives, the primates will naturally appear to do things that recall what humans do. In studying them, though, do we learn anything about humans that wouldn't be better learned from studying humans themselves?

The first thing to recall, if we want to consider the relationship of human to primate behavior critically, is that there are two kinds of relationships to be drawn between animals and humans. All cultures have stories about the meaningful similarities between the natural world and our own lives. The most famous example of this in European literature is the work of the Roman writer Aesop, who used the crafty fox, the regal lion, the clever monkey, and many others to derive moral lessons for his readers (Chapter 3).

But Charles Darwin showed in the nineteenth century that there was another way to consider a comparison between animal and human. Instead of the connection between animal and person being literary or metaphorical, the connection could be real and physical, biologically deep, a product of the shared ancestry the two species have in common. This relationship came to be known as homology, while the symbolic relationship came to be known as analogy. Analogy can range from the literature of Aesop to the similarity between a bird's wing and a bee's wing. In both cases, the species have "solved a common problem" of leaving the ground by pushing against the air with broad appendages. This is a real biological relationship in the sense of bioengineering; but it is also importantly symbolic, however, in that the appendages in question are so different that it is more biologically misleading to call them both "wings." The fact that we have a word to apply to both can conceal just how very different functionally, anatomically, genetically, and developmentally they really are.

The same distinction exists when we compare behaviors across species, although it is even more vexing to tease out the difference between homology and analogy, given how much easier it is to change a behavior than a body part.

Perhaps the best example of this is our difficulty in understanding infanticide in primates. The act that involves an adult killing a very young member of the same species has been found across the primates. Some primatologists believe that young primates live under a constant threat of murder—not just by virtue of their overall vulnerability, but as a general behavioral fact of primate life—to which their mothers must adapt.

If we compare infanticide in langurs, chimpanzees, and people, however, we find notable differences. In langur monkeys (Asian colobines), which live in unimale groups, a new male will occasionally displace an older one and "take over" his females. Then he may kill the offspring, and she may become fertile, and he may father her next children. Some primatologists have argued that this is a "reproductive strategy" on the part of the male langurs; it is an act that helps them pass on their genes. Others contest whether it happens frequently enough to be considered a strategy at all, requiring constant attention, or whether it is like getting struck by lightning; whether it is part of the "normal" behavioral repertoire of langurs, or a pathological result of environmental disturbance and high population density; whether it is overreported by virtue of being inferred by primatologists far more frequently than it is actually witnessed; and whether it actually does induce the female to become fertile more quickly than if the babies were left alone.

Suffice it to say we are not about to resolve those questions here; but being good evolutionists, we might seek to gain a deeper understanding of the phenomenon by comparing it in different species.

So we take a look at infanticide in chimpanzees. Once again, we find it a rare, but reported, occurrence. We find that most known instances involve a group of males encountering a female from a different group—of whose child they are very unlikely to be the father. Then, in a highly aggressive state, the baby is wrenched from the mother, and killed and eaten. Then there was the case of Passion and Pom, a mother-and-daughter pair who were believed to be responsible for the deaths of many infants in their own group at Gombe, catching the mother by surprise and killing and eating her child.

The differences between langur infanticide and chimpanzee infanticide are as striking as the fact that the grisly behavior has been seen in both (and many other) species.

And what about humans? In our species, most infanticide is perpetrated by the mother herself, or by someone acting on her behalf, for economic or social reasons (she *cannot* have a baby now). And it is carried out remorsefully, rather than aggressively.

The devil, the old saying goes, is in the details. Langur infanticide occurs during a male takeover; chimpanzee infanticide is generally a group of males attacking a lone neighboring female, except for the best-known episode, which involved females attacking females in their own group, and culminates in cannibalism; and human infanticide is carried out ostensibly for the mother's (or the family's) interests.

Are these "the same"? Are these behaviors homologous?

Or are they fundamentally different, to the extent that the misleading thing is that we apply to all of them the same label, "infanticide"?

If there were a good answer, it would appear right here. But all we can do is use this to illustrate the basic difficulty in comparing the "same" behaviors across primate species and in trying to relate them to human behaviors, which may be (at least) superficially similar.

And yet a best-selling popular book of science enjoins us to recognize that

> [a]mong our darker qualities, murder has now been documented in innumerable animal species, genocide in wolves and chimps, rape in ducks and orangutans, and organized warfare and slave raids in ants (Diamond 1992, 170).

Is whatever chimps and wolves do really genocide, or is it "genocide"? Do orangutans rape, or do they "rape"? Is slavery in ants really basically the same as what happened to African people in the seventeenth century, or is that just a metaphor, an evocative literary device? These questions are crucial for understanding the evolutionary significance and relationship of these behaviors to their human counterparts.

This dichotomy reflects the two basic kinds of models for using primate behavior to try and illuminate human behavior. One focuses on evolutionary proximity, and the inference that behaviors seen are homologous, and thus focuses on the chimpanzee as the key to human behavior. The other focuses on an ecologically meaningful similarity, and uses the baboon as a focus.

BABOONS IN THE SIXTIES, CHIMPS IN THE NINETIES

The baboon model was popular in the 1960s and noted that baboons have secondarily descended from the trees, just as early humans had. Being fairly closely related, the baboon and human perhaps afforded an opportunity to show how life on the ground posed problems that were answered in similar ways by these different primates. And perhaps those answers involved social patterns familiar to Americans in the early 1960s and that were apparently replicated in baboons: the males fought, or at least competed, conspicuously—for resources, or females, or just for status in the troop. They were out at the forefront defending the troop against predators, while protecting the females and offspring. So perhaps, to a generation searching for unity instead of division, these paternalistic themes of baboon society echoed the common themes of a shared humanity.

And perhaps the only reason they didn't evolve into us is that the baboon males were satisfied being vegetarians, and our males developed a taste for meat and the skill to hunt.

But the deeper the baboons were examined, the more alien they appeared. Yes, the males fought, but there was a good reason—they didn't grow up together like the females did. The fact that male baboons transfer troops at adulthood, and females do not, means that the adult females are more strongly socially bonded, having grown up together, than the males are, having had to enter a new troop. The females had a dominance hierarchy too, but it was more subtle; and it was also more stable. Moreover, the baboons did hunt occasionally.

So not only were the similarities illusory, but so were the supposed key differences.

By the 1990s, the baboon as model for human evolution had given way to a model based on phylogenetic proximity: the chimpanzee. Jane Goodall's famous work at Gombe Stream Reserve in Tanzania, beginning in 1960, had produced a wealth of information, much of it visually documented in magazines, television shows, and popular books; and a steady stream of scientists came to work along with her.

Goodall's writings had always emphasized how nearly human the chimpanzees were; it is hard to look at chimpanzees, especially their facial expressions, and *not* be struck by their similarity. The chimpanzees are male bonded, and although there are competitive plays for individual status, the males band together into coalitions and look for trouble—perhaps to hunt, kill, and eat some colobus monkeys; or perhaps to patrol a territorial boundary, looking for an unfamiliar chimpanzee who may have strayed onto their turf; or to bump off a member of a neighboring group. Parallels rapidly began be drawn from those nasty, male-bonded apes to anything from human inner-city gang warfare, to football games, to primitive war, and modern genocide.

And because they shared our history until just a few million years ago, we might well be watching our ancestors.

But once again, some circumspection is called for. In the first place, chimpanzees are the only apes with multimale groups and females with prominent visual signals of fertility. Clearly some key aspects of their social behavior, then, are very likely to be highly derived. And if those features are highly derived, then they probably evolved in chimpanzees after we parted evolutionary ways with them—so they may not be part of our own heritage at all. And in the second place, their closest relatives, the bonobos, seem to be different in many interesting ways: more peaceable, less male bonded, less territorial—maybe they are the ones that represent human ancestry instead? Or perhaps we just have a very diverse array of behavioral capacities in the genus *Pan*, which precludes any easy inferences about the origins of human behavior from them. And of course, the giant peaceful gorilla, usually found in single-male groups, can't be dismissed so easily either.

LOOKING ELSEWHERE FOR CLUES ABOUT HUMAN EVOLUTION

The twenty-first century brings with it a call to higher level of sophistication in using nonhuman primates to understand human evolution and behavior. No single species will do; they each have their own evolutionary histories and unique adaptations. Instead of looking at particular species as grand models by which to understand humans, the more modern reasoning would focus on particular biosocial traits in the nonhuman primates and see what their evolutionary correlates are, and then relate it to human evolution.

Thus, for example, some lemurs live in female-dominant societies. Although there are no known matriarchies in the human species, there is considerable variation in the kinds and amount of social power that women can wield. Might lemurs be able to shed some light on what it takes to run a matriarchy successfully?

One of our closest relatives, the bonobo, engages in far more nonreproductive sexuality than other primates do. They are also female bonded and have very low levels of aggression. Likewise, the muriqui monkey of Brazil has very low levels of aggression. Might it have something to show us about the needs of a pacifist society?

Of course, one needs to retain caution. A government bureaucrat said in 1991 that he thought that inner-city ghettoes reminded him of rhesus monkey society because they have "removed some of the civilizing evolutionary things that we have built up," making them resemble "jungles." Mixing up cultural and biological evolution, he didn't seem even to realize that ghettoes are an historical consequence of urbanism, poverty, and social marginalization, and are thus very recent in human history, and consequently represent some of the most "civilized" places on earth. After all, you can't be crime ridden without a prior concept of crime, which implies the existence of law. You can't have poverty without money and without vast inequality of wealth. In other words, ghettoes are not at all like jungles, which are metaphors for the complete absence of civilization, not for its products and discontents!

THE APE MIND

Ever since they became familiar to scientists in the eighteenth century, the apes were seen to be very smart. How could they not be, if they resembled us physically in so many ways?

Yet while they could be taught many amazing tricks and behaviors, they could not be taught to speak. Was this because they were too stupid?

One way to tell would be to distinguish between speech (the act of producing meaningful sounds) and language (the cognitive, mental processes involved in making sense of those sounds). Since they could understand many things a person said (even better than your dog understands "Sit!"), perhaps they had the mental equipment, but just lacked the muscular and neural capabilities of speaking. This hypothesis was tested in the 1960s in a famous study by psychologists who taught a chimpanzee named Washoe to communicate in American Sign Language. Shortly thereafter, other apes were taught to communicate the same way, and still others were taught to use customized computer keyboards to communicate.

We now knew that the apes could use aspects of human language to communicate. But were they doing more than a really smart dog with prehensile hands could do? After all, it wasn't entirely clear that the apes could combine more than three signs, or that they had much to say beyond demanding candy or a tickle, and identifying things. In a well-controlled study, a chimpanzee named Nim Chimpsky gave little evidence of linguistic capabilities, without the prompting and translation that accompanied the accomplishments of the other apes.

The widely reported stories of a gorilla named Koko and a bonobo named Kanzi are among the most familiar ape intelligence studies still proceeding. Both of them have been raised as virtual humans, and both seem to have developed crude linguistic capacities. This work, however, tends to downplay the scientific in favor of the experiential—just watch them and you'll see how human they are! The problem is that a puppy raised in a human household becomes a family member; becomes sensitive to the desires, emotional states, and voices of humans; and can be trained to do remarkable things. So are the minds of these apes essentially those of supersmart, well-trained dogs, or are they essentially those of very dumb people?

Of course, as just phrased, the dichotomy is a little absurd. Everybody acknowledges that the apes are biologically much more closely related to humans than dogs are, and have central nervous systems very similar to our own, and brains one-third the size of ours. But the dichotomy encapsulates the crucial issue with regard to human evolution: Have humans evolved something mentally that is fundamentally different from the capacities of other animals, or are our mental and linguistic capabilities shared in some rudimentary form by the apes?

This turns out to be something that requires carefully controlled experiments to determine. If, for example, you take a rhesus monkey, and paint a red dot on its forehead, then place a mirror nearby, the rhesus monkey will react to its own reflection as if were simply another monkey with a red dot on its forehead. It gives no indication that the reflection is itself. A chimpanzee, on the other hand, usually responds by touching the red dot (which it can only see in the mirror), apparently knowing that the reflection is indeed itself, and using the mirror to examine parts that it could not otherwise see.

All humans can do this by age three to four. But some apes never get it. What this suggests is that whatever property the "mirror test" is testing—we can call it self-consciousness—is polymorphic in the apes, and may even have been lost in some. This in turn suggests that some of our assumptions about intelligence—that it is a species-specific trait, and self-evidently adaptive—may be too simplistic.

It is also fairly clear that the kinds of experiments designed to test the linguistic or mental capabilities of apes tell us next to nothing about how apes think or communicate while they are in the wild, just being apes. There is no evidence to suggest that they use anything like the words and signs of human invention to conduct their own affairs in the forest.

This raises an additional question: What value do these experiments have in helping us understand ape life or ape thought? We learn from them what the apes may be capable of under highly contrived circumstances, but we are left to field primatologists to get at what they actually do. What they actually do is of course far less strikingly human than what they are able to do in human surroundings and with human inventions. Interestingly, some of the most cleverly designed experiments, to distinguish whether when solving a problem, chimpanzees are using a simple or complex algorithm, seem to show chimpanzees consistently using a simple one.

CULTURE

Anthropology was to a large extent founded on the division between the group traits that are biologically based and those that are socially learned—"race" and "culture." Indeed, that was the distinction drawn by the British anthropologist E. B. Tylor when he first popularized the concept of culture to the English-speaking world, as "that complex whole which includes knowledge, belief, art, morals, custom, and any other capabilities and habits acquired by man as a member of society." In the hands of the German-American anthropologist Franz Boas, culture acquired a slightly different usage, referring to the things we learn that unconsciously shape our perceptions and experiences. Tylor's "culture" was something that all societies have to a greater or lesser extent, and can be observed and tabulated; Boas's "cultures" are possessed equally by all societies, and must be experienced and interpreted to be fully understood.

One significant property of culture is that it is learned, not instinctive or innate; and consequently, since different people in different places learn different things, those things come to characterize and differentiate the groups of people from one another.

Appropriating the anthropological term, ethologists (students of animal behavior) began to define "culture" solely in terms of its properties of being learned and locally specific. Consequently, they began to identify "culture" outside of the human species, most famously in chimpanzees, orangutans, and macaques. That intelligent, long-lived, social creatures would have learned local traditions should come as no surprise to any student of human evolution.

Chimpanzees, for example, have characteristic greeting gestures, food preferences, hunting styles, and tool use patterns, which differ from group to group. While this is not "culture" in the anthropological sense, it is certainly interesting, and a testimony to the intelligence of the chimpanzees and the intensity of study by scientists. The drawback, however, is that it has given rise to a sterile debate over whether chimpanzees "have" culture. They do as the word is used in ethology, but not as the word is used in anthropology.

The sad thing is that arguing about whether chimps really have "culture" or "language" obscures the interesting question, which is: What do they have? Certainly apes do not behave or communicate as humans do, so whatever the difference between human and ape behavior and communication actually is, it must be described in words, and the words "language" and "culture" seem as good as any. However, if we decide that apes have both of these, then we must come up with other labels to describe what humans have.

CONSERVATION

No apes are being imported from the wild for scientific research in the United States any more, for they are all endangered species—as are many prosimians and monkeys. Recent years have seen a great deal of interest in the plight of endangered primates. Scientific research was never much of a threat to them (the biggest scientific threat involved the depletion of local populations of rhesus monkeys in the 1950s as the polio vaccine was being developed)—rather, the threat has come principally in the form of the encroachment of human societies around them, destroying the forests and natural habitats of the primates, accompanied by human diseases, illegal hunting or poaching for trophies, and even the hunting of primates as exotic food or "bush meat."

Since it is specifically the economic development of the human societies that threatens the apes, it is difficult to look someone in the eye and tell them that their own plight is less important than that of the apes. The solutions seem to lie in developing conservation programs that bring revenues into the community and give the local people an economic incentive to conserve the primates. In Bwindi, in Uganda, a small town has developed near a group of rare mountain gorillas, and the cash from "eco-tourism" is benefiting both the people and the gorillas.

A more radical solution involves arguing that the notion of "human rights" should be extended to the great apes, endowing them legally with the rights to life, liberty, and freedom from torture. This position is advocated by the Great Ape Project, led by animal rights activists and supported by some primatologists. Of course nobody is in favor of torturing or enslaving apes, so at a very fundamental level, this is merely rhetorical. But it is unclear just what the rhetoric might actually imply. Is, for example, a colony of apes in a zoo being denied their rights to liberty?

Could an ape's right to life be violated by another ape, or can it only be violated by a person? And what manner of discomfort to an ape constitutes torture?

Perhaps the saddest part of the Great Ape Project is that, while resonant with sensitivity to the welfare and preservation of the great apes (orangutans, chimpanzees, and gorillas), it casts a blind eye to the endangered lesser apes—the gibbons of Southeast Asia—and to the many other prosimian and monkey species also threatened.

Primate conservation is one of the pressing issues of our age—not only for the fact that we are dealing with sentient and emotionally complex creatures, more similar to ourselves than to any other forms of life—but also because of the complex entangled issues of globalism, economic development, and the rights and interests of indigenous peoples and sovereign nations. Of course, a scholarly interest in primate conservation also emerges from becoming aware of the impoverishment to our understanding of our own roots that would result from the loss of these species. One important area where primate conservation and anthropology overlap is in the study of how local peoples and primates adapt to sharing the same space with one another. This multidisciplinary research involves different anthropological skill sets, since it involves both humans and nonhumans, and both ecological and economic relations. In cultural anthropology, this is part of a new intellectual area called multispecies ethnography. In biological anthropology the intellectual area is called ethnoprimatology.

REFERENCES AND FURTHER READING

Corbey, R. 2005. *The Metaphysics of Apes: Negotiating the Animal-Human Boundary*. New York: Cambridge University Press.

Corbey, R., and A. Lanjouw, eds. 2013. *The Politics of Species: Reshaping Our Relationships with Other Animals*. New York: Cambridge University Press.

Di Fiore, A. 2003. Molecular genetic approaches to the study of primate behavior, social organization, and reproduction. *Yearbook of Physical Anthropology* 46:62–99.

Fossey, D. 1983. *Gorillas in the Mist*. Boston, MA: Houghton Mifflin.

Fuentes, A. 1999. Variable social organization: What can looking at primate groups tell us about the evolution of plasticity in primate societies? In *The Nonhuman Primates*, ed. P. Dolhinow and A. Fuentes, 183–188. Mountain View, CA: Mayfield.

Fuentes, A. 2012. Ethnoprimatology and the anthropology of the human-primate interface. *Annual Review of Anthropology*, 41:101–117.

Goodall, J. 1971. *In the Shadow of Man*. Boston: Houghton Mifflin.

Goodall, J. 1986. *The Chimpanzees of Gombe*. Cambridge, MA: Harvard University Press.

Haraway, D. 1989. *Primate Visions*. New York: Routledge.

Hart, D., and R. Sussman. 2005. *Man the Hunted: Primates, Predators, and Human Evolution*. New York: Westview Press.

Hausfater, G., and S. B. Hrdy, eds. 1984. *Infanticide: Comparative and Evolutionary Perspectives*. New York: Aldine.

King, B. J. 2013. *How Animals Grieve*. Chicago: University of Chicago Press.

Marks, J. 2002. *What It Means to Be 98% Chimpanzee*. Berkeley: University of California Press.

Martin, R. 2013. *How We Do It: The Evolution and Future of Human Reproduction.* New York: Basic Books.

Mitani, J. C. 2009. Cooperation and competition in chimpanzees: Current understanding and future challenges. *Evolutionary Anthropology* 18:215–227.

Palombit, R. A. 1999. Infanticide and the evolution of pair bonds in nonhuman primates. *Evolutionary Anthropology* 7:117–129.

Pavelka, M. 1999. Primate gerontology. In *The Nonhuman Primates,* ed. P. Dolhinow and A. Fuentes, 220–224. Mountain View, CA: Mayfield.

Povinelli, D. 2012. *World Without Weight: Perspectives on an Alien Mind.* New York: Oxford University Press.

Pruetz, J., and P. Bertolani 2007. Savanna chimpanzees, Pan troglodytes verus, hunt with tools. *Current Biology* 17:412–417.

Radick, G. 2007. *The Simian Tongue: The Long Debate about Animal Language.* Chicago, IL: University of Chicago Press.

Ray, E. 1999. Social dominance in nonhuman primates. In *The Nonhuman Primates,* ed. P. Dolhinow and A. Fuentes, 206–210. Mountain View, CA: Mayfield.

Rees, A. 2009. *The Infanticide Controversy: Primatology and the Art of Field Science.* Chicago, IL: University of Chicago Press.

Richard, A. F. 1985. *Primates in Nature.* New York: Freeman.

Sperling, S. 1991. Baboons with briefcases: Feminism, functionalism, and sociobiology in the evolution of primate gender. *Signs* 17:1–27.

Strier, K. B. 1994. The myth of the typical primate. *Yearbook of Physical Anthropology* 37:233–271.

Strier, K. B., ed. 2016. *Primate Ethnographies.* New York: Routledge.

Strum, S. C. 2012. Darwin's monkey: Why baboons can't become human. *Yearbook of Physical Anthropology* 55:3–23.

Strum, S. C., and L. M. Fedigan, eds. 2003. *Primate Encounters: Models of Science, Gender, and Society.* Chicago, IL: University of Chicago Press.

Sussman, R. W., James M. Cheverud, and Thad Q. Bartlett. 1994. Infant killing as an evolutionary strategy: Reality or myth? *Evolutionary Anthropology* 3:149–151.

Tuttle, R. 2014. *Apes and Human Evolution.* Cambridge, MA: Harvard University Press.

de Waal, F. B. M., ed. 2002. *Tree of Origin.* Cambridge, MA: Harvard University Press.

Wallman, J. 1992. *Aping Language.* New York: Cambridge University Press.

Whiten, A., J. Goodall, W. C. McGrew, et al. 1999. Cultures in chimpanzees. *Nature* 399:682–685.

Wrangham, R., and D. Peterson. 1996. *Demonic Males: Apes and the Origins of Human Violence.* Boston, MA: Houghton Mifflin.

Wynne, C. 2004. *Do Animals Think?* Princeton, NJ: Princeton University Press.

CHAPTER 9

Being and Becoming
(On the Relevance of Humans
to Understanding Humans)

THEME

By overemphasizing the similarities between human and ape, we run the risk of failing to appreciate the unique position of the human species in the natural order, which for humans is really a natural-cultural order. To understand the evolution of our species, we have to see the ways in which we have come to differ from the apes in fundamental biological and ecological ways.

HUMAN NATURE

One of the most contentious issues in the area of intersection among biology, anthropology, and philosophy is that of human nature. Is there something special and unique about us, something innate and unwavering, something that we each possess as a boon or curse simply by virtue of being human? Many aphorisms and witticisms have been penned about it through the ages, but the Darwinian revolution of the late nineteenth century made it an empirical issue. Humans evolved by natural processes from an ape ancestor; the genetic differences between us and the living apes constitute the basis of uniquely human attributes; and our extensive shared ancestry with them constitutes the basis for understanding the biological substrate on which our human features were inscribed.

Of course, that doesn't necessarily help identify particular features of human nature. After all, any person thinking about the issue is doing so not just as a product of the biological evolution of their species but also as a member of a national history, an economic class, an ethnic tradition, a gender, and so forth. Is it feasible to think that we can disentangle what is human nature from what is the product of social, cultural, and economic forces on the history of the thinker?

It is hard, but in principle, we could—if we found regularities that transcended history, geography, class, tradition, and basic rationality. After all, we readily agree that speaking English, eating with a fork, going to church, and dodging falling boulders are hardly human nature. The first three are accidents of history, and the last is a reflexive act of self-preservation. Is there something in between the ephemeral and the trivial that we can identify as human nature?

This is where things get tricky. To see the problem, we must return to a philosophical distinction we drew in Chapter 1: ontological versus epistemological issues. Certainly, evolution would dictate that any features that are human autapomorphies—uniquely derived traits, or evolutionary novelties specific to the human lineage—must be human nature. And obviously a host of such features must exist. But epistemologically, how do we identify them as such, without mistaking them for the more parochial and historically shallow things we are so familiar with in our day-to-day existence?

Perhaps we could focus on broad uniformities in human thought and deed. But broad uniformities raise problems. Let's say that we find 85% of humans do something. Can we say it is human nature? If so, what does it mean about the 15% of people that do not? Are they thereby not human? Or, if we decide that *both* the act (what 85% do) and its opposite (what 15% do) are human nature, then haven't we simply made a trivial statement?

These issues are compounded by two additional facts: demographic and historical. The most widely spoken language in the world is Mandarin Chinese, spoken by nearly a fifth of the human species. Is that because it is deeply rooted in a basic human nature to speak Mandarin Chinese, or because there are so many people in Asia that the number is simply a demographic accident, rather than a manifestation of human nature? Alternatively, we may observe that about one-third of the people in the world are Christians. Is that a basic fact of human nature, or rather, just a consequence of aggressive evangelism?

In the cases of Christianity and Mandarin Chinese, the answers are pretty obvious, for a religion and a language are clearly acquired during the course of one's life. But what about something hazier, such as what features a person finds attractive in a sexual partner?

Some scientists believe that it is human nature for a man to be attracted to a woman with a 2:3 ratio of the waist measurements to the hip measurements. After all, when you show silhouettes of women's figures to men all over the world, you find them to express a preference for a 2:3 waist-to-hip ratio. A more critical observer notes that a 2:3 waist-to-hip ratio is the glamorized figure of Hollywood starlets ("36-24-36"), and wonders whether that broad male preference is a facet of human nature or simply a reflection of the universal exposure of men to the movies. To test that hypothesis, anthropologists working with a short, stocky group of people known as the Matsigenka, living high in the Peruvian Andes, asked them the same questions about their preferences in women's figures. And they found, contrary to the uncritical assertions about human nature, that the Matsigenka men preferred women shaped just like their women are shaped—and not like Marilyn Monroe! A similar study among the tall, thin Hadza in East Africa found a similar result.

Thus it seems that this "universal preference" is merely an expression of cultural globalization, not of human evolution—for the people least exposed to Hollywood tastes have preferences least like the glamorized Hollywood ideal.

There is a crucial cautionary tale underlying this research, however. Much of the generalization about presumptive human nature comes from human samples that are Western, Educated, Industrialized, Rich, and Democratic (or WEIRD) and not at all representative of the diversity of the human experience. These kinds of critical experiments are becoming more and more difficult to perform, as the economic and social forces enmeshed in American popular culture reach even the most remote peoples on earth. When everyone has been exposed to the same cultural information and values, it will be impossible to tell those broad uniformities that are the result of being human from those regularities that are the result of living in a homogeneous society!

All of which is not to say there is no such thing as human nature, of course. If we had the genes of a dog, we would go "woof woof" and run on all fours. Our own genes compel us to learn to walk on two legs and say "blah blah blah anthropology." And that is the root of something very real, a biologically rooted human nature. The problem is epistemological—figuring out what we can reliably infer about this human nature.

THE MOST FUNDAMENTAL HUMAN ADAPTATION: BIPEDALISM

In the early twentieth century, it was unclear which of the major skeletal differences between humans and apes—bipedalism, reduction of the canine teeth, and expansion of the brain—came first. Some versions of the evolutionary story had all three proceeding at approximately the same rate; others had the brain leading the way, with a remote ancestor that was an ape who became smarter, and whose descendants then came to walk erect and reduce their canines. We now think that the very first of the three traits under discussion to arise in the ape lineage was bipedalism—in other words, there existed a distant ancestor with the teeth of an ape, and the brain of an ape, but walking upright like a person.

It was once thought that bipedalism arose very gradually and incrementally, with a long series of descendants standing more and more erect. It is more likely, however, that the intermediate postures are unstable, so bipedalism is essentially a binary switch. We see living chimpanzees walking upright while carrying things, for example. Presumably, then, the shift to habitual bipedalism began as a behavioral option, which was then facilitated by the spread of mutations that affected the growth and modeling of bone under new sets of stresses caused by the adoption of the new posture and locomotor habits. The result involved widespread changes throughout the body that serve to diagnose the bones of a terrestrial bipedal ape from an arboreal, quadrumanual ape. These changes are principally associated with the feet, legs, and pelvis now bearing the full weight of the body.

Let us consider these differences from the bottom up. Where an ape foot has grasping toes and very flexible ankles—essentially two more hands—a human foot is redesigned not so much for grasping, but for bearing weight. The ankle or tarsal bones themselves are large, and the ligaments binding them are strong, forming a rigid "arch." The metatarsal bones are straight and stout; the end of one of them is expanded into a "ball;" the hallux or big toe is aligned with the rest of the toes; and its distal phalanx is enlarged. An ape walking upright does so with its knees pointing outward; a human does so with its knees facing forward. Consequently, the inner part of the knee is larger in humans, bearing the body's weight to a much greater extent; and the entire joint is rotated inward, orienting the hip, knee, and ankle in the same direction. If we look at the shin bone, or tibia, we find that it is considerably longer in a human (reflecting the human body proportions, which evolved a few million years after the acquisition of the bipedal habit). Moreover, since this bone connects the knee and ankle, although its shape is very similar to the ape's homolog, the ends of the bone are slightly differently oriented with respect to one another. This twisting or "torsion" of the tibia helps to distinguish a bipedal creature on the basis of the relative orientations of the ankle and knee. Likewise, the medial or inner portion of the upper knee joint, the distal end of the femur or thighbone, is enlarged to help support the body's weight. And the relationship between the knee and the hip is altered by the inward orientation of the knee. The hip socket (or acetabulum) is larger and deeper, and the head of the femur, which fits into it, is larger and rounder as well. The neck of the femur is also thicker in the human. The pelvis itself assumes a bowl shape, with the blade of the ilium becoming more short and broad. The spinal column has an extra curve in the lumbar (lower) region, which serves to keep an already arched backbone balanced vertically. This reorients the human sacrum, just above the coccyx or tailbone, which now lies in front of the hip socket rather than behind it. The rib cage is now positioned fully in front of the vertebral column, rather than dangling down at all from it. The rib cage assumes a more barrel-like form, rather than the conical shape it takes in apes.

Moreover, since the human head sits atop the spinal column, rather than suspended somewhat in front of it, we find smaller spinous processes on the human cervical vertebrae, for the attachment of smaller nuchal muscles. And the foramen magnum (Latin for "big hole"), where the spinal cord enters the skull, is located more centrally, as are the occipital condyles, which balance the head on the first cervical vertebra, or atlas. Finally, we can compare the front limbs. The ape's are longer, especially the forearms. The human hand has a longer thumb and relatively shorter other fingers, which are thinner and straighter than those of the ape. Of course, where apes support themselves on the ground with their fingers flexed, the human hand is not a weight-bearing part of the body, and itself has been refashioned for increased dexterity.

Why Be Bipedal?

One of the most vexing questions in the study of human evolution is what prompted the assumption of an upright posture and a striding gait. Given that our whole skeleton had to be remodeled to accommodate the habit, and that it appears in the fossil record before the other recognizable distinctions of our lineage, it is clearly fundamental to human existence and to understanding human origins.

So why is it there? After all, it is not a terribly efficient way of getting around. Being bipedal seems to have meant that now our ancestors could be outrun by pretty much any animals they encountered.

Decades ago, some biologists explained the origin of bipedalism as "having freed up the hands for tool-use." The problem is that bipedalism precedes recognizable tool use by up to four million years, so it is hard to imagine how the trait could have hung around for so long before finally becoming useful. Obviously, since evolution has no foresight, the trait would have had to be helpful immediately to remain; if it made its bearers less efficient at moving about, it would presumably be eliminated by natural selection, unless the costs associated with the trait were outweighed by some other hidden benefit.

What might that benefit have been? Possibly it was the ability to carry things in one's arms over fairly lengthy distances. Alternatively, it might have been just a good way to get from one food source to another in an environment in which forests were receding and were becoming separated by increasingly large tracts of flat plains or savannas.

Perhaps the oddest suggestion is that bipedalism arose as an adaptation initially for wading or swimming, rather than for walking and running. This "aquatic ape hypothesis" posits the buoyant properties of water as a transformative force on the gene pool, reorienting the center of gravity, and obliging our ancestors to be more vertical (to keep their heads up and avoid drowning) than their land-lubbing ape cousins. This theory also purports to account for other seemingly disparate facts: the subcutaneous fat layer of humans (analogous to blubber?); our lack of body hair; and the ease with which humans take to the water, in contrast to apes. But this union of seemingly random facts is also the theory's weakness. Why would an aquatic life lead us to develop a layer of blubber like many aquatic mammals, but *not* lead our nostrils to migrate upward, like so many aquatic mammals? Why would we lose our body hair like many marine mammals, yet *retain* hair in the smelliest parts of the body—in an aqueous environment where olfactory cues would be useless?

And finally, why would we have gained so many sweat glands in our skin, making it our major mode of heat dissipation—unlike our panting, hairy ancestors? After all, what use is evaporative sweating in the water?

The aquatic ape hypothesis, in pulling together diverse facts and arbitrarily ignoring other related ones, actually raises more questions than it resolves. Consequently, it is not a particularly well-regarded idea, because there is not much that scientists can do with it. This highlights once again the crucial difference between ontology and epistemology (Chapter 2) in understanding science. While the aquatic ape hypothesis may have elements of truth, there is little in the way of data that can be collected in order to prove it likely. After all, does finding fossil ancestors near marine paleo environments (and in the 1980s, a dolphin's rib from an East African site called Sahabi was transiently mistaken for an ancestral ape's clavicle!) mean that they were adapting aquatically, or simply that they needed a reliable source of water to survive? Any feature that can plausibly be linked to a watery origin will be invoked by its advocates, and any feature that can't be linked to such an origin, but *ought to be,* will be conveniently ignored. It is simply an interesting story.

Ultimately, we are faced with being able to describe the anatomical changes associated with habitual bipedalism far more readily than we can explain them. In other words, the more reliable scientific inference concerns *what* happened and *how* it happened, but not *why* it happened.

Even so, another controversial area involves the immediate substrate on which the bipedal habit was founded. How was the immediate bipedal ancestor getting around? On its forelimbs and knuckles, like present-day gorillas and chimpanzees—a very specialized way of locomoting in its own right? Or rather more like an orangutan, perhaps a more generalized ape—who is on the ground only very rarely, and then shambles about, bearing its weight on the fists rather than specifically on the knuckles?

What is clear is that diverging from the apes by becoming bipedal—for whatever reason—had long-term consequences. One consequence is that our own ancestors are far more plentiful in the fossil record than their contemporary ape cousins. This is most easily explained by a movement from forested environments to drier, warmer ones, which favor the preservation of fossils. The other consequence is that indeed it permitted our ancestors to explore the possibilities in exploiting the environment technologically, through the more persistent use of tools that living chimpanzees use sporadically now—and presumably that our distant pre-bipedal ancestors used sporadically as well.

THE SECOND FUNDAMENTAL HUMAN ADAPTATION: THE TEETH

When you compare the teeth of a human and an ape, you are struck principally by one feature: the size of the canine teeth. Not only are the canines larger in the ape's mouth, but they produce other structural consequences as well. The ape's canines must interlock for the jaws to close, which means there must be a space (diastema) in which the upper teeth can sit when the jaws are shut. Further, the ape's first lower premolar itself is shaped very differently from its human homolog. A human first lower premolar has two cusps of about equal size; hence, your dentist refers to it as a "bicuspid." By contrast, the same tooth in an ape has cusps of very unequal size (a sectorial premolar), and the upper canine sharpens itself against the larger one. Further, the large canine teeth come at the corners of an ape's mouth, followed by chewing teeth positioned in nearly parallel rows. Having much smaller canines, the human tooth row is far less squared off, and generally forms a simple semicircle. Because the ape's large canines interlock, it is harder for an ape to chew in a side-to-side motion; consequently, the pattern of wear on an ape's teeth is quite different from that found on human teeth. And finally, although the occlusal (chewing) surfaces of the molar teeth are quite similar between a human and ape, the cross-sectional thickness of the enamel varies quite considerably. Humans have thick enamel, chimpanzees and gorillas have thin enamel, and orangutans have enamel of medium thickness.

Why Reduce the Canines?

Not only do the apes have stout, projecting canine teeth, but those teeth are sexually dimorphic as well. Males may have canine teeth twice the size of a female's, which tends to coincide with a sexual dimorphism in body mass as well. A male ape is bigger, and also has bigger canine teeth, than a female ape. The reduction in canine tooth size and its lack of sexual dimorphism seems to have arisen between 4 and 5 million years ago in the human family, only shortly after the emergence of bipedalism.

But why should males and females be so different in their canine teeth at all? The explanation seems to lie in the auxiliary theory of Charles Darwin's called "sexual selection." Where natural selection invoked competition for survival and reproduction as an engine to generate adaptive differences between populations, sexual selection invokes a different kind of competition—for access to mates—as an engine to generate differences between males and females, or sexual dimorphism. Here, through some combination of male display and female choice, the males with the more prominent apparatus—from a peacock's tail to a gorilla's canines—are favored by a bias in reproductive opportunities; and as a result, subsequent generations tend to exaggerate such dimorphic appearances.

Among the apes, the gibbons are unique in having little obvious competition for mates among the males—as they live in pair-bonded groups—and males and females have long, slender canines of the same size and have about the same body mass. Humans, however, emerged from a larger-bodied stock, allied to the orangutans, gorillas, and chimpanzees, in each of whom the males are larger and have large, stout canines.

Most likely, then, the reduction of human sexual dimorphism in canine tooth size is related to a reduction in the kind of competition for access to mates that characterizes other great apes. What social changes might have resulted in such a lessening of competition? Perhaps the multifaceted and universal cultural institution of marriage, which generally binds the families of a male and female together in a long-term commitment, was one such social change. Another might be the fashion in which such competition was displayed—while physical features and prowess characterizes the bulk of male-male competition in the apes, the ancestors of humans came to play out such competition in less biological, and more symbolic, ways. By inventing such things as prestige, status, wealth, manners, charm, flattery, a good family, and love, human ancestors broadened the attributes that would influence a female's choice of mates. The net effect would have been to reduce the selection for physical attributes on which so much of primate sexual dimorphism is based.

Indeed, while human males remain at least some 25% larger than females on the average (a figure often exaggerated by cultural values that glamorize beefy he-men and waifish fashion models), we are also sexually dimorphic for other features that have no parallel in the other primates. This would include facial hair, body hair, body composition (proportions of fat and muscle), and the expansion of specific body parts, notably the breasts and penis. Presumably some other aspects of sexual selection came into play to produce these patterns of sexual dimorphism unique among the primates.

There are, of course, also things we call beauty and sexiness—but they are too locally specific, culturally determined, and temporally transient to be of evolutionary significance. Nor is there any evidence that unhandsome or unsexy people consistently reproduce any less successfully anywhere. And finally there is the possibility that canine reduction in both sexes was needed to accompany the evolution of speech, and had little or nothing to do with sexual selection at all. Unlike a gibbon's long, sexually monomorphic canine teeth, ours are very small in both sexes. It's a good thing, too, because it is very hard to speak intelligibly with long, interlocking canine teeth. And reducing the canines comes at a cost: for protection and social threat displays, as the apes use them now. Without those large canine teeth, our early bipedal ancestors would have been at least more vulnerable. Perhaps the earliest forms of speech afforded them new and powerful mechanisms of defense, and the possibility of replacing threat displays with actual threats.

THE THIRD FUNDAMENTAL HUMAN ADAPTATION: THE BRAIN

The other crucial difference lies in the size of the cranium and its contents. Whereas the brain of a human contains, on the average, about 1,500 cubic centimeters of volume, an ape would be considered well endowed with only a third of that. Most of that growth has occurred in the cerebrum, superimposing a growth of additional neocortex upon the more "primitive" parts of the brain. Indeed, even the difference in volume may underestimate just how different the brains of human and ape have become, for the human neocortex is also highly folded, or convoluted, which exposes a larger number of its cells to the surface of the organ.

In addition to growth in size or folding, certain parts of the brain are more expanded than others. Thus, the evolution of the human brain has seen a particular expansion of the parietal and temporal lobes (on the sides), relative to the frontal and occipital lobes. And further, the human brain is detectably asymmetric; but if such corresponding asymmetries exist in the brain of an ape, they are at best subtle.

Of course, the most obvious correlates of brain growth are left in the archaeological, rather than in the paleontological, record—namely, tools and the technological products of culture. As the brain increased in size, so did intelligence, and along with that came technological complexity. However, most cultural evolution in our species has only occurred in the last 10,000 years, long after the first appearance of modern people. This highlights a paradox of the relationship between the brain and the intellect: We tend to infer a relationship between brain size and intellect, as judged by the increasing complexity of cultural forms, in the early evolution of the genus *Homo*, from about 2.5 MYA (million years ago) to about 100,000 years ago. But once modern people had settled in, their cultural forms seem to have evolved independently of changes in either brain size or intelligence.

This is a principal reason why anthropologists generally disdain the inference of intellectual differences from craniometric differences among modern people: Anatomically modern humans appear in the fossil record close to 200,000 years ago, but leave no traces of being culturally modern for more than two-thirds of that span. But once those traces begin to appear, they change rapidly and progressively. Culture, as anthropologists have long noted, now evolves independently of people—it has become a "superorganism."

Why Be Big Brained?

Following the precepts of the eighteenth-century's "Enlightenment," the earliest modern scholars to speculate on the origin of the most obvious endowment of our species—our enlarged brain—saw it as an organ of rationality. If the brain was the center of rational thought, which it obviously was, then it followed that humans were the most rational species around, and the forces that made us human must have emphasized our powers of problem solving.

Two lines of evidence stood in the way of this hypothesis, however. In the first place, humans don't have the biggest brains out there. As anthropologist Matt Cartmill notes, elephants and whales have larger brains than we do, so it couldn't be just raw size that makes our brains so unique. Perhaps, as scholars sought a way to make us peerless among the world's brains, it wasn't just the size, but the size in relation to the body weight that matters. But once again, humans still don't come out on top, for small-bodied mammals (like mice) have large brains in proportion to their body weight. Obviously we are smart, and obviously we have large brains, but there doesn't seem to be a simple algorithm explaining that relationship.

The second line of evidence came with the development of the field of psychology. The brain isn't just an organ of problem solving, or rationality. After all, humans also have the most extensively *irrational* thoughts we know of. Whether it is in dreaming of a better life, praying to invisible powers, crying over fictitious events, or just basic insecurities and phobias, humans have far more *irrational* thoughts than other kinds of animals too, also a product of our large brain. And since human history shows quite well that people can be very highly motivated by those irrational thoughts, it becomes difficult to argue that they would have been less of an impetus in our evolution than the *rational* thoughts are.

And once we start confronting the other functions of the human brain beyond rationality, we realize that the brain is preoccupied with other functions. One important function is, of course, language. We don't know precisely when recognizable language emerged, but we see at best rudimentary homologs in our closest relatives, the apes. The emergence of language required the mental capabilities to store large vocabularies, and to combine them into grammatically sensible groups of words according to specific rules, to recognize appropriate sounds and statements, and distinguish them from inappropriate ones.

More than that, the very fact of opening up a new and powerful medium of communication raised a host of problems, since for every true statement that could now be communicated linguistically, there were many more false statements that could be communicated just as easily. Certainly there had to be a premium placed on the cognitive ability to distinguish truths from lies or from mere ignorance. Consider, by way of analogy, the development of the Internet—also a new and powerful means of communication. As we scan the Internet for useful information, we are faced with unwanted spam, pop-ups, viruses, and the propaganda, advertisements, and simple falsehoods that misrepresent themselves as information. Consequently, we are obliged to develop software and high degrees of discernment to protect our computers (and our minds). Quite possibly, this is technologically replicating the biological pressures that arose in response to the initial development of language itself.

A chimpanzee has to make strategic decisions about whom to be allied with in a specific situation. But it doesn't have to decide which of two or three individuals who say "Trust me, I'm your real friend" is telling the truth. Nevertheless, as soon as language evolved, its possessors would have had to do just that—which would have placed a strong premium on developing the cognitive apparatus to make sense of the volume of information and misinformation coming in.

Other prominent scenarios for the evolution of human braininess attempt to relate the growth of intelligence to the ability to manipulate others strategically in a complex network of primate social relations ("Machiavellian intelligence"); or to a feedback loop that began with the intensive exploitation of a new food source and procurement strategy—meat and tools. Obviously, these are not at all mutually exclusive.

SOCIAL AND LIFE-HISTORY NOVELTIES

Perhaps the most far-reaching uniqueness of the human condition is also exceedingly subtle, and involves a slowdown of our rate of maturation. A four-year-old chimpanzee, while not fully mature, is nevertheless able to take care of itself, and while it still hangs around its mother, it could survive without her. Its brain is as big as it is going to get. A nine-year-old chimpanzee is sexually mature, socially mature, and nearly full grown, and long-since cut off from its ape apron strings.

A human child, however, is nowhere near as mature. A four-year-old's brain is still growing, and the child is still entirely dependent on adults for its survival. A nine-year-old human is neither sexually nor socially mature, and still far from fully grown. Obviously somewhere in human evolution there has been a significant extension of the period of dependency, effected by slowing down the rate of maturity, and nearly doubling the time that young humans have to learn to communicate, to adapt to their surroundings, and to be a successful participant in a social group.

What might have caused this delay of maturation? Perhaps it was the emergence of this new way to communicate, both immensely powerful and also highly complex, and incidentally also requiring a long time to master.

Of greater significance, however, were the consequences of prolonging this childhood. A chimpanzee generally gives birth without assistance; a human generally cannot. The human infant's head is so large that it can only pass through the birth canal by rotating its body, and having the skull bones be soft and movable. Needless to say, it seems to be a far more painful experience for a human mother than for a chimpanzee mother. Moreover, the young infant—human or ape—is very dependent on its mother for everything, paramount among them being nutrition and protection.

A mother ape has stopped nursing her first offspring by the time it is four years old, and she is ready to have another. The four-year-old is still reliant, but is able to fend for itself. A human mother, however, has an exceedingly less capable four-year-old child, and if she has another, she will be saddled with not one, but with two, effectively helpless tykes. Their survival (the mother and offspring) will effectively depend on their ability to secure some kind of reliable assistance in provisioning them. This assistance can come from two principal sources.

The first source would be the young mother's own mother, or older relatives. In addition to extending the period of juvenility, humans also have extended the full life span, compared to apes. A forty-five-year-old ape is nearing the end of its life; a human at that age still has a ways to go. But the end of child-bearing years is roughly the same in both species. What that means is that a chimpanzee female is essentially giving birth to offspring until she herself dies; but a human female is facing a couple of decades of life without fertility— postmenopausal. If she is no longer having children of her own, yet is still physically competent, she is an obvious source of assistance for her own daughter's offspring. This "grandmother hypothesis" might help explain the survival of a species that has encumbered its adult females with far greater burdens than its zoological relatives must bear.

A second source of assistance would be from the adult males. An adult male chimpanzee has little interest in helping out a female with an infant; ordinarily he is little more than passively tolerant. Of course, when she becomes fertile, he knows it, and he becomes far more solicitous of her attention. A human male, on the other hand, has far less of an idea when the female is fertile, so there is no radical change in the behaviors of men and women at that time. Not only that, but with her enlarged breasts, the human female visually seems to look as if she might be lactating at any given time, and would therefore be permanently infertile. Since the male has few cues as to the female's actual reproductive state, his reproductive/evolutionary interests might best be served by bonding to particular females over a long term and thus hopefully ensuring that any offspring she bears are his.

He is bonded to another female, however, although in a significantly different way. Primate *dispersal* means that, at puberty, young males or females transfer into another social group; thus opposite-sex siblings rarely go through sexual maturity together. The especially slow growth of humans—taking nearly twice as long as chimpanzees for their wisdom teeth to erupt, for example—dramatically lengthens the time brothers and sisters spend growing up together. The development of a rule governing (prohibiting) their sexual conduct will be a broadly human adaptation to this problem, and extended to other family members as well, creating a symbolic universe of acceptable and unacceptable sexual partners that seems to be unfamiliar to apes. This emergence of rule-governed sexual behavior—an incest taboo—coevolved with the divorce of human sexuality from reproduction.

There are many ways of being non-reproductively sexual, and to exploit them is almost quintessentially human. Here, although we are talking about the primordial roots of marriage, it is a human cultural practice broadly legitimizing both sexuality and reproduction in the ritual establishment of a family. While it is most familiarly between a youthful man and woman, it can take many forms ethnographically, where legitimizing either sexuality or reproduction (or other roles, such as companionship or formalizing in-laws) may be most important.

This need on the part of early hominid mothers for greater assistance in child rearing than modern apes, has an interesting behavioral consequence, noted by Sarah Blaffer Hrdy. Human mothers are simply more tolerant of other people handling their offspring than, say, chimpanzee mothers are. No one but the mother holds a chimp baby, and any attempt to do so is greeted with a threat by the mother. But all kinds of people handle a human baby: fathers, grandparents, in-laws, doctors and nurses, nannies, doulas, wet-nurses, and even other relatives and friends. This maternal mellowness, combined with the material assistance offered by postreproductive women and possible husbands, may have ultimately permitted the success of the human species.

PHYSIOLOGICAL AND SEXUAL NOVELTIES

Some physiological oddities of the human species appear early on and persist throughout life. Our prominent eye whites, or optic sclera, seem to communicate aspects of our social or emotional states. Psychologists have recently found that dogs are better at following a human's gaze than chimpanzees are; the implication is that we have selectively bred dogs to be sensitive to the kinds of facial cues that we evolved after diverging from the apes.

Our skin, with the same density of hair follicles as the apes, but which yield only thin small wisps of hair, is also conspicuous. Within it lie copious sweat glands, which help us dissipate heat (and wouldn't be nearly as effective on a hairy body, for the hair traps moisture rather than allowing it to evaporate). Possibly the need for a new mode of heat reduction arose when the neuromusculature of the mouth and tongue began to get remodeled as language developed, and were no longer much good for panting. On the other hand, our continuously growing hair on the head also has no parallel in the apes; without some form of grooming (cutting, tying, brushing) it would obscure our vision and be a real nuisance. It would seem that our head hair would have had to coevolve with the cultural mechanisms of dealing with it.

Humans also have a suite of odd features that appear at puberty. Beginning with a dramatic increase in the rate of growth (known as the adolescent growth spurt) in the young teenager, the physical transition from juvenile to adult is marked by a series of changes that diverge markedly from the apes.

Although menstruation is known throughout the Catarrhini, the human female, as noted earlier, develops a layer of subcutaneous fat behind the nipples and on the hips and buttocks. While highly variable in humans, it marks a departure from the condition of adult female apes. In parallel, and beginning slightly later, but extending over a longer period of time, the human male develops a pendulous penis, adds muscle mass, and begins to grow a beard. The hair on the body grows, but more so in the genital and armpit regions, and more so in men than in women. Again, these are all variable traits across the species, and are commonly augmented or altered culturally because of the symbolic meaning they carry.

Symbolic meanings notwithstanding, the evolution of breasts has attracted considerable attention. The breasts of an ape female are only enlarged when she is nursing, and is thus infertile. She is also not at all interested in sex, and neither are the resident males. The nursing mother is sending a clear signal about her fertility status—not fertile!—and since the apes generally mate only when the females are fertile, the males don't take too much sexual interest in her. But suppose females had permanently enlarged breasts, whether or not they were fertile? Then the males would have far less information about the fertility status of the females. Indeed, that loss of reliable information about the fertility status of females seems to be a prominent feature of human evolution, and may be related in a straightforward fashion to the decoupling of sexuality from fertility that characterizes human sexual activity.

Of course there is also continuity with the other primates in some ways. The fact that maturation is accompanied by physical growth, even if not in an obvious spurt, and by conspicuous changes in vocalizations and complexion, are also characteristic of the chimpanzee.

WHAT DOES IT TAKE TO MAKE A SCENARIO OF HUMAN EVOLUTION VALUABLE?

Obviously there is much we do not yet understand in the history of the human species and its divergence from the ape ancestor. And just as obviously there are many possible explanations, or scenarios, for the emergence of these human features.

And yet, although they are all unverifiable, they are not all equal. We use several rules of thumb for deciding which kinds of scenarios to favor. For example, we give little credence to a scenario that has extraterrestrials coming in and doing genetic modifications on apes. Why not? First of all, there is no compelling evidence of such a visitation; and second, the fossil record shows the gradual emergence of human skeletal features over the last several million years, which is not what you would expect from a genetic intervention.

Another rule of thumb is that any explanation must be consistent with the known biology of the apes and humans. The "naked ape" theory, popularized in the 1960s, had front-to-front sex as the great causal agent in human ancestry (it was, after all, the sixties!), but bonobos and orangutans have front-to-front sex, and humans are, frankly, more diverse in the spectrum of their sexual activities than the theory gave them credit for.

Another general rule of thumb is that single grand theories are unlikely to account for as much as they purport. Human history is too complex and too long, and there are too many divergent lineages to be explicable under a single grand umbrella. We have already dismissed the aquatic ape hypothesis as an overarching explanation for human evolution, although it is certainly conceivable that some part of it is true.

Similarly, some scholars have promoted the idea that we are "just" apes whose development has been generally retarded, so that we are for all intents and purposes like very young apes. Again, there may be a grain of truth in the recognition that ape infants have small vertical faces and relatively large, rounded skulls; however, detailed studies of the anatomy of humans and apes shows that for every trait in which humans look like baby apes, there is another for which we look like geriatric apes. In other words, like the "aquatic ape" scenario, this theory picks the data that seem to support it, and conveniently ignores the data that don't. The truth in this theory is that it probably has gotten to the core of a mechanism by which anatomical evolution has occurred in our lineage—by changes in the relative rates of growth of different body parts—but still doesn't tell us the reason that the relationship between the body parts needed changing.

CULTURAL EVOLUTION

Certainly the most zoologically unique aspect of the human species is the fact that we have expanded all over the earth, adapted to its harshest climates, and still show no signs of declining. In other words, our adaptation works remarkably well. Indeed, the only species that could be considered comparably successful are those that adapt by following us around, such as dogs, rats, cockroaches, and the HIV virus.

But our present mode of adaptation leaves no paleontological evidence. It leaves archaeological evidence; the only thing the comparative anatomy of the primates can help to tell you about it is that humans have gone from the Stone Age to the computer age with no apparent change in anatomy. Therefore, anatomy, it seems, is largely irrelevant to the study of cultural evolution. It is obviously relevant to the study of cultural *origins*, for this seems to be predicated on achieving a certain brain size and conformation, and the manual dexterity to match. But once it arose, culture seemed to take off in an evolutionary mode all its own, unrelated to the anatomy or to the body that produced it; when we track the evolution of culture, we are studying artifacts, not body parts.

Culture could consequently be regarded as having an existence outside the body (an "extrasomatic" existence), evolving by its own means, at its own pace, and in forms and directions not predictable from biological data. It marks the transformation of ape ecology into human economy, and creates an environment of its own to which the human species and the human body itself must ultimately adapt.

Indeed, one of the most remarkable aspects of cultural evolution is that it returns in both obvious and subtle ways to affect the body itself. In the first place, we find that culture commonly compels us to do things to our body as a means of identifying ourselves in a social universe; as a member of a class, religion, nation; or even just as an individual—things like makeup, haircuts, shaving, and even dressing. Beyond that, there are more invasive products of culture inscribed in our bodies, like dental work, cosmetic surgery, circumcision, tattooing, scarification, foot binding, and head binding.

Moreover, there are subtle ways in which culture affects us biologically: urban life and high population density make infectious diseases more of a threat; an agriculturally based society generally has women spend much of their lives in reproduction and caretaking; while an industrialized society commonly has women menstruating five to ten times more often during the course of their lives than their grandmothers did. A modernized economy has men and women maturing earlier and getting fatter, therefore making obesity, hypertension, and heart disease far more common causes of death.

Since culture inscribes itself throughout our bodies, we are all to some extent, as the cultural theorist Donna Haraway observes, cyborgs. A *cyborg* or "cybernetic organism" is a hybrid—a partly synthetic, partly natural creature. And although we may think of it principally in terms of artificial limbs or bionic strength, that is actually only the far end of the range. It is continuous with wearing red ochre on your body to symbolize your status, or displaying pierced shells or animal teeth around your neck, or braiding your hair, as humans seem to have been doing for tens of thousands of years. And no other species does.

We thus observe that the most paradoxically natural aspect of the human condition is that it resists being identified as "natural," for anything we can see or measure about the body has been coproduced by, and exists in, a context of culture, itself in turn a product of human evolution and human history.

REFERENCES AND FURTHER READING

Barnard, A. 2016. *Language in Prehistory*. New York: Cambridge University Press.

Cartmill, M. 1990. Human uniqueness and theoretical content in paleoanthropology. *International Journal of Primatology* 11:173–192.

Chapais, B. 2008. *Primeval Kinship*. Cambridge, MA: Harvard University Press.

Crompton, R. H., and M. Günther. 2004. Humans and other bipeds: The evolution of bipedality. *Journal of Anatomy* 204:317–330.

Fortes, M. 1983. *Rules and the Emergence of Society*. Occasional Paper #39: Royal Anthropological Institute of Great Britain and Ireland.

Fuentes, A., and A. Visala, eds. 2017. *Verbs, Bones, and Brains: Interdisciplinary Perspectives on Human Nature*. Notre Dame, IN: University of Notre Dame Press.

Haraway, D. 1991. *Simians, Cyborgs, and Women: The Reinvention of Nature*. New York: Routledge.

Hare, B., M. Brown, C. Williamson, and M. Tomasello. 2002. The domestication of social cognition in dogs. *Science* 298:1634.

Hawkes, K., J. F. O'Connell, N. Blurton Jones, H. Alvarez, and E. L. Charnov. 1998. Grandmothering, menopause, and the evolution of human life histories. *Proceedings of the National Academy of Sciences, U S A* 95:1336–1339.

Hill, K., M. Barton, and A. M. Hurtado. 2009. The emergence of human uniqueness: Characters underlying behavioral modernity. *Evolutionary Anthropology* 18:187–200.

Hrdy, S. B. 1981. *The Woman That Never Evolved*. Cambridge, MA: Harvard University Press.

Hrdy, S. B. 2009. *Mothers and Others*. Cambridge, MA: Harvard University Press.

Krogman, W. 1951. The scars of human evolution. *Scientific American* 185 (6):54–57.

Lancaster, J. L. 1991. A feminist and evolutionary biologist looks at women. *Yearbook of Physical Anthropology* 34:1–11.

Lieberman, D. 2013. *The Story of the Human Body: Evolution, Health, and Disease*. New York: Vintage.

Lovejoy, C. O. 1981. The origin of man. *Science* 211:341–350.

Malik, K. 2002. *Man, Beast and Zombie: What Science Can and Cannot Tell Us about Human Nature*. New Brunswick, NJ: Rutgers University Press.

Marks, J. 2015. *Tales of the ex-Apes: How We Think about Human Evolution*. Berkeley, CA: University of California Press.

Morgan, E. 1972. *The Descent of Woman*. New York: Stein and Day.

Morris, D. 1967. *The Naked Ape*. New York: McGraw-Hill.

Richmond, B. G., D. R. Begun, and D. S. Strait. 2001. Origin of human bipedalism: The knuckle-walking hypothesis revisited. *Yearbook of Physical Anthropology* 44:70–105.

Schultz, A. H. 1949. Ontogenetic specializations of man. *Archiv der Julius Klaus-Stiftung* 24:197–216.

Thierry, B. 2005. Hair grows to be cut. *Evolutionary Anthropology* 14:5.

Thorpe, S., R. Holder, and R. Crompton. 2007. Origin of human bipedalism as an adaptation for locomotion on flexible branches. *Science* 316:1328.

Ungar, P. S. 2014. *Teeth: A Very Short Introduction*. New York: Oxford University Press.

de Waal, F. B. M., ed. 2001. *Tree of Origin: What Primate Behavior Can Tell Us about Human Social Evolution*. Cambridge, MA: Harvard University Press.

Wells, R., and J. McFadden, eds. 2006. *Human Nature: Fact and Fiction*. London: Continuum.

White, T. D. 2009. Ladders, bushes, punctuations, and clades: Hominid paleobiology in the late twentieth century. In *The Paleobiological Revolution: Essays on the Growth of Modern Paleontology*, ed. D. Sepkoski and M. Ruse, 122–148. Chicago, IL: University of Chicago Press.

Yu, D. W., and G. H. Shepard. 1998. Is beauty in the eye of the beholder? *Nature* 326:391–392.

CHAPTER 10

If History Is Humanities, and Evolution Is Science, What Is Paleoanthropology? (On the Assumptions of a Diachronic Science)

THEME

Paleontology has to rely more on the serendipitous field discovery than on the controlled laboratory experiment. Moreover, not being able to control scientific variables, the interpretations placed on paleoanthropological data are often more creative and less mutually exclusive than those in experimental sciences. Nevertheless, the principal elements of the story of our origins lie in the fossil record, which comes with its own set of epistemological and cultural issues.

SCIENTIFIC INFERENCES ACROSS TIME

There are two ways we can study natural phenomena scientifically: looking at the relationships among things at the same time (a synchronic study) and tracking the same entity at different times, or through time (a diachronic study). Synchronic studies offer the advantage of lending themselves to controlled experiments; while diachronic studies offer the advantage of yielding direct information on things that may take place on a different timescale than the duration of the average experiment, or the average career in science.

The two kinds of studies are complementary, for it is widely observed that "the present is the key to the past"—in other words, scientific inferences based on phenomena that are observable and manipulable (such as the muscles involved in movement and how they relate to the form of different parts of the body) are what permit us to understand things that happened long ago (such as inferring bipedalism from the form of the australopithecine pelvis).

One question for which synchronic data are especially valuable is in allowing us to gauge how physically different two populations of primates are, when we would call them different species, based on the classic interbreeding criterion. Since no fossils can interbreed with one another, it follows that the only way we can decide how different two fossils have to be before we can call them different species is by consulting those kinds of data in living species.

And why should we bother to worry about it? Because that is the crucial issue in understanding the fossil record. *How do we interpret the anatomical variation we encounter?*

Given that no two fossils, or animals, are ever exactly alike, how do we make sense of the differences that we see? The answer to that question will affect every other question we ask about the fossil record: questions such as the major patterns of evolution, and the demography and life history of the species we identify. To understand our fossils fully, then, we need to know details of anatomy to understand what part we have, how it fits into other parts, and what that says about that animal's behavior and lifestyle. In addition, however, we need to know how those parts differ from person to person and the patterns of variation that we see in living populations. These are the kinds of features that assist paleoanthropologists in understanding the nature of the material they are analyzing, and of course, they also help forensic anthropologists identify individuals from their bony remains.

SKELETAL BIOLOGY

Sexual Dimorphism

To a crude first approximation, adult humans in any group come in two sizes, large and small. That is to say, there are males and there are females, and the males tend to be larger than the females. While there is certainly overlap, if you have a small adult body part, and you assign it to a female, you have much better than a 50:50 chance of being right.

Along with greater body size comes greater musculature to move the larger body parts. In general, a larger muscle will leave a larger mark where it attaches to the bone, so a male bone will be thicker and larger and have larger ridges and grooves than the corresponding part of a female. We call the former condition "robust" and the latter "gracile," although these are obviously relative terms—one male skull can obviously be more robust than another male skull. One neck muscle, called sternocleidomastoid, attaches to a bump of porous bone behind the ear. This bump, the mastoid process, is generally noticeably larger in men than in women, and gives a very effective way of quickly identifying the sex of a human skull. Other features of the skull that are useful in this way are the slope of the forehead (women generally more vertical), brows (generally more pronounced in males), the margin of the eye orbit (more blunt in males), the angle of the jaw (more square in males), and the region in the back of skull where the nuchal muscles attach (more rugged in males). Any one of these traits, taken alone, could well mislead; but taken together, one can make a strong case for the sex of a particular skull.

Sex can be determined even more reliably from the pelvis, since the female pelvis has adapted secondarily to having a large-headed infant take a one-way trip through it.

Ontogeny

When born, a human being not only has thin, small bones, but most of them have tips of cartilage. The process of ossification—replacing pliable cartilage with hard bone—goes on throughout childhood. The degree of ossification helps to tell how old the person who once surrounded the bone was. Likewise, the sutures between the bones of the skull fuse and ultimately become obliterated during the course of a person's life—and while it doesn't mean anything while alive, it can help an anthropologist tell how old the person was when they died.

Certainly the best indicator of age is the teeth. Like most other mammals, we have two sets of them, and they erupt in very regular patterns. The baby teeth, or deciduous dentition, consists of four sets of five teeth—the same five teeth in the upper, lower, left, and right parts of the mouth—for a total of twenty. These are composed of two incisors, one canine, and two molars in each jaw quadrant.

Around age five or six, these teeth begin to be replaced by a set of eight teeth per quadrant, a process that continues until about age eighteen, when the last molars, or "wisdom teeth" erupt. Once again, there is a high degree of regularity in the pattern of eruption, so that a knowledgeable anthropologist can tell the age of a human being under the age of about twenty very reliably from the teeth alone. After all of the teeth are in, however, it becomes more difficult, for now the teeth just wear down—and it is consequently much more difficult to assess the age of a fully adult skull with the same degree of precision.

Geographic Variation

In addition to the obvious features of skin color and hair form that vary across populations around the world, there are also features of the skull that can help to identify the geographic or "racial" origin of a skull. Thus, some populations tend to have wide, flat faces—such as the peoples of northern Asia; others tend to have the jaws situated slightly forward relative to the face (alveolar prognathism)—such as the indigenous peoples of Australia; and still others to have a prominent bridge of the nose—such as the peoples of northern Europe. The significance of these features is unknown, and of course there is considerable overlap; but once again, they give us a bit of information.

Like any knowledge, a little bit of this can be dangerous. The fact is that these geographic cranial variations are subtle, and many are responsive to the conditions of life and are not fixed by the genes. Thus, when a 9,500-year-old skeleton called "Kennewick Man" turned up in Washington State in 1996, and appeared to have some characteristics associated with the skulls of northern Europeans, it was used as a fulcrum to unbalance the law that mandates Native Americans having control of the skeletons of their ancestors (Chapter 14). The argument ran that the skull looked "Caucasoid" and thus could not have been the ancestor of Native Americans, who are "Mongoloid." They even found likeness to the captain of the Enterprise in "Star Trek: The Next Generation"—Jean-Luc Picard, a character of French ancestry played by the English actor Patrick Stewart. Kennewick Man consequently spawned some fanciful reconstructions in the popular literature of the Americas being primordially populated by prehistoric Frenchmen before the Asian ancestors of Native Americans arrived. Amid considerable controversy, the skull was restudied and found to resemble Polynesians even more than the English or French; and later its DNA looked Native American, as the skull should have. What this story really tells us is that the human skull varies from place to place and time to time, its variations are subtle, and the cranium of an ancient American can resemble modern Europeans or Polynesians in some ways (and even peoples from other parts of the world) and yet still be a close relative of modern Indians.

Paleopathology

The study of variation in the form of the body also involves the effects of trauma on the skeleton. Sometimes the trauma is in the form of long-term stress, such as nutritional imbalance; or short-term stress, like a broken bone. A healed fracture is easily recognized on a bone, and many diseases, if left to run their course, leave characteristic lesions on the skeleton: tuberculosis and syphilis, for example.

It is generally straightforward to distinguish between healed trauma, skeletal trauma incurred around the time of death (and obviously being a possible cause of death), and the breakage of bone after death (commonly due to weathering, gnawing by insects, or crunching by carnivores).

The microscopic structure of the teeth can reveal periodic episodes of famine or more general growth retardants, whereas their macroscopic structure can show aspects of how they lived (wear patterns), or what they ate (gritty versus soft foods), or technology (repair or decorative inlays), or even crude ancestry (as in the shape of the incisors, which varies somewhat around the world).

SOURCES OF MORPHOLOGICAL VARIATION

Ultimately all inferences about the fossil record begin with a knowledge of the physical structure of the body, and of the normal (and abnormal) range of variations that affect it. To try to understand the relationship between two fossils, which look slightly different from one another, we are forced to make decisions about the relative probabilities of different sources of morphological variation.

The first possibility is that the two fossils we are looking at are actually parts of two distinctly different evolving lineages, representatives of two different species. Here we infer that the two specimens in question exploited their environments in slightly different ways, or would not identify one another as members of the same reproductive community. This, of course, is based on the amount of physical difference between the two specimens, and is, to some extent, a judgment call, although based on reasonable analogies to species of living primates.

Alternatively, the difference between them may not be of taxonomic significance at all, but of differing degrees of maturity. After all, as noted in Chapter 6, growth and development does not entail merely expansion, but is accompanied by a change of form as well. If we only have a child's skull, how can we predict what an adult would look like? That was in fact the problem faced by Raymond Dart, who described the first australopithecine, the skull of a child, in 1925, from a site in South Africa called Taung (or Taungs). Given its fascinating juxtaposition of ape-like (a small brain) and human-like (small front teeth and large back teeth) traits, Dart promoted it as a "missing link." He was probably right. On the other hand, so were his critics, for they knew that young apes look more human than adult apes do, and it was over a decade before an adult specimen was discovered, showing clearly that the key features of the fossil were indeed its human-like traits.

Knowledge of the patterns of dental eruption can also yield interesting insights into the fossil record when combined with new technologies. After the Taung child had been reliably established as similar to humans in key ways, and belonging to a lineage of bipedal primates with small canine teeth and, yet, small ape-like brains, its age at death was determined to be about four or five years, based on its teeth. A CAT scan, however, revealed the unerupted adult teeth embedded within the fossil jaws. In a human, the first incisor and the first molar erupt around the same time; but in a chimpanzee, the first molar erupts up to two years before the first incisor. The CAT scan of the Taung child showed an unerupted first incisor that was considerably less developed than the unerupted first molar. This suggested that its dental eruption pattern, and schedule of maturation, was likely to be more like an ape's than a human's, in spite of the obvious human-like features it bore. As a result, we now believe the Taung child probably died closer to three years of age.

A third source of variation is sexual dimorphism. We know that the skeletons of male and female humans look slightly different from one another. Oddly, the pattern of skeletal sexual dimorphism in humans is quite different from that in apes, where the male has much larger canine teeth, muscle attachments, and over-all body size. Consequently, if you find a fossil skull, and it looks slightly different from another fossil skull, might they just be male and female of the same species?

Consider the case of *Aegyptopithecus zeuxis*, a catarrhine dating from the Oligocene of Egypt, about 30 million years ago. As with the vertebrate fossil record generally, most of what is found has been teeth, and the molar teeth are diagnostic of this fossil animal. The molars are found attached to a diverse array of cranial remains, but most significantly, they are attached to either small canines or large canines. That tends to suggest that we are seeing sexual dimorphism here, along the lines of what we see in living catarrhines generally.

On the other hand, the robust and gracile australopithecines of South Africa (Chapter 11) were considered by some to reflect sexual dimorphism, with one larger, more muscular form and a smaller, more delicate form. But this idea did not catch on, for the presumptive males and presumptive females lived in different places and at different times. More importantly, the larger ones considered to be the males actually had smaller canines than the ones considered to be the females. They would have been the only catarrhine primates known to show such a pattern, so the inference was probably false. They are more likely two evolutionary lineages.

Another source of variation is temporal. We know that a single lineage changes through time, sometimes genetically, sometimes not. The introduction of farming, and a heavy reliance on prepared food, affected the growth of the jaws and structure of the face in a similar fashion all over the world. Likewise, economic development and modernization seem to lead to people getting larger and maturing earlier all over the world. Consequently, Japanese of the present day look as "Japanese" as their ancestors 100 years ago, they but are not physically identical to those ancestors—they are (among other things) taller and heavier.

Once again, finding two skulls to be slightly different in appearance may merely indicate that they are representatives of the same lineage at different times.

A fifth source of variation is geographic. A broadly distributed species, such as rats or people, often contains populations adapted to local conditions and more or less isolated from populations of the same species that live far away. What then do we make of two fossils, similar but slightly different in form, but from thousands of miles apart?

An example here is *Homo erectus,* known from Tanzania, China, and Java. The form from Java was originally called *Pithecanthropus erectus;* the one from China, *Sinanthropus pekinensis;* and the one from Africa (OH-9), *Homo erectus.* Are there three genera? Probably not—just a single species whose populations looked slightly different, as the present-day people of Tanzania, China, and Indonesia do.

A sixth source of variation is simply the normal range that exists among any population of organisms, especially people. Any group has taller and shorter, or thinner and fatter representatives. All the parts of the body vary to some extent from one person to the next. Might the two fossils be different simply by virtue of falling within a range of variation on the part of a single species?

Seventh, there is also an abnormal range of variation. Some of it is genetic— such as achondroplastic dwarfism. Some of it is the result of trauma or disease. How do you know whether the two fossils differ because they are different species, or whether you have just discovered the skeletal remains of the Pleistocene equivalent of John Merrick, The Elephant Man?

The answer is that such genetic conditions are quite rare; and consequently, the chance of finding an individual so afflicted in the fossil record would have to be quite low. Of course we can't rule it out entirely. Thus, when the nineteenth-century racist biologist Ernst Haeckel proclaimed that the fossil discoveries of "Neanderthal Man" and "Java Man" were evidence not just for the human past (Chapter 3), but for the inevitable future dominance of the Nordic militarized state as well, it placed his academic rival Rudolf Virchow in the difficult position of having to deny *both* the fossil's significance and the political agenda. He ended up suggesting that they were some sort of pathologically afflicted people from historic times, which carried a surprising amount of clout, since he had pretty much invented the modern medical field of pathology.

We do encounter the afflictions of aging, such as arthritis and decaying teeth, throughout the later evolution of our family. In another famous misinterpretation, the French paleontologist Marcellin Boule correctly reconstructed a famous fossil skeleton from the French site of La Chapelle aux Saints as standing somewhat stooped; and this caught on as a reconstruction of Neandertal posture, in spite of the fact that the fossil skeleton from La Chapelle was that of an old man with arthritis, and not representative of all Neandertals!

And finally, over the millions of years a fossil lays in the ground, lots of things can happen to it. It can be eroded, crushed, and otherwise distorted or deformed by the geological processes acting on it. A crushed skull gives an anatomist some degree of freedom in reconstructing the animal—it has been likened to attempting a three-dimensional jigsaw puzzle with most of the parts missing. Sometimes the deformations are more subtle, and sometimes the knowledge that a specimen is distorted does not accompany the circulation of its photographs. We can call these sources of variation "post-depositional," and they will include everything from being trampled by buffalo shortly after dying, through the endurance of the massive forces of the earth's crust, to the ways in which the parts are assembled.

One recent example involves a 7-million-year-old fossil known as *Sahelanthropus tchadensis*—the most widely publicized photo made it look like it had a brow ridge very similar to later hominids; others made it look like the fossil had had a stroke, showing considerable facial asymmetry and distortion. It will require a bit of reconstruction before we know what it really looked like.

Another notable example involved a famous fossil discovered in 1972 by Bernard Ngeneo, a member of Richard Leakey's expedition on the eastern side of Lake Turkana in Kenya. It came to be known as ER-1470 (after "east Rudolf," the former name of the lake), and attracted considerable attention for the claim that it was in some sense anomalous: too modern, too early. Reconstructed from over 100 small bits of fossil by Alan Walker and Meave Leakey, the skull was initially photographed with the face pushed in, reinforcing its modern look; but more recent pictures of it show the face pushed out, and looking more primitive. Initially the point of contact between the facial parts and the cranial parts was not clear, so a case could be made for the vertical face—although making it look like the other known hominids of the time was always the safe conservative choice. Moreover, the specimen is no longer anomalously early, but its brain is still on the high side for its time.

LUMPING AND SPLITTING

Our survey of the sources of variation in the fossil record is associated with two poles of taxonomic practice. The first would be represented by those scholars who tend to maximize the taxonomic diversity, interpreting the variation between the fossils as being indicative of different species. We can call them "splitters" (Chapter 7) because they tend to split the fossils into possibly too many distinct taxa. The other pole would be represented by those scholars who tend to maximize the amount of variation attributable to those other sources. We call them "lumpers" because they tend to lump the fossils into possibly too few distinct taxa.

Most primate groups have gone through faddish cycles of lumping and splitting. As we noted in Chapter 7, the primates are currently undergoing a cycle of splitting, encouraged by the needs of conservation. Perhaps the most celebrated examples of lumping involved compressing what we now see as 20–30 ape genera of the Miocene into simply *Dryopithecus;* and Donald Johanson and Tim White in 1974 studying the assemblages from different hominid fossil sites in East Africa around 3 million years of age, and calling them all *Australopithecus afarensis.*

The human lineage is currently going through a cycle of splitting, but for reasons peculiar to it. We can understand it by considering the "moral economy"—the professional assets and liabilities—of splitting in paleoanthropology. What does a scholar stand to gain or lose one way or the other? By calling a new fossil the "first X," you get headlines, grants, and promotions; by calling a new fossil "the twelfth Y," you get to continue to labor in obscurity. By acknowledging someone else's fossil as the "first W," you get their good will, which is always nice to have if you want to examine their fossils. And furthermore, splitting creates enough taxonomic "space" for all the major players to have the found the first *something.*

While this problem is faced to some extent in paleontology generally, it is magnified in paleoanthropology. The reason is that paleoanthropology deals with our ancestors and relatives, and one of the oldest anthropological discoveries is that nobody looks at their ancestors and relatives with objectivity and dispassion. What they do—and what we do—is tell stories about who they are and where they came from. Ancestors are always somewhat sacred.

Our scientific stories are unusual, in that we formulate them with the goal of maximum accuracy, and according to a series of guidelines for achieving that goal. Nevertheless, our narratives have considerable leeway, while still being constrained by data points. Extinct people, for example, can be made to look less apelike with eyewhites and head hair and clothing, none of which fossilize and thus are a "perhaps" for any given part of our lineage. Simply calling us "apes" as a shorthand for "our ancestors were apes" has far more rhetorical than scientific value, since we are not our ancestors; and to say that we *are* our ancestors is a strongly bio-political statement. Likewise, a "splitter" narrative contains themes of competition, diversity, and extinction; while a "lumper" narrative is one of universalism, continuity, and survival. With so much flexibility in the narrative emerging simply from the number of species we sort the fossil material into, this is where "human paleontology" transforms into "palaeolithic archaeology" and becomes a more self-consciously humanistic endeavor. The stories are no longer about the history of life generally, but about your particular history and identity, which have resonance far beyond the boundaries of science. The ideological aspects of archaeology, for example in the service of nationalism, are well known.

Another scientific practice favoring splitting is cladistics (Chapter 6)—which is based on the idea that sharing a derived trait is indicative of recent common ancestry. Unfortunately, however, cladistics doesn't work below the species level, where a derived trait can be transmitted from group to group by gene flow, rather than by common descent. Further, cladistics requires that parallel evolution be rare in relation to divergent evolution, so that a shared derived trait most likely reflects the intimacy of common ancestry, rather than the coincidence of similar environmental pressures or similar mutations. But similar characteristics often do crop up in parallel in divergent populations: blond hair among indigenous Swedes and Australians; relatively small jaws and teeth in many peoples; short stature; copious male body hair; or a prominent bridge of the nose. If these fossil assemblages reflect one or a few species, then the methodology of cladistics may simply not be applicable to them, for whatever traits they share may not be the result of recent common ancestry. But, elevating fossils to the species level makes the methodology of cladistics appear more appropriate, and can make the whole enterprise look more rigorous and objective than it actually may be. Rather than the metaphor of diverging tree branches, which underlies cladistics, a more appropriate metaphor for human prehistory might be a mesh, or river delta, or railroad trellis, or capillary system.

The recent discovery of fossils from a site in Georgia called Dmanisi has suggested that the current splitting cycle may be ending, for at the same time (1.5 million years ago) and place (eastern Europe) there apparently lived early humans with an unexpectedly wide range of cranial variation.

FOSSILIZATION

There are three things a primate must do to become a bit of data for paleoanthropology: (1) die, (2) fossilize, and (3) be found.

The first is easy, rather too easy for most modern primates.

The second, however, is quite tricky, for it is generally opposed by the elements: Not the elements of the modern periodic table, but the old elements—earth, air, water, and fire. A dead animal on the African savanna does not last very long—between the hyenas, vultures, and insects, there might be no trace remaining of the animal in a matter of days. So we need to imagine an animal dying, but not being entirely devoured. Even if not wholly devoured, though, exposure to the sun, wind, and water may be enough to disintegrate the remains. So we need the dead animal to elude the scavengers, and be buried quickly, out of harm's way. But it had better choose soil that is not too acidic or alkaline, for otherwise the natural chemistry of the ground will cause it ultimately to dissolve.

Moreover, the ground must be mineralized, for the process of becoming a fossil is not so much preservation as it is transformation. Unlike insects in amber, which retain their physical integrity by being insulated from everything external, the process of fossilization involves the substitution of the atoms of the ground for the atoms of the animal. Little by little the organic (that is, carbon-based) cells and protein matrix that comprise bone (and very rarely, the soft organs too) become their own inorganic replicas. The fossil, then, is not the animal itself, but a rock in the perfect form of the animal.

This, of course, takes many tens of thousands of years.

For dead animals a few thousand years old, the process of fossilization is incomplete, and sometimes DNA can be extracted, as has been carried out on 2000-year-old extinct lemurs from Madagascar and 40,000-year-old Neandertals.

The speed of the process of fossilization depends on the conditions of preservation, and the fossilization of bone might occur at a very different rate than the degradation of cellular DNA.

Finally, the fossil must be found. That's the hard one.

Obviously paleontologists can't dig a big hole half a mile deep to find fossils of the desired age, but must rely on geological processes to expose the ancient ground, either vertically or horizontally. Then they must make sure that there are fossils contained within this exposure. And once paleontologists have an exposure of the right age, and know that it has fossils, they must scour the ground to see what is weathering out—they can't very well bulldoze the whole region. Hopefully the fossils will include some primates—if that is what they're looking for—and not, say, example after example of antelope molars.

But once found, the fossils are rendered meaningful by the paleoanthropologist. That meaning is going to lie in the areas of taxonomy (what species they represent); phylogeny (where they fit in the evolutionary story); and broader patterns of adaptation, speciation, and extinction. The geological context and anatomical features are only part of the picture: the spatial relationships in which the bones lie, the ecology, and (after about 3 million years ago) the artifacts associated with the fossils, are all sources of important information in understanding human evolution fully. Thus, paleontology needs to be informed not only by anatomy and geology, but also by archaeology, paleoecology, and taphonomy (the study of what happens to a fossil between the time it dies and is found).

OTHER CONSIDERATIONS

One other problem that needs to be considered is that the hot, dry climate that is best for fossilization is generally not a great place to live; and discovering things in the ground is most efficiently accomplished where there aren't too many people around. Consequently, the discovery of fossils most commonly takes place in areas that are remote, sparsely populated, forbidding, and often downright dangerous. The badlands of Montana yield fossils of early primates, about 45 million years ago; the deserts of Chad yielded an early ape known as *Sahelanthopus,* from 7 million years ago; another known as *Ardipithecus* came out of the deserts of Ethiopia. And not only are these places hard to get to, and hard to work in, but there commonly are hurdles involved in getting the appropriate authorizations to conduct research and protecting your group from robbers, paramilitary forces, local warlords, corrupt administrators, and political insurgents.

Even so, there are also global political issues to be considered. In many regions of the world, paleoanthropology has been a handmaid of colonialism. After all, most of the fossils of early hominids are from Africa, and most of the people studying them are white; it doesn't take a rocket scientist to figure that one out. (Actually, perhaps, it takes a *social* scientist.)

In some countries, the government now insists that the original fossils remain in the country and that the scientist agrees to train students from that country.

The fossils themselves, as early ancestors, become national relics—symbolizing the autochthonous roots of the nation and its importance in the global history of our species.

One interesting example of the significance of these fossils in constructing a national identity and origin myth is South Africa, where the first australopithecines, and some of the most important fossils generally, came to light. But when the National Party took over power in 1948 and built up the racist policies they called apartheid, they were faced with some possible embarrassments. First of all, they were allied with the Dutch Reformed Church, and were committed to a literal, creationist reading of the Bible. And second, they were actively dehumanizing the indigenous peoples of the area, whose rights to the land might be symbolically legitimized by having the human species rooted there. No exhibits on human evolution were permitted in their museums, and paleoanthropology itself was largely hidden from view as well. But when the government changed in 1994, so did both of those factors; being a "cradle of our species" was now celebrated; and the indigenous peoples now could take pride in having "their ancestors" be admired by scientists the world over. Nelson Mandela, the new president, addressed a paleoanthropological convention in 1996, and the paleoanthropologist Robert Broom had a stamp issued in his honor. More recent fossil discoveries have made the paleoanthropologist Lee Berger a national celebrity.

A more infamous example involved the discovery of "Peking Man" by a Canadian anatomist named Davidson Black, teaching in China in the 1920s. After Black's death, the research in China was supervised by Franz Weidenreich, himself an expatriate from the Nazi regime. By the late 1930s, the caves at Zhoukoudian had yielded the fossils of about 40 individuals, now known as *Homo erectus* and seen as ancestors by the Chinese. When the Japanese threatened to invade Manchuria, they also made it clear that they intended to destroy those very Chinese ancestors and leave their victims rootless. What was the concerned paleoanthropologist to do?

Weidenreich decided that the best course of action was to send the fossils to a safe haven. Fine, detailed casts of the specimens had already been made and sent to museums around the world. Now Weidenreich's Chinese colleagues painstakingly wrapped and crated the original fossils and prepared to send them off to the safest place in the area, the American naval base in Hawaii, transported by a detachment of US Marines on the *S.S. President Harrison*.

Badly timed, as it turned out. The fossils were to leave China on December 8, 1941 (December 7 on the other side of the International Date Line), for the American naval base, which was called "Pearl Harbor." But the Japanese attacked the American Pacific fleet that day, the Marines were captured, and the ship they were supposed to be on was sunk. To this day we don't know whether the fossils were actually on the ship when it sank, or whether they are hidden away in the care of some obscure anonymous collector. The actual fossils haven't been seen since then.

The Chinese blame the Americans for their loss; the Americans blame the Japanese.

A third example of the role that global and national politics can play involves research at a site called the Tugen Hills, in Kenya. For over two decades, through dramatic political changes in the country, Andrew Hill of Yale had conducted paleoanthropological research there, getting the appropriate permits through his government contacts, and painstakingly mapping the geology of the region, but finding no significant fossils. Then a French team led by Martin Pickford and Brigitte Senut got permits to work in the same region, from different government contacts, and shortly thereafter discovered *Orrorin tugenensis,* which may well be the earliest known biped, at 6 million years of age. Quickly, news of a turf war broke out in the pages of the leading science journals, as Hill's American group quite reasonably accused the French group of encroachment—of not respecting the general ethical protocols of the field, which try to discourage rival groups from excavating in the same area (it's a big world, after all!). Pickford and Senut responded, also quite reasonably, that it was just sour grapes. And to some outsiders, it looked very odd that two groups of white researchers would be arguing vehemently over who had preferred rights to a tract of land in Africa. This helps remind us of the intimate historical relations between paleoanthropology and colonialism.

And finally, all academic fields have their stories of uncollegial behavior. Mark Twain reputedly once said that the reason academic disputes are so vicious is that the stakes are so small. But the story of Jon Kalb may represent the nadir of unscrupulousness. Kalb was a geologist working in Ethiopia, and part of the research team that found the fossil called "Lucy" in the early 1970s. But when it became clear that the area indeed held important fossils, the group fragmented into a French team and two American teams, one from Berkeley and one from New York University and Southern Methodist University, headed by Kalb. Soon Kalb found his permits being revoked, his grants being rejected, and his life in jeopardy. He later learned that his rivals had spread the rumor that he was a CIA agent, and everything else had cascaded from that act.

The point is that research does not take place externally to a matrix of culture, especially in the exercise of political power. And for a field that trades in people's conceptions of who they are and where they came from, their identity and descent, the competition and pressure will be very great, and the cultural influences will likely be very great, too.

RIGHTS AND RESPONSIBILITIES IN PALEOANTHROPOLOGY

One notable outgrowth of the rigors involved in field paleoanthropology is that it demands a specific set of aptitudes, and it is not uncommon that the person who finds the fossils (or for whom the actual finder works) may not be the most qualified to interpret it. The best interpreter of the fossils may be the one who spends more time in museum basements comparing specimens, or working on the cutting edge of experimental anatomy and physiology.

While fieldworkers are accorded the respect that comes with discovery, and the first rights of publication and interpretation, it is often the *re*interpretation of the specimen that makes more sense of it. After the fanfare that greets the discovery of "the earliest X" dies down, scholars with different training and specialization can determine whether it is indeed earlier than all the other X's, or whether it is indeed an X at all and what its differences from Y's may mean.

But that means that sometimes the finder's initial interpretation needs to be revised, which may be a little embarrassing. Some museum paleoanthropologists have recently begun publicly airing their frustration over the reluctance of some field paleontologists to allow their colleagues to see and examine their specimens in a timely fashion. On the one hand, all parties agree that credit for discovery and "first dibs" on publication is a recognition of the fieldworker's risky business.

But with those rights, are there any responsibilities incurred? Does the fieldworker have an obligation to publish the material in a timely fashion, and allow colleagues to see and photograph the new specimen? If so, how does that responsibility get enforced?

Some researchers found themselves denied permission to examine the original specimens of *Ardipithecus,* stored in Ethiopia. Further, they voiced their complaint about the discovery of a full skeleton of *Ardipithecus,* found in 1995, but eventually published only in 2009 by Tim White's group from Berkeley. While those charges are not those of misconduct, nor of the breach of any formal ethical standards, they do raise the issue of the adequacy of the old informal code of rights and obligations that worked well enough back when paleoanthropology was a small and gentlemanly pursuit. Public disputes over the control and care of fossils from Liang Bua, Indonesia (called *"Homo floresiensis"* or The Hobbit) also broke out. And of course, the flip side of the community's impatience with the publication of *Ardipithecus* is that the laboratory work involved in extracting, preserving, and rebuilding the delicate and valuable fossils is very costly and time consuming, if you want to get it right. On the other hand, the specimens of *Homo naledi* in South Africa were discovered in 2013 and admirably published within two years; but even more importantly, the scholars used the technology of the internet to disseminate their papers and fossil casts rapidly and broadly to interested colleagues.

KINDS OF EVIDENCE

Paleoanthropology straddles traditional disciplinary boundaries by demanding expertise both in the hard sciences of anatomy and geology and in the soft sciences of inferring behavior and social relations from a distribution of artifacts. The primary research conducted by paleoanthropologists reflects this breadth. In addition to excavating for fossils and recognizing the anatomical features they encounter, scholars interested in paleoanthropology must use other diverse data and methods.

Superposition and Association

Two "laws" govern the interpretation of diachronic materials. First, more geologically recent materials are generally found physically on top of older materials. This relationship is known as superposition, and holds except in the cases of odd geological formations and the human propensity for burying the dead. Digging a grave and placing a body at its bottom means that the body is now somewhat younger than the material six feet above it. But this has been going on for tens of thousands of years, and necessitates careful examination of the site.

And second, two artifacts (biological or cultural) found in the same geological layer or stratum are about the same age. This relationship is known as association, and generally holds except for the human intervention noted above.

With these two "laws" internalized, we can begin to make sense of the fossil record, at least in one place—by applying the logic of superposition and association and establishing the relative dates of fossils and artifacts, from oldest (lowest) to youngest (highest). The strata and associated remains from any specific era can then be studied for paleoecological information. Palynology (the study of fossil pollen) can tell you what kinds of plants were present; and the kinds of plants can tell you about the local environment. Associated fauna, especially of diverse and widespread mammals like pigs and rodents, can permit the correlation of one site with another.

These correlations are crucial for understanding the relationships and the relative ages of fossils. For example, in the 1930s, a British archaeologist named Dorothy Garrod excavated a site in modern-day Israel called Mt. Carmel. In one cave were the remains of Neandertals, in another cave were the remains of humans. The stratigraphy, or natural layering of the earth, was complex, and Garrod took the fossils to be the same age. This shaped our views of Neandertals for half a century—the apparent side-by-side coexistence of humans and Neandertals. It wasn't until the 1980s that subsequent archaeologists came to realize that the stratigraphy indicated that the bones in one of the caves were 30,000 years older than those in the other!

One important implication of the concept of association is the ability to make inferences about the ecological setting of our fossil ancestors by analyzing the remains of the things they lived with. In another famous example, Richard Leakey's fossil ER-1470 (see above) was thought initially to be 2.6 million years old, which would make it considerably older than other similar fossils. But the pig fossils from the site correlated perfectly with pigs from other sites that were only 1.8 million years old. Arguments about the age of the fossil raged for about a decade; but we now realize that the pigs were right, and the fossil hominid is no longer considered so anomalous.

Dating

Superposition and association help us to understand the relative ages of fossils—that is, which came first—but still doesn't help us to tell just when the species lived. For this, we need other kinds of techniques that became available in the latter half of the twentieth century. Prior to that time, fossils were grouped according to their geological eras, and the origins of the human lineage were thought to lie anywhere from 500,000 years ago to 20 million years ago.

The development of radiocarbon dating changed all that. If you know the rate of decay (5,370 years for half of ^{14}C to break down), the proportion of ^{14}C the animal started with, and you can measure the amount of ^{14}C the specimen has, you can estimate how long it has been dead. When coupled with good conditions of preservation and careful selection of the material for dating (seashells are not good because they absorb inorganic carbon and thus appear artificially ancient, while charcoal from the art on a cave wall is very good because it is was living vegetable matter until the cave painter burnt it and ground it for pigment), radiocarbon dating quickly became the foundation for our understanding of the spread of anatomically modern peoples in Europe, and stimulated the development of other absolute dating methods that can reach back in time farther than the 50,000 or so years of radiocarbon's utility.

DOING THE BEST WE CAN WITH LOST DATA

Certainly the most significant aspect of paleoanthropology is what is lost and not directly recoverable, but can only be deduced and inferred (but not, of course, merely "guessed at"). We have already noted one such problem: that of determining what the species are, and assembling the fossil materials into their fundamental ecological and evolutionary units. Since we cannot apply the interbreeding criterion to fossils (the criterion itself is not foolproof, but certainly is a handy guide to discerning the species), we can only match up degrees of anatomical variation among living species with those of a fossil assemblage, and decide whether the fossil assemblage represents two spectra of variation, or only one.

This is a crucial epistemological issue—for our inferences about macroevolutionary diversity, rates of change, and broader trends in evolution are going to be predicated on our knowledge of what the species are. This is not to say that we are flying completely blind—but simply that the species we identify right now may only approximate the species identifiable in the fossil record. Species that may strikingly differ principally by their pelage (hair) and chromosomes, like modern vervet monkeys and gibbons, may not be discernible as multiple species in the fossil record. Or conversely, species that are highly physically diverse but nevertheless comprise a single gene pool, like domestic dogs, may not be discernible as a single species in the fossil record.

On balance, however, we use our knowledge of modern species to inform our inferences of ancient ones, and hope that whatever mistakes we make will balance each other out, or ultimately be corrected by new discoveries.

The second directly unrecoverable item is physiology. Although rarely the "soft parts" like the brain or other organs can be fossilized, we are usually at the mercy of biological inferences from the skeletal system alone. To the extent that muscles are attached to the bones and commonly leave marks on them in proportion to their size, we can make rigorous inferences about the muscular system as well.

But what of the neurological system? Or the digestive system? Or the respiratory system? Here we are forced to mine the primate body for any kinds of relationships that might obtain between the form of the skeleton and relevant aspects of the missing parts of the body. Sometimes the relationships are quite good, such as the between the skull and the brain inside it. In a well-preserved fossil it is possible to make an endocast of the inside of the skull and see the size and shape of the lobes of the brain and the meningeal arteries on either side of it. More often, however, the relationships are obscure, and the proposed anatomical correlations simply don't hold up. It was recently suggested, for example, that we might get a skeletal handle on whether a fossil was capable of speech by virtue of the size of the groove in the skull base through which the hypoglossal nerve passes. It was soon appreciated, though, that the relationships are just too complex to draw a solid conclusion from that skeletal datum.

The third directly unrecoverable item is behavior. Not only does an animal stop behaving when it dies, but it hardly if ever freezes while in the middle of doing something. We may have preserved the conditions of its death, but that doesn't automatically tell us about the conditions of its life. Once again, our knowledge of behavior is limited to what we can infer from the bones. Some anatomists, for example, maintain that there is nothing anatomical about the hand bones of *Paranthropus* that would preclude it being a toolmaker over a million years ago, like our own genus, *Homo*. This of course does not necessarily mean that it was a toolmaker, but simply that, to the extent that the neuromuscular control necessary for the activity leaves its imprint on the skeleton, the imprint appears to be indistinguishable between them and us.

Inferences such as that can help us at least to place boundaries around our scenarios of the lives of extinct species, by helping to establish what they were more or less likely to have been capable of doing. In most other cases—such as social behavior or sexual behavior—our inferences are doomed to be very crude, leaving the space for imagination vast and open.

The fourth directly unrecoverable information is the full range of species diversity in the past. Given the difficulties of becoming a fossil and being found, it should not be surprising that our knowledge of extinct species is a small and biased sample—biased toward species that have preservable parts (like oysters and unlike jellyfish), toward species that happened to live in conditions favorable to preservation, and toward species that we find interesting and worth looking for. This problem—the spottiness of the fossil record itself—accounts for the instability of the phylogenetic hypotheses we put forward.

Consider two similar fossil species, *A1* and *B1*, which lived at different times. You infer that they are genealogically related because they look alike, and that the earlier one (*A1*) is likely to have been an ancestor of the later one (*B1*). But was the species *A1* itself the ancestor of species *B1*, or was species *A1* simply one member of a group of species of the genus *A*, another member of which was the ancestor of the founder species of the genus *B*?

Once again, this situation poses an epistemological problem. Given the difficulty of entering the fossil record, and then of being found, we believe that only a tiny sample of the species that have ever lived have actually been discovered. So it is probably very unlikely that any particular known species directly evolved into any particular other known species, without having diverged into several intervening species as yet unknown. So if we know of two species, which stand in a close physical relationship, and which make a plausible ancestor–descendant sequence, on the one hand, we cannot simply pretend that they represent six species; and yet we also cannot pretend that it is likely that one directly evolved into the other.

What we do, then, is adopt a shorthand in which we draw the two known species in a sequence, but we interpret it loosely as "this species, or one closely related to it, evolved into this other species." Ultimately, that statement lies at the limit of our knowledge, given the difficulty in knowing about species we have not found, which is unfortunately most of them.

The last unrecoverable item, however, is both the most vexing and the most exciting loss of information: phylogeny. The relationship among ancestors and descendants is never directly observed in the fossil record, it is always inferred. You never see the fossilized remains of a mother of one species giving birth to an infant of another species. Rather, you see a fossil assemblage representing a species at one point in time, and another fossil assemblage exhibiting slightly different anatomical features at a later time; and you decide whether or not to draw a connecting line between them.

If your line connects them directly, then you are inferring that the older is the ancestor and the younger is the descendant—a parent–offspring relationship; if your line connects them indirectly, then you are inferring that they are more distant relatives of a common ancestor—more like cousins. You could also choose not to connect them at all—the position of "creationism"—but that would raise more problems in interpreting the data scientifically than it would solve. Where did the later species come from? Why does it look so much like the earlier species? Is that resemblance just a coincidence? And if all of geology is wrong, and the earth is only 6,000 years old, then why bother to study geological data at all, if all it does is lie?

MAKING SENSE OF HUMAN ANCESTRY

Once the morphologies of the relevant fossils have been studied, and their remains assembled into species, the most basic units of macroevolutionary analysis, what do we do with the species? We generally envision a three-step process in understanding our biological history.

The first step involves grouping them according to the distribution of synapomorphies (Chapter 6), the derived traits or evolutionary novelties that come passively along with descent from a recent common ancestor. Species that share many such features will be one another's close relatives; and the resulting diagram depicting the distribution of shared derived traits is called a cladogram.

One important feature of a cladogram is that it has no time dimension. It is a chart of the relationships of species in terms of their shared evolutionary novelties. In Figure 10.1, we see several species that lived at different times: humans (*Homo*), an extinct primate called *Proconsul,* the so-called sabre-toothed tiger (*Smilodon*), *Tyrannosaurus rex,* a bald eagle (*Haliaetus*), and *Archaeopteryx.*

The derived features of the first two would include the hands and eyes that allow us to identify them as primates; the next is joined by virtue of skeletal features of the jaw and middle ear that identify it as a mammal. On the other side, the eagle and Archaeopteryx are united by possessing feathers; and the two of them join up with *T. rex* as Ornithischia, by virtue of their cranial and pelvic structure.

Notice that we can construct this figure without reference to the fact that we have vastly different ages represented. The cladogram is thus a chart of relatedness, not of ancestry. There is no information provided on whether humans are likely to be the descendants of *Proconsul, Proconsul* is likely to be the descendant of humans, or both are descended from something else.

Once we add the dimension of time, in the second step, we are able to eliminate at least one of the alternatives. Since *Proconsul* lived 17 million years ago, and humans have only been around for the last 200,000 years, it is hard to see how *Proconsul* could be our descendants. On the other hand, *we* could be *its* direct descendants, or we might both be descended from another undiscovered species.

Adding the temporal dimension allows us to produce a chart with additional inferences, a phylogenetic tree or phylogeny. (See Figure 10.2.) Here we link together the species in a genealogical arrangement, incorporating the relationships established in the cladogram, but adding additional data about time and inferences about descent.

Thus, if *Proconsul* itself wasn't our ancestor, then nevertheless something rather like it, as part of an early ape radiation 15 million years ago, was. The sabre-toothed tiger (order Carnivora) diverged from the two representatives of the Order Primates perhaps 60 million years ago, shortly after *T. rex* went extinct. And *Archaeopteryx,* being a 150-million-year-old feathered reptile, was certainly in or close to the ancestry of the living birds.

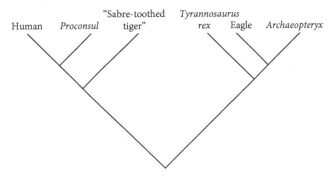

Figure 10.1. Relationships of six taxa.

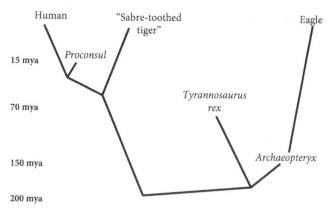

Figure 10.2. Temporal and inferred genealogical relationships of the same six taxa.

The third and final step involves fleshing out the phylogeny with adaptive scenarios about the key features, divergences, and lifestyles of the animals. We can see the left side of the tree reflecting the arboreal adaptations of the primates, with humans becoming secondarily adapted to the ground. The other mammals, the sabre-toothed tigers, became specialized for ground predation, somewhat convergently with the extinct reptile *T. rex*. And the animals on the far right side of the chart developed feathers rather than scales, and took to the air.

This will be the same strategy we use to understand the human fossil record itself: decide on the taxa, map the relationships based on shared derived features, add time, and flesh out the scenario.

CLASSIFYING THE LIVING APES
AND FOSSIL ANCESTORS

As we already noted, classification is a linguistic device that facilitates communication among scientists, as well as being a framework that imposes meaningful order on species in nature. The classification we are adopting in this book is a traditional one, emphasizing the adaptive divergence of humans—bipedal and reliant on technology and language—from the other living members of their clade. Consequently, for the reasons discussed in Chapter 7, we classify humans, our closest relatives, and the living apes as shown in Table 10.1.

This classification is fairly simple (partly because we are omitting all the extinct ape genera here), and allows us to recognize two extinct genera within the family Hominidae, or hominids: *Australopithecus* and *Paranthropus*. Here *Australopithecus* is an ancestral or stem group that gave rise to *Homo* and to *Paranthropus,* and is itself paraphyletic (Chapter 6). Using this scheme, we will talk about our extinct ancestors and close relatives as hominids, that is, as other members of the family Hominidae.

Table 10.1. Traditional classification, in which the extinct genera of bipeds are called "hominids."

SUPERFAMILY	FAMILY	GENUS
Hominoidea	Hylobatidae	*Hylobates*
	Pongidae	*Pongo*
		Pan
		Gorilla
	Hominidae	*Australopithecus*
		Paranthropus
		Homo

Table 10.2. A cladistic classification, in which the extinct bipeds are "hominins" (see Table 7.1).

SUPERFAMILY	FAMILY	SUBFAMILY	TRIBE	GENUS
Hominoidea	Hylobatidae			*Hylobates*
	Hominidae	Ponginae		*Pongo*
		Homininae	Gorillini	*Gorilla*
			Panini	*Pan*
			Hominini	*Australopithecus*
				Paranthropus
				Homo

It is important to note, however, that there are other ways of classifying these species, which emphasize other elements. One way that we presented in Chapter 7, and currently enjoying a vogue among some paleoanthropologists and textbooks, highlights two different principles: the genetic similarity of humans and living apes, and the desire to purge classification of paraphyly. (See Table 10.2.)

Here, all the living apes are placed in the family Hominidae, to reflect their genetic similarity. The subfamily Ponginae is used to separate the Asian orangutan from the three closely related African genera—chimpanzees, gorillas, and humans—which are now clustered together as a subfamily. Then a new level is introduced, the tribe, to distinguish the three groups of African genera from one another. Thus, humans and our extinct relatives are now discussed as members of the tribe Hominini, that is, as hominins.

The difficulty with this classification is that it is more cumbersome, with the introduction of a new level; it is inconsistent in defining the paraphyletic Pongidae out of existence, but retaining the paraphyletic *Australopithecus;* and it privileges the genetic similarity of the living genera over their adaptive anatomical and ecological differences. The living hominoid that stands out is the first to have diverged (the orangutan), not the strangest (the human).

And how do we make sense of the extinct branches of our family tree? Under the older system, which calls this group of species "hominids," we have some taxonomic space in which to theorize the relationships among these extinct species.

We could, for example, juxtapose bipedal small-brained species against bipedal big-brained species—as encoded in the classic "australopithecine" versus "hominine." Under the new system, we are already near the bottom of the taxonomic hierarchy, so pretty much the only thing we can do with the "hominins" is to list their genera and species. And as we will see in Chapter 11, the proliferation of species names can make those lists very imposing.

More important, though, is the assumption that a classification should privilege the genetic relationships over all others. Just because a biochemist can't tell a human from a chimpanzee, it doesn't mean that nobody can—you can tell them apart quite easily, for example, by looking at their feet instead of at their genes. The purpose of a classification is to summarize the overall relationships of the animals, and the traditional way seems to do a better job of it, given the conflicting demands and consequent compromises, than the newer alternatives. Consequently, although most textbooks today give the "hominin" classification, the group that published and promoted *Ardipithecus* as a human ancestor in 2009 very conspicuously called it a "hominid." If you believe that (1) the ecological divergence of the human is zoologically more significant than the temporal divergence of the orangutan; and (2) the genetic similarity between human and ape is outweighed by their behavioral, anatomical, and ecological differences, then you should call it a "hominid" too. I do.

REFERENCES AND FURTHER READING

Abu el-Haj, N. 2001. *Facts on the Ground*. Chicago: University of Chicago Press.
Ackermann, R. R., A. Mackay, and M. L. Arnold. 2016. The hybrid origin of "modern" humans. *Evolutionary Biology* 43 (1):1–11.
Berger, L. R., and J. Hawks. 2016. *Almost Human: The Astonishing Tale of Homo naledi and the Discovery That Changed Our Human Story*. Washington, DC: National Geographic.
Butler, D. 2001. The battle of Tugen Hills. *Nature* 410:508–509.
Cartmill, M. 2002. Paleoanthropology: Science or mythological charter? *Journal of Anthropological Research* 58:183–201.
Clark, G. A., and C. Willermet, eds. 1997. *Conceptual Issues in Human Origins Research*. New York: Walter de Gruyter.
Dalton, R. 2004. Anthropologists rocked by fossil access row. *Nature* 428:881.
Delisle, R. 2007. *Debating Humankind's Place in Nature, 1860–2000: The Nature of Paleoanthropology*. Upper Saddle River, NJ: Prentice Hall.
Eldredge, N., and I. Tattersall. 1982. *The Myths of Human Evolution*. New York: Columbia University Press.
Falk, D. 2011. *The Fossil Chronicles: How Two Controversial Discoveries Changed Our View of Human Evolution*. Berkeley, CA: University of California Press.
Foley, R. 2001. In the shadow of the modern synthesis? Alternative perspectives on the last fifty years of paleoanthropology. *Evolutionary Anthropology* 10:5–14.
Fuentes, A. 2017. *The Creative Spark: How Imagination Made Humans Exceptional*. New York: E. P. Dutton.
Gibbons, A. 2003. Africans begin to make their mark in human-origins research. *Science* 301:1178–1179.

Gottschall, J. 2012. *The Storytelling Animal: How Stories Make Us Human*. Boston: Houghton Mifflin Harcourt.

Henke, W., and I. Tattersall, eds. 2015. *Handbook of Paleoanthropology* (online). doi: 10.1007/978-3-642-27800-6. Berlin: Springer.

Kalb, J. E. 2001. *Adventures in the Bone Trade: The Race to Discover Human Ancestors in Ethiopia's Afar Depression*. New York: Copernicus.

Kuljian, C. 2016. *Darwin's Hunch: Science, Race, and the Search for Human Origins*. Johannesburg, South Africa: Jacana.

Landau, M. 1993. *Narratives of Human Evolution*. New Haven, CT: Yale University Press.

Lordkipanidze, D., M. S. Ponce de León, A. Margvelashvili, et al. 2013. A complete skull from Dmanisi, Georgia, and the evolutionary biology of early Homo. *Science* 342:326–331.

Montagu, A. 1971. *The Elephant Man: A Study in Human Dignity*. New York: E. P. Dutton.

Morrell, V. 1995. *Ancestral Passions: The Leakey Family and the Quest for Humankind's Beginnings*. New York: Simon and Schuster.

Pilbeam, D. R. 1969. Tertiary Pongidae of East Africa: Evolutionary relationships and taxonomy. *Peabody Museum of Natural History, Yale University, Bulletin 31*.

Pyne, L. V., and S. J. Pyne. 2012. *The Last Lost World: Ice Ages, Human Origins, and the Invention of the Pleistocene*. New York: Penguin.

Schmalzer, S. 2008. *The People's Peking Man: Popular Science and Human Identity in Twentieth-Century China*. Chicago, IL: University Of Chicago Press.

Schwartz, J. H. 2003. Another perspective on hominid diversity. *Science* 301:763.

Schwartz, J., M. Collard, and C. Cela-Conde. 2001. Systematics of "humankind." *Evolutionary Anthropology* 10:1–3.

Shipman, P. 1981. *Life History of a Fossil*. Cambridge, MA: Harvard University Press.

Simpson, G. G. 1951. The species concept. *Evolution* 5:285–298.

Sommer, M. 2008. History in the gene: Negotiations between molecular and organismal anthropology. *Journal of the History of Biology* 41:473–528.

Susman, R. L. 1988. Hand of *Paranthropus robustus* from Member 1, Swartkrans: Fossil evidence for tool behavior. *Science* 240:781–784.

Tattersall, I. 1992. Species concepts and species identification in human evolution. *Journal of Human Evolution* 22:341–349.

Thomas, D. H. 2000. *Skull Wars*. New York: Basic Books.

Ward, C. 2003. The evolution of human origins. *American Anthropologist* 105:77–88.

White, T. D. 2000. A view on the science: Physical anthropology at the Millennium. *American Journal of Physical Anthropology* 113:287–292.

White, T. D. 2003. Early hominids—Diversity or distortion? *Science* 299:1994–1997.

White, T. D., B. Asfaw, Y. Beyene, et al. 2009. *Ardipithecus ramidus* and the paleobiology of early hominids. *Science* 326:64, 75–86.

Zerubavel, E. 2012. *Ancestors and Relatives*. New York: Oxford University Press.

CHAPTER 11

The Dental and the Mental
(On Making Sense of the Early
Diversification of the Human Lineage)

THEME

The proper classification of hominid fossils is presently unclear, with estimates ranging from three species to nearly twenty. The reasons are both cultural and empirical. A productive way to think about the human fossil record is at the genus level, where we can infer the emergence of three sets of adaptations: walking in the basal genus *Australopithecus,* chewing in *Paranthropus,* and thinking in *Homo.*

THE SHADOW OF PILTDOWN MAN

In 1912, the history of the human species was being uncovered in Europe. The Germans, Belgians, and French all had their ancient fossils, from sites like La-Chapelle-aux-Saints, Spy, and the Neander Valley itself, which gave its name to a curious and ancient race of people, known from their oddly shaped fossil remains and primitive tools. While the sun had not yet set on the British Empire, the British were faced with being a remote outpost of human prehistory, an ephemeral presence.

All that changed with the announcement in 1912 that the remains of a "dawn man" had been found by an amateur naturalist named Charles Dawson, at a place called Piltdown, in England. He was neither fully man nor fully ape, resembling the former in his cranium, and the latter in his jawbone. He combined a manlike brain (and even left some tools to cinch it), with apelike teeth—a cunning yet vicious adversary for any would-be attacker. Some skeptics doubted whether the jaw and the cranium actually belonged together, but the following year, more fossils were discovered, which seemed to settle the matter.

England was now a central player in the story of our species—not just politically and economically, but historically as well. The scholars most closely associated with Piltdown Man were honored, and several were knighted. And the story Piltdown Man told was that the origin of man, at least on the British Isles, was led by brains and followed by brawn.

And yet in the 1920s and 1930s, discoveries in Africa and Asia began to tell a different story: the earliest identifiable ape-men had teeth rather like a human, yet a primitive brain! These were hard to reconcile with the morphology of Piltdown Man. Either (a) the new discoveries were wrong and Piltdown Man was right, or (b) Piltdown was wrong and the others were right, or (c) perhaps evolution from the apes occurred independently on different continents. Unsurprisingly, many British scholars clung to (a) as long as they could; a few German scholars opted for (c). But ultimately, the weight of scientific evidence by 1950 suggested everyone could benefit by taking a closer and more critical look at Piltdown Man, as suggested by (b).

When they did, they found that chemically, the skull and jaw appeared to be of different ages; that the brown paint on one of the teeth to make it look like a fossil was peeling off; and that the marks left by filing down the molar teeth could clearly be seen.

To this day we don't know who pulled it off, or why, although many accusations have been leveled through the years. It might even have begun as a publicity stunt for a novel called *The Lost World,* published by the local celebrity author, Sir Arthur Conan Doyle, at the same time as the discovery of Piltdown Man—and which featured conversations about scientific fraud and a fight between people and ferocious ape-men. But regarding Piltdown Man as a whodunit misses the important point. It was successful because it played to nationalistic expectations, because the scholars became too heavily invested in the specimen to regard it skeptically, and because nobody dared to challenge the authorities. And most importantly, it sent the scholarly community thinking incorrectly about human origins for several decades.

The story of how our species arose is predicated on knowledge of (1) our differences from the apes, (2) the order in which they evolved, and (3) their plausible survival value for our ancestors. Different scholars have emphasized various aspects of our *differences* from the apes as central themes of their particular story of our biohistorical *divergence* from the apes. While this gives paleoanthropology a strong flavor of "connect the dots," it is important to appreciate that the position of the dots constrains the picture we can draw.

We now know—or at least we are pretty sure—that bipedalism and small canine teeth were the first detectably human traits to emerge in our ancestors. Why? Simply because creatures with brains like apes, teeth kind of intermediate between apes and people, and the pelvis and legs of a person were alive between 3 and 4 million years ago; and there is a lot of evidence for them. But there is no evidence for the existence of a contemporaneous creature with the brains of people, but the teeth and legs of apes. The discovery of such a creature—sounding rather like Piltdown Man!—would require us to rethink our scenarios of human evolution. But in the absence of such a discovery, the scenarios we now discuss are those in which bipedalism and canine reduction lead the way.

A HOMINID ORIGIN

The living apes are but a tiny relic of a widespread radiation of brachiating apes of the Miocene. Apparently, however, the forest was a less conducive environment to the fossilization process than the drier open savanna. Thus, the record of the latest Miocene, when one group of animals became habitually bipedal, and traveled over long tracts of ground, rather than exclusively through the trees, is very heavily biased in their direction. In fact, we have virtually no fossil record of the living apes. While a literal reading of these data might imply to a creationist that humans had evolved, but apes were specially created, we will instead regard this absence of data as an artifact of preservation.

One difficulty in trying to find the earliest evidence of bipedalism is that we don't know precisely what directly preceded bipedalism. As we observed in Chapter 7, if humans, chimpanzees, and gorillas are very closely related, and each shares an intimate bit of biological history with the other, then we can understand the fact that chimpanzees and gorillas both knuckle-walk as a unique bit of their shared ancestry, and not necessarily as a precursor of hominid bipedalism. But if, on the other hand, the radical interpretation of the genetic data is right, and humans and chimpanzees are each others' uniquely closest relatives, then knuckle-walking in chimps and gorillas is harder to make sense of. Either the trait evolved separately in both lineages, or else it was the ancestral condition out of which bipedalism arose in the hominids, and was passively retained in chimps and gorillas.

The three late Miocene candidates for early human ancestry—*Sahelanthropus*, *Orrorin*, and *Ardipithecus*—are all complex in their own ways. Originally thought to resemble the younger and better-known *Australopithecus* very closely, *Ardipithecus* was given its own genus name shortly after its original publication. The fossil genus is officially known from assorted teeth, even some deciduous, and miscellaneous postcrania, including a bit of the clavicle or collarbone, humerus, and a toe. But that was just a tantalizing morsel, since a large part of an *Ardipithecus* skeleton was published in 2009.

Two Ethiopian localities have yielded *Ardipithecus* remains about a million years apart, sufficiently similar to one another that researchers initially designated them as different subspecies, a category rarely used in paleoanthropology. Indeed, some challenge whether it should even be used in the systematics of *living* species! Consequently, a few years later, they changed the distinction to the species level. And when the skeleton was finally revealed in 2009, its most interesting features appeared to be a very apelike foot, and small, sexually monomorphic canine teeth, perhaps suggesting that social changes or even early speech preceded the emergence of obligate bipedalism—or else that there was parallel evolution in different ape lineages for the reduction of canine dimorphism.

DISCOVERY OF THE AUSTRALOPITHS

If we assume bipedalism only evolved in the African ape clade once, then we can put all bipeds in our own subclade, the hominids (or hominins). We will recognize three groups, which we will designate as genera, within them. These are the genus *Australopithecus*, the stem group of bipedal apes; the genus *Paranthropus*, one group of their descendants, who developed hypertrophic specializations of the teeth and jaws; and *Homo,* the other group of descendants, who developed hyper-trophic specializations of the brain. The genera *Australopithecus* and *Paranthropus* are generally grouped together apart from *Homo,* and called australopithecines, or commonly now, australopiths.

The australopiths first came to light in 1924, when workers for South Africa's railroad company blasted a fossil skull from the wall of a nearby limestone cave at a place called Taungs; a geologist from the University of the Witwatersrand brought it to the Johannesburg home of his anatomy colleague, Raymond Dart. Dart named his fossil *Australopithecus africanus,* or "southern ape of Africa"— thus emphasizing its apelike qualities, but promoting it as a "missing link" between people and apes. He published the fossil in the journal *Nature* in 1925, and noted that the vertical position of the brainstem indicated that it carried itself upright. More importantly, however, the rear teeth were very large, and the front teeth, in-cluding the canine teeth, were very small. This is not the pattern we find in living apes. Most of its teeth were deciduous, and only the first adult molar had erupted. However, for a human child at that stage of dental maturity, its brain was quite small, and seemed to be more like a young ape's in size. It seemed to present a brain like that of an ape joined to teeth like those of a human.

Significantly, this was the opposite suite of features that seemed to be present in Piltdown Man—which sported an apish jaw and a humanish skull. It was over a decade before more fossils like the Taung Child would be found, by a Scottish paleontologist in South Africa named Robert Broom. A devout Christian, Broom believed in the direct intervention of good and bad angels in the history of life on earth; but he did not let his faith interfere with his study of evolution. Between 1936 and 1947, Broom and his colleagues drilled in limestone caves in South Africa, and found remains of adult *Australopithecus* specimens. There appeared to be two kinds of australopithecines: one at cave sites known as Sterkfontein and Makapansgat, and another at cave sites called Swartkrans and Kromdraai.

A visit to South Africa by the American paleontologist William King Gregory began to swing scholarly opinion in favor of *Australopithecus,* although it took the British another decade before coming around. Broom published a detailed schol-arly monograph on the fossils in 1946, and the great Oxford anatomist Wilfrid E. Le Gros Clark visited South Africa to see the specimens for himself in 1947. Even the aged anatomist Sir Arthur Keith, who had helped establish his reputation on Piltdown Man, came around to accepting *Australopithecus* as a human ancestor.

By the early 1950s, the only thing standing in the way of a new clear under-standing of human evolution, centered on African prehistory, was Piltdown Man. A reanalysis now showed the brown paint peeling off the canine tooth and the marks where the teeth had been filed; and finally, a chemical analysis of the remains indicated that they were from two different organisms. Clearly Pilt-down Man had been a hoax from start to finish, and was no longer a piece of the puzzle—except as a cautionary tale about how easily even scientists can be fooled when their expectations and ideologies coincide with the data they are presented with.

Attention now shifted to Africa as the "cradle of humanity," where Louis and Mary Leakey had been searching for hominid fossils for decades at Olduvai Gorge, Tanzania. In 1959, their patience was rewarded with Mary's discovery of *"Zinj"* (short for *"Zinjanthropus boisei"*), a nearly complete skull, well dated to 1.8 million years ago, and similar in form to the australopithecines known from Swartkrans and Kromdraai in South Africa. Other discoveries soon followed, paralleling to a large extent the South African fossils. The East African fossils, however, had the advantage of not coming out of limestone blocks from cave walls, but of being, rather, embedded in softer matrix, with clear contextual relationships to other fossils found, and in datable sediments.

Other major excavations began in Kenya, Ethiopia, and other areas along the geological fault known as "The Great Rift Valley," and continue to the present day. Fossils are also being found again in South Africa, and the recovery of human ancestry is a source of national pride for the new government of South Africa. The South African material has tended to be overshadowed by the East African material because the latter are more reliably dated, correlated with one another, and often better preserved. Nevertheless, in the 1990s, an older section of the Sterkfontein cave yielded a cranium and skeleton of *Australopithecus,* probably about 3.5 million years old. Like *Ardipithecus* (unfortunately), it has been a long time in being fully described, but is nicknamed "Little Foot" and may well play a considerable role in future understandings of human evolution.

After some other South African fossils found in the 1940s, some scholars have begun to call Little Foot *"Australopithecus prometheus,"* even though it has not yet been fully described. As we noted earlier, these named species may seem like biological entities, but they are at least as much units of origin story as they are units of ecology or genetics. It is consequently probably a mistake to imagine that the species of the paleoanthropologist are, or ever could be, equivalent to the species of the zoologist. To ask whether any of these paleoanthropological species is zoologically "real," then, is probably a meaningless question, for they are not fundamentally zoological elements. These fossil names generally designate a particular fossil assemblage with minor anatomical distinctions, a chunk of the human story. As such, they are units of nature/culture, of our origin narrative; not units of nature. There were of course species back then, but we cannot tell how well the names of our ancestors map on to the zoological species of Pleistocene hominids. We will try to make more sense of human origins at the genus level.

AUSTRALOPITHECUS: BASAL BIPEDS

The Kenyan *Australopithecus anamensis* appears to have been walking upright by about 4.2 million years ago. At the Tanzanian site of Laetoli, several different kinds of animals walked through some shallow thick mud, composed of a mixture of rain and volcanic ash, about 3.8 million years ago. The mixture hardened and preserved their footprints; and they were discovered by a team led by Mary Leakey in 1978. Among the footprints were those of two hominids, a large one and a small one, walking side-by-side, whose feet left the imprints of a heel, arch, ball, and enlarged and aligned big toe—all hallmarks of bipedalism; and no evidence of forelimbs touching the ground. I tend to think that the early hominids walking through the volcanic ash had not yet fully evolved language, for if they had, they might have paid attention to the frenzied shouts of their conspecifics: "There's a volcano erupting! Run for your life!"

The bad news is that there are no *Australopithecus* fossils known from precisely that age, for *A. anamensis* is about half a million years older, and *A. afarensis* is about half a million years younger. So who made the footprints? Something rather like them. Perhaps something very much like the remains discovered by a French team in Chad—the jaws of an early australopithecine that lived about 3.5 million years ago, extending the range of the group farther north and farther west than had previously been known, and still quite early in the history of this lineage.

In the mid-1970s, a French-American team led by Yves Coppens was working in Ethiopia, when graduate student Donald Johanson found a knee joint that gave clear indications of having come from a biped. They soon found bits and pieces of several individuals, which they nicknamed "The First Family"; and finally, about 40% of the skeleton of a single individual, whom they nicknamed "Lucy."

At 3.2 million years of age, Lucy was notable for being (into the 1980s) the clearest and oldest evidence of bipedalism, and therefore, of the origin of the human lineage. Although the body parts of australopithecines were already known—for example, a foot from Olduvai Gorge, and a pelvis and vertebrae from Sterkfontein—Lucy was the earliest indicator of what the parts of a single individual looked like.

Only from the parts of a single individual can you tell body proportions, for example. Whereas a modern human has long legs relative to arms, and an ape has long arms relative to legs, how do you know where an australopithecine falls if all you have are arm bones and leg bones from individuals of various sizes? With Lucy, that situation became rapidly clarified: She had relatively long arms and short legs, like an ape.

In other ways, however, notably in the structure and orientation of her knees and pelvis, we can tell she walked upright, unlike any ape, and rather like us. Indeed, Lucy is a classic "missing link"—if by that term we mean something that partakes of both ape and human qualities. In this way, she reminds us that she is, all told, unlike any creature we are intimately familiar with.

At 3½ feet tall, Lucy is made of the smallest parts known of her species, *Australopithecus afarensis*. It is principally on this basis that we regard her as a female; given what we know of primate biology, if she were a male, there would have to be even smaller, as yet undiscovered, members of the species. But her pelvis, which would give unambiguous signals of her sex if she were fully human, gives no indication that she was female. Why not? The modern woman's pelvis is the result of a compromise between the biomechanics of bipedal walking and the logistics of passing a big-headed baby through the pelvic canal. But Lucy faced no such obstetrical dilemma, for her babies, like her, were small-headed; consequently what we just described as a structural compromise had not yet been worked out, for it was not necessary. Lucy's pelvis is that of a biped, pure and simple; our own pelves are the ones that have been otherwise compromised.

What Lucy does show clearly is that the divergence of humans from apes was not a continuous transformation of the whole body. Rather, it took place piecemeal, and the earliest species of fossil hominids possessed suites of characters that were partly ape, partly human, and partly intermediate. Thus *Australopithecus afarensis* shows a mosaic of features (so, of course, did Piltdown Man—since that is what we would expect to find!). In addition to the apelike limb proportions, Lucy had an apelike brain; but her molar teeth were large and had thick enamel, like those of humans. Her pelvis and knee were decidedly like those of humans, but her toes and fingers were long and curved like an ape's, and her ribcage was conical, neither precisely like known apes nor humans.

Among these basal australopithecines we should also include the fossil skull called "*Kenyanthropus platyops*" found near Lake Turkana in 1999 and dated to 3.5 million years. Although broken into hundreds of small bits, it is clearly the head of a small-brained biped with small front teeth and large rear teeth. The significance of its peculiarly flat face remains uncertain.

Australopithecus africanus has become something of a problem for obsessive taxonomists and creationists, each of whom has their own difficulty in coping with the morphological continuities between its ancestor, *Australopithecus afarensis*, and its descendant genera, *Paranthropus* and *Homo*. For the taxonomists, the physical intermediacy of *A. africanus* places a premium on intuition in allocating individual specimens, and makes it difficult to define the species in terms of its own unique derived traits—both of which are necessary. For creationists, the physical intermediacy of *A. africanus* seems to be another classic example of what they maintain did not and could not happen—the transformation of a species with one set of physical features into another species with another set of physical features, over a span of geological time.

Over the course of their biological history, the early bipedal australopithecines appear to have become more specialized in two different directions: dental and mental. Recent studies have shown that this evolutionary crossroads may have been established with a relatively simple genetic switch. Nevertheless, both sets of specializations enabled their bearers to exploit new sources of food, or make more efficient use of old kinds of food resources, as the climate of Africa underwent a prolonged period of cooling, and grasslands expanded at the expense of forests. Those hominids that developed dental adaptations emphasized a great expansion of the molar teeth, and the associated bones and muscles, which permitted them to grind down vegetable foods, like leaves, grasses, and seeds, that are rarely fully exploited by primates. And those that developed mental adaptations emphasized non-biological ways of broadening the Pleistocene smorgasbord—by cutting, collecting, and cooking.

Both of these adaptations were present to some extent in the basal australopithecines, who had large molars and broad cheekbones to frame their chewing muscles and also had at least the cognitive capacities of chimpanzees, who can use natural objects as tools in various ways, and even crack nuts with stones. Indeed, a species discovered and named in the late 1990s, *Australopithecus garhi,* shows elements of both of those specializations at about 2.5 million years. Its teeth lie in between the dentally specialized "robust" australopithecines and the earlier basal or "gracile" australopithecines; and it seems to have left evidence of having used stone tools on gazelle bones. The anatomically similar remains of *Australopithecus sediba* in South Africa at about 2 million ago left no direct evidence of stone tool use, but very human-looking hands.

PARANTHROPUS: THE DENTAL ADAPTATION

Robert Broom recognized by the late 1930s that there were two kinds of "ape-men" coming out of the limestone quarries in South Africa: one of these had very large cheek teeth, and had even co-opted the premolars to become essentially more molars. It had very wide cheekbones to accommodate the chewing muscles that passed through them, and even had a ridge of bone down the midline of its head for these strong, thick chewing muscles to be anchored. When Louis Leakey got a look in 1959 at the fossil his wife, Mary, had discovered—with a complete set of upper dentition—he dubbed it "Nutcracker Man."

We now follow Broom in recognizing it as occupying a fundamentally different ecological niche than our own ancestors occupied. Its brain was slightly larger than a chimpanzee's, but its principal means of acquiring the necessities of life involved rather less chewing them over, and rather more simply chewing them. There is no doubt that it was bipedal, although no associated skeletons have yet been able to tell us about its overall body proportions.

Perhaps the most interesting thing about the dental adaptations of *Paranthropus* lies in where it falls on a chimpanzee-to-human axis. Relative to chimpanzees, humans have thicker enamel on their molars, much smaller canine teeth, and smaller incisors as well, indicating a general overall emphasis on the back teeth relative to the front teeth. On such a scale, *Paranthropus* comes out as more human than humans: it has smaller canines, smaller incisors, thicker molar enamel, and a much greater emphasis on the rear teeth. This group took one aspect of the human-ape differences and ran with it, quite successfully, for about a million years.

The *Paranthropus* fossils were found limestone caves at Swartkrans and Kromdraai, and thus faced the same problems of dating and association that the *Australopithecus* fossils from Sterkfontein and Makapansgat did. It was quickly clear, however, that the collection sorted into two related, but different, groups on the basis of their teeth. *Australopithecus* had bigger back teeth than we do, but was nevertheless humbled by *Paranthropus.* At roughly the same body size as *Australopithecus, Paranthropus* had immense rear teeth, the muscles to drive them, and the jaws to hold them. *Australopithecus,* with its smaller and less muscle-bound head and face, came to be called "gracile"; and *Paranthropus* to be called "robust." These, however, are relative terms, and both of these forms are quite "robust" when compared to our own direct ancestors of the genus *Homo*. The earliest representative of this robust lineage is WT17000, more colloquially known as "the Black Skull" for the literal color of the fossil, due to the manganese in the ground. At 2.6 million years of age, it has a very prominent set of crests to anchor its chewing muscles, showing that the basic specialization was established early in the history of this lineage. Its face juts out farther than the faces of its descendants, and the base of its skull is very similar to that of the early australopithecines; but the shape of the cheeks and size and strength of the chewing machinery place it squarely in the *Paranthropus* lineage.

How did *Paranthropus* live? The dental emphasis on the grinding teeth tells us that it was probably exploiting a food source that other apes only rarely rely on: nuts and seeds. These are foods that are small and well protected, and consequently are difficult to extract efficiently. It takes a lot of work for relatively little reward; you're far better off lying back and munching on a stalk of celery, like a gorilla. The emphasis on the molars that characterized a robust australopithecine—the size, the thickness of the enamel, and the massive jaw muscles—made its mouth into a walking mortar and pestle. This certainly expanded the range of foods it could cope with, and presumably explains its million-or-so-year survival as a human cousin.

The other thing the robust australopithecine teeth tell us is that its social organization may have been quite different from those of other living apes—perhaps in a lineage stretching as far back as *Ardipithecus*. Other apes have extensive degrees of sexual dimorphism in the canine teeth, with males having much larger ones than females, baring them in threat displays, and using them in fights. It is hard to imagine how the teeth of a robust australopithecine could have been used in that way—its canines were neither very dimorphic nor intimidating, and you would have to look far too deeply into its mouth to be intimidated by its molars. The sexual dimorphism believed to be represented by comparing the presumptively female skulls (from Drimolen in South Africa, and from Kenya) to the other robust australopithecine skulls combines no canine dimorphism with a modest amount of dimorphism in body size (as reflected in face size). This is the pattern we see in modern humans when we compare them to apes.

Consequently, whatever competition for mates occurred in these hominids would have to have been of a very different order than what we see in other species of apes. In modern humans, that competition is played out symbolically and culturally—in terms of wealth, beauty, status, reputation, family, body decoration, bonds of marriage, and so on. Did *Paranthropus* make tools? A careful examination of the hand bones associated with robust australopithecine teeth shows that their degree of manual dexterity was probably no less than that of their smarter contemporaneous relatives. And certainly the discovery of butchered gazelle bones with the early australopithecine *A. garhi* lends additional support to the idea that different hominid lineages relied on tools, even with brains one-third the size of ours. But after about 1.2 million years ago, the teeth and tools of *Paranthropus* were insufficient to withstand the competition from technology-reliant cousins—or perhaps from a more distant vegetarian specialist species—and they became extinct.

EARLY *HOMO:* THE MENTAL ADAPTATION

In contrast to *Paranthropus,* another group of australopithecines developed specializations useful in food processing. These specializations were rooted in the size and structure of their brain, nearly twice as large as that of their cousins. In addition to the physical continuity that exists between *Australopithecus africanus* and the robust lineage, there is also physical continuity between *Australopithecus africanus* and the origins of the genus *Homo.* This is probably most easily seen in the taxonomic allocation of key specimens, which have occasionally leapt from the category "very gracile australopithecine" to "early representative of the genus *Homo*" or vice versa.

The earliest indications of the genus *Homo* seem to occur about 2.5 million years ago in East Africa, about the same time and place as the earliest proliferation of recognizable stone tools. While it is reasonable to associate these two facts causally, we must also be wary of the chauvinism it involves.

Stone tools may well reach back to *Australopithecus,* as suggested by a Kenyan site 3.3 million years old. The earliest recognizable stone tools are known as *Oldowan,* and consist only of small rocks on which another rock has been used to knock off a few pieces, thus forming a sharp edge. It's not much, and certainly not likely to afford much protection from a leopard, but distinctly different from naturally formed broken rocks. When the Leakeys published the *Zinjanthropus* skull in 1959, they attributed the Oldowan tools to the only hominid they knew there, the robust australopithecine. Five years later, they took the tools away from "*Zinj*" and attributed them instead to the new species *Homo habilis.*

The principal working assumptions were that (1) there was only one species making the tools, and (2) it must have been the one most like ourselves (the one with a smaller face and larger brain). The second assumption is predicated on the first, and it is not clear that the first is necessarily true, either archaeologically or anatomically. We are consequently obliged to remain open to the possibility that several different hominid species saw merit in hitting stones together to form sharp edges, augmenting their sharpened bone shafts and sticks, which are harder to identify in the fossil record, but were probably used as well.

And what did they do with these tools? Anything they could, as one uses a Swiss Army knife. While there might well have been some advantage in hunting or fighting, the greater value was probably in food procurement (such as digging for roots and tubers), and processing (such as slicing tendons to remove meat from a carcass).

From about 2.4 to 1.8 million years ago, we find the co-occurrence, then, of physically diverse bipedal primates, with larger brains than australopithecines and a reduced chewing apparatus. These we collectively call "early *Homo,*" and although they could be split into a number of different species, it is simplest to identify one broad evolutionary lineage with anatomical continuity to earlier australopiths, and call it *Homo habilis,* and another with continuity to later *Homo erectus,* and call it *Homo ergaster.* Whether these are really even two separate species comparable to two closely related living species, like *Pan troglodytes* and *Pan paniscus,* is of course open to considerable debate—which emphasizes again that the basic classification of extinct hominids is itself theory laden, for it encodes an interpretation of their diversity, ecology, and evolution.

The most famous specimen of the *Homo habilis* lineage is undoubtedly ER-1470, found in 1972 by Bernard Ngeneo, a member of Richard Leakey's expedition, working on the eastern side of Lake Turkana in Kenya. While the skull is very complete, it was nevertheless reconstructed from literally hundreds of tiny pieces, and has always been seen as morphologically rather unique, with a large brain (about 735 cc, about half the size of ours) and an odd, flat face. The following year their colleague Kamoya Kimeu found skull ER-1813, in many ways a better fossil—more anatomically representative of the lineage, and more intact, and with a brain only about 600 cc. This group of fossils also includes material from Olduvai Gorge and other East African sites, as well as material originally called "Telanthropus" from South Africa.

The most interesting feature of this lineage is undoubtedly its facial reduction and cranial increase (compared with the australopithecines), but coupled with the limb proportions of the australopithecines—long arms and short legs. This measurement requires the association of teeth for identification of the species, and enough of the leg and arm from the same body to estimate the limb proportions; but in the few specimens that permit this, they seem to place *Homo habilis* with the apes and australopiths.

Homo ergaster, however, is a different story. The 1974 discovery of ER-3733, also by Bernard Ngeneo, firmly established the idea that about 1.8 million years ago there were several lineages of hominids coexisting, which simply could not be accommodated within a single species, however broadly conceptualized. As long as the only known hominids were a very robust one (*Paranthropus boisei*) and a very gracile one (*Homo habilis*), we could still retain the idea of a single lineage existing at the time, even with a ridiculously high level of musculoskeletal sexual dimorphism and a weird pattern of canine dimorphism. Skull ER-3733, however, had a cranial capacity of about 850 cc, considerably larger than any previously known skull of that age, and a somewhat elongated shape, reminiscent of *Homo erectus* a million years later. This was identical to neither of the known forms, and therefore, unless there were three sexes of hominids in East Africa at the time, it made the case for taxonomic diversity.

The clear establishment of taxonomic diversity coexisting in the hominid lineage made it impossible to see human evolution as a linear ascent from the apes. Rather than looking like a bamboo shoot, the prehistory of the human species began to appear like a bush, with different adaptive survival strategies evolving in different related lineages. (Of course, the degree of "bushiness" varies with the amount of taxonomic splitting one is inclined to invoke; and while there are representations of Pleistocene hominid diversity as bushy as a berry farm, it is generally good in science to err on the side of conservatism.)

Another fossil skull, ER-3883, looked quite similar to ER-3733, but in 1984, Richard Leakey's field assistant Kamoya Kimeu found the first part of the big prize: from a site called Nariokotome, on the western side of Lake Turkana, a nearly complete skeleton of an adolescent male who lived and died about 1.6 million years ago. While it has never attained the cult status of Lucy or ER-1470, the skeleton known as WT-15000 is arguably the best fossil of them all.

Where Lucy stood 3½ feet tall about 3.2 million years ago, scarcely a million and a half years later the Nariokotome Boy stood about two feet taller. Although Lucy was female and Nariokotome was male, he was also not fully grown, either— he had fresh second molars, and unerupted third molars; an upper canine tooth in the process of erupting; and bone shafts not yet fused to their epiphyses, or tips— all telling us he was an adolescent, perhaps 12 years old. Fully grown, we might see the Nariokotome Boy as a strapping Pleistocene six footer.

Even more striking than his absolute size, however, are the proportions of his limbs. Whereas earlier bipeds appear to have had long arms and short legs, a retention from apehood, *Homo ergaster* has developed the long legs and short arms of a human. Obviously bipedal primates got along well on two legs for millions of years with long arms, and the distribution of their body weight making them a bit top heavy. Why the change? Perhaps this physical change involves the incorporation of running, especially over long distances, into the hominid locomotory repertoire and concomitant fine tuning of the body to facilitate it. It also suggests the possibility of not having to climb trees for safety at night, like apes do, because they now had something that could keep terrestrial predators away at night: namely, fire. We may also note that long, heavy, muscular arms are probably less beneficial for the fine-scale manipulation of natural objects that will become the hallmark of this lineage's adaptive strategy.

While each specific body part has minor features that enable us to see it wasn't from a modern human, the skeleton nevertheless looks much more familiar than Lucy's, and each part closely approximates the human form in both relative and absolute size and form. Indeed, the Nariokotome Boy's head is probably his most distinctively different part, with a face jutting forward, no forehead to speak of, a ridge of bone looking like eyebrows, and a brain just over half the size of a modern human's (in a nearly full-sized body, of course).

The forward setting of the jaws, or prognathism, provides the most striking contrast to the modern face. The browridge, or supraorbital torus, is a consequence of the relations between the size of the face and the forehead. We see these features in diverse forms throughout human ancestry, and even variably in modern people (although these are structural convergences, not throwbacks!).

Perhaps the most notable aspect of the postcranial skeleton is the fact that, while being the size of a modern human, he was not enervated like one. The spinal cord passing through his vertebral column was somewhat narrower than a modern human's, and it has been suggested that his motor skills were comparably poorly developed. Indeed, perhaps something as basically human as the ability to coordinate breathing with speaking might have been compromised in a species whose central nervous system was literally smaller than a human's at the same body size.

A less complete skeleton, ER-1808, also found by Kamoya Kimeu, has skeletal lesions consistent with a form of food poisoning. These bone lesions, which healed over, are argued to be the result of consuming a massive dose of Vitamin A, which is concentrated in the liver of carnivorous animals. The story read into these bones is one of experimentation with carnivory, and care for the sick.

Two of the most interesting fossil assemblages of early *Homo* come from Dmanisi, Georgia (*"Homo georgicus"*) and from Dinaledi Cave, South Africa (*"Homo naledi"*) The Georgian fossils are dated to about 1.8 MYA and display a surprisingly wide range of craniofacial diversity. The South African material is copious, remarkably well preserved, strikingly homogeneous, and exhibits a mixture of *Australopithecus*-like and *Homo*-like features throughout its body.

As we have already noted, whether they represent zoologically real species or not is a poorly framed scientific question, because it presumes that a human origin story must be populated by zoological elements that are inaccessible to us, but which nevertheless are the focus of the question. This represents a widespread, basic confusion of categories. Here the scientist is a mythmaker, whose role is to create a coherent and meaningful narrative out of the available themes and motifs, as the anthropologist Claude Lévi-Strauss described; and names like *Homo georgicus* and *Homo naledi* constitute those elemental themes and motifs, or bricolage. Indeed, *Homo naledi* has a particular origin story associated with it. Since the Dinaledi Chamber is so difficult to reach—even other species didn't die there, just these hominids—then how did they get there? Might these small-brained ancestors have dragged their dead kin to this place, and deposited them to rest in this remote and inaccessibly deep cave? That might associate them with the ritual mortuary practices that are so distinctively human, and grant them the earliest signs of human symbolic thought and behavior.

Or perhaps there was once another way into the cave that hasn't yet been identified.

THE BEGINNING OF CULTURAL EVOLUTION

By 2.6 million years ago, our early ancestors had crossed a threshold no species had before. In addition to modifying soft, perishable objects to aid in food procurement and processing, or in aggressive displays and personal defense, they began to modify hard, permanent objects as well. These early stone tools, known as Oldowan, are distinguished by shape, but generally cluster into two categories: the "flake" (a smallish piece of rock with a sharp edge, knocked from a larger piece) and the "core" (the larger leftover piece of rock, also with a sharp edge). Both were probably used.

A bonobo named Kanzi was taught to make such Oldowan tools, but showed little interest in using them (bonobos are not avid tool users in the wild). Early

African hominids, however, had taken such a keen interest in the possibilities inherent in their edged rocks that they began to carry good ones with them over fairly long distances, as can be seen by mapping where the tools were found in relation to where the raw material came from.

This marks the point of divergence between paleontology and archaeology, where the objects of study are no longer simply anatomical or biological, but cultural as well. In some ways, they remain affiliated, since early in cultural history we will be making strong associations between particular types of tools and particular types of toolmakers. This is a valuable association, for example, at the Kenyan site of Olorgesailie, about 0.7 million years old, where tools are very abundant, but hominid fossils are very rare.

By about 1.6 million years ago, however, a different and novel ecological relationship began to form. The hominids who had been making these pebble tools for a million years began to do something a little different to them—taking a rock that began flat, they knocked flakes off not just one side, but off the opposite surface as well. These bifacial tools required a bit more labor than their predecessors, as well as a bit more foresight. It seems to have been the first identifiable example of improvement: doing what you've been doing, but a bit more, a bit differently, and a bit better. This will become the hallmark of cultural evolution.

This technology is clearly an outgrowth of the Oldowan, but as Mary Leakey originally noted, it connects the Oldowan to the technology that will conquer much of the world over the next million years, the Acheulian.

Beginning about 1.4 million years ago, hominids began making a special triangular kind of biface, known to archaeologists (somewhat problematically) as a "handaxe." The name is unfortunate, as it conjures an image of a hominid holding it by the butt end and hacking down at something. But the butt end is sharpened also, so if used in such a fashion, a hominid would be more likely to lacerate the hand than to hack effectively at anything. Quite possibly, the handaxe was a prepared core, from which many uniform and predictable small flakes could be made whenever they came in handy—and those flakes were the principal tools. In other words, the "handaxe" may not be what the hominid set out to make, but was merely a means to an end, namely, the flakes—and what was left over when the toolmaking was done.

The advantage would likely have been a faster and more reliable way to make simple, sharp tools of a particular shape as needed. And this cyclical process, which we take for granted now—innovation, adoption, improvement—becomes the basis of a new kind of survival strategy. This ecological strategy of survival via technology produced two basic patterns for anthropologists to confront.

First, changes in form or complexity of the tools can be studied largely independently of any aspects of the creatures that produced them. In other words, the artifacts assume their own distinctive evolutionary changes, which can be tracked without recourse to changes in the biology of the makers. This will be as true for studying changes in the styles of chipped rocks as it is for studying changes in the structure of the airplane.

Second, technological evolution is progressive. Wherever we look, we find early tools are more simple and crude, and later ones are finer and more effective. This is the area of cultural change in which variation is not equivalent, for some technologies are better than others (that is to say, they allow you to do more things more efficiently—but they still may contain other trade-offs, such as the relative ease of disposing the waste products of stone tools versus nuclear reactors).

Why do we find this pattern? Imagine two groups of hominids encountering one another, with one possessing a superior technology. If their encounter is peaceful, then the tools might well give one group a long-term edge in survival and reproduction; or the other group may adopt the new technology. Either way, the better technology is perpetuated. And if the encounter is aggressive, who is more likely to emerge victorious? The one with the better technology.

It is useful at this juncture to reflect on the nature and extent of coevolution in our ancestry over the last few million years. Those (inorganic) technologies of stone or metal coevolved along with the (organic) hands and brains making them—that is to say, the tools coevolved with the manual dexterity to produce them. Moreover, our organic bodies, brains, and genomes have been coevolving with new social relations, which connect bodies to one another, and are thus properties of something other than the bodies themselves, and we can call them superorganic. Human social relations are fundamentally structured by kinship. This is rooted in the evolutionary novelty of marriage, which serves many functions: sanctioning sexuality, legitimizing children, establishing a new residential, economic, and legal unit (that is, a family), uniting unrelated families as in-laws, formalizing love, acknowledging obligations of support and companionship. Since these diverse roles may be differently weighted in different societies, marriage can assume many forms ethnographically. But it is quite different from pair-bonding in, say, gibbons or gorillas.

So we have the organic (biological) evolution, the superorganic (social) evolution, and the inorganic (technological) all proceeding together over the course of human emergence in the last million or so years. Among the technological innovations around this time was fire, as interpreted from some charred fossil animal bones at several sites in East and South Africa. Fire would have three salutary uses: to cook food, to scare off predators, and to warm up. Warming up would be more necessary in temperate climates, which may be why we seem to find the earliest evidence for fire at sites in South Africa. Scaring off predators with their fires might be what allowed our ancestors to come to the ground to sleep, and to lose their upper-body climbing specializations entirely.

Cooking, however, can broaden the spectrum of edible food possibilities in the environment. While we tend to think in terms of roasting antelopes, it is very possible that vegetable matter, such as tubers, constituted the bulk of what was being roasted. The need for more food may have been stimulated by the physiological cost of growing a big brain in the first place. Leslie Aiello and Peter Wheeler have suggested that having a big brain is so metabolically costly that a higher-quality diet was required, and food preparation took over some of the role of the digestive system, so that the size of the gut was consequently reduced. They point to a different shape of the rib cage (barrel-shaped and apelike in small-brained Lucy; broad and flattened in the large-brained Nariokotome Boy) as evidence that the nervous system of early *Homo* was expanding at the expense of its digestive system.

The interest in and the ability to transform the things around you into *useful* things around you becomes the hallmark of this lineage. In consequence, humans become the species whose survival will rely on the leveling of environmental variation—using technology, language, and social relations to essentially take their environment with them, wherever they go. The human ecological niche is thus itself a cultural niche, constructed from the choices and accomplishments of earlier generations. The fundamentally successful nature of this adaptation is shown by the fact that early *Homo* comes to thrive in Africa at the expense of the other hominids, and indeed to expand its geographic range beyond Africa. By 1 million years ago, its tools and bones are found at sites outside of Africa, and *Homo erectus* is—arguably, at least—the only hominid or hominin species left.

REFERENCES AND FURTHER READING

Aiello, L. C., and P. Wheeler. 1995. The expensive-tissue hypothesis. *Current Anthropology* 36:199–221.

Antón, S. C., R. Potts, and L. C. Aiello. 2014. Evolution of early *Homo*: An integrated biological perspective. *Science* 345:45.

Berger, L. R., D. J. de Ruiter, S. E. Churchill, et al. 2010. *Australopithecus sediba*: A new species of *Homo*-like australopith from South Africa. *Science* 328:195–204.

Berger, L. R., J. Hawks, D. J. de Ruiter, et al. 2015. *Homo naledi*, a new species of the genus *Homo* from the Dinaledi Chamber, South Africa. *eLife* 4:e09560.

Bramble, D. M., and D. E. Lieberman. 2004. Endurance running and the evolution of *Homo*. *Nature* 432:345–352.

Clarke, R. J. 1998. First ever discovery of a well-preserved skull and associated skeleton of *Australopithecus*. *South African Journal of Science* 94:460–463.

Dart, R. 1925. *Australopithecus africanus*: The man-ape of Southern Africa. *Nature* 115:195–199.

Flannery, K., and J. Marcus. 2013. *The Creation of Inequality: How Our Prehistoric Ancestors Set the Stage for Monarchy, Slavery, and Empire*. Cambridge, MA: Harvard University Press.

Fuentes, A. 2015. Integrative anthropology and the human niche: Toward a contemporary approach to human evolution. *American Anthropologist* 117:302–315.

Gundling, T. 2005. *First in Line: Tracing Our Ape Ancestry*. New Haven, CT: Yale University Press.

Harmand, S., J. E. Lewis, C. S. Feibel, et al. 2015. 3.3-million-year-old stone tools from Lomekwi 3, West Turkana, Kenya. *Nature* 521:310–315.

Hill, A., S. Ward, A. Deino, G. Curtis, and R. Drake. 1992. Earliest Homo. *Nature* 355:719–722.

Johanson, D. C., F. T. Masao, G. G. Eck, et al. 1987. New partial skeleton of Homo habilis from Olduvai Gorge, Tanzania. *Nature* 327:205–209.

Johanson, D. C., and T. D. White. 1979. A systematic assessment of early African hominids. *Science* 203:321–329.

Leakey, L., P. V. Tobias, and J. Napier 1964. A new species of the genus Homo from Olduvai Gorge. *Nature* 202:5–7.

Leakey, M. D., and R. L. Hay. 1979. Pliocene footprints in the laetolil beds at Laetoli, northern Tanzania. *Nature* 278:317–323.

Lévi-Strauss, C. 1962. *The Savage Mind*. Chicago: University of Chicago Press.

Lordkipanidze, D., M. S. Ponce de León, A. Margvelashvili, et al. 2013. A complete skull from Dmanisi, Georgia, and the evolutionary biology of early *Homo*. *Science* 342:326–331.

Maclarnon, A., and G. Hewitt. 2004. Increased breathing control: Another factor in the evolution of human language. *Evolutionary Anthropology* 13:181–197.

Marks, J. 2016. The units of scientific anthropological origin narratives. *Anthropological Theory*, 16 (2–3):285–294.

McCollum, M. A. 1999. The robust australopithecine face: A morphogenetic perspective. *Science* 284:301–305.

McHenry, H. M., and K. Coffing. 2000. *Australopithecus* to *Homo*: Transformations in body and mind. *Annual Review of Anthropology* 29:125–146.

Potts, R. 1996. *Humanity's Descent: The Consequences of Ecological Instability*. New York: William Morrow.

Schwartz, J. H., and I. Tattersall. 2015. Defining the genus *Homo*. *Science* 349:931–932.

Skelton, R., and H. McHenry. 1992. Evolutionary relationships among early hominids. *Journal of Human Evolution* 23:209–349.

Smith, B. H. 1986. Dental development in *Australopithecus* and early *Homo*. *Nature* 317:525.

Spencer, F. 1990. *Piltdown: A Scientific Forgery*. New York: Oxford University Press.

Stedman, H. H., B. W. Kozyak, A. Nelson, et al. 2004. Myosin gene mutation correlates with anatomical changes in the human lineage. *Nature* 428:415–418.

Tattersall, I. 1986. Species recognition in human paleontology. *Journal of Human Evolution* 15:165–175.

Tobias, P. V. 1991. *The Skulls, Endocasts and Teeth of Homo habilis*. Vol. 4 of *Olduvai Gorge*: Cambridge, England: Cambridge University Press.

Tobias, P. V. 1997. Ape-like *Australopithecus* after seventy years: Was it a hominid? *Journal of the Royal Anthropological Society* 4:283–308.

Ungar, P. S., and L. Hlusko. 2016. The evolutionary path of least resistance. *Science* 353:29–30.

Walker, A., and R. Leakey. 1978. The hominids of East Turkana. *Scientific American* 239:54–66.

Walker, A., and R. Leakey, eds. 1993. *The Nariokotome* Homo erectus *skeleton*. Cambridge, MA: Harvard University Press.

Ward, C. 2003. The evolution of human origins. *American Anthropologist* 105:77–88.

Ward, C., M. Leakey, and A. Walker. 1999. The new hominid species *Australopithecus anamensis*. *Evolutionary Anthropology* 7:197–205.

White, T. D., C. O. Lovejoy, B. Asfaw, J. P. Carlson, and G. Suwa. 2015. Neither chimpanzee nor human, *Ardipithecus* reveals the surprising ancestry of both. *Proceedings of the National Academy of Sciences, USA* 112:4877–4884.

Wood, B. A., and M. Collard. 1999. The human genus. *Science* 284:65–71.

Wood, B. A., and T. Harrison. 2011. The evolutionary context of the first hominins. *Nature* 470:347–352.

Wrangham, R. 2009. *Catching Fire*. Cambridge, MA: Harvard University Press.

CHAPTER 12

What to Do When
Confronted by a Neandertal
(On Continuity and Discontinuity)

THEME

The fossil record of the genus *Homo* over the last million years involves a dialectical tension between physical continuity and discontinuity. On the one hand, several distinct taxa in the human lineage can be discerned on the basis of key morphological features. But on the other hand, the differences are subtle, and "missing links" connecting the taxa, far from being missing, are nearly ubiquitous, which is why the classification of these ancestors and relatives has proven to be difficult.

In 1945, the distinguished paleontologist George Gaylord Simpson published a magisterial synthesis of mammalian systematics. A corner of the order Primates, however, was troubling. "Perhaps it would be better for the zoological taxonomist to set apart the family Hominidae and to exclude its nomenclature and classification from his studies," he wrote.

Simpson could afford to be a bit sarcastic, as the world's expert on the classification of mammals. But his point resonates: hominid classification is beyond help, and will probably always be. Maybe it is because of the logical contradiction of trying to classify yourself objectively (when the act of classifying makes you the subject as well as the object); or because of the meaning-ladenness that is carried by all narratives of human kinship and descent; or because of the moral economy of hominid classification (Chapter 11) that favors splitting; or even that the training of human paleontologists is often in medical anatomy more than in systematic biology. Maybe it's a combination of them. What is important is that the classification of the human lineage generally seems to reflect less "biological reality" than does the classification of other lineages. And, as Simpson recognized, it's unavoidable.

Consider the first point, that the act of classifying makes you a subject and an object, a different situation from classifying fruit flies, where you are the subject and *they* are the object. This is a gap that can never be bridged, for in order to classify humans "objectively," you must begin by becoming nonhuman yourself.

Yet that is manifestly impossible—the one incontestable biological fact in this enterprise is that you are human. It makes no sense to begin an ostensibly scientific enterprise by denying the one obvious fact that everybody agrees on: We are humans classifying humans, and it can never be otherwise.

Nevertheless, even if it has no scientific merit for being idiotic, there is rhetorical value in pretending to be nonhuman while classifying humans. Thomas Huxley was the first to make this argument, as he tried to persuade his readers that humans and apes were actually more alike than his readers might be inclined to think:

> Let us imagine ourselves scientific Saturnians, if you will, fairly acquainted with such animals as now inhabit the earth, and employed in discussing the relations they bear to a new and singular 'erect and featherless biped,' which some enterprising traveller, overcoming the difficulties of space and gravitation, has brought from that distant planet for our inspection, well preserved, may be, in a cask of rum. . . . We should undoubtedly place the newly discovered tellurian genus with [the apes].

Huxley is actually constructing a very clever argument here. "Maybe I can't really convince you that humans and apes are so similar," he is saying, "but if there were biologists on Saturn, they would vouch for me."

But since there are no biologists on Saturn, we have only Huxley himself to tell us what they think.

In the 1920s, the paleontologist Henry Fairfield Osborn—who was both a leading Darwinist and a leading racist—wrote for a popular audience:

> If an unbiased zoölogist were to descend upon the earth from Mars and study the races of man with the same impartiality as the races of fishes, birds, and mammals, he would undoubtedly divide the existing races of man into several genera and into a very large number of species and subspecies.

Once again, the message is a strange one: Invoking science fiction to make an ostensibly scientific point. And the point again, is, I can't really demonstrate this, but the Martians would vouch for me. (In this case, however, it seems as though the Martian biologists are considerably less competent than the Saturnian biologists.)

And the argument is still powerful. In 1992, the biologist Jared Diamond wrote, "A zoologist from Outer Space would immediately classify us as just a third species of chimpanzee." It ought to be sufficient to rebut this argument with, "No, they wouldn't," for your knowledge of the thought processes of extraterrestrials is the same as his.

There is, however, a subtler and more insidious point here. Anthropologists have long been documenting the diverse ways in which people divide and classify the things that are important to them—relatives, colors, kinds of snow, kinds of illnesses, and kinds of diarrhea—and they do so in locally meaningful ways. That is to say, they are classifying because they are interested in these objects, and they impose order upon the objects by arranging them according to the criteria they think are important. Thus, the Bible explains how to classify the animals of the world (Chapter 6). The reason is very explicit: to tell the Hebrews what they could and couldn't eat. The criteria are explicit, too: animals are to be classified by where they live and by how they move. Thus, the primary division will be in the air, on the land, or in the sea. Of the airborne animals, there are those that fly and those that swarm; the land-dwelling animals are divided into those that have hooves, those that have paws, those that creep or swarm, those that travel on their belly, and those with many feet. And the sea-dwelling animals are those with fins and scales, and those without them.

The criteria are arbitrary, but they render the universe meaningful or sensible—they give it order. So what of the scientific argument that aliens would classify the world just as the speaker would? It is probably more likely that the extraterrestrials would classify us by how we taste. The speaker does not even appreciate the breadth of *human* ingenuity in imposing order on things, much less the scope of alien ingenuity!

The second point is that all classification is value-laden, and a scientific classification of our place in the natural order, particularly our historical place, is meaningful in ways that classifying other species simply is not. When the lawmakers of Tennessee made it illegal to teach evolution in the 1920s, they specified whose evolution they were particularly concerned about. It wasn't the barnacles that Darwin actually worked on, or the dinosaurs that have captured our imaginations, or the fruit flies that have told us about speciation. Rather it was made illegal specifically "to teach any theory that denies the story of the Divine Creation of man as taught in the Bible, and to teach instead that man has descended from a lower order of animals."

As we noted in Chapter 10, during World War II, the Japanese sought to destroy the fossils of Peking Man, and thus destroy the Chinese people's ancestors. And in modern-day Ethiopia, Kenya, and South Africa, being a key part of the scientific story of the human family is a source of national pride. Indeed, as we noted in Chapter 11, national pride was probably a contributing factor to the success of the Piltdown Man fraud.

The point is, how we make sense of the human family—our ancestors and cousins—is subject to symbolic pressures that other biologists don't have to deal with. That is simply the price tag that comes with working on something so interesting as human origins. Indeed, we may see ourselves as the subjects of an anthropological generalization: The ancestors are always sacred.

The third point is the moral economy of splitting. As noted in Chapter 10, the most basic kind of analysis to publish is a cladistic study of the features of the relevant fossils. But since cladistic analyses don't work in principle below the species level, it makes sense to increase the number of species you recognize, so you can analyze them *as if they were* species. Further, multiplying the number of species democratizes the process, so that more scientists control key specimens, more museums and more curators are more important, and more egos are thereby massaged. Taxonomic splitting thus becomes not an act of caprice, but a strategic practice—the rising tide that lifts all academic boats (and careers).

Another thing to consider is the epistemological problem caused by the existence of a gap in the human fossil record. You devote your career and life to plugging it, and you succeed, and name it for yourself or your benefactor, or for your people—but at what a scientific cost! You have now created two gaps, one on either side of the new fossils, both of which now have to be filled, where there was formerly only a single gap. And so they will be, by someone else, who will name the new species, and create four new gaps. This is a game you can never win—if you are the one representing "biological reality"—like the Greek myth of Sisyphus, condemned to roll a boulder up a hill, but to never quite get there.

And finally, remember that we are dealing with broadly distributed species, over geologically short periods of time—certainly much shorter than those we invoke for the australopithecines. The patterns of ancestry and descent may indeed be very complex for populations that lived in this fairly narrow span of geological time, but in widely different places, looking subtly different, but quite possibly able to interbreed quite freely with one another. Does the shape of nasal bones of Neandertals and humans really mean that they should be placed in different species, as some paleontologists have suggested—or does it mean that the scientists have been cooped up in the basement of museums studying the fine structure of the nasal bones for too long, and need to get some fresh air?

For these reasons, hominid (or hominin) taxonomy is in a comparable position to the time when Simpson wrote. Some paleontologists recognize nearly twenty species simply in the genus *Homo*. If this even approximates biological reality, that would mean that technology couldn't have been that great an adaptation, since 95% of the species that had it have gone extinct in only the last 2.6 million years!

Many of the species currently recognized are chronospecies (an evolving lineage that ends up different enough from the way it began, with enough continuity evident, to call it one thing at the beginning and another thing at the end). This is very likely the nature of the relationship between *Homo ergaster* and *Homo erectus*. Others exist primarily to accommodate anomalous specimens, such as *Homo rudolfensis*. Still others really do plug those morphological gaps, such as *Homo antecessor*, a western European pre-Neandertal—although the objection can always be raised that those gaps, which are narrowly localized in time and space, are not species-level gaps, but subspecies-level gaps. And other species may exist only in the essentializing mind of the scientist, in whose professional interests it may be to see novelty and immortality where there is only difference.

Certainly the most bizarre aspect of all this para-biological classification can be seen in comparing the recent suggestions of two groups of geneticists. One group maintains that chimpanzees are genetically so *similar* to us that we should recognize them as another species of the genus *Homo*. Another group maintains that Neandertals were genetically so *different* from us that we should recognize them as another species in the genus *Homo*.

What's the problem? Chimpanzees are simply a heck of a lot more different from us than Neandertals are, any way you measure it. These two suggestions, therefore, cannot both be right. One, or the other, or possibly both, must be wrong.

THE HUMAN LINEAGE

*Early Homo—let's call it Homo ergaster—*makes a great discovery: the rest of the world. With the technology to exploit it, *Homo ergaster* makes its way through diverse climates in Eurasia by 1.2 million years ago. The climatic diversity of Africa is often underemphasized; old racists used to argue that the challenges posed by Eurasian climatic variations promoted the rise of intelligence, but this ignores the fact that australopiths are found near Johannesburg and Dar-es-Salaam, thousands of miles and many climatic zones apart! What this first African diaspora did was to promote genetic drift, by vastly expanding the territory into which hominids could live in their small bands. This seems to be a situation eminently suited to Sewall Wright's model of drift and selection working together (Chapter 5).

Two important things now occur, although the precise details and mechanisms are not well established. First, the other hominid species become extinct, and *Homo ergaster* (or its descendant, *Homo erectus*) establishes an effective monopoly on the bipedalism/technology niche. Second, Acheulian bifacial stone tools can be found most commonly in Africa and Western Asia, although not invariably, with the *ergaster-erectus* lineage.

The reason for the imperfect relationship between the tools and the species is probably that the technology is a cultural feature, and may be adopted or not for various reasons, ranging from dire necessity to the availability of the appropriate kinds of raw materials to simple aesthetics and tradition. Further, simpler tools are more easily made and are still very useful.

Notice also that the timescale of human evolution is beginning to collapse. Where the features of human evolution discussed in the last chapter occurred over millions of years, now we are dealing with hundreds of thousands of years, and a broader swath of the world. Further, dating techniques for the geological context of these fossils are not as reliable as potassium-argon (for older material) or radiocarbon (for younger material, up to about 50,000 years ago), and we tend to rely on a convergence of different approaches for dating the material in this middle range.

Smaller physical differences now tend to become exaggerated in significance in the minds of the scientists studying them, since the fossils themselves are so rare and consequently each one is so meaningful. And relationships of australopiths to the ancestry of our own species are now gone: while being diagnosably different from us, these more recent hominids are overwhelmingly similar in brain and body to ourselves, and are consequently that much more compelling to mythologize in our narratives of ancestry.

The nineteenth-century German evolutionist Ernst Haeckel had predicted the discovery of an ape-man who would be bipedal but unable to speak, and even named this hypothetical ancestor *Pithecanthropus alalus,* or "mute ape-man." A young Dutch physician named Eugene Dubois settled in Java (then a Dutch colony) with an ambition to find those elusive "missing link fossils." In 1891 and 1892, his efforts were rewarded with a femur, skullcap, and two teeth, found fairly close together at a site called Trinil.

These first remains of "Java Man" sparked the curiosity of the scholarly community, and a lively debate about their meaning ensued. The femur had some pathological growths (or exostoses), but was essentially human; the teeth were human in form, but somewhat larger than human; and the skullcap was smaller, thicker, and more angular than a human skull. Some skeptics argued that the skull was that of a "microcephalic idiot" (they were wrong); some argued that the skull was that of an ape (they were also wrong); and some argued that the parts represented more than one species (they were trivially right). The thighbone does appear to have come from an old modern human; but the skull is from neither ape nor person; it is from a species that did walk upright, but on slightly different legs than a modern person's.

Subsequent discoveries in the 1930s by G. H. R. ("Ralph") von Koenigswald, from a site called Sangiran in Java, resembled the original Trinil material very closely. By 1940, there was a sample of four adult skulls, a child's skull, and two jaws from these Indonesian sites.

Coincidentally, Davidson Black, an anatomist teaching in China, was brought a molar tooth that he recognized as slightly different from a human counterpart. In 1927, he published it as a new genus and species, *Sinanthropus pekinensis* ("Chinese man from Peking"), and made arrangements to excavate the cave it came from, at a site now known as Zhoukoudian, about 20 miles south of Beijing. The excavations were led by Black and by the Chinese paleontologist Pei Wenzhong, who found a skull there on December 2, 1929. Black died in 1934 and was ultimately replaced by Franz Weidenreich, a distinguished German anatomist who had been obliged to emigrate because of his Jewish ancestry. Excavation continued until 1937, when the Japanese Empire invaded China.

Against the backdrop of civil and political unrest, Weidenreich and the Chinese made excellent casts of the fossil material that had already been discovered, which amounted to five skulls and many more jaws and cranial fragments, teeth, and postcrania. In 1939, von Koenigswald and Weidenreich compared the material from Java and China side by side and concluded that they were very similar; but global events soon overtook them. As we noted in Chapter 10, the Chinese fossils disappeared on Pearl Harbor Day and haven't been seen since.

There have, of course, been many other *Homo erectus* fossils found in the intervening decades, from sites in North Africa, South Africa, East Africa, South Asia, Indonesia, and various sites in East Asia, including more remains from Zhoukoudian. Perhaps the most noteworthy of these newer finds is a skull bone recovered in 1966 from the Peking Man site, whose cranial sutures match perfectly with those of one of the skulls cast by Weidenreich—clearly a part of the same individual, and a testament to the precision and accuracy of the Peking Man casts.

Homo erectus, as identified anatomically from the classic Asian and African material, does not seem to have made it very far northwest into Europe. Fossils discovered in the 1990s from Gran Dolina in Spain, and Ceprano in Italy, serve to illustrate the anatomical continuity that renders it so difficult to impose taxonomic categories on these recent fossil hominids. Regardless of how we allocate these southern European finds (and some scholars would split them into yet another fossil hominid species, *Homo antecessor*!), they form a strong anatomical bridge between classic *Homo erectus* in Asia and Africa and the earliest *Homo sapiens*.

THE MENTAL AND SOCIAL LIFE OF *HOMO ERECTUS*

Earnest Hooton (Chapter 1) very likely overstated the primitiveness of the mental qualities of *Homo erectus* when he wrote a couplet that rhymed its occipital torus with "no ideals with which to bore us." It is, however, with *Homo erectus* that archaeology begins to detect aspects of what we may call the life of the mind. The earliest evidences are always the most equivocal, and of course fire was presumably used and controlled long before it could be produced on demand and fully mastered. But by the time that *Homo erectus* begins to be replaced by archaic *Homo sapiens,* a few hundred thousand years ago, we find evidence for hearths—which in turn implies the things that people do with fires, from scaring off predators, to cooking, to staying warm, and even telling "campfire stories" (or a primitive equivalent with its attendant social correlates).

The features of the human brain that are grossly associated with language, such as its basic asymmetrical structure, and regions known as Broca's area and Wernicke's area, are all present in the brain of *Homo erectus*. These features are arguably present in the brains of earlier ancestors, but whatever debate exists about their brains ends with those of *Homo erectus*.

Migrating into more northerly latitudes brought *Homo erectus* into contact with unfamiliar animals and cooler environments. Consequently, we tend to associate with *Homo erectus* the construction of shelters, and wider adoption of clothing. While the most famous *Homo erectus* sites are caves, those caves were also occupied by hyenas, bears, and other animals whose archaeological effects are difficult to disentangle from human activity. Thus, does the fact that the Peking Man skulls are generally missing the softer cranial base imply that the brains were eaten in a cannibalistic frenzy, or by hyenas?

There is little doubt that *Homo erectus* was a successful hunting species, and that this cultural exploitation of resources helped it spread rapidly over the Old World. This demographic expansion, however, yields a paradox, given the longevity, low fertility, and difficult parturition characteristic of our lineage. As the brain expanded, birth became harder and put mother and child at considerably greater risk than their ancestors faced. Moreover, associated with this brain growth is a longer period of immaturity. An eight-year-old chimpanzee is physically mature and able to fend for itself; but an eight-year-old human is still highly dependent on others. How could a young human mother fend for herself and her child (as a young ape mother must), as well as for her previous children, who are still very highly dependent on her (while the ape mother is no longer burdened by them)?

In other words, the growth of the brain, which we often take to be self-evidently beneficial, came with attendant problems that needed to be addressed if this evolutionary strategy was to succeed. The answer to these problems seems to lie in the coevolution of biological specializations and social forms in the human lineage, the "grandmother hypothesis" (Chapter 9). A strengthening of the maternal lineage, with older, nonreproductive females assisting their own daughters and granddaughters, was one solution to this problem. An independent solution came with the development of the now-universal institution of marriage, which generally includes responsibilities for joint provisioning of offspring. It seems reasonable to associate the development of these new social forms, and their attendant obligations, with the demographic and geographic expansion of *Homo erectus*. (A recent study finds that advanced age only became common later in the fossil record, which might even make the obligations associated with marriage the first solution, and grandmothering the second.)

HOMO SAPIENS, THE WISE SPECIES

The continued expansion of the brain produced groups of hominids about 400,000 years ago with cranial capacities well within the normal range of modern humans, but outside the range of modern human morphology in other respects. We generally take this to mark the emergence of our own species, *Homo sapiens*, in an archaic form, although with obvious strong continuity to *Homo erectus*.

We can call the earliest representatives of our species *Homo sapiens heidelbergensis*, after a jaw discovered in Germany in 1907, which may be nearly half-a-million years old. Not only are the dating techniques often imprecise here, especially for material recovered decades ago, but so, of course, is the taxonomy. Nevertheless, similar remains are known from Spain (Atapuerca), England (Swanscombe), Greece (Petralona), and France (Arago), all several hundred thousand years old. In fact, fossils of very similar form have been found as far away as India (Narmada), Ethiopia (Bodo), Zambia (Kabwe), China (Maba), and Indonesia (Ngandong).

Homo sapiens heidelbergensis presents a form at once strikingly familiar, yet also strikingly primitive. Its head is larger and rounder than *Homo erectus*, and its skull bones somewhat thinner. And yet its face is massive and juts forward, and the lack of a forehead results in enormous browridges, the thickest we encounter in the hominid record.

One striking aspect of the archaeological record of tools is the extent to which it diverges from the paleontological record of bones. For all of the well-known (and perhaps overinterpreted) discrete anatomical variations among these hominid taxa, the toolkits they made and used exhibit extensive continuity, both locally and globally. And although there are general associations to be made between skull forms and toolkits, there are many sites at which the tools do not match the skulls. In other words, people are never simply doing, in one place, everything that they are capable of, which is why we cannot easily infer the intellectual capacities of the inhabitants from what we happen to find at any particular site. Further, since the longest-studied and best-known stone tool assemblages are from Europe, we tend to interpret lithic technologies from the rest of the world in a "Eurocentric" framework. However, they may not be strictly comparable, insofar as any technology must be adapted to the locally available raw materials and to the specific requirements of the climate, available prey, and other environmental particulars.

These archaic *Homo sapiens* populations were smart enough to appreciate the Mediterranean, and many Middle Paleolithic sites have been excavated in southern Europe. At Terra Amata in France, a group of hominids 300,000 years ago left evidence of simple structures there, containing pits of ash that are reasonably interpreted as hearths. Stone tools associated with these kinds of hominids have yielded evidence that they were used to scrape hides. A Middle Paleolithic site in Israel showed the occupants to be roasting and eating the available nuts in the area.

One descendant population of *H. s. heidelbergensis* became adapted to the rigors of the glacial ages in Europe; these are known as Neandertals, or *Homo sapiens neanderthalensis*. These specializations included a short, stout, muscular body; a rounded but elongated head, and a narrow, forward-projecting face.

The Neandertals were the first extinct members of the human lineage to be discovered, and have consequently been studied the longest, and scrutinized the most extensively. Subtle but regular differences from modern people have been discerned in virtually every part of the Neandertal's body, from the bridge of its nose to the tips of its fingers. It is hard to evaluate the significance of any of these features either to the Neandertal's survival or to its taxonomic status, but one thing is clear: they occupied a unique position, being both "like us" and "not like us," the ambiguity of which has given them great cultural power, for it is against the Neandertals that we contrast ourselves in the most basic zoological way. Whether we see them as a species or as a subspecies, they are the lowest-ranked zoological group against which we can contrast ourselves. Their anatomy lies outside the range of modern human variation, but not very far outside it.

NEANDERTAL LIFE

The anatomical features we identify as Neandertal are found on fossils from Europe and the Mediterranean area, from about 250,000 to about 30,000 years ago. The skull is low, like *Homo erectus,* but rounded rather than angular, and at least as large as a modern human's. The Neandertal skull, however, retains its greatest width near the bottom. All of its long bones are short and stout, often with impressive grooves and ridges for the attachment of prominent muscles. Although their bones are often diagnosably different from modern human bones, Neandertals walked fully erect, in contrast to caricatures of the "cave man" (although whether they used wooden clubs to subdue mates is tantalizingly unknown).

Many Neandertal bones show signs of healed fractures. This seems to demonstrate two things: One, the harshness of Ice Age life, and two, a system of support that permitted the injured to be cared for and to survive. The most famous example, which inspired the Jean Auel's novel *The Clan of the Cave Bear,* involved an adult male (Shanidar 1) who had survived an arm amputation and considerable trauma to his head and body. Indeed, Neandertal arm bones are also very bilaterally asymmetrical, with one side (the right) generally being far more robust than the other, to an extent only seen in modern tennis players. That suggests repeated, strenuous, asymmetrical motion; perhaps spear thrusting. Many Neandertal teeth commonly have enamel hypoplasias, indicative of uneven growth rates, as occurs in humans who suffer from periodic dietary deficiencies.

A unique pattern of dental wear on the anterior teeth suggests the working of hides and sinews through the teeth, as arctic populations of humans have done quite recently. The rear teeth differ from our own principally in their position; their third molars (wisdom teeth) erupted vertically, with more than enough room so that there is actually a "retromolar space" between the back edge of the last molar tooth and the front edge of the ascending ramus of the jaw. Our own teeth have regressed so far back that our last molar is generally hidden behind the ascending ramus when it erupts, and consequently is often impacted.

Matching the tools to the raw materials from which they were made suggests the existence of trade networks, or at least of highly mobile populations with extensive social relations.

Although many of the most famous impressions of Neandertals appear to have been based on romanticized overinterpretations of the archaeological evidence, it is clear at least that they commonly buried their dead. This implies something, although it is not clear what: Belief in an afterlife? Disgust at scavenger activity on the bodies of loved ones? Discouragement of cannibalism? A taboo on dead bodies? Regardless of which cognitive property we assign to it—awe of death, disgust, forethought, or a division of the sacred and profane—we are recognizing some kind of high mentality in these extinct beings, a recognition we cannot make with any other form of life.

Australopiths and early *Homo* are associated with the Oldowan industry; *Homo erectus* with the Acheulian industry (characterized by an abundance of handaxes in Africa and south Asia, but less so in East Asia); and Neandertals with an industry known as Mousterian. Mousterian points represent a high degree of refinement in lithic technology when compared to earlier choppers and flakes. They are smaller and more precise, suggesting both a higher degree of manual dexterity and a more ambitious final product. Mousterian tools also show attention to small, fine work at the edge.

The Neandertal's body build was probably an adaptation to the glacial climates, as cold-adapted peoples today are also stockily built, for that shape retains heat efficiently. However, Neandertals also lived in Iraq, where it is not, and was not, particularly frigid. Consequently, it is probably unwise to identify too many aspects of their appearance casually as "adaptations" to cold climate.

Likewise, we tend to think of them as "big game hunters" relying on reindeer herds, or other animal sources of subsistence, as arctic populations of humans tend to. Archaeologically we find that Neandertals were indeed skilled hunters, and that their combination of physical strength, ingenuity, and technology enabled them to bring down rabbits, rhinos, and anything in between. And yet, when available, they also ate some seafood. In other words, they were able to adapt to local circumstances and live successfully off what was available, as contemporary foragers do.

Their own meatiness, and their proficiency at hunting, raises the question of whether they occasionally dined on one another. This is difficult to assess because the two most general taboos in human society are cannibalism and incest, and imagining a society in which one or the other taboo did not exist is a common literary theme, since it explores a presumptive boundary between humans and other forms of life (which presumably lack such rule-based governance). Where (non-starvation) cannibalism is known ethnographically, human flesh is not being eaten for its nutritional value, but for its symbolic properties—for healing, for power, for life, for remembrance. At several Neandertal sites, the bones show unmistakable marks of having been defleshed—stone tool marks on the same parts of the body that one finds them on other animal bones, where sinews are sliced to facilitate the removal of meat. But does this mean that the body was defleshed *and eaten*? Or simply that they had their own reasons for transforming corpses into skeletons for mortuary practices, as many people do ethnographically? The first alternative symbolically renders the Neandertals behaviorally nonhuman (since the consumption of human flesh lies on the symbolic boundary of human behavior); the second symbolically renders them as more human, since it invokes thought and ritual. And if Neandertals were eating one another, were they doing it because they were hungry (unlike, chimpanzees, who don't eat adults of their kind, even when they are hungry), or because they had divided the universe into profane and sacred domains, and were deriving spiritual value from consuming the remains of one of their own?

And since defleshing has been argued for hominid material as far back as *Homo erectus* 600,000 years ago, our interpretation of the practice may be important in understanding the origin of the human mind. This highlights the problems faced by Paleolithic archaeologists as they explore the complex relationship between thoughts and their material expression.

ANATOMICALLY MODERN PEOPLE

Our own lineage, all over the world, is marked by a dramatic reduction and recession of the face. Along with this comes a shift in the shape of the brain, assuming a more globular form. The result yields our two most familiar features: a forehead and a chin. There is also evidence to suggest that growth and maturation in our lineage occurred up to 30% more slowly, as contrasted to archaic *Homo sapiens*, from the pattern in which layers of enamel on the teeth (known as perikymata) were deposited.

Another feature is well known to college students: overcrowded wisdom teeth pushed far back into the jaws, so that they cannot grow in properly and are "impacted." We might wonder what William Paley, the nineteenth-century author of *Natural Theology*, would have made of a wise "designer" who made our jaws too small for our teeth!

We find the first evidence for people like these—robust, yet physically modern people—nearly 200,000 years ago in East Africa. By 90,000 years ago, their remains are found in the Middle East and southern Africa. Over the next 50,000 years they will make it to China, Australia, and eastern Europe.

Although humans coexisted with Neandertals for 50,000 years in the Middle East, that coexistence in western Europe was considerably shorter—about 10,000 years—and the physical contrast was more striking. All modern populations more closely resemble one another than they resemble the archaic human populations that once lived there. We all, for example, have the body shape of the Africans of 200,000 years ago, not of Europeans of 200,000 years ago. However, it is not uncommon to find that certain traits characteristic of local archaic populations are occasionally found in later, otherwise normal modern people in the same area. Certainly the most obvious of these is the prominent jutting mid-face of Neandertals, which is approximated in some northern Europeans.

One interesting pattern is that the earliest modern human populations in Europe and the latest Neandertal populations show some signs of convergence, although still readily separable. Early modern Europeans, for example, generally had elongated heads: not shaped as strikingly as a Neandertal head is, but certainly on the "very long" end of the modern human range. Various early modern skulls have significantly large brows and jaws to go along with their diagnostic foreheads and chin, and the late Neandertal site of Vindija in Croatia has Neandertals with smaller browridges and jaws. A 36,000-year-old mandible from Romania is diagnostically modern, yet has a single feature generally found on Neandertal jaws. At a 25,000-year-old site in Portugal called Lagar Velho, archaeologists found an anatomically modern child with the stout muscular body of a Neandertal; was he just a stocky modern kid, or evidence for ancient contact between the two populations?

Ultimately, though, we see only people with foreheads and chins after about 30,000 years ago. What permitted these anatomically modern humans to survive and to flourish, while the Neandertals perished? Was there something we had and they lacked, which effectively fated the outcome—or, rather, if we replayed the movie of life, might they just as easily have survived at our expense? (The latter is actually the plot of a series of fun novels by the science fiction writer Robert J. Sawyer.) The question is important, because it frames how we see the Neandertals—whether as imperfect or not fully formed versions of ourselves, or as a highly successful and well-adapted population. The first alternative has held a powerful sway over our scientific narratives for generations: One group of scientists recently suggested that the Neandertals died because they all had a thyroid condition—as if our job was to identify just what was "wrong" with them. This approach, however, is difficult to square with the fact that Neandertals existed for a longer duration than modern humans have!

Actually it is conceivable that the success of modern humans was due not so much to a biomedical advantage, as it was to a discovery, a cultural advantage. For 100,000 years, anatomically modern humans had lived pretty much as their Neandertal cousins did. But about 50,000 years ago, they began making a new kind of stone tool—long, thin, sharp "blades" to contrast with Neandertal "flakes." They also began to work with other kinds of raw materials, such as bone (which may have begun in Africa close to 100,000 years ago); and to decorate themselves with the products of their labor, such as pendants and beads. By about 35,000 years ago they were painting the walls of caves.

The Neandertals, however intelligent they were, had never seen anything like this. Although they sometimes buried their dead, and have been associated with caches of natural pigments, there is little evidence that they buried anything with the corpses, or that they ever actually colored anything (except perhaps themselves). Perhaps the new artifacts came with status and set the owner above other members of the group. Perhaps they were a very powerful means of establishing widespread social relations and systems of obligation that enabled the bearer to participate in widespread trade networks that would have been beneficial to all. In any event, they effectively signaled social statuses, and bound people strongly to the social group, via the shared meanings and values that we mean by "culture."

Interestingly, a few thousand years later the Neandertals were doing it too, for example, at a site called Grotte du Renne in France. Archaeologists dispute whether they borrowed it from anatomically modern people, or whether they hit on these ideas themselves independently. Actually, there is a third alternative, called "stimulus diffusion" by the American anthropologist Alfred Kroeber in 1940. Two groups, aware of each other's existence and perceiving themselves as rivals, monitor each other carefully. One (say, the United States) develops something useful (say, an atomic bomb). The other (say, the USSR) decides they have to have one. The United States is not going to sit down and teach them how to make an atomic bomb; nor are the Soviets hitting on the idea independently. Rather, stimulated by what they saw of the US version, they used their own ingenuity and technology (and spies) to develop their own atomic bomb.

Perhaps that is what Neandertals did as well. Indeed, archaeologists can show that the holes that the Neandertals drilled to make bone pendants were made differently from the way that contemporary modern humans drilled holes for their bone pendants. They seem to have adapted techniques they were familiar with to the new task at hand. Disentangling cultural processes from biological processes now becomes paramount for anthropologists interpreting the record of past behavior, after hundreds of thousands of years of fairly tight association between cultural and biological forms.

One of the hallmarks of the material culture of modern humans is its rapid change after about 40,000 years ago. Like the earlier lithic traditions, Neandertal tools were remarkably stable over a long period of time, close to 200,000 years. Our own stone tools, however, develop such great diversity and specialization that we need a glossary of names to describe them all: Aurignacian, Magdalenian, Solutrean, Gravettian, and so forth. And yet, the Chatelperronian, once thought to be a modern human technology, is now widely held to have been a Neandertal development from the Mousterian—and thus, evidence of a more intimate relationship between the stone tools of Neandertals and moderns. Perhaps our cousins were actually on board at the beginning of the ride of the Upper Paleolithic cultural roller coaster.

Moreover, it is important to remember that cave painting is first known from about 35,000 years ago at Chauvet in France, while the best-known sites of Lascaux (France) and Altamira (Spain) are only about 14,000 years old. In other words, nearly twice as much time elapsed between the sites of Chauvet and Lascaux, with little discernible difference in style, as elapsed between Lascaux and Picasso. We consequently cannot regard the painting of cave walls as a biological innovation, for humans existed long before they painted cave walls; nor can we necessarily see rapid cultural change as a biological mutation, as features of human culture were quite stable for unfathomably long periods of time. Rather, discoveries and rates of behavioral change appear themselves to be culturally driven.

There is a hundred-thousand-year lag between the emergence of the anatomically modern human form and the discovery and spread of art, our principal indicator of behaviorally and mentally modern people. While some have argued that this lag indicates a genetic evolutionary change separating early modern humans from later modern humans, that is probably as unnecessary as inferring a genetic evolutionary change from the 30,000-year lag between the emergence of cave painting and writing. Writing is obviously a latent property in all people, even in those who lived before it was invented; what reason is there to regard art any differently?

At any rate, the distinctive Neanderthal morphology (large, narrow, projecting face; no chin; short, muscular body; and low, long cranium) disappears around 30,000 years ago and is replaced by the anatomically modern human form. It is an irony of prehistory that these originally African populations seem to have done to the indigenous occupants of Europe what their European descendants would do to other indigenous populations many years later.

THE EMERGENCE OF ART

Some sort of symbolic representation or decoration can be found in all human populations, although not preserved from the same time and not necessarily along with the initial peopling of the area. The ubiquity of this feature, indicating the expression of latent abilities in all peoples, must have had some obvious value to have been so widely adopted. Perhaps the real novelty lay in the permanence of drawing, carving, and sculpting, and the abilities were not so much long latent, as expressed earlier on less durable media (like wood) or in other ways.

It is hard to know whether these artistic activities were gendered—that is to say, made principally by men, women, or both. It is clear, however, that from the outset of their detectable expression, both carving and painting are done very skillfully, which may again suggest a transfer of media more than an unprecedented innovation.

Like the development of modern language, with which it may be connected, the development of art (or more broadly, symbolic representation) has several different and complementary functions, any of which might be its most significant feature at any particular time and place. These functions are (1) the material or utilitarian value that permanently inscribed or decorated objects might serve, such as marking territory, ownership, or some form of familiarity, or marking the recurrence of regular natural events; (2) the social value that such goods would have as markers of status and identity, and in the establishment of trade networks and alliances; (3) the symbolic and aesthetic value that emerges from a shared understanding of the meanings of the objects, and the ingroup membership that such understandings imply; and (4) the numinous value, that is to say, the non-rational, spiritual, and even mystical feelings that such objects can evoke under the appropriate settings, instilling courage into the meek, belief into the dubious, loyalty into the wavering, or just calling forth a warm and fuzzy feeling.

The philosopher Hans Jonas sees three kinds of mental processes evident in different kinds of human symbolic activities: making tools, images, and graves. The *tool*, which serves a useful purpose, reflects the imposition of a mental image on a lump of raw material, requiring both the mentality to think it and the dexterity to execute it—which apes have only in rudimentary form. The *image* is less utilitarian but more evocative, and implies the development of an un-apelike thought process—meaningful similarity, depicting what something seen or imagined was significantly like. The *grave* also implies the development of human social, as well as cognitive, processes—ancestry and descent, beliefs and rituals, and the contemplation of death.

Aside from geometric incisions, such as parallel grooves or regular notches in bone, the earliest widespread examples of symbolic art are game animals, anthropomorphic figures, and pregnant women—that is to say, indicating strong interests in food, ritual, and reproduction. But pendants and beads also become common in the Upper Paleolithic, representing other evidences of labor, decoration, aesthetics, and value.

The cave painting from Upper Paleolithic Europe is striking in many ways, not least of which is its awesome beauty. Also, however, we have the stability of style for tens of thousands of years—as if to say "this is the way it is done properly; no room for self-expression here!" This is common in all but fairly recent European tradition—the artist tries not to emphasize individual style or uniqueness, but rather to do a job the way it is supposed to be done (witness the uniform Egyptian artistic style over hundreds of years). Further, the cave paintings demonstrate, within the stylistic constraints, the recognizably modern feature of caricature—meaningfully exaggerating key features of particular subjects—the horn of the rhinoceros, the animal head or mask of the anthropomorphic figure, the swollen breasts of the pregnant woman.

Another common theme on the cave walls is the outline of a hand, presumably the artist's. Ninety percent of the time the hand on the wall is a left hand, suggesting that the artist used the drawing hand to trace the other—which also reflects the proportion of right-handedness in modern human groups.

As many of the caves were used for thousands of years, we find that the pictures commonly overlay one another. Contours of the shape of the wall, and physical features such as cracks in the cave wall, were commonly incorporated into the figures, and the fact that they are located in deep recesses of caves suggests that they weren't really meant to be seen, except on very special occasions. Then, convening in the spooky glow of torchlight, the tribe might have proceeded "slaking their ravenous thirst with the hot blood of victims and greedily devouring livid writhing flesh," to put some of the most famously purple prose in anthropology into a slightly different context (this was actually Raymond Dart's misanthropic vision of early australopiths). Or more likely, they just danced a bit, said some mumbo-jumbo, and went home to a restful sleep—contented, secure, and at peace with the Pleistocene universe.

THE POLITICAL NATURE OF ANCESTRY

In 2002, President Thabo Mbeki of South Africa gave a speech at the australopith cave site at Sterkfontein, and called it "an important area that traces the evolution of the significant part of our Earth as well as the interdependence of peoples, plants and animals, thus, in many ways teaching all of us how we can co-exist and ensure enduring prosperity for all species." He continued: "The sequence and diversity of evidence that is found here in Sterkfontein and in other sites, belongs not just to South Africans, but also to the whole of humanity. This is the window through which we get a glimpse into our shared past."

Beyond simply the pride that nations such as China, Kenya, and South Africa take in regarding themselves as the "cradle of humanity" because some of the most famous fossils were discovered there, it is important to acknowledge that human ancestry is filled with cultural meaning. The stories that we tell about our origins and our relationships to other groups of people may legitimize or delegitimize their very existence.

For example, in an age of empire and racism, the statistical geneticist and devoted social Darwinist (Chapter 3) Karl Pearson wrote, "a capable and stalwart race of white men should replace a dark-skinned tribe which can neither utilize its land for the full benefit of mankind, nor contribute its quota to the common stock of human knowledge." Where non-Europeans were reviled as "backward" (that is, they had not participated in the history of Europe, but instead had their own history), the empire needed a constant source of cheap raw materials to import and a market for its exports, and human life (especially that of non-Europeans) was considered cheap, and biologists were easily able to co-opt scientific narratives of ancestry and nature to rationalize land grabbing and genocide.

Closer to home, the 1950s and 1960s were turbulent times in the United States. Older standards of behavior were being threatened by rock and roll and by the civil rights movement. The intellectual backlash they engendered in the scholarly community came initially from a psychologist named Henry Garrett (from Columbia University), an anatomist named Wesley Critz George (from the University of North Carolina), and a wealthy former airline executive named Carleton Putnam. They used their expertise and organizational skills, and money from racist philanthropies, to argue publicly against the integration of public schools.

In the early 1960s, they found an ally in a prominent anthropologist at the University of Pennsylvania named Carleton Coon, a relative of Putnam.

Coon had devised an idiosyncratic interpretation of the fossil record, which held that the five kinds of modern people he could identify were detectable as such in *Homo erectus*. Each of them, he believed, evolved largely independently into *Homo sapiens*—Europeans first, Australian aborigines last. This, Coon felt, explained why whites were the "most civilized" of peoples—they had been members of the modern species for longer than anyone else. His ideas were quickly taken up by his segregationist allies, who wrote, "When the President of the American Association of Physical Anthropologists, a magna cum laude graduate of Harvard and a native of New England, states that recent discoveries indicate the Negro is 200,000 years behind the White race on the ladder of evolution, this ends the integration argument."

Actually, it doesn't; and fortunately, it didn't. Coon's ideas were shown to be anthropological bunkum, and he ended a distinguished career in embittered isolation. Nobody else was confident that subspecific variation in *Homo erectus* could be identified with such clarity, much less matched up to patterns of biological variation in modern people hundreds of thousands of years later. Moreover, levels of civilization were recognized to be contingencies of social history, and not genetic endowments of nature. There was in fact nothing solid to suggest that any human group was any "less human" or "less evolved" than any other, and certainly nothing to suggest we should base social legislation on such ideas.

Ironically, scholars on both the political right (such as the psychologist Henry Garrett) and on the political left (such as the geneticist Theodosius Dobzhanzky; Chapter 5) recognized the political value of Coon's work. The only one who denied it, in a pathetically self-interested stance, was Coon himself. The important point we take away is that our stories of who we are and where we came from do not exist, and have never existed, in a de-politicized world. They are laden with value, and consequently we are obliged to be very certain about our authoritative scientific pronouncements, and we bear a burden of responsibility for their use and application.

It is particularly ironic, in light of the claims made by racists in the 1960s, that we began this section with a scientifically literate quotation from South Africa's (black) President, Thabo Mbeki. His (white) American counterpart, George W. Bush, simultaneously expressed the regressive view that creationism should be taught in school as science.

TESTING PALEONTOLOGICAL MODELS GENETICALLY

It is not uncommon to hear that genetic data can solve social problems (by studying nonexistent genes for stupidity, crime, and other antisocial traits), or that they can resolve our conflicting interpretations of prehistory by extracting simple patterns from the gene pool. Usually the interpretation of the genetic patterns turns out to be just as conflicted: for example, it has been argued, based on genetic data, that Paleo-Indians entered the Americas from Siberia in one wave, two waves, three waves, and more than three waves!

However, a landmark study in 1987 attempted to answer the question of whether or not global patterns of DNA variation could be meaningfully related to human evolution. Rebecca Cann, Mark Stoneking, and Allan Wilson pioneered the use of mitochondrial DNA (mtDNA; Chapter 4) as a marker of ancestry.

Mitochondrial DNA has several properties that make it a useful tool in genetic studies. First, it is easily separable from the bulk of the DNA, the nuclear genome. Second, it is small (16,500 bases) and well characterized. Third, it is inherited clonally, from mother to offspring. Fourth, there is no recombination, so the mtDNA molecule is passed on across generations as a single intact genetic unit. Fifth, it accumulates mutations rapidly, so a sample of humans (as long as they are not all close relatives) will likely have detectable differences. And sixth, the we now understand the two principal forces governing the population dynamics of mtDNA: random lineage extinction (families with all boys are mitochondrially extinct, even if they are very prolific) and selective sweeps (since the mtDNA molecule is passed on as a single unit without recombination, any period of positive selection on any part of the mtDNA molecule would carry the rest with it, and essentially wipe out all the variation in the mtDNA gene pool).

Cann, Stoneking, and Wilson found that the sample of Africans subsumed the diversity of the people from other parts of the world; and that humans had relatively little genetic diversity to work with in the first place. These data were more compatible with the idea that modern humans had arisen fairly recently from a population in Africa, than with the idea that people have evolved pretty much where they are now, from ancient, local populations. The creative use of genetic data, therefore, was able to distinguish between two hypotheses generated from the paleontological data. This of course does not mean that the question of how modern human evolution proceeded is closed, for we now know that there are more complicated scenarios that can account for the genetic pattern, but it helps to show that there can be points of contact between the diachronic science of paleoanthropology and synchronic science of genetics.

Indeed, a study published a decade later by Svante Pääbo's research group in Germany showed that trace amounts of mtDNA could be recovered from Neandertal bones and compared to human DNA. They found that it lies outside the range of modern human variation, and thus possibly merits taxonomic distinction. The genetic difference between human and Neandertal mtDNA seems to be comparable to that between subspecies of chimpanzees.

Geneticists, however, sometimes have been known to overstate their results. The earliest studies of Neandertal DNA showed that there was no genetic contact between their gene pool and ours; more recent genomic analyses suggest that living peoples may have up to 4% of their genomes derived from the Neandertal gene pool. The geneticists also find DNA from an inferred group of Siberian Neandertals, or Denisovans, to be principally residing in the genomes of living New Guineans, in spite of the biogeographical problems posed by that inference. The rest of us don't quite know what to make of it.

Another kind of statistical analysis using global variation in mtDNA sequences asked about the pattern we might expect to see if we compared everyone to everyone else and tabulated the detectable differences each time. Such a "mismatch distribution" predicts a different pattern characteristic of a population that has steadily increased in size, compared to a relatively stable population that experienced a major surge of growth at some point in time. Sure enough, the pattern of mismatches in human mtDNA seems most consistent with an explosive rate of growth about 60,000 years ago, and roughly coincident with the development of the artistic, symbolic cultural forms we have come to associate with modern humanity.

Genomic studies of nuclear DNA have supported the findings first established with mtDNA quite strongly. Indeed, the study of genetics has produced three well-established patterns about human prehistory. First, living humans have a small fraction of the genetic variation we find in chimpanzees and gorillas, our closest relatives. This strongly suggests a different demographic history, and is most readily explained as a combination of founder speciation events in the human lineage, and selective sweeps.

Second, we don't find humans clustering into a small number of large and fairly discrete groups, our popular conception of what "races" ought to be. We do seem to cluster genetically into local populations, but larger agglomerations are elusive and unstable, and thus not "natural."

And third, we find an elaboration of culture as a marker of orientation and identity in parallel with a reduction in biological diversity. Two and a half million years ago there were arguably three genera of hominids; 100,000 years ago there were arguably just three subspecies (aside from a relict prehuman population in Indonesia, *Homo floresiensis*). Now there is just one subspecies, and there is no argument about it. There is so little taxonomic structure within extant *Homo sapiens,* and so little genetic variation detectable, that the groups we tend to acknowledge are either bounded culturally (for example, nations or religions) or not actually bounded at all (for example, pigmentation classes, blood groups, or skull shapes).

REFERENCES AND FURTHER READING

Arsuaga, J. L., I. Martínez, L. J. Arnold, et al. 2014. Neandertal roots: Cranial and chronological evidence from Sima de los Huesos. *Science* 344:1358–1363.

Benazzi, S., V. Slon, S. Talamo, et al. 2015. The makers of the Protoaurignacian and implications for Neandertal extinction. *Science* 348:793–796.

Bermudez de Castro, J. M., M. Martinon-Torres, E. Carbonell, et al. 2004. The Atapuerca sites and their contribution to the knowledge of human evolution in Europe. *Evolutionary Anthropology* 13:25–41.

Cann, R. L., M. Stoneking, and A. C. Wilson. 1987. Mitochondrial DNA and human evolution. *Nature* 325:31–36.

Caspari, R., and S. Lee. 2004. Older age becomes common late in human evolution. *Proceedings of the National Academy of Sciences, U S A* 101:10895.

Chase, P. G., and H. L. Dibble. 1987. Middle Paleolithic symbolism: A review of current evidence and interpretations. *Journal of Anthropological Archaeology* 6:263–296.

Churchill, S. 1998. Cold adaptation, heterochrony, and Neandertals. *Evolutionary Anthropology* 7:46–61.

Cowgill, L. 2011. One year in biological anthropology: Species, integration, and boundaries in 2010. *American Anthropologist* 113 (2):213–221.

d'Errico, F. 2003. The invisible frontier: A multiple species model for the origin of behavioral modernity. *Evolutionary Anthropology* 12:188–202.

Douglas, M. 1966. *Purity and Danger: An Analysis of Concepts of Pollution and Taboo.* London: Routledge and Kegan Paul.

Duarte, C., J. Mauricio, P. Pettitt, et al. 1999. The early Upper Paleolithic human skeleton from the Abrigo do Lagar Velho (Portugal) and modern human emergence in Iberia. *Proceedings of the National Academy of Sciences, U S A* 96:7604–7609.

Etler, D. 1996. The fossil evidence for human evolution in Asia. *Annual Review of Anthropology* 25:275–301.

Goren-Inbar, N., N. Alperson, M. Kislev, et al. 2004. Evidence of hominin control of fire at Gesher Benot Ya'aqov, Israel. *Science* 304:725–727.

Henshilwood, C., F. d'Errico, M. Vanhaeren, K. van Niekirk, and Z. Jacobs 2004. Middle Stone Age shell beads from South Africa. *Science* 304:404.

Jonas, H. 1996. *Mortality and Morality.* Evanston, IL: Northwestern University Press.

Klein, R. 2003. Whither the Neanderthals? *Nature* 299:1525–1527.

Kroeber, A. L. 1940. Stimulus diffusion. *American Anthropologist* 42:1–20.

Kuhn, S. L., M. C. Stiner, D. Reese, and E. Gulec. 2001. Ornaments of the earliest Upper Paleolithic: New insights from the Levant. *Proceedings of the National Academy of Sciences, U S A* 98:7641–7646.

Manzi, G. 2004. Human evolution at the Matuyama-Brunhes boundary. *Evolutionary Anthropology* 13:11–24.

Manzi, G., F. Mallegni, and A. Ascenzi. 2001. A cranium for the earliest Europeans: Phylogenetic position of the hominid from Ceprano, Italy. *Proceedings of the National Academy of Sciences, U S A* 98:10011–10016.

Meyer, M., M. Kircher, M.-T. Gansauge, et al. 2012. A high-coverage genome sequence from an archaic Denisovan individual. *Science* 338:222–226.

Pääbo, S. 2015. The diverse origins of the human gene pool. *Nature Reviews Genetics* 16 (6):313–314.

Plummer, T. 2004. Flaked stones and old bones: Biological and cultural evolution at the dawn of technology. *Yearbook of Physical Anthropology* 47:118–164.

Qin, P., and M. Stoneking. 2015. Denisovan ancestry in East Eurasian and Native American populations. *Molecular Biology and Evolution* 32:2665–2674.

Ramirez Rossi, F. V., and J. M. Bermudez de Castro. 2004. Surprisingly rapid growth in Neanderthals. *Nature* 428:936–939.

Schmitz, R. W., D. Serre, S. Feine, et al. 2002. The Neandertal type site revisited: Interdisciplinary investigations of skeletal remains from the Neander Valley, Germany. *Proceedings of the National Academy of Sciences, U S A* 99:13342–13347.

Schwartz, J., and I. Tattersall. 1996. Significance of some previously unrecognized apomorphies in the nasal region of *Homo neanderthalensis. Proceedings of the National Academy of Sciences, U S A* 93:10852–10854.

Shea, J. J. 2003. Neandertals, competition, and the origin of modern human behavior in the Levant. *Evolutionary Anthropology* 12:1730187.

Shea, J. J. 2013. *Stone Tools in the Paleolithic and Neolithic Near East: A Guide.* New York: Cambridge University Press.

Simpson, G. G. 1945. The principles of classification and a classification of mammals *Bulletin of the American Museum of Natural History* 85:1–349.

Spikins, P. 2015. *How Compassion Made Us Human*. London: Pen and Sword.

Stoneking, M. 2017. *An Introduction to Molecular Anthropology*. New York: Wiley.

Trinkaus, E. 1983. *The Shanidar Neandertals*. New York: Academic Press.

Trinkaus, E. 2003. Neandertal faces were not long; modern human faces are short. *Proceedings of the National Academy of Sciences, U S A* 100:8142–8145.

Trinkaus, E., S. E. Churchill, and C. B. Ruff. 1994. Postcranial robusticity in *Homo*. II: Humeral bilateral asymmetry and bone plasticity. *American Journal of Physical Anthropology* 93:1–34.

Vernot, B., S. Tucci, J. Kelso, et al. 2016. Excavating Neandertal and Denisovan DNA from the genomes of Melanesian individuals. *Science* 352:235–239.

Wilford, J. N. 1998. Neanderthal or cretin? A debate over iodine. *New York Times*. December 1.

Yellen, J. E., A. S. Brooks, E. Cornelissen, M. J. Mehlman, and K. Stewart 1995. A Middle Stone Age worked bone industry from Katanda, Upper Semliki Valley, Zaire. *Science* 268:553–556.

CHAPTER 13

Just How Different Is Different?
(On Race)

THEME

The study of human diversity involves a negotiation between objective patterns of difference and subjective perceptions of otherness. It is consequently an inextricably biocultural endeavor, and fundamentally anthropological. Patterns of human genetic diversity do not map well onto patterns of behavioral diversity, which suggests that behavioral genetics has a very limited range of applicability to human behavior.

RACE

There are fewer terms so widely used, considered so important, and yet so imprecisely conceptualized as "race." While all ancient people with some travel or trade experience recognized that people far away looked different from them, they invariably interpreted that variation in local terms. Indeed, real variation in physical form was often impossible to disentangle from mythological variation, as writers from ancient Rome through medieval times wrote of people here and there who had heads in their chests, or one leg, or no nose, or some such. By the mid-1600s, however, European scholars had a pretty good idea of what kinds of people were real and where they lived. This knowledge had come as a consequence of the maritime exploration, trade with, and conquest of much of the rest of the world.

The opening of long-distance sea voyages raised an interesting optical illusion about travel. In the old days, you took boats over short distances and did most of your travel over land (like, say, Marco Polo in the thirteenth century). You might note the subtle differences in physical form from place to place, but you were not struck by significant discontinuities. Now, however, you got on board in, say, Lisbon, and got off a few weeks later in the Caribbean, where the people looked and acted quite different from the last people you saw. You might naturally start thinking about those considerable differences and the large gap that separates you from one another, both mentally and physically.

Further, the political and economic relations between Europeans and other people had also taken a curious form. Back in Europe, you had a centralized government regulating an area with fixed boundaries, a nation-state. Now you want to trade with, or exploit, or subjugate people elsewhere. How do you deal with them, if they don't have the recognizable political forms with which you are familiar, but rather have more fluid forms of social and political organization? Once again, you might naturally start thinking about them as being largely undifferentiated and homogeneous, in stark contrast to your own frame of reference.

This kind of thought, of course, might be neither formal nor conscious, but just a natural way of making sense of the world that Europeans were perceiving in the 1600s. And thus it was that a French physician and traveler named François Bernier in 1684 became the first to propose that the human species came naturally divisible into just a few basically different kinds of people.

Who were they? The people of Eurasia (including Native Americans), East Asia, sub-Saharan Africa (excluding the southernmost part), the Cape of Good Hope in southern Africa, and the Lapps of Scandinavia.

Wait a minute—who are the Lapps of Scandinavia?

Actually the Lapps (or Sami) are—stereotypically, at least—stockily built reindeer herders, ethnically distinct from other Scandinavians. Of course, they don't look all that different; but they were considered an "other" against whom Europeans could contrast themselves. The peoples of the Cape of Good Hope are known as KhoiSan (and formerly, as "Hottentots" and "Bushmen"), herders and hunter-gatherers who are both somewhat smaller statured and lighter complected than their Bantu-speaking agrarian neighbors to the north.

It is not clear what Bernier thought he had discovered. The descendants of different Adams and Eves, perhaps? In 1655, a scholar named Isaac de la Peyrère had written a widely noted book on "pre-Adamites"—people who may have been separately created by God elsewhere and earlier, independently of the provincial story recounted in the Bible.

Bernier's new idea, however, was "good to think with"—a fairly sensible way of conceptualizing the peoples of the world: they came packaged into a small number of fundamentally and geographically distinct varieties. When the great Swedish naturalist Carl Linnaeus (Chapter 2) considered the place of humans within the primates, and within the mammals, it naturally occurred to him to incorporate the variation within the human species itself into his framework. Following Bernier, a geographically based division of the human species into subspecies seemed quite natural.

Linnaeus, however, was proud of all forms of Scandinavian heritage, and embraced the Sami as part of the European subspecies. The Asian subspecies now encompassed the entire continent, as did the African subspecies. And finally, the native peoples of the Americas became a subspecies of their own. So, there were now four formal, geographically based subdivisions of the human species; and Linnaeus even color coded them for your convenience—Europeans white, Asians yellow, Africans black, and Americans red.

It is not clear what Linnaeus thought he was describing, either. Why would the boundary of a continent create human homogeneity within it, and categorical difference outside of it? In fact, Linnaeus was working with two importantly pre-modern concepts. The first is the idea that an ideal imaginary form underlies real living groups of animals, and that the task of the scientist is to describe that ideal form by studying the real variation in nature, and imagining just what it is that each particular creature is a deviation from. This is called essentialism (Chapter 3), and is rooted in the ideas of Plato and Aristotle. That is why Linnaeus could define *Homo sapiens europaeus albus* (white European *Homo sapiens*) as having blue eyes and flowing blond hair. The fact that most Europeans did not have those features was irrelevant; Linnaeus was describing something eternal and metaphysical, the essence of the European, not something earthly, like the attributes of real Europeans. What his "European" meant, where it came from, or even where it is, are not questions he addressed.

The second pre-modern idea applied here by Linnaeus is that the microcosm (the small universe) maps directly on to the macrocosm (the big universe). Linnaeus was trained in medicine, and doctors in the eighteenth century were taught that the body is composed of four fluids or humors: blood, bile, black bile, and phlegm. These were familiar especially in their classical Greco-Roman names: *sanguis*, *chole*, *melanchole*, and *phlegma*; and had to be present in a proper balance for the body to be in good health. Imbalances led to personality flaws and poor physical and mental health. Linnaeus transferred this idea to the human species as a whole, assigning each of his four human subspecies a dominant personality from each of the four humors. Europeans were hearty, or sanguine; Americans irascible, or choleric; Asians serious, or melancholy; and Africans lazy, or phlegmatic.

Thus, Linnaeus inscribed the human body itself on the human species, at least as both were understood in the eighteenth century. While this is obviously highly culturally inflected, Linnaeus had such an immense impact on biology through his breakthrough in ordering and classifying the natural world that his basic approach became the basis for understanding human diversity as well.

Outside the corridors of academia, however, Linnaean taxonomy was resisted by the great French naturalist and writer, Count de Buffon (Chapter 2). Buffon also resisted any such organizing theory below the level of the human species, describing the continuous variation of the human species as consisting of local "races"— a term he used with no precise meaning, in the sense of a "strain" or "lineage," and certainly not to denote a formal taxonomic category of people. But Linnaeus's system and approach eclipsed Buffon's work, because it obviously worked very well for most of the natural world.

By the end of the eighteenth century, Johann Friedrich Blumenbach became the foremost student of the human form and, like Buffon, was struck not so much by the discontinuities as by the continuities—as indeed most scholars had traditionally been, until scarcely a century earlier. But in order to study natural variation scientifically, one had to follow Linnaeus and classify. Thus, Blumenbach could paradoxically write, "one variety of mankind does so sensibly pass into the other, that you cannot mark out the limits between them" and yet proceed to mark out the limits of five of them. He named them after their most beautiful representative skulls, and called them Ethiopian, Mongolian, Malay, American, and (his most famous category) Caucasian.

Scholars of the early nineteenth century proceeded to take Buffon's informal word ("race") and fuse it with Linnaeus's formal concept ("subspecies"), thus constructing a pseudotaxonomy of human populations that might sometimes privilege geography, or language, or skin color and hair form, or ethnic identity—or any of the other biocultural criteria that human beings use to sort themselves into groups. The scientific study of human diversity consequently became the study of how many different kinds of people there are and how they differ. For the next 150 years, however, scholars couldn't agree on what traits were most important, how many groups there really were, or who might be in them. What they did not question was their assumption that race was the most important organizing principle in understanding how human groups differ from one another.

PATTERNS OF CONTEMPORARY HUMAN VARIATION

By the end of World War II, in which mystical ideas about race figured prominently in Nazi ideology, scholarly thought about race had changed in a significant way. Earlier essentialist approaches envisioned race as a part of a person, as their core identity. Thus even Harvard's Earnest Hooton could write that a person might look white and "really" be black, or vice versa; to him race was a matter of diagnosis. A newer concept of race, a "population" concept, reversed the relationship, conceiving of people as parts of races, rather than races being parts of people. How could you now look one thing and "really" be another? You were part of a geographical group, or perhaps of multiple geographic groups, and that was that. Race was ancestry—it was just geography and genetics, which left nothing to diagnose. And race was real people, not abstract ideas.

The new concept of race was more empirically based, but soon also collapsed under its own weight. After all, populations can be subdivided endlessly; was there anything biologically natural about juxtaposing "Africans" against "Europeans" racially, but *not* juxtaposing West Africans against East Africans racially, or northern Europeans against southern Europeans racially? What of the peoples of Pakistan or Sri Lanka, who facially resemble Europeans, are darkly complected like Africans, and are from the continent of Asia? What about the Pygmies, the Basques, the Polynesians, and all the other local variants of the human race? What makes a difference count? Without a clear or "objective" answer to this, the number of racial categories that specialists recognized could become quickly multiplied.

Moreover, they were now seen by outsiders to be loaded with cultural value, and not at all reflective of natural patterns of variation. For example, the geneticist William C. Boyd wrote a review in the journal *Science* in 1963 in which he identified thirteen races of people. The "European group" comprised five races: (1) Basques, (2) Lapps, (3) Northwest Europeans, (4) Eastern/Central Europeans, and

(5) Mediterraneans. The sixth race was Africans; the seventh, Asians; the eighth, Indo-Dravidians; and the ninth, American Indians. Finally, the "Pacific group" comprised (10) Indonesians, (11) Melanesians, (12) Polynesians, and (13) Australians.

But what could possibly be natural about seeing five kinds of Europeans and only one kind of Asian? By what stretch of the imagination could the Basques of the Pyrenees Mountains be considered the taxonomic equivalent of the Africans?

In fact, the entire enterprise was riddled through with cultural values about "how different is different" and what differences "count," in addition to the cultural problem identified by Blumenbach, namely, forcing yourself to draw formal divisions where none exist in nature.

Perhaps race needed to be "unthought" as a concept, and human variation examined outside the Linnaean framework of formal nested categories. When anthropologists did that, not coincidentally around the time of the civil rights movement, they once again identified the pattern that had been obscured since the earliest days of colonialism: namely, that people differ gradually from one another geographically. We call this pattern "clinal," and the anthropological geneticist Frank Livingstone summarized its rediscovery epigrammatically in 1962: "There are no races, there are only clines."

The introduction of genetic studies in the 1960s provided some valuable quantitative data, but also provided a data set that (unlike physical appearance) was generally not modifiable culturally, and not subject to the same crude set of intellectual biases that had beset classical anthropological studies, which were invariably based on how people "looked." Yet the patterns between phenotypes and genes were highly concordant. Everywhere you studied, you found people blending into one another physically and genetically.

In other words, to a first approximation, people are similar to those close by, and they are different from those far away—but that no more tells you there are three kinds of people than it tells you there are five, or twenty, or one hundred.

Why does this pattern exist? Quite simply, it is the human mode of life: trade, sociality, and interbreeding. Natural selection adapts populations to their environments, which vary locally; genetic drift makes local populations slightly different from one another; and gene flow connects them. The pattern of difference that we see between populations is principally local variation. Interestingly, even that difference is a small part of the picture of how humans differ—for most of our variations can be found within a single population.

Consider the ABO blood group (Chapter 4) in which three principal alleles are known. And yet, all populations have them (Native Americans have lost nearly all their B alleles, and are overwhelmingly O, but they are exceptional in this regard). What they differ in is simply the relative proportions of the three alleles. There are also rare alleles found in some members of some populations, but neither of these maps well on to ideas of race; and it seems to be paradigmatic for the way genetic variation is structured in our species.

Anthropologists had long known that far more diversity exists within any human race than between them, but had never been able to quantify that observation. Beginning with a classic study by Richard Lewontin in 1972, it turns out that whatever genetic system you study—protein variations, mtDNA, short redundant segments of nuclear DNA—you find that 85%–95% of the variation exists within populations, and only 5%–15% distinguishes populations from one another (and of course, much of that is local differentiation, not global). There is geographical structure to the small amount of between-group variation, but even that is patterned principally clinally and locally. The most significant implication of the genetic work is that the gene pools of large human groups are not at all discrete, and overlap tremendously.

A more important consideration, however, is what the conditions of the modern world in the last 500 years, perhaps twenty generations, have done to the human populations of the world, even the most remote ones. A major consequence of colonialism was the large-scale resettlement of people away from their "ancestral" land and into major communities elsewhere. This resettlement runs a gamut from voluntary migration, through economic or political coercion, to capture and enslavement. The result has been the development of enormous diaspora populations, many of which have existed for centuries (the term "*diaspora*" is an extension of a word that initially referred to the forced dispersal of the Jews from their homeland into the Babylonian Empire, after being conquered by Nebuchadnezzar in the sixth century BC).

Not only are diaspora communities interesting to cultural anthropologists, but they have been interesting to biological anthropologists as well. Members of such communities develop physically somewhat differently in their new land (see below), and may also face particular new biomedical problems. Diaspora communities also create high rates and new patterns of gene flow, making the human population more homogeneous.

In addition to immigration, the consequence of colonialism, there is also an effect of industrialism, namely, the movement of enormous numbers of people away from their rural homes and their coalescence in urban centers. However strong the tradition of endogamy, or marrying your own kind, might be, the coalescence of large numbers of diverse people in small areas also increases the rate of gene flow tremendously.

Indeed, these two demographic factors—immigration and urbanism—products of the political economics of colonialism and industrialism, have changed the biology of the human species enormously. What does it mean to produce a "racial map" that shows America to be the land of Indians, Africa the land of Africans, and Europe the land of Europeans, when the large majority of people in the United States are of principally European descent, 12% self-identify as having principally African ancestry, and less than 2% claim to have any Native American ancestry at all? Such a map would be entirely disconnected from the modern world.

The bio-demographic issues assume even greater significance in the hotly political arena of land rights issues. If we agree that indigenous people have been, and in many cases still are being, unfairly stripped of their land and possessions, and are entitled to something for it, who counts as indigenous? Is there a statute of limitations that permits us to declare that a South African KhoiSan (itself a category reflecting the mixture of two peoples who once saw themselves as distinctly different from one another) is more indigenous than a Bantu speaker, whose ancestors entered the area a few thousand years ago, and even more so than a Boer, whose ancestors have been living there for over 300 years? How far back do your roots have to go before you can stop being an invader and start being considered as native?

In short, races—as large, taxonomic groups of people—are optical illusions, the result of imposing cultural categories of meaning upon natural patterns of variation. Categories of identity will always be with us, but those identities have evolved, and will continue to change, for they are categories of political salience, not categories of biological transcendence.

WHY DO WE SEE RACES?

The pattern we find in human genetics is known as isolation by distance—the farther away two populations are, the more different they appear. Suppose we were to bring large numbers of people from three very different parts of the world together; what would we see?

We would obviously see a few different kinds of people. Clearly, that is something like what took place in American history, with large numbers of immigrants from West Africa, northern Europe, and east Asia superimposed on an indigenous population.

American theories of race are naturally related to the history of American slavery. In the decades before the Civil War, slavery's defenders were able to martial the earliest American physical anthropology for their cause: the polygenist theories (Chapter 2) of Josiah Nott and George Gliddon, authors of *Indigenous Races of the Earth*. This work, by a physician and a diplomat, purported to show that the races are as they always have been—made separately by God. Nott and Gliddon made use of an old interpretation of Noah's ark, which held that after the ark landed, Noah's three sons went off in different directions to found their own continents. Writing before the development of modern theories of heredity or evolution, Nott and Gliddon maintained that the descendants of Ham became Africans, the descendants of Shem became Asians, and the descendants of Japheth became Europeans. Their essential differences were passed on intact over the generations since the Flood, and where the descendants later came into contact, they produced intermediate races.

Polygenism, then, held that the races partook of fixed differences, inscribed by God, whether they were inherited from different sons of the same patriarch, or were (in a slightly different version) simply products of different creative acts. Monogenism, by contrast, took biblical literalism—we are all products of the same creative act, Adam and Eve—as a justification for the abolition of slavery. The monogenists bolstered their position empirically with the recognition that humans interbred freely all over the world.

Neither position is really "right"—since both are based on pre-modern concepts. However, the racist position does yield some testable hypotheses: Was there ever a time when people occupied Norway, Nigeria, and Cambodia, but not the places in between? Of course not; the earliest evidence we have for modern people comes precisely from those in-between areas, east Africa and west Asia!

Indeed, even today, it is common to hear people naively think of West Africans, East Asians, and northern Europeans as being the purest or most ancient representatives of their respective continental races. But actually the traits we identify as "racial"—skin color, hair form, facial contour—are the results of selection and drift, so that the people furthest away simply look the most different. But they are by no means the purest, or most primordial peoples; they are simply the farthest apart.

We know very little about the origin or possible adaptive significance of hair form or facial contour (e.g., northern Europeans tending to have long, narrow noses; east Asians tending to have wide, flat faces; Africans tending to have tightly curled hair). But we have learned something about skin color. Modern humans seem to have become depigmented as they moved into northerly (and southerly) latitudes, owing to the reduction in sunlight, and in particular, of ultraviolet rays in those latitudes. People need to produce vitamin D, which is stimulated by ultraviolet light. Where there is plenty of sunlight, in the tropics, the dark skin pigment melanin screens out the surplus, preventing skin cancer (triggered by too much ultraviolet light). The ultraviolet light also breaks down a chemical called folate, too little of which can cause birth defects. But where sunlight is at a premium, especially seasonally, it was apparently adaptive to lose the melanin and allow the body to maximize the production of vitamin D.

Consequently, skin color follows a cline that maps very closely onto the amount of ultraviolet radiation that can penetrate the atmosphere at different latitudes.

Given the history of slavery, of course skin color has become an important marker of identity in America. In earlier times, when it was illegal for whites and blacks to marry (a situation called "miscegenation" in the parlance of the age), our society was legally obliged to define who fell into each category. We adopted the "one drop of blood" rule, whereby any amount of non-white ancestry—usually a single great-grandparent—would place you in the non-white category. That obviously enlarged the category "black" to include people of varying degrees of diverse ancestry. In North America, "black" and "white" became exclusive categories, and the ancillary rule of "hypodescent" (if your parents are of different races, you belong to the one with the lower social status) kept the categories qualitatively discrete and distinct.

This is a cultural system of heredity that maintains races by patrolling their boundaries vigilantly and by defining intermediacy out of existence. It is a workable system of heredity and descent, but hardly bears a relationship to biological reality.

The racial system that emerged in Latin America is different. There, subtle social rankings emerge from nuanced categories of skin color. In other words, they have "race" there too, but conceptualized in a very different way.

It is the flexibility of racial categories and conceptualizations, both across nations and through time, that permits us to see that the basis of the concept of race is culturally complex, rather than a simple observation from nature. And it is one of the fundamental aspects of anthropology to recognize that the way things appear to be commonly depends more upon the cultural lenses with which you examine them than upon the way they "really" are.

The cultural practice of assigning people to fixed, discrete racial categories, in defiance of actual patterns of biological diversity in our species, is one facet of a more general cultural practice known as "naturalizing difference." This involves rationalizing social distinctions via an argument that those distinctions are actually the products of genetics or biology or some constitutional endowment, rather than being products of history or human agency. This is the logic that commonly sets pharaohs or emperors above their subjects, aristocrats over peasants, and conquerors over victims. We encounter it again when we examine gender.

Another way to gain an appreciation for race as a cultural construction is to consider the way in which racial categories come into existence and pass out of existence over a few generations—like ideas, not like natural entities. At the turn of the twentieth century, most Euro-Americans distinguished not only blacks and whites racially, but also other marginalized Europeans, notably Irish and Jews. Many Jews originated in eastern Europe, and the Irish obviously originated in northwest Europe, and since we know that geography is a significant determinant of human variation, they both looked physically distinct. But those physical distinctions were greatly augmented by stylized forms of posture, dress, movement, attitude, and speech, which exaggerated their physical distinctiveness. (We now refer to the latter kinds of attributes as ethnicity.)

Over the course of the twentieth century, not only was there some intermarriage among the groups, but more importantly, as Irish and Jewish immigrants to America entered the middle class in large numbers, their physical distinctiveness seemed to diminish with economic and social assimilation, and they simply lost much of the "otherness" by which they had been formerly set apart as racially distinct. Nowadays we recognize Irish and Jewish as ethnicities, but not as races. Of course, some people "look Irish" or "look Jewish"—but many more members of both groups don't. And even people with "the look" may not even know if they had ancestors belonging to those groups!

The opposite situation is also instructive: the category "Hispanic," which was not a category a hundred years ago (even though such people obviously existed!), but is a very important one in America today. Yet consider the very name, which denotes a group of people defined by language, not by biology or geography. One can be Hispanic and (due to colonial history) have ancestry principally from peoples of nearly anywhere—Spain, Mexico, the Caribbean, South America, West Africa, the Philippines. With such an un-biological basis, it is nevertheless also true that people can sometimes be identified as Hispanic by their "looks." Hispanic, as a category of demographic and political salience, has become "racialized" in American society, to the extent that many Americans have no problem in considering "Hispanic" to be a race.

This caused some problems on the 2000 US census. The census takers wanted to tabulate the Hispanic population, but also quite reasonably did not want to call Hispanics a race, recognizing it as a category defined by language. So one question asked whether you are Hispanic, and the next question asked for your race. But many people who self-identified as Hispanic proceeded to skip the next question, because they figured that they had just answered it. The 2010 Census specified, "For this Census, Hispanic origins are not races."

Once again, this is not to say that there are no patterns of biological variation in humans. Rather, these patterns of biological variation do not map easily on to racial categories. The racial categories are fictions, but biological variation is real; and even more real are the social consequences of the pseudo-biological racial categories.

RACE AS A BIOCULTURAL CATEGORY

The cultural theorist Donna Haraway has said that "race is a verb." What she means is that race is a process of cultural assignment, involving arbitrary decisions about what categories are to be recognized, what criteria are used in assigning people to those categories, and ultimately who is to be placed in them. It is not a fact of nature, but an act of culture, a social construction and a means of naturalizing difference. This does not, however, mean that everyone is the same. Anthropology is predicated on the study of human difference. If everyone were the same, there could be no anthropology. Rather, recognizing that race is a social construction means that whatever patterns of biological variation are "out there" do not map readily on to the social categories articulated by race, and thus are not relevant to explaining the social differences that race encodes, nor to explaining much of the variation in the lives and fortunes of ordinary people.

Thus, race is a biocultural category, that is to say, the facts of biological difference rendered sensible by cultural perceptions of otherness. Culture not only informs us "how different is different"—that is to say, what kinds of people need to be placed into different categories—but also exaggerates the differences among groups beyond simply genetic features. The biological variation is in the form of the gene pool and body, and the cultural variation is in the form of the speech patterns, body movements, typical attitudes and behaviors, diet, and other non-genetic markers of social identity. We refer to these as ethnicity, and drawing the distinction between these two dimensions of variation was a major contribution of anthropology in the twentieth century.

It was the great anthropologist Franz Boas who demonstrated that the physical features that distinguish groups from one another constitute a far larger universe than the *genetically determined* physical features that distinguish groups from one another. He studied Italian immigrants to New York from Sicily and Jewish immigrants from eastern Europe. The form of the head, ranging from globular (brachycephalic) to elongated (dolichocephalic), was known to differentiate peoples from one another and to have some kind of biological basis. But Boas showed that the act of immigrating to a new country (and circumstances of growth) can change the shape of the head dramatically. Long-headed Jews were more round headed the younger they had immigrated, and their children who grew up in America were more round headed still. And the opposite situation was found for the Sicilians. Obviously people weren't just morphing into one another, but subtly different aspects of the conditions of life apparently worked to exaggerate the physical differences of the different populations in their native lands.

Boas initiated the study of immigrants, and his findings were soon replicated for many other groups of people, most notably Japanese immigrants to Hawaii. There, Harry Shapiro and Fred Hulse found that Japanese who had immigrated to Hawaii were physically statistically different from their relatives who had stayed behind; and their children who had been born in Hawaii were more different still. At a certain level, this was a trivial finding, that the environment contributes to the development of phenotypes. But at another level, it was very disconcerting to students of race, who had generally assumed that any regularly visible difference in appearance must have a genetic etiology. It was becoming clear that the universe of genetically based differences was only a small subset of the universe of visible differences between groups of people.

One such difference that has succumbed to scientific scrutiny is the difference that one commonly finds among different groups of people in IQ. The IQ, or intelligence quotient, is a number that is calculated from the performance on a standardized test. Obviously something as complex and multifaceted as intelligence cannot really be collapsed into a single number, with different people linearly ranked according to how much of it they have. Linearization is itself a highly cultural value. Equally obviously, your performance on a test can't be determined by your genes, but must also reflect in part the educational experiences of the subject. After all, if you've never been exposed to the word "rhododendron," how could you reasonably be expected to know what it means? (It's a flower.)

We now know that IQ is very sensitive to the social environment, and the effects of social prejudice can be significant and consistent. Koreans fare consistently worse than Japanese on such tests in Japan, where they are an underprivileged minority, but equal to Japanese in America, where their social status is equivalent. Likewise, the gap between the IQ of blacks and whites in America vanishes the more carefully that social variables are evened out, or controlled. There seems to be no good reason to regard group-average differences in IQ to be innate, other than a malicious desire to "naturalize difference."

It was generally held by the 1960s that race was a "natural" category, and ethnicity was a "cultural" one. That distinction was important, but we now realize that it was an oversimplification. We now know that race is also a category culturally constructed in other ways, but still significantly different from the constructed differences we call ethnicity. Moreover, if we accept the dichotomy between natural and cultural variation, it is hard to know into which category to put differences in head shape, which have a genetic and an environmental component. The dichotomy, then, is a false dichotomy, but the difference it highlights is a crucially important one.

ASKING SCIENTIFIC QUESTIONS ABOUT HUMAN DIVERSITY

Knowing what we do, how can we study human diversity scientifically if race is not its basic organizing vector? In fact, there are four broad strategies of scientific research on human variation that show not only how human variation can be studied without race but also how race would be positively misleading if it were considered uncritically to be a genetic feature.

The first study involves the commonly social origin of race-based disparities in health matters. To the extent that blacks and whites are at different risks for being afflicted by certain diseases and how they run their course, nearly all of these disparities are eliminated by controlling the data for economic status and access to healthcare.

Some are not, however, such as hypertension in men (blacks at a significantly higher risk) and low birth weight in women (again black mothers at a significantly higher risk). Both of these have been regarded as genetically based, since even when controlled for the variables that even out other differences, these two are still there.

On the other hand, in the case of hypertension, we find that African blacks don't have the same high risk; only American blacks do. That makes it sound a bit less genetic. And in the case of low birth weight, a cohort of black African immigrants to America has a distribution of baby birth weight that parallels that of white American mothers, not black American mothers. Once again, that makes it sound a bit less genetic; indeed it looks as if the different experience of growing up black in America versus growing up white in America might be a source of significant biomedical difference.

Notice, however, that these differences are both racial (in that the sample was constructed racially, contrasting blacks and whites) and probably non-genetic. This can tell us rather little about the categories of race, but it can tell us a lot about the effects that different racialized life experiences can have on a person; or in other words, about the effect of a disparity of social circumstances on generally rather evenly matched bodies. This is the study of *embodiment*, how racism (a political act) becomes inscribed into the biological human organism.

A second area of study involves the origin and basis of those physical features that we key on, for example, skin color. It has long been thought that perhaps six or so genes control skin color variation in humans. But even with the Human Genome Project completed, and several relevant genes identified, we still have only a minimal idea what they actually do. How can we study them? Obviously we need to contrast very dark people to very light people. In this case, however, you would have to sort people by the literal color of their skin, not by their racial category. Contrasting the extremes will get you what you need, but relying on the broad categories of race would be a significant hindrance to the project.

A third research problem is the geographic distribution of human traits, both genetic and phenotypic. Suppose we wish to study, once again, skin color—how valuable is race for such an endeavor? Actually, again it is quite intrusive. After all, skin color is clinally distributed, and contrasting the most depigmented peoples of Eurasia against the rest of the world hardly reproduces race. Very darkly pigmented people are found in central Africa, south Asia, Australia, and Melanesia; very lightly pigmented people are found in northern Europe and Asia, and people of intermediate complexion over the whole world—of what use is race here?

Or alternatively, we could look at the distribution of a genetic trait, such as the allele for sickle-cell anemia. In America, it is found disproportionately in African Americans (1 in 13 being a carrier). But a large number of cases occur in people with no known or identifiable African ancestry. Why? Because the allele spread in connection with malaria resistance wherever humans began irrigating fields to grow crops (except in the Americas). Consequently, people of south Asia, the Middle East, and the Mediterranean have elevated frequencies of the sickle-cell allele. None has it as high as the populations of west and central Africa do, and the KhoiSan of southern Africa do not seem to have elevated frequencies. So once again, how does race help us understand sickle cell? Of course, race is important for getting information to the social communities at greatest risk; but it doesn't help us understand sickle-cell anemia or treat it.

Finally, to understand the causes, make a proper diagnosis, and have medical services available to any populations at elevated risk for any genetic disease are important scientific projects. But again, race fails us, because the diseases are invariably nonracial. Consider cystic fibrosis, which affects principally people of European ancestry (1 in 25 is a carrier, as opposed to 1 in 100 Asians), but is a greater risk for northern Europeans than for southern Europeans. Although the data have been collected racially, the clinal nature of the real patterns of variation makes the risk of cystic fibrosis different for natives of northern France and southern France, much less Denmark and Turkey. So imposing race on these data simply obscures the real pattern that exists because of the structure that is present within any of the large "racial" categories.

Ashkenazi Jews (from eastern Europe) have slightly lower risks of cystic fibrosis than the grand European average, but in line with what would be expected from southeastern Europeans. But they also have a cluster of disease at high frequencies, several of them on the same physiological pathways, involving the metabolism of molecules in neurons. The most well-known of these is Tay-Sachs disease, with a carrier rate of 1 in 30 Ashkenazi Jews, about ten times higher than the rest of the world.

But how does racializing Tay-Sachs help us? First of all, no knowledgeable student of human diversity would call Ashkenazi Jews a race. Second of all, 29 in 30 have no connection to the disease at all. This is a disease, like many, for which certain populations are at higher risk than others; but this is a biological correlate of a group membership that is not itself biologically based. Indeed, Tay-Sachs is also elevated among French Canadians and Cajuns.

RACE IS TO ETHNICITY AS SEX IS TO GENDER, BUT NOT QUITE

In the mid-twentieth century, it began to be appreciated that the issues around which the civil rights movement coalesced were not really about race, that is to say, about presumptive genetic differences. Rather, they were about exclusion, prejudice, economic inequality, and access to the opportunities for upward mobility. These issues were not faced by black people alone, but by various immigrant and non-immigrant groups: Jews, Irish, Asians, Italians, Latinos, women, homosexuals.

The idea of "ethnicity" came to represent those non-biological features that identify people as members of groups in transplanted or urban populations. Some aspects of those identities may be tangible and physical, such as patterns of scarification, hair style, and overall bodily comportment. Others may be related to subtle patterns of social prejudice, such as expectations about what one is "supposed" to be good at, or dietary stress. And still others are the organizing minutiae of everyday life—such as the clothing, speech pattern, or belief system.

The women's movement in the mid-twentieth century adopted a dichotomy to parallel race and ethnicity. Certainly the most familiar biological distinction in the human species is the universal division of people into two types: women and men. And yet that natural biological distinction is augmented culturally in profound ways, from early life. Girls are taught culturally appropriate feminine behaviors and attitudes, and boys are taught culturally appropriate masculine counterparts.

Of course, what attitudes and behaviors are considered to be masculine and feminine vary widely cross-culturally, as Margaret Mead showed in her 1935 classic, *Sex and Temperament*. Those cultural features, which are overlaid on the male-female biological dichotomy and serve to reinforce it, came to be known as gender. Thus twentieth-century anthropology called attention both to the cultural reinforcement of racial difference and in parallel to the cultural reinforcement of sexual difference, and called them, respectively, ethnicity and gender.

This equivalence, however—that race is to ethnicity as sex is to gender—is becoming increasingly strained. After all, sex is a far more "natural" category than race. While categories such as hermaphrodites and transsexuals expand the range of natural categories of sexes, they account for a small proportion of the people of the world. That situation is quite different from the situation with respect to race, which is much less partible—that is, readily divisible. And while sex is indeed beginning to be reconceptualized as a spectrum, rather than as a binary, the relevant issue again is that of equality, not of biology.

WHAT IS INNATE?

Nevertheless, the analytic separation of the "natural" group attributes from the "cultural" ones was a major advance for twentieth-century anthropology. One of the major tasks for the twenty-first century is to put them back together intelligently, and see how they merge into each other. Thus, for example, we may ask how the average difference in body composition and size between men and women affects their social roles, for example, in the division of labor.

But understanding the nature of the separation must precede putting them back together. And unfortunately, there is an important convergence of interests that may lead to overstating the role of "nature" or "biology" or "genetics" in thinking about why groups of people act as they do. First, there is political capital in overstating group differences in behavior and mentality. To the extent that such differences are caused by social inequities, it stands to reason that social reforms comprise the solution; thus, overstating the innateness of those differences erases the need for social reform by denying that the problem is real. This was the argument of an infamous 1994 book, *The Bell Curve*, coauthored by a psychologist and a right-wing political theorist. The money "saved" by not "wasting" it on social programs could then be redirected, for example, toward war or tax cuts, while the barriers between social classes widens. Second, geneticists themselves may perceive their own interests to be served by having people believe that the most important differences are genetic. This was certainly the case in the 1920s, when geneticists signally failed to criticize the pronouncements of eugenics (that sterilizing the poor and restricting immigration into the United States were needed on account of the bad genes of the poor). Indeed, many eugenics enthusiasts were themselves geneticists. And third, sadly, there are still old-fashioned racists and sexists who have neither a lofty political agenda, nor a knowledge of genetics, yet sustain deep prejudices about the innate inequality of large groups of people.

This field, then, is so contentious because it is a significant area in which science intersects with political action, and consequently, it is hard to know what "scientific discoveries" about human behavioral genetics to take a face value. In theory, the study of identical twins separated at birth should be able to tell us what is innate and what is learned, since identical twins are genetic clones, and having been raised in different environments, their detectable differences might reasonably be assigned to their different environments. In practice, however, separated identical twins are usually raised nearby, and by other relatives, or are put in carefully screened adoptive homes, and consequently have very strongly correlated environmental backgrounds as well.

A major study of identical twins separated at birth was undertaken in the 1930s by a British psychologist named Cyril Burt, who was later knighted for his influential work. Burt believed that intelligence was principally an innate quality, and claimed that over a span of decades, he got consistently identical results on the innateness of intelligence as his sample of identical twins separated at birth grew larger. Unfortunately, it turned out that Burt was something of a "nutty professor"— he invented colleagues to praise his own work, and invented lots of his twins as well. Consequently, in the 1980s, another major research program into identical twins separated at birth, based in Minnesota, began to generate notoriety. This group of psychologists were doing their science with funding from a private right-wing foundation with a record for supporting eugenicists and segregationists; and these scientists talked freely about the role not only of genetics but also of ESP and the psychic contact of identical twins. But these subjects are not taken as seriously as science, so it is hard to evaluate their other claims pertaining to genetics, especially given the political source of the financial support.

Since identical twins are the subjects of such pervasive cultural mythologies, it is actually rather difficult to draw any serious inferences about nature and nurture from them. It is quite simply a lot easier to make assertions about the innateness of different human qualities in different groups of people than to demonstrate anything in the area with a reasonably high degree of rigor.

One common argument is that behavioral "universals" must be innate. This is not necessarily useful or true, however, since there are few such universals, and nearly every generalization about human behavior has notable exceptions. If universality is a sign of innateness, is the exception a mutant?

More importantly, the social, economic, and political processes grouped together as "globalization" work to homogenize diverse cultures, and thus to universalize behaviors and attitudes without inscribing them in the genes. Does the fact that Marilyn Monroe is universally recognized as beautiful mean that she evokes an innate human response, or that mid-twentieth-century American standards have diffused to the rest of the rest of the world through the cultural power of the entertainment media? One way to tell would be to look at the way in which standards of beauty vary through time and across cultures—and to many, someone who looked like Marilyn Monroe would be considered sickly and in need of fattening up. In the other direction, female movie stars of the 1920s commonly appear flabby to a contemporary culture that values "buff."

The attempt to separate "innate" from "learned" behaviors and attitudes is another good example of a false dichotomy. For some of our most profound evolutionary adaptations, we have evolved to be innately predisposed to learn things. Consider, for example, walking. You are not born doing it; but you actively learned it around the age of two, from watching those around you and practicing it yourself. If you had not had those role models and worked at it, you would probably not walk as you evolved to, as the stories of abandoned babies raised apart from human contact seem to show.

Likewise, we evolved to speak, but we have to learn a language. We have an innate drive to do it, but without exposure and practice, we would not be able to exercise this capacity. And of course, the innate drive to learn language does not result in everyone learning the same language, but in learning one or a few variants of the many possible languages.

In other words, juxtaposing the "natural" against the "cultural" or the "innate" against the "learned" is a useful first approximation as a dichotomy, but doesn't stand up very well under closer scrutiny. We need to be wary of those who overstate what is innate, because it commonly is politically motivated, and one of the major roles of twentieth-century anthropology has been to show how malleable what superficially seem like innate differences can actually be.

PATTERNS OF HUMAN GENETIC
AND BEHAVIORAL VARIATION

This obviously does not mean that there is no genetic effect on human behavior, or that everybody is exactly the same. Those would be pretty weird positions to take, although occasionally ascribed to anthropology by people who don't know what they're talking about, or are trying to confuse the issues. As we noted above, anthropology is predicated on human differences; if everyone were the same, there could be no study of anthropology. At issue is not *whether* humans differ, but *how* they differ—the patterns we encounter in studying human differences rigorously. Similarly, whether there are genetic influences over behavior is uncontroversial; at issue is whether genetic variations are causal in explaining any significant features of variation in human behavior.

The most fundamental recognition is that the gross patterns of human biological variation and behavioral variation do not map well onto one another. We have already reviewed in this chapter the patterns of biological variation in our species: human groups blend into one another physically and genetically, and the bulk of detectable genetic variation is located within any particular group.

What about the patterns of behavioral or cognitive variation? Obviously everybody doesn't have the same thoughts or act the same way. Let us consider something obvious, like the mode of dress. Look around you; everyone is dressed differently. But are they really so different? Do you see anyone wearing a sari? A grass skirt? A loincloth? A set of chain mail? A toga? In fact, if you think about it in the context of the many things people have worn or can wear, everyone you can see is dressed quite homogeneously. Actually, the mode of dress is a fairly good indicator of where (and when) a person is from. That is because it is a marker of ethnicity, a purely culturally constituted aspect of group identity.

Indeed, so are most other aspects of everyday thoughts and acts. How we speak, what we consider funny, what we consider appropriate, even what we consider edible (insects and horses, for example, being nutritious, but not eaten by Americans). How we think about the world, how we interact with others, how we express respect and to whom we express it, what we consider sacred or taboo—these are the kinds of things that we have come to call "culture," and which constitute the major features of variation in human thought and deed. A contemporary anthropology classroom might contain Americans of very diverse ancestries, but their minds and actions vary only within very narrow limits, when we think about the array of behavioral and cognitive variation presented by our species as a whole. In that classroom, a medieval Frank, pre-Dynastic Egyptian, an Olmec from Mexico, a Khoi from Namibia, a Sherpa from Nepal, or a Roman centurion would stand out very readily. One would probably not even have to call the roll to identify them.

If cultural features (that is to say, group-level or ethnic differences) comprise the bulk of our behavioral and mental variation, what role does genetic variation play? Here is a thought experiment. If we take any of the people just mentioned—say, the Sherpa—and place them in your class, it is clear that their own expectations, experiences, and thought processes would be considerably different from everyone else's. Now let us give them an absurdly readily expressed genetic mutation that affects their thought, and makes them be very happy and laugh a lot. Let us imagine further that someone else in the class also has that "happy" mutation—say, a white university student from Texas. Aside from both being happy, very little about them would be similar. They would still dress differently, eat differently, walk differently, entertain themselves differently, and probably not even be able to communicate with one another. In fact, they probably wouldn't even be friends, since their "happy allele" might well lead them to laugh inappropriately in each other's company, a well-known source of offense!

In other words, the major features of human cognitive and behavioral variation are immune to genetics. There are certainly alleles that affect aspects of mood and personality, but like all the genetic variation we already know of in our species, nearly all the variation for these genes will be found in nearly all populations. And the cultural manner in which human behavior is structured shows a completely different pattern from the manner in which our gene pool is structured. Thus, the principal features of human behavioral variation are non-genetic in origin, and serve to distinguish one group of people from their neighbors quite readily in many different ways, all in the absence of genetic distinctions. These are cultural or ethnic differences. On the other hand, the principal feature of human genetic variation is polymorphism, or within-group variation; and the between-group variation is structured clinally, rather than permitting discrete distinctions to be found or made. *It is consequently impossible for genetic variation to be a major source of behavioral or cognitive variation in the human species.*

This does not deny a role for genetics in human behavior, but necessarily relegates it to explaining only the differences in thought and deed that can be found among members of the same population—who, in the great scheme of things, are very behaviorally homogeneous to begin with!

Thus, knowing a bit about the patterns of human genetic variation allows us to understand the broad irrelevance of "human behavioral genetics" to the major features of human behavioral variation. Human behavioral genetics is only equipped to deal with a small bit of the spectrum of human behavioral and mental variation—the within-group variation—and even then it must still compete with other factors, such as education, life experiences, and family history. It consequently has little to say of relevance to anthropology, whose focus has traditionally been on the differences between groups of people.

REFERENCES AND FURTHER READING

Abu El-Haj, N. 2007. The genetic reinscription of race. *Annual Review of Anthropology* 36:283–300.

Barkan, E. A. 1993. *The Retreat of Scientific Racism*. New York: Cambridge University Press.

Baum, B. 2006. *The Rise and Fall of the Caucasian Race: A Political History of Racial Identity*. New York: NYU Press.

Bethencourt, F. 2014. *Racisms: From the Crusades to the Twentieth Century*. Princeton, NJ: Princeton University Press.

Bliss, C. 2012. *Race Decoded: The Genomic Fight for Social Justice*. New York: Stanford University Press.

Boas, F. 1912. Changes in the bodily form of descendants of immigrants. *American Anthropologist* 14:530–562.

Bogin, B. 1988. Rural-to-urban migration. In *Biological Aspects of Human Migration*, ed. C. G. N. Mascie-Taylor and G. W. Lasker, 90–129. New York: Cambridge University Press.

Boyd, W. C. 1963. Genetics and the human race. *Science* 140:1057–1065.

Brace, C. L. 2005. *"Race" Is a Four-Letter Word: The Genesis of the Concept*. New York: Oxford University Press.

Cartmill, M. 1998. The status of the race concept in physical anthropology. *American Anthropologist* 100:651–660.

Fields, B., and K. Fields. 2012. *Racecraft: The Soul of Inequality in American Life*. New York: Verso.

Fish, J., ed. 2002. *Race and Intelligence: Separating Science from Myth*. Mahwah, NJ: Erlbaum.

Gould, S. J. 1981. *The Mismeasure of Man*. New York: W. W. Norton.

Greene, J. C. 1954. Some early speculations on the origin of human races. *American Anthropologist* 56:31–41.

Haller, J. S., Jr. 1971. Race and the concept of progress in nineteenth century American ethnology. *American Anthropologist* 73:710–724.

Hannaford, I. 1996. *Race: The History of an Idea in the West*. Baltimore, MD: Johns Hopkins.

Harris, M. 1970. Referential ambiguity in the calculus of Brazilian racial identity. *Southwestern Journal of Anthropology* 26(1):1–14.

Harrison, F. V. 1995. The persistent power of "race" in the cultural and political economy of racism. *Annual Review of Anthropology* 24:47–74.

Hartigan, J. 2015. *Race in the 21st Century*. 2nd ed. New York: Oxford University Press

Hauskeller, C., S. Sturdy, and R. Tutton. 2013. Genetics and the sociology of identity. *Sociology* 47 (5):875–886.

Hooton, E. A. 1926. Methods of racial analysis. *Science* 63:75–81.

Hudson, N. 1996. From "nation" to "race": The origin of racial classification in eighteenth-century thought. *Eighteenth-Century Studies* 29:247–264.

Hulse, F. S. 1962. Race as an evolutionary episode. *American Anthropologist* 64:929–945.

Ignatiev, N. 1996. *How the Irish Became White*. New York: Routledge.

Jablonski, N., and G. Chaplin. 2000. The evolution of human skin coloration. *Journal of Human Evolution* 39:57–106.

Jackson, J. P., Jr. 2005. *Science for Segregation*. New York: NYU Press.

Joseph, J. 2015. *The Trouble with Twin Studies: A Reassessment of Twin Research in the Social and Behavioral Sciences*. New York: Routledge.

Kaufman, J., and S. Hall. 2003. The slavery hypertension hypothesis: Dissemination and appeal of a modern race theory. *Epidemiology and Society* 14:111–126.

Koenig, B. A., S. S.-J. Lee, and S. Richardson, eds. 2008. *Revisiting Race in a Genomic Age*. Piscataway, NJ: Rutgers University Press.

Kuper, A. 2003. The return of the native. *Current Anthropology* 44:389–402.

Lewontin, R. C. 1972. The apportionment of human diversity. *Evolutionary Biology* 6:381–398.

Lancaster, R. N. 2003. *The Trouble with Nature: Sex in Science and Popular Culture*. Berkeley: University of California Press.

Little, M., and K. A. R. Kennedy, eds. 2010. *Histories of American Physical Anthropology in the Twentieth Century.* Lanham, MD: Lexington Books.

Livingstone, F. B. 1962. On the non-existence of human races. *Current Anthropology* 3:279–281.

Marks, J. 2017. *Is Science Racist?* London: Polity Press.

Mead, M. 1935. *Sex and Temperament in Three Primitive Societies.* New York: William Morrow.

Meloni, M. 2016. *Political Biology: Science and Social Values in Human Heredity from Eugenics to Epigenetics.* New York: Springer.

Montagu, A. 1997. *Man's Most Dangerous Myth: The Fallacy of Race.* 6th ed. Pleasant View, CA: AltaMira Press.

Painter, N. I. 2010. *The History of White People.* New York: W. W. Norton.

Panofsky, A. 2014. *Misbehaving Science: Controversy and the Development of Behavior Genetics.* Chicago: University of Chicago Press.

Shapiro, H. L. 1939. *Migration and Environment.* New York: Oxford University Press.

Shapiro, H. L. 1944. Anthropology's contribution to interracial understanding. *Science* 99:373–376.

Smedley, A., and B. D. Smedley. 2005. Race as biology is fiction, racism as a social problem is real. *American Psychologist* 60:16–26.

Sussman, R. W. 2014. *The Myth of Race: The Troubling Persistence of an Unscientific Idea.* Cambridge, MA: Harvard University Press.

Teslow, T. 2014. *Constructing Race: The Science of Bodies and Cultures in American Anthropology.* Cambridge: Cambridge University Press.

Tucker, W. H. 2002. *The Funding of Scientific Racism: Wickliffe Draper and the Pioneer Fund.* Urbana: University of Illinois Press.

Washburn, S. L. 1963. The study of race. *American Anthropologist* 65:521–531.

Yudell, M., D. Roberts, R. DeSalle, and S. Tishkoff. 2016. Taking race out of human genetics. *Science* 351:564–565.

CHAPTER 14

Nature/Culture, or How Science Manages to Give Little Answers to Big Questions (On the Non-reductive Core of Anthropology)

THEME

Humans are uniquely biocultural animals. Everything we do is rendered meaningful within a contextualizing environment of economy, social relations, and ideas. That environment changes rapidly, and not only do we change to fit it, but also the practice of science, and especially of biological anthropology, changes with it as well.

ADAPTABILITY AND THE HUMAN CONDITION

The hallmark of the human condition is not so much our particular adaptations, but the extent to which our intelligence and long periods of growth and immaturity allow us to be adaptable. Natural selection molds the gene pool of species to conform to the stresses of the environment; but the adaptations wrought by natural selection are long term and largely irreversible. That is what we generally mean by "adaptation" in an evolutionary sense.

Human populations have adapted in this evolutionary sense mostly in fairly subtle ways. The least subtle is of course the depigmentation of human skin in nontropical latitudes, allowing ultraviolet light to stimulate the production of vitamin D (Chapter 13). But those examples seem to be quite rare. We find geographical regularities in body build across mammalian species, and these seem to hold as well for human populations. Short, stocky bodies retain heat more efficiently than lean, lanky bodies, and consequently you tend to find lean animals in the tropics and fat ones in the arctic. Interestingly, this generalization (known as Bergmann's Rule) also seems to hold for human populations, at least crudely, in the extremes. One finds lean, lanky people in East Africa, and short, stocky people in Greenland. (Obviously other factors are also at work, since officially the tallest population today is the Dutch.) Similarly, Allen's Rule relates limb length to climate among vertebrates, with cold-adapted species having shorter limbs; and again we tend to find the longest-limbed peoples in hot areas, and the shortest-limbed peoples in the coldest areas.

Another well-known, but subtle, genetic adaptation is lactose tolerance, the ability to digest milk beyond childhood. This ability does not exist in most people—at least 70% of the people in the world. Far from being a "disease," lactose intolerance is polymorphic everywhere, and is the majority condition among everybody except Europeans and other people with a history of cattle herding, like some East Africans. The mutation permits people to metabolize lactose, the sugar in milk, and thus to derive sustenance from a food that would otherwise give them gas and diarrhea. This mutation, then, seems to be an adaptation to the availability of a source of nutrition—milk—that ordinarily requires fermentation into cheese or yogurt to be digestible.

And even more subtle are the adaptations of the human gene pool to the environmental pressure of infectious disease. The gene pools of peoples in malarial environments have developed elevated proportions of certain alleles that afford some measure of protection from that debilitating disease (Chapter 5). Other diseases have been suggested as pressures (such as cholera, bubonic plague, and tuberculosis), having corresponding effects on the gene pools of certain populations, but with far less convincing evidence. Presumably the ravages of historical pandemics, like the bubonic plague in Europe from 1348 to 1350, have an effect on the gene pool at least in the genes governing immune responses or assisting in disease resistance, but the specifics are unknown; or even whether other alleles may have been "carried along" under the intense selection for disease resistance. It is certainly not terribly difficult, however, to imagine the mutations that may confer resistance to HIV infection having a subtle effect on the human gene pool over the next several generations.

The diverse other ways in which humans come to respond to environmental pressures, and form a "fit" with their surroundings, constitute the study of adaptability. After all, there is also genetic control of physiology, as first explored in depth by the biologist C. H. Waddington (Chapter 6). Human bodies are characterized by developmental plasticity, that is, they are sensitive to the conditions of growth, so the adult form of the body can be affected by long-term stresses quite strikingly and regularly, without being directly a consequence of the genetic program. In this sense, the body is adapting to an environmental stress, but it is not doing so through the gene pool in geological time, but rather, over the course of a single lifetime by virtue of the body's reactive properties. While these physical modifications are not passed on per se, the persistence of the stressor across generations causes the bodies of ancestors and descendants to develop in a consistent and similar fashion.

In this category we can place the changes in head form and body that occur as a result of immigration, described in the last chapter. A major environmental stressor is hypoxia, or reduced air: people who live at high altitudes, or whose mothers smoked heavily while pregnant, commonly have "stunted growth"—their bodies have physiologically adapted to the lower oxygen levels and have altered their growth trajectories accordingly.

These physiological adaptations are nongenetic, since they are direct responses to specific environmental pressures. But they are also permanent; once the bones grow in a certain way, over a certain period of time, they are stuck with that form within very narrow limits. Thus, the practice of cradle-boarding (tying the infant's head to a cradle with a flat surface) results in a very flat rear of the head. This is such a regular feature of some populations that it had once been classified as a racial type—the "Dinaric" skull form. But it is due simply to a cultural practice.

Similarly, the binding of women's feet by traditional Chinese society, or the lifetime of repetitive motion by women grinding grain in agricultural societies, affect the skeleton in very characteristic ways.

In addition to adapting genetically and developmentally, humans adapt facultatively to short-term stresses. These adaptive physiological responses are generally reversible, such as tanning, callousing, or increasing the blood flow to cold parts of the body. Athletes preparing for competition at high altitudes will commonly train at high altitudes for precisely that reason, to acclimate their bodies to the new stressor. These short-term physiological responses are another aspect of the adaptability of the human condition.

A third kind of nongenetic adaptation, also widely shared with other animal species, is behavioral adaptation. Many animals—especially mammals—learn what to eat, how to hunt, how to hide from predators, how to act around other members of their social group, and even how to use tools to accomplish specific tasks. The key element here is the transmission of information. (Ethologists sometimes refer to this as "cultural," but that reflects a different use of the term than in anthropology.)

Obviously humans also learn things, and use objects to help them survive. But in humans, as noted in the last chapter, these objects take on an evolutionary trajectory of their own. They constitute an extrasomatic (external to the body) adaptation and superorganic mode of evolution. There is certainly nothing mystical about this: after all, you use things, but how many of those things have you actually made yourself? Mostly they were made by others, independently of your organic existence, and quite possibly before you were even born. You read English, but you didn't invent it; English was there before you, and you essentially were born into it; and it will be there when you die, although very slightly changed.

To the extent that people invent new things or coin new words, those are minor perturbations, roughly analogous to mutations; cultures change through the large-scale social process of adoption, which is often difficult to predict. Cellular phones and the Internet, now impossible to imagine being without, were almost inconceivable a generation ago; so was a global and domestic war against an enemy called terrorism. And a world in which America drives Edsels and listens to quadrophonic music was certainly conceivable; it just never materialized.

The point is that human culture is not merely a response to environmental problems, but comprises a complex environment in and of itself, which necessarily entails its own set of responses. And those responses come partly from you as an individual—learning how to act appropriately in your own time and place—but also from us as a social collectivity. I have "written" this book, for example, only in the very narrow sense of having composed it; but I didn't chop down the trees, make the pulp, press and cut the paper, blend the ink, cast and set the type, print it, and bind it! Clearly, even the most basic things we take for granted are formed and exist within a complex network of economic, political, and social forces and are well beyond the capabilities of any individual person.

This is what anthropologists mean by culture. It is not the learned behaviors themselves, but the invisible matrix of social relations, meanings, technologies, and histories within which those behaviors are embedded, as well as their visible products. That is the difference between a beaver dam and Hoover Dam; and it is presently the most powerful force in our own adaptation and survival, without precedent in the history of life.

FOLK THEORIES OF HEREDITY

All cultures have ideas about why people are different, how those differences are patterned and inherited, where family resemblances come from, and what it all means, or how to structure one's life according to one's beliefs and practices. This extends to the cultures of science, in which it is not uncommon to encounter theories of human behavior that fail to acknowledge human adaptability—nongenetic adaptations—as the hallmark of our species, and that assume that natural selection has been busily crafting aspects of our gene pool governing everything from walking to raping!

At the dawn of modern anthropological fieldwork, the social anthropologist Bronislaw Malinowski found that the Trobriand Islanders, near New Guinea, among whom he lived during World War I, didn't acknowledge a relationship between sex and procreation. The Trobriand Islanders also were matrilineal, tracing family relationships just through the mother's side—which the denial of biological paternity served to reinforce. Their theory held spirits of the driftwood as responsible for pregnancy, and the proximity of the husband as responsible for family resemblance. While wrong, their theory was logical and reasonable, given their beliefs.

In premodern Europe, it was widely held that if a woman had sex outside of wedlock, the imprint of her lover could be retained in her womb, so that when she later married, her children would resemble her former lover rather than her husband. This idea, known as *telegony*, reinforced popular beliefs about the importance of female chastity, although it is wrong. (Some animals—for example, fruit flies—are able to retain sperm, so the first consort may indeed be the father of eggs laid after subsequent matings over the course of a lifetime: But not us.)

The inheritance of acquired characteristics (Chapter 2) has perennially been revived by scholars with a Marxist political bent, since it seems to be compatible with the goal of progressive social improvement, at the core of Marxism (and many other humanitarian social philosophies). This is counterbalanced by the overemphasis on innate inequalities by the eugenicists and later genetic enthusiasts. The point is that there are popular ideas about heredity that may sound scientific, but are based not so much on modern scientific knowledge as on cultural ideologies. As such, they may be difficult to identify, because, like the prejudices of the 1920s' eugenicists, the cultural ideas may be encrypted into the science itself, and then read back out.

We can identify three major sets of contemporary cultural prejudices, or folk ideologies, of heredity. All are popularly thought of as scientific in some circles, but actually represent the gray zone where science and culture mingle. They are empirically false, or at least only true in a peculiarly narrow sense, yet are important to biological anthropology as illustrations both of the intersection of the biological and the anthropological realms and also of the inherent difficulties in understanding the human condition scientifically, when the subject is so highly value laden.

The first folk ideology of heredity is taxonomism, the idea that the human species is naturally divisible into a small number of relatively discrete groups, equivalent to zoological subspecies. We showed in Chapter 13 how this is empirically not so. Making groups and assigning people to them is a fundamental part of human social life, but human biological variation is clinal, and the groups we make are biocultural. That is why the categories of Latino, Jew, Italian, or Native American are important both as identities and as cultural and social groups. They are groups of political salience and personal meaning, and while sometimes correlated with biological features, the categories are not biologically demarcated or defined. Likewise for the category "black," the color is a metaphorical label, but there is no biological coherence to any group it embraces—in America, it can refer to anyone with any ancestors at all from Africa. Taxonomism entails a theory about the structure of the human gene pool; and to that extent, it is empirically false, and recognizably another manifestation of the process of "naturalizing difference" (Chapter 13).

The groups themselves, of course, are no less real for not being natural subspecies; and that is another testament to the cultural nature of human life. In some cases, the cultural history of the groups has placed them at higher risk for some health problems. For example, African American males are at higher risk for high blood pressure and its cardiovascular consequences. And yet, one does not see the same pattern among Africans; it appears to be a biological consequence of growing up black in America, rather than a direct phenotypic consequence of the African gene pool.

Other cultural issues may have genetic consequences. Millennia of enduring periodic bouts of persecution and genocide have left Ashkenazi (eastern European) Jews with elevated proportions of otherwise rare alleles, including those that are implicated in breast cancer and neurological disease, such as Tay-Sachs, Gaucher's, and familial dysautonomia. While other microevolutionary factors may be at work, the genetic homogeneity of the Tay-Sachs genotype (about 75%–80% of detectable alleles are copies of exactly the same one) suggests a major role for the founder effect, a presumable genetic consequence of the history of persecution.

The second major category of folk heredity is racism, the idea that a person is an embodiment of group attributes, which are often themselves imaginary. If the group is considered to be a race, then this becomes racism in its most familiar form; otherwise it shades into other kinds of group-level animosities (such as anti-Semitism, sexism, or homophobia), based on the nature of the perceived identities. This is also a folk theory of heredity, not only because of the common assumption of the innateness of these group attributes, but also because there is no opportunity for an individual to escape the group's stigma, regardless of actual ancestry or genetic constitution. These perceived group-level attributes tend to be undiluted by intermarriage, and yet are not inherited probabilistically, like genes. (A good example of this is the belief that black athletes are naturally endowed with basketball skill, yet independently of the complexion or actual ancestry of the particular athletes, much less of their life experiences and self-expectations.) These are cultural processes, with aspects that mimic genetics, but are quite distinct from biological properties and processes.

The final category of folk taxonomy is genetic essentialism, the reductive construction of identities on the basis of broad key features presumed to be innate. Here, however, the identities are not group-level, or population-specific, identities. Instead, the pseudogenetic categories are applied to within-population variation, most often to nebulously defined features with complex etiologies, such as intelligence, aggression, sexual orientation, novelty seeking, alcoholism, or depression.

The truth value of these claims is generally quite low, in part because they seem so commonsensical that they are easier to accept uncritically (for a brief time, at least). But these are precisely the kinds of claims—the ones that reinforce what we already think we know—that must be subjected to the highest degree of scrutiny. And unfortunately many are never replicated, and even the most well-supported claims account for only a tiny fraction of the behaviors. The infamous "gay gene" on the X chromosome, which was the subject of cover stories in major magazines and newspapers in the early 1990s, was only suggested to explain about 5% of homosexuality, and then only in men; but in any event, we can see that it does not actually seem to exist, now that the Human Genome Project is complete. Needless to say, this enterprise carries strong political implications for "naturalizing difference."

Even worse, this kind of work is often promoted by groups with an explicitly anti-egalitarian agenda, on the (incorrect) belief that evidence for genetic differences in behavior *within* groups counts as solid evidence for genetic differences in behavior *between* groups. But it should be fairly obvious that the differences in genetic endowments that may underlie some children's divergent performances in the same classroom cannot be reliably invoked to explain the gross difference in performance between students in a suburban prep school and those in an understaffed and overcrowded slum school. Likewise, the differences that may lead one frat guy to drink too much too often, and another not to, probably have little to do with explaining the difference in drinking patterns between Navajos and Mormons.

THE STATE OF THE SPECIES

Modern *Homo sapiens* is a cultural creature in ways that are so fundamental and pervasive as to be almost too obvious to see. Human demography, for example, is far less species specific than it is for other primates. Thus, when we examine agricultural societies, we find that they tend to have high growth rates, and a higher proportion of children than either hunting-and-gathering peoples or industrialized peoples. In other words, features that are biological in other species are predicated on one's economic system in humans.

Significantly, then, we cannot talk about "natural" human demography, for human demography does not exist outside the context of an economic system.

This problem can be seen in reverse as well. What could be more "natural" than menstruation? Once a month, when fertilization has not occurred, hormones begin to rage, and the endometrial lining of the uterus is shed, along with some blood: inconvenient, perhaps; irritating, perhaps—but *natural*. And yet, women in industrialized society reach sexual maturity earlier and menopause later, have fewer children, spaced more closely together, and they generally do not breast-feed on demand—compared with women in other times and places. If you do the math (and know that breast-feeding on demand stimulates the production of a hormone that inhibits ovulation), you discover that modern women are having 5–10 times more menstrual periods than any women have ever had. How "natural" does it look then?

It is a further testimony to the adaptability of the human body, yet also makes us appreciate the environmental uniqueness provided by contemporary culture. Sometimes this appreciation is mass marketed as a "lack of fit" between "what we evolved for" and "the modern condition." This is misleading, however, for two reasons: (1) the human condition is generally characterized by extreme adaptability, not by particular adaptation—humans have a remarkable ability to *make* themselves "fit"; and (2) to the extent that Pleistocene environments are what our ancestors evolved *in*, those environments were quite heterogeneous in space and time, and thus the hypothetical environment that we evolved *for* is simply an abstraction, another elusive Platonic essence.

Obviously we evolved in an environmental context that lacked sanitation, antibiotics, stressful jobs, and Big Macs. The first two contribute to extending the life span, so that we no longer die of the infections and contagions that threatened our ancestors. The latter two (stress and high-fat foods) contribute to the heart disease that (along with cancers) are major causes of death in modern society, at ages that our ancestors rarely made it to.

Does that mean it is "unnatural" to be fifty years old? Probably not. Rather, it means that a highly adaptable organism, faced with new circumstances and stimuli, develops and reacts in harmony with its cultural surroundings. If those surroundings produce a larger proportion of elderly individuals, then that is simply part of the human condition. The real issues are not about evolution, nor even about extending the human life span. The issues are entirely cultural: How to integrate a growing proportion of elderly into a society that alienates those it already has! What, after all, is the point of living to 120 in a society that doesn't care adequately for its eighty-year-olds?

Like other problems of human adaptation, this one is caused by cultural factors, and will require a cultural solution. The biology of aging is a relatively trivial issue in comparison.

We see similar patterns in many ostensibly biological features. The process of industrialization or modernization, which entails technological changes, economic changes, dietary changes, and lifestyle changes, carries biological consequences to the population. For example, children mature earlier and grow to larger body sizes. This phenomenon has been found in diverse populations, and is not genetic in etiology. We call these "secular trends," and once again they testify to human adaptability.

They have little to say about human "adaptation," however. To the extent that there is a lack of fit that may be discernible, it would seem to be between the social system that identifies people as socially adult only at age 18 or 21, when they have been physically adult for possibly the latter third of their lives. Once again, "nature" is not at fault, and is only very passively involved in the problem; culture is both the cause of the problem and the source of the solution.

And it need hardly be noted that trying to tell teenagers that sexuality is bad and should be avoided is a vain endeavor; not so much because of the neurobiology that makes it feel good, but because of the hypocrisy of the message when everyone else is so obviously enjoying sex. Once again, the problem and the solution are cultural; biology is a largely passive player in the drama.

THE ANTHROPOLOGY OF SCIENCE

Other animals eat; we dine. Other animals breathe; we snort with derision, we smoke. Other animals look and see; we adapt transparent materials to allow us to gaze in admiration, and to read. Other animals get wet; we construct shelters.

We humans have evolved away from the brachiating apes, and into a new ecological niche without precedent in the history of life. That niche was initially one that simply involved manipulating and modifying natural objects to serve useful ends, something done by many animal species to a limited extent, most notably primates. Our lineage, however, developed a coevolutionary relationship with those modified natural objects. As they helped our ancestors to survive and reproduce, our ancestors in turn developed the capability—both manual and mental—of making even finer, more efficient, and more diverse tools. With the emergence of anatomically modern *Homo sapiens*—forehead, chin, and all—the tools took on an evolutionary trajectory of their own. Ultimately, the products of human invention have come to create their own environment to which humans in turn adapt.

Of course the products of human invention extend beyond simply tools, to the social and ideological spheres—the interpersonal interactions and the sense we make of the world. Culture constitutes an environment into which we are born, and consequently to which we must accommodate ourselves in order to survive. In the narrowest sense, culture dictates the kinds of ways in which we can earn a living, thus providing us with the biological basics of existence. Culture dictates the appropriate behaviors to particular people, which facilitates both toleration and cooperation. More broadly, culture gives us identities as members of nations, religions, or ethnicities, which may also have a profound effect on our survival, in addition to governing the minutiae of our daily lives.

In more subtle ways, however, culture gives us a coherent view of the world, which gives meaning to our lives and satisfies the intellectual curiosity we all have, as a byproduct of the large brains we evolved. And yet the particulars of that coherent view vary from place to place and from time to time, that is to say, "culturally." Contemporary science provides one set of such views, formulated according to the basic guidelines discussed in Chapter 1, and can consequently be readily characterized as unstable (by virtue of its "self-correcting" nature) and spiritually unrewarding (by virtue of its materialism or naturalism, which deliberately shields it from "spirituality").

On the other side of the ledger is the fact that science provides the most accurate and empirically valid set of ideas about the universe.

The fact that science has shown itself to explain the universe well and to apply that knowledge for useful ends means that scientific explanations have earned a reputation of authority, at least in our culture. One consequence of having earned such authority is that it may be invoked inappropriately, to make a political view sound more rhetorically convincing. This rhetoric may be obvious or subtle. The late nineteenth-century elitist movement known as Social Darwinism (Chapter 3) fizzled out because its anti-union, anti-welfare sermons were so transparently a self-rationalization for the greedy excesses of the privileged classes.

On the other hand, during the eugenics movement, the scientists themselves held the popular racist and classist views that supported congressionally restricting the immigration of Italians and Jews, on account of their "bad germ-plasm" (1924), and judicially permitting states to sterilize their citizens involuntarily, also on account of their "bad germ-plasm" (1927). Here the biologists themselves were the vanguards of the mass political action, and hardly questioned or noticed the vulgar cultural prejudices that were actually motivating them.

As a result largely of the eugenics movement, and particularly as it found ideological compatibility and expression in the Nazi movement in Germany in the 1930s, science after World War II came under intense scrutiny by the public, and ideas of scientific responsibility and bioethics were developed. Prior to World War II, it was tacitly assumed that the progress of scientific knowledge, the march of science, was inexorable and that nothing should be allowed to impede it. But the Nazis, who were advancing science through torturing people, showed that indeed something should be allowed to impede it. When science comes into conflict with human rights, human rights wins.

In fact, the problem did not end with the Nazis, either. The eugenicists in America were intellectual kin of the eugenicists in Germany. And the infamous

Tuskegee experiments showed that a concern for human rights in American bio-medical practice needed to be articulated and formalized as well, for a lack of concern for those rights did not end at the boundaries of Germany. American scientists were curious about the ultimate progress of syphilis, which damaged many physiological systems as its course progressed through the body, until the victim was either treated, or died. As doctors, if someone came to them with syphilis, they had to treat them. But that precluded the study of the ultimate destructive effects of syphilis. So they arranged to *study* poor black men in Alabama with syphilis, but *not* to *treat* them. They satisfied the letter of the Hippocratic oath—"first, do no harm"—after all, they had not infected the victims, but were merely monitoring them. The subjects were physically no worse off for having participated. On the other hand, the doctors were dehumanizing their subjects by regarding them as not worthy of treatment; they were relating to these men as if they were mere things, or animals. Didn't they have spouses and children? And these experiments were carried out from 1932 to 1972 in America.

We now commonly refer to the study of the cultural practices of science as "the anthropology of science." Like more traditional areas of anthropology, this often subsumes ethnographic work (observing and interviewing scientists), analytical work (understanding how some interesting ideas undergo a transformation into accepted facts), and archival work (studying historical documents). In this view, science is neither good nor bad, but both simultaneously, and more importantly, science is a unique and peculiar set of thoughts and acts, or discursive practices.

Science is clearly here to stay, and has the power to enrich our lives immensely. But like any form of social power, it can readily be co-opted. Part of the anthropology of science strives to call attention to the political implications of science, the financial conflicts of interest and ideological convergences of interest, and the non-normative behavior of scientists—those actions that go against what scientists are supposed or commonly expected to do. Biological anthropology, which assumed the role of an authoritative scientific voice on race and human origins in the twentieth century, is situated right at the convergence of science and politics.

BIOETHICS

The field of bioethics arose as a guide to the practice of human sciences in the wake of World War II. The Nuremberg Code was formalized in 1947 (and subsequently revised, most significantly in the 1979 "Belmont report") to set international standards for the study of human beings in scientific research. One of the principal ideas in ethical research today is that the researcher has the responsibility to obtain the "voluntary informed consent" of any participant in a scientific study. A participant cannot be coerced in any way, and the cooperation must be secured through an open and honest explanation of the plusses and minuses of participating. And securing this consent honestly, in a non-coercive manner, is the responsibility of the scientist.

Of course, this all presumes that there is a fundamental concordance between the scientist and the subject—that they speak the same language, hold the same basic values, and share basic ideas about how the world works and about science. But what about people peripheral to the sphere of contemporary European and American cultural values?

In other words, how do you do ethically acceptable work with people, having received their voluntary informed consent, who do not share your ideas about life, death, health, the body, and science? This indeed was the problem faced by the organizers of the Human Genome Diversity Project in the mid-1990s (Chapter 5). While we tend to think of blood as a replenishable, if sometimes messy, resource, most peoples believe it to be a highly sacred substance, full of spiritual power. That is, after all, the basic belief of the Christian Eucharist.

If blood is a magical substance—charged with the cosmic forces behind blood brotherhood and menstrual taboos—then you are going to have to give people a pretty good reason to part with theirs. In the 1950s, you could give poor people five bucks, or sick people a shot of penicillin, in exchange for their blood. But that won't work today—for an exploitative economic or medical relationship is (quite reasonably) considered coercive. Nowadays, the burden falls on you, the scientist, to be honest about what you want, why you want it, what you're going to do with it, and to explain it all to people in terms they can understand, so that they are in a position to give their fully informed consent.

In the case of the Human Genome Diversity Project, they were trying to coordinate on a grand scale what anthropologists had been doing on a small scale for decades. But the publicity they were generating cast a bright light on practices that had been flying beneath the bioethical radar. Thus, for example, once the scientist had gotten the native to agree to give blood, the blood traditionally became the property of the researcher, who might do many other kinds of studies than the ones that the natives initially were told about when they agreed to participate. That no longer satisfies most bioethical standards.

Yet not only had the practice of taking native blood for scientific research without their full understanding been bypassed by modern bioethical sensibilities, but the political and economic circumstances had changed as well. With the opening up of biotechnology and the patenting of genes and cells, exotic blood might suddenly now have market value. If a remote tribesman had a rare allele, his cells might by patentable and the products obtained from them might be valuable. But this opened up another can of worms: Having been economically exploited for the local knowledge of the plants and animals around them, indigenous peoples were now possibly targets for the economic exploitation of their very bodies. Certainly that's not what science is about, is it?

The Human Genome Diversity Project was not interested in financial gain, but unfortunately also did not know how to deal with the fact that there were indeed financial aspects, quite possibly significant ones, in what they wanted to do. They also soon learned that their principal interest—the microevolutionary history of the human species—was of little interest to the native peoples whose blood they sought. In many cases, science flat-out contradicted their own ideas of their origins. So how could they be persuaded to participate without lying to them? One solution was to emphasize the ultimate biomedical benefits of genetic research, such as curing diseases like diabetes and alcoholism. But those are diseases with complex causes, and whose treatments are not likely to be based on genetic knowledge.

These issues have not yet been resolved, yet they cut to the very core of the scientific enterprise as it applies to human beings. A few decades ago, you could not hope to get rich doing genetics; now you can. All you need is some skill, a lot of luck, and cheap raw materials, in the form of the DNA of indigenous peoples. Unfortunately that recreates the most embarrassing aspects of the colonial enterprise, which would give modern science a bad name. Time was that many aspects of the relationship between industrialized nations and indigenous peoples involved taking resources cheaply, adding value to them but not sharing the profits, not training the local people, and even slandering or otherwise dehumanizing them as a means of rationalizing the economic exploitation. Nowadays we frown on such modes of intercultural contact as "colonial science," and it would certainly not do any great credit to contemporary science to recreate them.

Worse still, greedy insensitive geneticists can be rebuffed by funding agencies, or by their own university's oversight panels, or institutional review boards; but if the geneticists work for greedy pharmaceutical companies, or other private interests, there is hardly any ethical control over what they can do.

Certainly the most unanticipated consequence of the Human Genome Diversity Project was the development of a marketable product at nearly the same moment that genomics was transforming into a corporate science. That product, now for sale, is ancestry.

There are particular genetic variations associated with any ethnic group as a result of its microevolutionary history—but the associations are always statistical, not absolute. From the fine pattern of genomic variation among indigenous populations, the scientists can make a quantitative, probabilistic estimate of your ancestry—by your genomic similarity to those populations. And there are certainly questions that genomics can answer reliably: Is your child at risk for sickle-cell anemia? Are you a dead tycoon's last living relative? Are you the father of that baby boy? But the corporate world is often less circumspect than the scholarly world. The twin primary goals of this science are accuracy and sales—not just accuracy. And if there is, as P. T. Barnum famously said, a sucker born every minute, then why shouldn't corporate genomics benefit from that demographic fact as much as the rest of the corporate world?

Consequently, even though there are genomic tests available to tell you whether you have the Y-chromosome of Moses, or your child has the aptitude to be a world-class sprinter, or you are descended from a Zulu warrior, or a European Pleistocene clan mother, or you are 6% Native American, you shouldn't necessarily take them at face value just because they are science. The genomic tests specify that they are for recreational use only, and you can surely guess why.

Indeed, sometimes the genomic ancestry tests are just a lure to get your information into the company's database, where it might actually turn out to be of some use, although of course not to you.

NATIVE AMERICAN GRAVES PROTECTION AND REPATRIATION ACT (NAGPRA): WHO OWNS THE BONES?

The relationship between biological anthropology and native peoples has been especially contentious. Biological anthropology began as an empirical science with the collection of diverse skulls and skeletons. Skulls and skeletons, however, can only be acquired in a limited number of ways, and the simplest is: Dig them up. Consequently, in the latter part of the nineteenth century, many great museum collections were built up through the wholesale robbing of Indian graves.

A hundred years later, public attitudes toward Indians had evolved, and in 1990, Congress passed a law called the Native American Graves Protection and Repatriation Act (NAGPRA) that mandated the tabulation and possible return of Indian bones and artifacts to the tribes from which they had been initially taken. This was intended as legislation acknowledging the coercive and callous fashion in which at least some of this material had been acquired, effectively in the interest of human rights.

Of course, more recently, most archaeologists and physical anthropologists have been consulting closely with the relevant native groups, and working together in good faith. Indeed, all those old skeletons have yielded interesting conclusions about prehistoric life and death. For example, it was once held that people changed from being hunter-gatherers to being food producers because they recognized the obvious merits of the latter way of life. But careful analysis of skeletons from the time of that economic transition (which occurred in different parts of the world at different times and with different foods) shows that growing one's own food brought with it a significant immediate decline in the health of the population, detectable in their skeletons. We now know that this is because associated with growing one's own food is a decline in the diversity of foods eaten, with consequent nutritional imbalances, more labor involved in growing and preparing the food, and more exposure to the effects of drought or famine. The skeletons tell us that people didn't adopt agriculture because it was obviously better; they did it in spite of making their lives harder. Most likely, then, they felt as if they were out of other options!

So studying skeletons can yield interesting results, and most anthropologists are very respectful of the sensibilities of the people whose ancestors they are studying. Nevertheless, they were dealt a serious blow when some reactionary scientists, who felt their livelihoods were being challenged by NAGPRA, filed a lawsuit claiming that their right to study a Native American skeleton was being violated by NAGPRA, the federal government, and the Indians. The skeleton in question was known as Kennewick Man (Chapter 10), and he died 9,500 years ago near a river in what is now the state of Washington.

While the skeleton has interesting and unexpected facial features, it was decided by Federal authorities that the skeleton was subject to NAGPRA, and that the Native American groups, who saw the skeleton as the remains of a distant ancestor, were its rightful owners. And they did not want scientists probing around the remains of their "Ancient One." The scientists responded with the claim that the skeleton's facial features were "Caucasoid" (an obsolete anthropological term that used to be applied to indigenous inhabitants of Europe and southwest Asia), while Indians are "Mongoloid" (an equivalent obsolete term applied principally to peoples of East Asia)—therefore (with implausibly creationist logic) he could not have been their ancestor.

Actually, though, since Kennewick Man was found with a large spear-point embedded in his pelvis, he was not very likely to have been *anyone's* ancestor in a literal sense. The issue actually boiled down to one of *symbolic* ancestry and descent: What was the composition of human groups 9,500 years ago and what is their relation to human groups today?

That is not an easily answerable question. The scientists maintained that the fluidity and migrations of American peoples over the last 9,500 years makes it exceedingly unlikely that Kennewick Man's people were the biological ancestors of the Washington tribes who claim him today. The tribes maintained that he is an ancient Native American who wandered on their land thousands of years ago, and they are Native Americans who are there now, and so he is their ancestor. With different notions of what constitutes ancestry and relationship, and no way of proving either set of claims, we would seem to be at an impasse. This is why an appreciation of anthropology is so vital to the practice of biological anthropology: one has to be sensitive to the culturally specific ways of thinking about things.

Consider the basic concept of personhood. You are a person, but your great-great grandmother is no longer a person. Her femur may still exist, but not as a part of her, for she no longer exists. Her parts are no longer "her," but instead are objects, things. Her thighbone is an "it." In other words, death marks a transition from personhood to non-personhood.

But suppose death does not mark a passage from personhood to non-personhood? Suppose you are the same person regardless of whether or not you are dead, and regardless of the state of decomposition or corruption of your body? If the femur remains part of the person through birth, growth, puberty, and marriage, why should death necessarily change its status? After all, even from a strictly biological standpoint, that femur might still contain great-great-grandma's cellular matter, and recoverable DNA. There may indeed be "life" in the old girl yet! In this sense, the femur would no longer be an "it," but would remain a "she" indefinitely—and that femur would become a very different kind of object.

Which notion of personhood is scientifically correct? Both, and neither, for personhood is a cultural and political concept and is not affected by scientific evidence, although it might seem superficially as though it ought to be.

Consider the immortality achieved by an African American woman named Henrietta Lacks. Over 99% of everything we know about human cell genetics we owe to her. But she's not on the class syllabus. In 1951, Ms. Lacks checked into Johns Hopkins Hospital in Baltimore with terminal cancer. As fate would have it, that just happened to be the time and place in which biologists were trying to develop the means to cultivate human cells in vitro, that is to say, "under glass" or outside of the body. And with her tumor cells, they finally succeeded. And since that time, her cells have proven to be more durable and prolific than any other human cell line; they are known by an abbreviation of her name: HeLa. Great medical fortunes and careers have been made on HeLa cells, but not by Henrietta Lacks—who never even agreed to have her cells removed and tinkered with—nor by her family. And yet there is a sense in which she—that is to say, her cells—outlived everyone who originally took them and transformed them into a biomedical commodity, and will very likely outlive us all. Yet the biotechnology fortunes that have been made on HeLa cells have never been shared with her family.

Indeed, conflicting notions of personhood are at the heart of many contemporary debates: Is a fetus a person? Can you take someone's parts after they die, to save a life or to make some quick cash, or is that indecent—even though they are dead? Is an adult clone a person? Is a dog a person? That is the context within which the Indian bones must be seen: Is an ancient femur a person? Obviously the question is mostly metaphysical—there are reasonable arguments to be made on both sides, which scientific data do not illuminate. The answer simply hinges on what criteria and values you adopt in ascribing the status of personhood. And that is a cultural issue, not a biological one.

Personhood is one aspect of a broader spectrum of issues on which people hold strong opinions that sound like they are based on biological or genetic facts, but are really rooted in cultural assumptions. In the case of Kennewick Man, when scientists were later permitted to study the skull, they "discovered" that he didn't look European after all, but more closely resembled a Polynesian. But if the skulls of Indians, Polynesians, and Europeans are so similar as to be readily confused for one another by experts, doesn't that undermine the ostensible scientific authority behind the determination of racial affinity by skull form?

Of course, that logical possibility was not raised; the Kennewick Man controversy was about unrestricted access to the bones by interested scholars, regardless of the sensibilities of the other people around. The nonscientists' thoughts about identity and ancestry were rendered trivial, if not outright false and stupid; although the initial contention of the scientists, that Kennewick Man's Caucasoid racial appearance precluded him from any Indian ancestry, was actually just as false and stupid. But invested with the voice of scientific authority, that contention was decidedly not trivial.

This raises another question unique to biological anthropology: how do we balance our scientific quest for knowledge and our belief in the accuracy of that scientific knowledge, against the ideas and sensibilities of the people whose cooperation (or at least, passive neglect) are necessary for our scientific work to proceed?

If we trivialize their beliefs and regard them contemptuously, why would they want to help us do science? If science is obnoxious and dismissive toward them, why should they cooperate? Wouldn't you expect them, rather, to impede such science wherever possible? Finally, in a strange epilogue, geneticists in 2015 managed to extract DNA and link Kennewick Man genetically to Native Americans, thus bringing us, via a very circuitous and costly route, back to Square One.

ORIGIN MYTHS, SCIENTIFIC AND OTHERWISE

If humans did not evolve, then there are tremendous implications for the relationship between the critical faculties we possess and the discernible evidence. In other words, if astrophysics and geology attest to the antiquity of the cosmos and the earth, paleontology attests to the history and succession of life, biology and genetics attest to the relationships among organic forms and the kinds of variations to be found, and anthropology attests to the origin and diversity of the human species, then what kind of a deity would create us as related in the Bible, and then make it look as if He hadn't? Why would He have endowed us with the capacity to study and reason, if only to mislead us with false trails of evidence? Or perhaps He created us biblically and permitted another powerful being to mislead us. Why would He do that? Would either of those beings merit your worship?

These are, of course, not questions that science can address. As we noted in Chapter 1, science is about asking questions whose alternative possible answers can be distinguished through the collection of material evidence. The world of material evidence and appearance, aided by technology and reason, are all we (as scientists) have to go on. Regardless of whether, for example, God created the cosmos as related in the Bible and constructed a false trail of evidences to make it look as if we evolved, or whether He permitted Satan to do it, in order perversely to test our faith, the fact remains that it looks quite unambiguously as if we evolved, and therefore science is obliged to proceed on that basis. If we didn't evolve, that would raise far more bizarre theological questions about why it looks so strongly like we did, and indeed would undermine the entire scientific enterprise of figuring out how the universe works by studying it rigorously—which nevertheless generally does seem to work.

If we accept the scientific explanation of our origin, we are immediately confronted with theological questions about the origin of our immortal souls. Either (1) we evolved (or became otherwise endowed with) souls after parting ways with the apes in the last 7 million years; or (2) the apes have souls, and by extension all species do (which is compatible with some religious traditions, such as Hinduism); or (3) we are organic physical beings, pure and simple, and do not have immortal souls.

These issues are important to many people, yet science cannot resolve them. More importantly, however, science cannot responsibly neglect the fact that it has raised these issues. Many thoughtful scholars have grappled with the theological or spiritual implications of evolution, from the Jesuit paleontologist Pierre

Teilhard de Chardin to the atheist biologist Richard Dawkins. In between lies a vast middle ground that subsumes the religious-philosophical reflections of the Russian Orthodox geneticist Theodosius Dobzhansky, deist paleontologist George Gaylord Simpson, agnostic biologist Julian Huxley, and evangelical Christian molecular geneticist Francis Collins. However unsatisfactory any of these metaphysical positions may be, to fail to confront the implications of evolution is to cede the ground of discussing what evolution really means to the biblical literalists and creationists. The tenacity and popularity of contemporary creationism in America is testimony to the significance that many Americans place in the theological implications entailed by a scientific understanding of our origins.

Anthropologists have long been aware that origin narratives fulfill diverse functions in society. When Darwin was in college, the scientists were themselves theologians, the earth was believed to be young, and death was believed to be caused by Adam and Eve's sin—that is, the origins of mortality and morality were intimately linked. A generation later, the earth was thought to be much older, people had arisen from apes, and death had been decoupled from sin. One could obviously retain the meaning of the story as metaphor; but it's no wonder that evolution has found such opposition—it is threatening to the very social order, at least as that order was understood in the nineteenth century.

Indeed modern creationists are a diverse lot, united simply in their discomfiture with the spiritual implications of Darwinism. Some reject all historical science and maintain a biblical literalist chronology of 6,000 years for the age of the earth and cosmos. Some accept astrophysics and geology on the age of the earth and cosmos, but reject the idea of common ancestry for species. Some accept common ancestry for large groups of animals, positing an ancestral divinely created progenitor of lions, tigers, lynxes, pumas, chervils, civets, and pussycats, but arbitrarily rejecting an association of cats with, say, other Carnivora or Mammalia or Vertebrata. Some accept the old earth and a common ancestry for life, but not for humans. And finally, some who self-identify as creationists accept the old earth, and a common ancestry for life, including humans, but maintain the guidance of the processes by spiritual forces. (Many who hold this view would self-identify as evolutionists, too!)

In other words, modern-day creationism stands *for* nothing, but simply *against* the proposition that the human species arose entirely by natural processes from other species, and that oppositional stance seems to have broad resonance. No area of science other than biological anthropology has to deal with a comparable situation.

However, biblical literalism is an extreme position within Protestant theology. Jewish and Catholic theology, for many centuries, has been predicated on interpreting the Bible properly for every age. Mainstream biblical scholars today study their subject as an important cultural document, and try to understand the meaning of creation to its authors and readers, without imagining it to be a literal chronicle.

Consider the study of Adam and Eve as a story about something, if not a history. The tree from which they infamously ate was called the Tree of the

Knowledge of Good and Evil (Genesis 1:17), and what they acquired upon eating it was a moral sense, specifically the recognition that being naked in public is wrong (Genesis 2:7). What is acceptable for animals is no longer acceptable for people. In other words, the story's climax is the origin of the moral order, not the natural order. One can easily see a message that is important—not as science, but rather about living. The message is: as an adult human, you have the choice between morality (good) and immorality (evil). Amorality (living in ignorance or isolation from moral ideas) is possibly acceptable in animals and children, but as a functioning member of society—any society—it is not an option for you. You need to know right from wrong and choose right, or else you won't be wanted anywhere.

An important lesson, and universally applicable.

BIOCULTURAL STUDIES, OR CYBORG ANTHROPOLOGY

Biological anthropology is embedded in a cultural matrix much more obviously than other sciences. This is expressed in four ways:

1. In common with all anthropology, we rely on the goodwill of our study material, for they are people (or other intelligent and sensitive primates).
2. Our work affects their ideas of who they are and where they come from, which form the basis of cultural identities, and which are by consequence intensely politically contested (think of the annual debates over celebrating Columbus and the Pilgrims, and over the role of slavery and genocide in building America).
3. We study the nature and pattern of human differences, and find that most meaningful differences are the product of human history and agency, and not rooted in nature—and because we recognize the political salience of our science, we call attention to the ways in which genetics and biology are co-opted as an explanation for social and political inequalities.
4. We face religiously based opposition to our very field of enquiry.

Biological anthropology thus assumes greater responsibilities and confronts greater obstacles than other sciences. In starting with the cultural nature of human existence as an evolutionary fact, we can see that categories of principal relevance to us are mental. Most observable physical or biological features (hair color, body build, height) are not those that we use to group people meaningfully, although we commonly do consider and study them. But our principal meaningful groupings—race and ethnicity—are largely cognitive ephemera, the products of a historical moment in European history. Today we see the emergence of new meaningful categories—for example, Gay, Hispanic, Slovenian, or Mormon—that were not categories a few generations ago, and yet now are identities significant enough to be tabulated and subject to legislation.

New identities emerge, and old ones evolve or are obliterated. There are no more Hittites or Scythians or Essenes among us, although their descendants or relatives may well be. They are just no longer on the identity map.

One thing we can predict with confidence, though, is that there will always be an interest in "naturalizing" those new identities. As long as biology is believed to lie at the root of difference, it can be invoked to justify existing inequalities, to dehumanize target groups, and to absolve oneself of responsibility for behaviors that would otherwise be intolerable. More importantly, it can be used to misdirect interest from the social patterns and convergences of interest that really govern the construction of identities, and that really are at the heart of social injustices.

Consider the well-documented "population explosion." The earth cannot indefinitely sustain all the people already alive, and more are coming every day. To this end, we must find new ways to feed the masses, and agricultural intensification through biotechnology is the way to solve the problem. Or so the agribusiness companies say. Their opponents think that that agribusiness is interested primarily in markets and profits, and are wary of the introduction of genetically modified organisms (GMOs) or "Franken-foods."

In fact, the "too many people" argument has been made by every generation since Thomas Malthus (Chapter 3), and casually ignores two important cultural factors. In the first place, with industrialization and economic modernization invariably comes a decline in the population growth rate, as women become educated, enter the work force, and choose to have two children instead of seven. In the second place, everyone does not have equal access to the food that already exists, which is quite enough to feed the world. Farmers are subsidized to lower production and keep prices up; grain is stockpiled in silos. The problem is really the distribution of resources, not the quantity of resources or the number of mouths to feed.

This is not to say that there is no population explosion, or that overpopulation is a good thing—but just that biotechnology may not be the answer to the problem, because the problem is misleadingly framed biologically rather than culturally.

One of the central features of anthropology is to permit us to see and understand the cultural aspects of ostensibly biological issues. In the modern world, this represents a "holistic" site for the improved understanding of the natural and cultural existence of human groups. This is commonly called "biocultural studies" from the standpoint of biological anthropology or medical anthropology, where the emphasis in on how culture and biology are blended as we analyze and solve problems of the human condition.

A similar point is made in cultural anthropology, with a graphic metaphor: the cyborg (Chapter 9). The phrase "cyborg anthropology" reflects the recognition that we are simultaneously creators of culture, products of culture, and symbionts with culture. We create culture in the obvious sense that human ideas and innovations are the basis of technological and ideological change. But we are also products of culture in crucial ways. Our social interface with the world, for example, involves the way in which we are seen by others; the way we move, and cover ourselves, and decorate ourselves—ranging from our speech, style, attitude, and clothing to our haircuts, tattoos, and cosmetic surgeries. And not only are we creators and products of culture, but we are also essentially symbiotic with culture—adapting culturally throughout our bodies, and rescuing or augmenting physical function by cultural means. Here, examples range from pharmacology, artificial insemination, and obstetrics, through glasses and dental fillings, and on to prosthetic limbs, joints, or organs. These three categories obviously overlap considerably; but the point is that we are thus inseparable from culture—people and culture *co-construct* one another—and any comprehensive scientific approach to human behavior, evolution, or existence must incorporate, or at least acknowledge, that.

The case of lactose tolerance (mentioned previously) shows the power of the cultural environment in shaping both our eating habits and gene pool. After all, the mutation to lactose tolerance could only be useful after one has domesticated cattle and has begun to breed them for milk production. It thus represents an adaptive genetic synergy with a situation constructed by culture, an availability of milk that doesn't need to be made into cheese to be enjoyed. And to the extent that lactose intolerant people in America may feel as though they are missing out on something, like pizzas and milk shakes, culture provides its own solution—lactase enzyme supplements.

If we can pause to consider the future of the human species, we have to imagine that we will continue to adapt culturally, rather than biologically. Natural selection will be too weak and gene flow too strong to permit much room for biological divergence. We can't expect to see much biological change in our species, then, until we encounter a new and presently unimaginable set of ecological circumstances to adapt to, and until some dramatic population crashes and founder events promote genetic drift. That will probably have to wait until the colonization of outer space.

REFERENCES AND FURTHER READING

Annas, G. J., and M. A. Grodin, eds. 1992. *The Nazi Doctors and the Nuremberg Code: Human Rights in Human Experimentation.* New York: Oxford University Press.

Braman, D. 1999. Of race and immutability. *UCLA Law Review* 46:1375–1464.

Eveleth, P., and J. Tanner. 1991. *Worldwide Variation in Human Growth.* New York: Cambridge University Press.

Fan, S., M. E. B. Hansen, Y. Lo, and S. A. Tishkoff. 2016. Going global by adapting local: A review of recent human adaptation. *Science* 354 (6308):54–59.

Gluckman, P., and M. Hanson. 2006. *Mismatch: Why Our World No Longer Fits Our Bodies.* New York: Oxford University Press.

Goodman, A., D. Heath, and M. S. Lindee, eds. 2004. *Genetic Nature/Culture.* Berkeley: University of California Press.

Haraway, D. 1991. *Simians, Cyborgs, and Women: The Reinvention of Nature.* New York: Routledge.

Jones, J. 1981. *Bad Blood: The Tuskegee Syphilis Experiment.* New York: Free Press.

Kroeber, A. L. 1917. The superorganic. *American Anthropologist* 19:162–213.

Lasker, G. 1969. Human biological adaptability. *Science* 166:1480–1486.

Marks, J. 2017. Anthropology and science. In *The Routledge Companion to Contemporary Anthropology*, ed. S. Coleman, S. B. Hyatt, and A. Kingsolver, 305–322. New York: Routledge.

Meskell, L., and P. Pels, eds. 2005. *Embedding Ethics: Shifting Boundaries of the Anthropological Profession.* Oxford, England: Berg.

Nash, C. 2004. Genetic kinship. *Cultural Studies* 18:1–34.

Reardon, J. 2004. *Race to the Finish: Identity and Governance in an Age of Genomics.* Princeton, NJ: Princeton University Press.

Reverby, S. 2009. *Examining Tuskegee: The Infamous Syphilis Study and Its Legacy.* Durham: University of North Carolina Press.

Sacks, J. 2011. *The Great Partnership: Science, Religion, and the Search for Meaning.* New York: Schocken Books.

Scheper-Hughes, N. 2001. Ishi's brain, Ishi's ashes: Anthropology and genocide. *Anthropology Today* 17:12–18.

Scheper-Hughes, N. 2006. Alistair Cook's bones: A morality tale. *Anthropology Today* 22:10–15.

Shepard, R. J., and A. Rode. 1996. *The Health Consequences of "Modernization": Evidence from Circumpolar Peoples.* New York: Cambridge University Press.

Silverman, S., and S. McKinnon, eds. 2005. *Complexities: Beyond Nature and Nurture.* Chicago, IL: University of Chicago Press.

Skloot, R. 2010. *The Immortal Life of Henrietta Lacks.* New York: Crown.

Stone, G. D. 2002. Both sides now: Fallacies in the genetic-modification wars, implications for developing countries, anthropological perspectives. *Current Anthropology* 43:611–630.

Thomas, D. 2000. *Skull Wars: Kennewick Man, Archaeology, and the Battle for Native American Identity.* New York: Basic Books.

Tobias, P. V. 2002. Saartje Baartman: Her life, her remains, and the negotiations for their repatriation from France to South Africa. *South African Journal of Science* 98:107–110.

Turner, T., ed. 2005. *Biological Anthropology and Ethics: From Repatriation to Genetic Identity.* Albany: State University of New York Press.

Zevit, Z. 2013. *What Really Happened in the Garden of Eden?* New Haven, CT: Yale University Press.

INDEX